TRANSLATING PAST TO PRESENT

TRANSLATING PAST TO PRESENT

Interpreters in the American West and Beyond

EDITED BY ANDREW OFFENBURGER
AND PATRICIA NELSON LIMERICK

UNIVERSITY OF NEBRASKA PRESS
Lincoln

© 2025 by the Board of Regents of the University of Nebraska

Transcript of "Interview with Vietnam Peace Talks Interpreter," featured in "Interpreting for and in Vietnam," was reproduced with permission from EU Interpreters, © European Commission 2003. Excerpt from "Lost in Translation," featured in "Interpreting for and in Vietnam," was reproduced courtesy of Doug Bekke. Transcript of "The Interpreters," directed by Andrés Caballero and Sofian Khan, 2019, featured in "Call Me Phillip Morris," was reproduced courtesy of Capital K Pictures.

All rights reserved

The University of Nebraska Press is part of a land-grant institution with campuses and programs on the past, present, and future homelands of the Pawnee, Ponca, Otoe-Missouria, Omaha, Dakota, Lakota, Kaw, Cheyenne, and Arapaho Peoples, as well as those of the relocated Ho-Chunk, Sac and Fox, and Iowa Peoples.

For customers in the EU with safety/GPSR concerns, contact:
gpsr@mare-nostrum.co.uk
Mare Nostrum Group BV
Mauritskade 21D
1091 GC Amsterdam
The Netherlands

LIBRARY OF CONGRESS CONTROL NUMBER: 2024059304

Designed and set in Garamond Premier Pro by Katrina Noble.

CONTENTS

List of Illustrations   vii

Acknowledgments   ix

Introduction   1
ANDREW OFFENBURGER AND PATRICIA LIMERICK

A Message and a Dance for Zebulon Pike   13

PART 1. INTERPRETING FOR AND WITH EMPIRE

1. From Indigenous Interpreters to Creole Control:
   Race, Translation, and Exclusion in Yucatan, 1560–1633   17
   MARK LENTZ

   Misinterpreting for James Wilkinson   39

2. Captains of Civility: The Indigenous Interpreters of North
   America Who Attempted to School Settler Colonists on the
   Ideals of Civil Community   41
   NICOLE EUSTACE

   Maungwudaus Maintains Peace   59

3. William Wells ... Interpreter?   61
   CAMERON SHRIVER

   Ma-Son-Ne John Simpson Smith   85

PART 2. ALONG THE BORDERS OF CONSOLIDATING POWER

4. Translating Slavery   89
   ALICE BAUMGARTNER

   Jeffrey Deroine, Freedman and Ioway Interpreter   108

5. The Interpreter Generation: Boarding School Survivors, Euro-American Scholars, and Chiricahua Apache History in the Twentieth Century 110
PAUL CONRAD

Changing Names 133

6. Diplomacy in the Aftermath of Pancho Villa's Raid: Consul Antonio Landín in Columbus, 1917–1920 138
BRANDON MORGAN

John Collier: No Hands Raised 153

7. Interpreters of Diné dóó Gáamalii Oral Histories 154
FARINA KING

Rough Interpretations 183

PART 3. INTERPRETING IN PRACTICE

8. "Do You Solemnly Swear to Interpret Accurately and Without Bias?": Professional Court Interpreting in the Twentieth and Twenty-First Centuries 191
TAYLOR COZZENS

Dueling Interpretations 222

9. Puente, Ɓɔ, Bridge: Interpreting for Social Transformation in Storm Lake, Iowa 227
ANDREW OFFENBURGER

Interpreting for and in Vietnam 243

10. Keeping Faith: Interpreters in the Global War on Terror 247
ZACH GUILIANO

Call Me Phillip Morris 262

Contributors 265
Index 269

ILLUSTRATIONS

1. George Henry (Maungwudaus) 60
2. William Wells 63
3. Jeffrey Deroine 109
4. Asa Daklugie 118
5. Samuel Kenoi 122
6. Helena Yellowhair 167
7. Graciela Vrieze 230
8. Pom Kavan 234
9. Phillip Morris 263

ACKNOWLEDGMENTS

This book would not have been possible without the support of a number of individuals and organizations at Miami University. The Department of History's McClellan Fund provided most of the financial assistance necessary to host a two-day symposium in April 2022, with additional funding from the Myaamia Center and the Humanities Center. Thank you to the History Department's wonderful faculty, students, and staff for their support, and especially to Wietse de Boer, Erik Jensen, Soren Powell, and Karon Selm.

Other folks with an imprint on this book's development and production are mentioned in the introduction that follows, but we wish emphasize here our appreciation for having this book appear with the University of Nebraska Press. Thanks especially to Bridget Barry, who has been equal parts supportive and flexible as this volume took shape. Matt Bokovoy also provided early suggestions on how to shepherd an edited collection through the publication process.

TRANSLATING PAST TO PRESENT

Introduction

ANDREW OFFENBURGER AND PATRICIA LIMERICK

Several years ago in Santa Cruz, California, beneath the city's wharf, a herd of sea lions found a comfortable place for repose and reflection. People were naturally curious about these intriguing and adorable creatures. And so officials carved an opening, a viewing area, into the wharf's deck. Through this fenced opening, folks could get a glimpse of the gregarious sea lions. And every now and then, humans would bring along their canine pals for walks on the wharf.

This diverse gathering of sea lions, humans, and dogs sometimes provoked a wondrous bout of misunderstanding. In the substructure of the pier, sea lions would bark. On the surface, dogs would come to attention, charged with the desire to know where that strange-yet-familiar vocalization had come from, unsure of its source. More often than not, this situation would evolve into a parody of misunderstanding, with two parties drawn into a stalemated dialogue, stuck in an exchange of remarks that *sounded* familiar but delivered only reciprocal bewilderment. At least that's how it seemed through human ears and eyes. People chuckled amid bilingual barking. It was, in a word, hilarious.[1]

As funny or charming as this scenario is, it is not unique. We humans find plenty of opportunities to laugh at our own miscommunications, when recognized. In everyday life, scrambled messages can cause confusion, and frequently anxiety, until five clarifying words—"But I thought you said . . ."—lead to a realization that can generate bouts of laughter, infused with the relief of comprehension. Humor and misunderstanding often go hand in hand.

But not always.

Miscommunication can be an equally great source of irritation, antagonism, anger, and even violence. Here is a lesson laid out in multiple chapters of the history of the American West and its bordering territories: *When two groups manifest an inability to cross a wide linguistic gulf, and when both groups presume to know the meaning of the other side's gestures, words, and actions, everyone in the vicinity is well-advised to run and duck for cover*. In the case of the Santa Cruz wharf, without safety fencing and leashes, the mutual barking of dogs and sea lions might soon turn to growls, with the flashing of teeth and claws.

For historians today, we can identify many such contingent moments in the past, when outcomes hinged on perceptions of understanding. These often, though not always, erupted in violence. In the long history of the American West, these historical inflection points frequently emerged due to trade, alliances, territorial control, the work of missionaries, the availability of arms, treaties (misrepresented or broken), relocations, government oversight, tribal sovereignty, resource extraction, and environmental activism. But what if, in a moment of precarity, an interpreter, equally endowed with linguistic fluency and with cultural acuity, were to travel back and forth over that wide linguistic gulf, taking careful steps on a wobbly tightrope? Might that interpreter anticipate and reduce the peril of the situation?

If that question strikes you as deserving serious thought, then you have picked up exactly the right book. In the past, interpreters—also known as cultural brokers and intermediaries—have been crucial figures in the shaping of Western American history. In untold encounters and exchanges, when groups who spoke mutually unintelligible languages tried to deal with each other, interpreters were critically important. Their role of facilitating communication frequently left them between parties, at least in theory. This often led to the interpreter's paradox: for all their significance, these folks—typically figures who originated on the margins but who relocated themselves to the center—did not do much to generate records that would help posterity track the stories of their own lives, their own views of events. The contributors to this edited collection want to change this, to refocus some attention on the women and men who interpreted in the past and do so in the present.

In the history of the American West and in the history of borderlands, at every juncture, interpreters were active and present, conveying meaning between mutually unintelligible peoples; bartering for goods and power along borders; and uncovering intentions from the cryptic hints supplied in gestures, acts, and words. They performed these strenuous maneuvers as artists as much as linguists, improvising their techniques of negotiation while guessing at the protocols in use in different settings.

Historians of the American West have rarely focused on these essential historical figures.[2] Research and writing on interpreters within zones of cultural exchange (frontiers, borders, and borderlands), while nascent in the context of the American West, have prospered among scholars of early modern Europe and

Asia.³ There is some good fortune in this timing. These predecessors have provided Western American and borderlands historians with a diverse range of approaches: studies of communication, verbal and otherwise; close examinations of the translation and distribution of texts, often in conjunction with travel to faraway lands; the consideration of interpreters as participants in acts of cultural mediation (or of subjugation); and/or inquiries into translation as a fundamental feature in the transmission of values.⁴

While scholars working with these other locales have explored historical episodes of interpretation and translation with illuminating results, the subject can still stay situated at the margins of other fields, fragmented by the customs of academic specialization. Such a variegated—and still sparse in comparison to its importance—historiography arises in part from a structural problem: interpreters and translators have had good reasons to strive for invisibility, in the historical record and in contemporary practice. Court-appointed interpreters today, for example, are trained to be as transparent as "a pane of glass."⁵

This edited collection calls into question this purported transparency, summoning interpreters from the margins of history to its center, to understand the role that they have played in various contexts of the history of the greater American West. Joined together in the first book to pursue this topic in the domain of Western American history, the chapters span broad geographies and chronologies, interweaving theory and practice, to conduct a conversation long overdue.

In addition to showcasing rigorous historical scholarship, this book calls attention to the subjectivity inherent in interpretive acts, a subjectivity that shapes the work of historians as much as it shaped the work of the message-carriers in the West's past. Recognizing the compelling reasons to face up to this subjectivity, several of our authors use the first-person pronoun in their chapters. We (the editors) encouraged this as a methodological intervention, to remind readers that the past will *always* be understood through the prism of present interpreters (a.k.a. historians!).

Indeed, we recognize the importance of acknowledging the researcher/writer's "positionality," and—even in chapters that avoid the first-person pronoun—we foreswear any attempt to masquerade as an omniscient narrator. In other words, we are asking all our fellow readers and historians to consider the role of actual interpreters in the past and then to overlay that with our roles as historical intermediaries. The authors of these chapters therefore deliberate together, with different outcomes, on the care and handling of the first-person pronoun. Each must balance narrative strategies between the pronoun's power to add force and clarity to an inquiry *and* its potential to distract from the stories and experiences of the historical figures under study. We hope that this approach will produce insights in the present, as broader society reckons with "positionality," while also helping the historical profession figure out how to manage the "I"-word in a pronoun-preoccupied era.

The contributors to this volume thus perform a doubled role: we are studying interpreters while acting as interpreters ourselves, transmitting messages from the people of the past to the people of the present and future. Because of this, our perspectives and points of view never approach a state of rest. It is a daunting challenge. At any particular moment, we are trying to understand what the members of Group A intended by their words and deeds. At the next moment, we are performing the same exercise with the members of Group B. And then comes the added exertion of figuring out what the members of Group B thought they had heard and observed in the words and deeds of Group A, dispatching us on the next task of figuring out what Group A, in turn, made of Group B's responses and reactions. With all of these findings competing for our attention, we must put the disparate layers of our inquiry together in a way that coheres in our own minds.

The reward for our labors? We embark on a quest for the words, sentences, and paragraphs that will effectively communicate the thoughts and actions of the people of the past to people who live in an entirely different era. This requires us to anticipate and adapt to the expectations, knowledge, and worldviews of the living and breathing audience who we are asking to enter a world that, if we do our job right, will strike first-time visitors as foreign and disorienting. In the unlikely event that, at any stage of this adventure, we might be tempted to congratulate ourselves on the progress we were making, that temptation will be cut short by a reckoning with the patchiness of evidence in our sources and the possibility of bias in the assumptions we bring to bear on those sources.

If all this seems like hard work, it is. But it is also turns out to be work with the power to transform a set of high-achieving individuals into a team of scholars with a shared—though far from homogenized—vision, resting on a deep appreciation of each other's undertakings.

Origins

In the late 1980s, at the Buffalo Bill Historical Center in Cody, Wyoming, Kenneth Haltman participated in a workshop led by Patty Limerick. Now a distinguished professor at the University of Oklahoma, Haltman at that time was a graduate student who had written a research seminar paper on interpreters and translators. Reading this paper, Limerick realized that this was a very promising topic, and that she was herself, by virtue of her own limited abilities in the arena of language-learning, a very unpromising candidate to take up this line of inquiry. And so Haltman's lively mind moved on to other subjects, and Limerick spent the next decades fitfully pleading with young scholars to pick up where he left off. Given the absence of archival collection guides that have categorized primary source material in files labeled "Interpreters/Translators," resistance to her pleading may well have been perfectly sensible.

And then, at a Western History Association conference just before the lockdowns of the pandemic, Western American historian David Wrobel, an indefatigable builder of bridges, introduced Limerick to Taylor Cozzens, a graduate student at the University of Oklahoma who also serves as a court interpreter for Spanish-speaking people. At long last, a young scholar responded with enthusiasm to Limerick's pleading! Cozzens quickly put Limerick in touch with Andrew Offenburger, who needed no convincing. His research and interests in global frontiers and borders predisposed him to the importance of interpreters to their relative transparency in scholarly studies. With support from Miami University's Department of History, the Myaamia Center, and the Menard Family Center for Democracy, contributors to this volume convened at a two-day symposium in Oxford, Ohio, in April 2022, to present working drafts and to engage in conversations pertaining to the theory, history, and practice of interpretation.

Under any circumstances, this gathering would have lodged in the memories of all the participants as a festival of lively and congenial conversation. But one moment especially stands out. After a very enjoyable welcoming dinner, we retired to rooms in a tranquil and serene historic hotel. Somewhere around 4 a.m., tranquility and serenity took a break, and a high-volume smoke alarm ordered us to evacuate. The moment presented many of us with a relevant question: Do we interpret the alarm as a real emergency, as a malfunction, or perhaps as the result of undergraduate antics? Only one of our members exercised appropriate caution, quickly getting dressed and racing down to the lobby. The rest of us piled pillows on our heads and committed to sheltering in place. Eventually, the alarm was accurately interpreted as an electrical malfunction. The squawks and beeps were silenced, and we edged back into sleep.

Until the scenario was repeated at 5 a.m.

When we assembled for a hearty breakfast, we learned that our early morning adventures had forged us into a community of comrades, even as we recognized the potentially perilous consequences of our own interpretations. (Yes, this could have qualified us for a Darwin Award for poorly adapted evolutionary behavior.) Instead, we had received a narrative foundation for the creation of a resilient community. Wielding pens, phones, laptops, and tablets of paper and screen, and fueled with coffee, we plotted a course to understand a topic that informed each of our subfields, a topic that had never received sufficient attention. The volume that you now hold in your hands, or see on your screen, originated from this symposium, as well as from subsequent Zoom meetings that served as periodic workshops.

It is our dream that this book will ignite interest in this history of interpreters, with innumerable scholars recognizing how much their own work has anticipated and touched on the preoccupations that drove us to see this project through to completion. But if we pretended to claim that our findings were exhaustive and conclusive, we would betray the whole spirit of this undertaking.

Approach and Methodology

Over two days at the symposium, we took our own research subfields, and we asked new questions of them. How did the presence, recruitment, or performance of interpreters shape events in a particular time and place? What were the benefits gained and the costs paid by people who relied on these interpreters? How would the stories we uncovered make a case for the significance of interpreters in the West, in its borderlands, and in the world as a whole? What connections and comparisons do these ten essays offer to our contemporaries in the historical profession, and, probably most important, how will they stir up the next generation of historians to ask their own questions? Inspired by such questions, we then gave preliminary feedback, forged alliances, challenged assumptions, and, yes, laughed at our own miscommunications. And we shared these early conversations and their results with students, staff, and the public at the Myaamia Center, the McGuffey House and Museum, and within the corridors of Upham Hall.

One question arose immediately in our conversations: How would we distinguish interpreting from translating? Common use seemed to suggest that "interpreting" related to aural expressions, while "translating" happened in writing. This distinction breaks down, however, when historians "interpret" the written record. And consider the example of Farina King's analysis—in conversation with her father—of a transcribed oral history interview translated (interpreted?) from Diné bizaad to English. Multiple levels of complexity similarly entangle the chapters that follow. To avoid confusion, our authors use the terms interchangeably, without distinction.

Here are two lines of thought for our readers to keep in mind as they move through these pages. First, our focus on the American West is shifting, and it is certainly not exceptional, nor the end point. In truth, it is not even the beginning point, since chapter 1 opens on the Yucatan Peninsula, with Mark Lentz focusing on a distinctive configuration in the recruitment and deployment of interpreters, hired and paid by the Spanish Crown. Lentz's findings invite readers into a world where a cohort of aspiring cultural and linguistic go-betweens jostled for service, patrimony, and compensation. Individual motivations and eccentric character traits, we are reminded, alter the contours of history with lasting consequences.

Lentz's work on the Spanish empire, in what would become Mexico, sets the stage for an argument that imperial borderlands provided fertile grounds for interpreters and interpreting. Alice Baumgartner's chapter on nineteenth-century definitions of slavery—in geographical and linguistic borderlands—furthers this endeavor. Similarly, Brandon Morgan's contribution also asks what messages might be, or should be, received from the raising of a single flag at a critical moment in borderland relations.

Two additional chapters, by Nicole Eustace and Cameron Shriver, extend these observations into the polyglot world of the Ohio-Pennsylvania corridor, lands profoundly shaped by the Indigenous peoples of the Great Lakes region, and by French, English, Canadian, and American actors. (Readers who puzzle over the relative lack of attention to the western U.S.-Canadian borderlands should know that this and other Pacific geographies will be addressed in a subsequent volume, currently in development.)

Second, the importance of interpreters defies boundaries in time as relentlessly as it extends across terrestrial borders. Where go humans, so goes the need for interpretation. For this reason, this edited volume emphasizes a broad chronology, from the sixteenth century to the present. The case studies in chapters 7–10 feature contemporary manifestations of interpretation, from the complex underpinnings of oral history research among the Diné (King) to the practice of courtroom interpreting (Cozzens), from the policework of community service officers in Iowa (Offenburger) to the role of linguistic middlemen in the global war on terror (Guiliano). This concluding extension into Afghanistan, a locale at once geographically distant and thematically proximate, raises powerful questions about the continuities between interpreters' and soldiers' experiences in the Indian Wars with those of participants today.

With such a chronological span, we invite readers to contemplate the continuities between imperial borderlands, the early American republic, and the present. The pressures that the individuals faced, in all of our chapters, shared roots in personal capabilities, power imbalances, individual motivations, short-term exigencies, and split-second interpretive decisions. The worlds of the interpreters in this volume, from the 1600s to 2000s, overlapped in profound ways, even as their names and divergent historical contexts appear inconsonant.

These two constructs—geography and chronology—shape this volume, while other themes appear and reappear, with thought-provoking twists and turns, throughout the book. Here are a few, posed as questions we frequently asked, along with our preliminary and suggestive results.

What range of official or makeshift roles did interpreters play, and why did some claim the standing of professionals (and exercise authority that they derived from that standing) while others preferred anonymity? Viewing this collection through the lens of roles, one can conclude that interpreters follow power, whether they are officially appointed or volunteered. On the one hand, the cases of unofficial interpreting—perhaps better understood as arising with support from below—can be seen in the examples of Taquatarensaly (Eustace) as well as the extended kin network of King, her father, and the Diné linguist Clayton Long. Such positions became more formalized with expanding states and cultural conflict, leading to imperial appointees (Lentz) and the subsequent "interpreter generation" (Conrad). The examples of Burrill Daniel's case with the U.S. Mexico Commission (Baumgartner) and court-appointed translators (Cozzens) remind us that government officials, and officialdom, interpret the law on a daily basis. And lastly, amid the full power of the state, governments rely on interpreters to minimize friction and maintain power/peace as much as possible, whether in the military (Guiliano) or in local police forces (Offenburger).

Given that interpreters, in many of the most compelling case studies, were complicit in the multiple disruptions brought into the lives of Indigenous peoples, what kind of power did they really wield? Whether we characterize the westward expansion of Euro-American populations as "invasion and conquest" or "settler colonialism," interpreters were essential figures in this process. They sometimes engaged in efforts to curtail—or least manage and restrain—eruptions of violence, but they consistently played a crucial role in efforts to the reconfigure the homes of Indigenous peoples into the property and sources of profit for intruders and invaders. Rarely positioned in a clear configuration of opposed and antagonistic interests, interpreters often inhabited a terrain of scrambled identities and affiliations; in King's article, the interpreters—and the speakers whose words underwent interpretation—are both Indigenous residents and believers in a religion transported to the West by settlers. Chapters by Eustace, Shriver, and Conrad further reveal how interpreters were themselves predisposed to multicultural worlds; one could never be fully, unquestionably, aligned with a single power. This would appear to be another iteration of the interpreter's paradox: their positioning between worlds made them indispensable and suspect at the same time.

How did this power fluctuate? When Indigenous leaders met with Army officers or senators or territorial officials, we might at first assume that power and authority were in the possession of the Euro-American officials. And yet, by a more realistic appraisal, the Euro-American officials were the least informed, the most naïve, and most conspicuously out of their element of all the people assembled on these occasions. As the channels transmitting messages from one cohort to another, the interpreters could be seen as operatively the most empowered of all the participants. If we shift the point of view, though, we might see how the interpreters were the most vulnerable of all the figures assembled, subject to arbitrary exercises of power by the officials, and sometimes even subject to the implementation of the mindset "destroy the messenger, if you don't like the message." With these complicated arrangements in mind, the concluding article by Zach Guiliano—on the United States' reliance on interpreters in the Afghanistan arena of the global war on terror—provided an essential, mind-stretching comparison that influenced the thinking of the authors of the articles set in North America.

What is the nature of the relationship, or the connection, between humor and misinterpretation? An element of humor suffuses many of these contributions. King identifies a chain of miscommunication between translator Phillip Smith, Matthew Heiss, and Helena Yellowhair, who, when asked about her "heart" and religious experience in a Mormon Temple, replied with a health-based response: "My heart is happy. But here, my foot has problems..."

Cozzens recalls a moment when he heard a defense attorney "change the crime of burglary (*allanamiento de morada*) to robbery (*robo*) because he did not know how to say the former," and how surprised the defendant must have been at the new charge. In addition to these examples, participants at our symposium identified many of the stories, some fiction, of cultural or linguistic misinterpretation.[6]

Perhaps humor emanates from the high stakes of interpretation. Laughing at a missed phrase or idea can feel a bit like whistling past the graveyard. Nevertheless, to add some levity to this collection, we have selected several vignettes to adorn our scholarly contributions. Irony abounds, as in the figure of John Collier, who asks (in English) of an audience of Quapaws and Osages, "Will those who do not understand English so indicate by raising their hand." Subtle resistance emerges in the case of Maungwudaus, an Ojibwe/Chippewa interpreter, who works to maintain the peace when an Ojibwe leader purportedly insulted British women in front of their husbands. These intermittent anecdotes also reveal the immense challenges posed by cultural presumptuousness, so clear in the vignette detailing Indian agents' struggles to translate Indigenous names for the purposes of allotment. Such precarity between worlds. How to avoid dismay?

As evident in these chapters and vignettes, we have approached the topic of interpretation with humility, never losing sight of the daunting challenges to overcome when human beings aspire to clear communication. Aware of the pitfalls appearing everywhere in our subject, we sought convergences of thought, while we also paid special attention to mutual misunderstandings. At times our conversations led to dead ends or abandoned trails; at others, we relished the jolt of the energizing insights unleashed by comparisons and juxtapositions. In the tumultuous 2020s, current events—from the local to the global—repeatedly reminded us that the study of interpreters only grows more relevant. We hope that this book will invite both imitation and irritation, elicit invigorating challenges and revisions (though we would not object to a compliment or two), and deepen understanding of the dynamics of communication in the past, present, and future. With artificial intelligence models now beginning to interpret sources with results varying from the preposterous to the compelling, the need for fresh thinking about the future of interpretation appears all the more pressing.

What does the future hold? No one can know. Not even Siri. At our symposium in April 2022, as participants discussed interpreters in the U.S.-Mexico borderlands, one scholar's Apple Watch misinterpreted a phrase for "Hey Siri" and interrupted the conversation to announce, in a tone at once confident and revealing, "I'm not sure I understand."

Touché.

Notes

1. Alas, on December 23, 2024, a good portion of the Santa Cruz Wharf collapsed, and the area where the sea lions sat is no more. May this anecdote therefore commemorate a wonderful moment of cross-species barking and interpretive contingency!
2. A few rare examples, in addition to other works cited in the chapters that follow, include Radbourne, *Mickey Free*; Hoig, *Western Odyssey of John Simpson Smith*;

Kawashima, "Forest Diplomats"; West, *Contested Plains*; and Szasz, *Between Indian and White Worlds*.
3. Burke and R. Po-Chia Hsia, *Cultural Translation in Early Modern Europe*; Davis, *Trickster Travels*; Di Biase, *Travel and Translation in the Early Modern Period*; Gilbert, *In Good Faith*; Krstic, "Of Translation and Empire"; and Rothman, *Dragoman Renaissance*.
4. de la Puente, "Many Tongues of the King"; Rubiés, "Ethnography and Cultural Translation in the Early Modern Missions"; Andrews, *Native Apostles*; and Metcalf, *Go-Betweens and the Colonization of Brazil*.
5. Norman Shapiro and Willard Trask, quoted in Venuti, *Translator's Invisibility*, 1, 7.
6. One ubiquitous urban legend known to most participants concerned (purportedly) Chevrolet Nova's failure to sell in Spanish-speaking markets because its name, *no va*, suggested it wouldn't run.

Bibliography

Andrews, Edward E. *Native Apostles: Black and Indian Missionaries in the British Atlantic World*. Cambridge MA: Harvard University Press, 2013.

Burke, Peter, and R. Po-Chia Hsia, eds. *Cultural Translation in Early Modern Europe*. Cambridge: Cambridge University Press, 2007.

Di Biase, Carmine, ed. *Travel and Translation in the Early Modern Period*. Amsterdam: Rodopi, 2006.

Davis, Natalie Zemon. *Trickster Travels: A Sixteenth-Century Muslim between Worlds*. New York: Hill & Wang, 2006.

Gilbert, Claire. *In Good Faith: Arabic Translation and Translators in Early Modern Spain*. Philadelphia: University of Pennsylvania Press, 2020.

Hoig, Stan. *The Western Odyssey of John Simpson Smith: Frontiersman, Trapper, Trader, and Interpreter*. Glendale: Arthur H. Clark, 1974.

Kawashima, Yasuhide. "Forest Diplomats: The Role of Interpreters in Indian-White Relations on the Early American Frontier." *American Indian Quarterly* 13, no. 1 (1989): 1–14.

Krstic, Tijana. "Of Translation and Empire: Sixteenth-Century Ottoman Imperial Interpreters as Renaissance Go-Betweens." In *The Ottoman World*, edited by Christine Woodhead, 130–42. London: Routledge, 2011.

Metcalf, Alida C. *Go-Betweens and the Colonization of Brazil: 1500–1600*. Austin: University of Texas Press, 2005.

de la Puente, José Carlos. "The Many Tongues of the King: Indigenous Language Interpreters and the Making of the Spanish Empire." *Colonial Latin American Review* 23, no. 2 (2014): 143–70.

Radbourne, Allan. *Mickey Free: Apache Captive, Interpreter, and Indian Scout*. Tucson: Arizona Historical Society, 2005.

Rothman, Natalie. *The Dragoman Renaissance: Diplomatic Interpreters and the Routes of Orientalism*. Ithaca: Cornell University Press, 2021.

Rubiés, Joan Pau. "Ethnography and Cultural Translation in the Early Modern Missions." *Studies in Church History* 53 (2017): 272–300.

Szasz, Margaret Connell, ed. *Between Indian and White Worlds: The Cultural Broker*. Norman: University of Oklahoma Press, 1994.

Venuti, Lawrence. *The Translator's Invisibility: A History of Translation*. London: Routledge, 1995.

West, Elliott. *The Contested Plains: Indians, Goldseekers, and the Rush to Colorado*. Lawrence: University Press of Kansas, 1998.

A Message and a Dance for Zebulon Pike

From the editors: Zebulon Pike's narrative of his famous travels from 1805–7, on behalf of the U.S. government, illustrates just how much he, like other European and American travelers, relied on government and Indigenous interpreters. In the excerpt below, Pike stays with the Oceti Sakowin Oyate (Sioux Indians) just south of present-day La Crosse, Wisconsin. He and his travel companions, including interpreter Pierre Rosseau, met with Wahpasha. Note the appearance of direct communication and the absence of the interpreter (in the narrative) as an intermediary. The apparent understanding contrasts with Pike's subsequent observations, when he witnesses a dance he does not understand.

Excerpt from *Exploratory Travels*

When I landed, I had my pistols in my belt and sword in hand: I was met on the bank by the chief and invited to his lodge; as soon as my guards were formed and centinels [sic] posted, I accompanied him. Some of my men who were to attend me I caused to leave their arms behind, as a mark of confidence. At the chief's lodge, I found a clean mat and pillow provided for me to sit upon; and the before-mentioned pipe, on a pair of small crutches, was placed before me. The chief sat on my right hand, my interpreter and Mr. Frazer on my left. After smoking, the chief spoke to the following purport.

"That notwithstanding he had seen me at the prairie, he was happy to take me by the hand amongst his own people, and there to shew [sic] his young men the respect due to their 'new father': that when at St. Louis in the spring his father had told him, that if he looked down the river he would see one of his young warriors coming up; he now found it true, and he was happy to see me, who knew the great spirit was the father of all, both the white and the red people, and if one died the other could not live long. That he had never been at war with their new father, and hoped always to preserve the same good understanding that now existed. That he now presented me with a pipe to shew [sic] to the upper bands, as a token of our good understanding; and that they might see his work, and imitate his conduct. That he had gone to St. Louis on a shameful visit, to carry a murderer; but that we had given the fellow his life, and he thanked us for it. That he had provided something to eat, but he supposed I could not eat it myself, and if not, desired I might give it to my young men."

I replied, "that although I had told him at the prairie my business up the Mississippi, I would again relate it to him: I mentioned the different objects I had in view with regard to the savages who had fallen under our protection, by our late purchase from the Spaniards;—the different posts to be established; the objects of these posts as they related to them; supplying them with necessaries, having officers and agents of government near them to attend to their business; and, above all, to endeavour to make peace between the Sioux and Sauteurs. That it was possible on my return I should bring some of the Sauteurs down with me, and take some of the Sioux chiefs to St. Louis, there to settle the long and bloody contest which had existed between the two nations. That I accepted his pipe with pleasure as the gift of a great man, and a brother. That it should be used as he desired."

I then ate of the dinner he had provided. It was very grateful. It consisted of wild rye and venison, of which I sent four bowls to my men. I afterwards went to a dance, the performance of which was attended with many curious manoeuvres. Men and women danced indiscriminately. They were all dressed in the gayest manner; each had in their hand a small skin of some description: they frequently ran up, pointed their skin, and gave a puff with their breath; when the person blown at, whether man or woman, would fall, and appear to be almost lifeless, or in great agony; but would recover slowly, rise, and join in the dance. This they called their great medicine, or, as I understood the word, the dance of religion: the Indians believing that they actually puffed something into each others['] bodies, which occasioned the falling, &c.[1]

Notes

1. Zebulon Montgomery Pike, *Exploratory Travels through the Western Territories of North America: Comprising a Voyage from St. Louis, on the Mississippi, to the Source of that River, and a Journey through the Interior of Louisiana, and the North-Eastern Provinces of New Spain* (London: Longman, Hurst, Rees, Orme, and Brown, 1811), 23–25.

PART 1

INTERPRETING FOR AND WITH EMPIRE

1

From Indigenous Interpreters to Creole Control

Race, Translation, and Exclusion in Yucatan, 1560–1633

MARK LENTZ

In 1605 the namesake and mestizo son of the conquistador Alonso Ruiz de Arévalo appealed for royal confirmation of the title to serve as one of two official interpreters general, due to the death of the previous holder, Gaspar Antonio Herrera de Chi. Arévalo had long served as a secondary interpreter in the shadow of Gaspar Antonio, the best-known interpreter of sixteenth-century Yucatan. Gaspar Antonio's illustrious career included teaching grammar in the Franciscans' school and a stint as the Indigenous governor of Maní. Arévalo, the *hijo natural*, or illegitimate son of a conquistador and likely a Chontal Maya woman, had dutifully served as an interpreter in remote locations to which the Mérida-based interpreter general, Chi, was not inclined to travel.[1] In 1607 Arévalo's petition met with success, and he received royal confirmation of his status as interpreter general.[2]

There was one major problem, however. Gaspar Antonio was not dead. Though Arévalo secured the title to interpreter general, Yucatan's governor don Carlos de Luna y Arellano continued to rely on Gaspar Antonio's expertise along with that of a second interpreter general appointed with less controversy in 1603. Gaspar Antonio and Diego de Mora investigated rumors that the heads of the pueblo of Yobain had led their community and residents of surrounding towns in forbidden religious practices and rebellion.[3] Although Arévalo had legal claim to the title of interpreter general, the notary Gerónimo de Yanguas identified Gaspar Antonio and Diego de Mora as "the interpreters of this court."[4] In 1607, again alongside Diego de Mora, Gaspar Antonio translated during an investigation into rumors of a conspiracy against Spanish rule in Yobain.[5] This was not Gaspar Antonio's final appearance as a translator for a protracted legal proceeding, either. Despite his ill health and advanced age, in late October of 1609 he began to translate in a nearly six-month investigation and trials following an uprising in Tekax, apparently his last major undertaking as the province's leading translator.[6] Though Gaspar Antonio was apparently quite ill during his final decade on earth and in office, he had not died, as Arévalo claimed. However, one or two such severe illnesses might have led his erstwhile protégé and recent rival for the post of interpreter general, with its accompanying salary, to write of his impending death as a fait accompli.

Gaspar Antonio was indeed in ill health. Exaggerated rumors of his infirmities may have reached Arévalo, leading him to pen a letter to the Crown based on a belief that by the time it reached Spain, Gaspar Antonio would indeed be dead. As early as 1581, Gaspar Antonio Chi had complained of his ill health in letters to the crown requesting payment of salary either owed him as a result of earlier decrees from Madrid or due to unpaid services. Still almost thirty years away from his death, Gaspar Antonio mentioned his old age (referring to himself as *viejo*), and twice referred to his constant infirmities.[7] In a series of seven *probanzas* and *cédulas* in support of Gaspar Antonio's claims to the position of interpreter general dating from 1581 to 1599, the term "enfermo" or "enfermedad" appears thirty-three times. Furthermore, witnesses offered detailed descriptions of his poor health and how it hampered his work, adding more evidence of thirty years of poor health that preceded his death.[8]

Arévalo's haste in confirming his succession as interpreter general based on premature claims around Gaspar Antonio's death, whether misinformed or malicious, took place at a time in which candidates fiercely contested each other in their efforts to be named the province's top interpreter. From 1560, when Arévalo first appears named as interpreter general, until 1610, when Gaspar Antonio stepped away from his duties one last time, intense competition characterized the fight to win nomination from the governors as interpreter general, an increasingly lucrative and respectable post. Though collaboration marked some of the overlapping terms of service, rivalries and disparaging claims against competitors also characterized the disputes. Many such contests for official recognition involved racially based arguments regarding the unfitness of opponents to hold the position. Yet racial politics did not consistently thwart efforts at upward mobility. Indeed, the fates of three mestizo interpreters and one Maya translator set the stage for a century in which the post of interpreter general served as a socially prominent, stable, and well-remunerated position. However, due to the attractiveness of the post, among other factors, the vast majority of their successors were of Spanish identity. This chapter explores the biographies of these intermediaries, suggesting that many factors led to the disappearance of Maya and mestizo interpreters and their displacement by Spanish-descent creoles. The Maya and mestizo interpreters of the sixteenth century were victims of their own success, as creoles sought the more well-established, remunerative, and respectable position for themselves.

Gaspar Antonio and Arévalo, one-time collegial co-interpreters and later competitors for the same royal appointment, were the last Maya and mestizo to hold the post of interpreter general before a generation of creoles of European descent monopolized the position. The gradual takeover by Spanish-descent settlers of a stable, salaried job once staffed primarily by Mayas and mestizos had multiple causes, though historians have failed to examine the transition in depth. A previous study by Caroline Cunill asserted that a wave of anti-mestizo legislation drove bilingual indigenous and mestizo intermediaries from the post. While growing sentiment in opposition to mestizos and restrictions on their career paths had some impact, more factors were at play than simply a series of *reales cédulas* (royal decrees) in the diminished presence of interpreters of Indigenous ancestry in the key office.

The lessened reliance on polyglot interpreters, the attraction of a stable salary, permanence in the post, a decimated population of Mayas, and growing creole bilingualism also played a role. As the seventeenth century wore on, more creoles exhibited fluency and literacy in Maya and Spanish. Knowledge of other languages became less important. Early mestizo and Maya interpreters often spoke or wrote more than one Indigenous language, making them useful in the early colonial period when Indigenous populations were in flux and a greater variety of native languages were spoken. Diminished demand for polyglot translators such as Gaspar Antonio and Alonso de Arévalo, who each spoke at least two Indigenous languages, lessened the reliance on multilingual translators. Expanding literacy and fluency in Maya among the descendants of Spanish conquistadors and early settlers also contributed to creole control of the position of the interpreter general. More creoles were inclined to put their linguistic talents to use as the pay, prestige, and stability of the interpreters general increased. Unlike the second half of the sixteenth century, when interpreters were hired and fired at the whims of governors, the seventeenth century witnessed longer and more fixed tenure on the part of these court translators, which attracted more creoles to seek employment in this capacity. Finally, the precipitous drop in the Maya population also led to the gradual disappearance of Mayas and mestizo interpreter generals.

Translation and interpreters in seventeenth- and eighteenth-century Latin America have received less attention from scholars, especially in English-language publications. Studies of interpreters in Spain's colonies skew heavily toward figures from the contact era or the early colonial period.[9] More recently, scholars have moved beyond contact-era intermediaries, notably in studies of Peru and Andean translators.[10] Despite a dearth of studies focusing on interpreters and translation in colonial Latin America in the middle viceregal period, recent monographs, books, and anthologies have addressed this gap, most notably in Spanish-language scholarship. Studies that move beyond the seventeenth century include Paulina Machuca's *Intérpretes y trasuntos* (2009) and several chapters in Caroline Cunill and Luis Miguel Glave Testino's edited volume, *Las Lenguas indígenas*.[11] The trend toward studying interpreters in Spanish-language scholarship focused on interpreters for the middle and late colonial eras has yet to be matched in English-language scholarship on the same periods.

Scholarship on translation in Yucatan consists primarily of two articles by Caroline Cunill that survey the interpreters of the sixteenth century as well as a few biographical sketches of Gaspar Antonio Chi.[12] In contrast to Cunill, this chapter examines the transition from the multiethnic array of interpreters of the sixteenth century who are the main focus of her studies to the transition from a mix of Maya, mestizo, and Spanish-descent translators to a cadre of interpreters general who were exclusively of Spanish ancestry from the seventeenth century onward. Cunill's legally oriented article attributed the diminished presence of mestizos and Mayas in governmental posts to prohibitions on mestizos and a general rising anti-mestizo sentiment, a significant cause of their removal and exclusion.[13] Ancestry alone did not disqualify interpreters from the post, though it did factor into rulings over appointments. While individual interpreters in Yucatan faced opposition that targeted their mixed ancestry in a way that coincided with broader legislation aimed at marginalizing mestizos, more factors also played a role in the diminished diversity of linguistic mediators in Yucatan. This chapter highlights how the efforts of Maya and mestizo translators elevated the prestige and pay of the interpreters to the point where it became highly desirable to creoles of high standing who were motivated to compete for the position. The expanding bilingualism on the part of Spanish-descent Yucatecans also contributed to the gradual creole takeover of the post of interpreter general.

Racially exclusionary politics peaked in the final decades of the sixteenth century. Though a decline in the social standing of Maya elites and mestizos with illustrious forebears and efforts to displace them did play a role, decrees passed in Madrid aimed at bringing order to its overseas empire tended to be "piecemeal," regionally specific, sporadically enforced, and often internally inconsistent.[14] As a result, many Maya and mestizo interpreters survived the purported anti-mestizo backlash with their positions intact. The Maya Gaspar Antonio and mestizo Arévalo both served into the first and second decades of the seventeenth century. Even the much-derided Antonio Nieto, a mestizo, served until at least 1597.[15] Legal restrictions were piecemeal and personalized. Indeed, economic attractions, the position's growing prestige, and permanence of the interpreters led creoles to pursue the position in a way that contrasted with their predecessors, who received less regular pay and were more subject to the whims of governors who came and went.

Opponents of mestizo translators often used a kitchen sink approach to criticizing mestizo translators. Two other mestizo interpreters, Antonio Nieto and Diego de Vargas, bore the brunt of racially charged accusations leveled against them, aimed at overturning their appointments as interpreter general. Arévalo, despite his mestizo ancestry, did not suffer such attacks. However, while the adversaries of Nieto and Vargas did use "mestizo" in an insulting manner, they focused on an array of character flaws in their efforts to depose the mestizo interpreters. Nieto's critics alleged that he solicited bribes and used his bilingualism to intimidate the Mayas and to coerce them into disadvantageous trading relations with him.[16] A 1580 cédula singled out Diego de Vargas as a "young mestizo, vice-ridden, of a bad lifestyle and habits."[17] The cédula alleged that he had caused much harm to the Mayas and harassed and took advantage of their women. It ordered his removal from the post of interpreter.[18] Accusations of personal misconduct, abuse of power, and corruption led to the downfall of Vargas and Nieto as much as the mestizaje in their ancestry. More sagacious interpreters of mestizo and Maya ancestry did not face such opposition or denunciations and continued to serve. Despite early attempts at a consistent, coherent legal system, petitions against mestizo interpreters and the resulting legislation often only applied in individual cases.

Mestizo identity and legal standing, given nuanced scrutiny in recent studies by Robert F. Schwaller and Adrian Masters, involved more than descent from Spanish and Indigenous parents. As Schwaller demonstrated, many children of conquistadors, such as three children of Francisco de Montejo, fell into a liminal category of "tacit *españoles*," receiving many of the legal privileges and inheriting much of the culture of their Spanish fathers.[19] Arévalo and Nieto likely fit into this category, though political rivals drew attention to Nieto's mixed ancestry to deprive him of his post of translator. Arévalo, on the other hand, appears just once in extensive documentation identified as a mestizo.[20] Moreover, he called upon many prominent Spaniards as witnesses in support of two *probanzas*, a "proof" or report of one's service to the crown, emphasizing his integration into Spanish society and distance from his Indigenous progenitors characteristic of "tacit *españoles*."[21] The fact that Arévalo's tenure lasted long beyond the supposed exclusion of mestizos from prominent posts indicates the importance of social standing rather than solely questions of racial identity. Furthermore, the application of exclusionary legislation was far from consistent.

As Adrian Masters demonstrated, the flurry of legislation dealing with the growing numbers of mixed-race subjects often repeated petitions word-for-word. In many instances the "petition and response system" addressed only local or regional conflicts over the legal and social status of mestizos.[22] A cédula ousting a mestizo interpreter in a particular setting did not mean that all mestizos, or Mayas for that matter, were banned from holding that post in the future. *Derecho indiano*, Spain's legal regime in its American imperial territories, was essentially casuistic, deferential to local and regional customs and traditions.[23] A general anti-mestizo thrust of legislation was not all-encompassing. Mestizos such as Arévalo and prominent Indigenous figures such as Gaspar Antonio escaped unscathed due to the inconsistent and case-by-case nature of the overall trend toward exclusion. Growing anti-mestizo legislation only provides a partial explanation for the creole displacement of interpreters of partial or full Indigenous ancestry.

Diminishing Diversity, Linguistic and Otherwise

The vast numbers of supporters who wrote endorsements and provided supportive verbal testimony for Gaspar Antonio makes it unlikely that racial animosity alone prevented a Maya successor from taking his place upon his death. Instead, the sharp decline of the Maya population meant that the number of potential inheritors of this position from the indigenous Yucatecans had dropped exponentially. During the pre-Columbian period, estimates of the Maya population of Yucatan range from 280,000 to eight to ten million for Yucatan before the arrival of the Spaniards. The most accepted estimate, by Sherburne F. Cooke and Woodrow Borah, stands at eight hundred thousand.[24] By the first decade of the seventeenth century, the number of Mayas had plummeted to around 163,000.[25]

A demographic disaster of this scale impacted society on many levels, including a significant reduction in the number of bilingual Mayas available to interpret.

Sixteenth-century mestizo interpreters typically descended from a conquistador father and Indigenous mother, with whom they likely had close ties. This cultural connection provided them with more social capital among Mayas, and they often spoke Maya as a literal mother tongue. As "mestizo" emerged as a distinct racial category, the social distance between Mayas and mestizos grew. During the seventeenth century cultural and linguistic affinities between Mayas and later mestizos, who usually were born to parents of mixed ancestry on both sides, decreased. Other prominent descendants of conquistadors married strategically into Spanish families, leaving their Indigenous ancestry unacknowledged. Though of partial Indigenous ancestry, they and their descendants became recognized as Spaniards. As Schwaller noted, the category of "tacit *españoles*" shrank during the final decades of the sixteenth century.[26] Their descendants' Indigenous ancestry, cultural ties, and linguistic abilities diminished generation by generation, making them less adept at crossing cultural and linguistic boundaries. Even Gaspar Antonio, a Maya, had descendants who moved into this class of ostensible creoles with Indigenous ancestry. His granddaughter Francisca Chinab Couoh de Herrera married a Spaniard, beginning a process by which Gaspar Antonio's descendants "continued to marry within Spanish society."[27]

This marriage came at the end of Gaspar Antonio's life, in 1609. Unlike the three mestizo interpreters—Nieto, Vargas, and Arévalo—Gaspar Antonio had no family ties to powerful conquistadors or their offspring to aid his ascent to the prestigious position of interpreter general. Instead, he stands out as a rare figure who counted on Maya, mestizo, and Indigenous central Mexican supporters as well as Spaniards from the ranks of encomenderos and friars who testified in his extensive petitions in support of his claim to serve as interpreter general. Gaspar Antonio benefited from unmatched broad support from a diverse array of political allies. Indeed, he stands out as Yucatan's best-known Indigenous intellectual, a polymath who spoke at least four languages and was likely literate in at least three. A polyglot interpreter, Gaspar Antonio not only spoke and wrote Spanish and Yucatec Maya but was also literate and fluent in Nahuatl as well as Latin, noted by ecclesiastical chroniclers. Several witnesses noted his fluency in all four languages, including friars such as fray Hernando de Sopuerta and Gaspar de Nájera and public officials such as the notary Alonso de Rojas and the cabildo member Martín de Palomar.[28]

Remarkably, he had survived the protracted conquest of Yucatan and was one of the few survivors of a Maya massacre inflicted on his dynasty—the Xiu—by the rival Cocoms in the 1530s.[29] As a descendent of Maya nobles, he commanded the respect of the native inhabitants of the land.[30] Though many Indigenous nobles eventually fell afoul of the domineering Franciscans, Gaspar Antonio deftly maneuvered through the turbulent early years of the Franciscans' political dominance of the peninsula, roughly 1544–63, first earning the favor of the friars before cultivating powerful patrons among the representatives of royal rule who came to tame the clergymen.

In a region that initially had no governor and in which power rested with the Franciscan prior, the young interpreter earned the respect of many churchmen in the turbulent 1560s, including both secular clergy and friars beginning with the infamous extirpator of "idolatry," fray Diego de Landa.[31] The priest and author Pedro Sánchez de Aguilar noted in his 1639 *Informe contra idolorum cultores del obispado de Yucatan* that Gaspar Antonio had served as interpreter, served briefly as cacique of Maní, and worked as a notary, among a variety of governmental posts. Sánchez de Aguilar's only slight against Gaspar Antonio was that he spoke Latin only "medianamente."[32] The friar López de Cogolludo, providing a historical Franciscan perspective decades after the interpreter's death, provided similar accolades of Gaspar Antonio but differed in his estimation of his aptitude in Latin, stating that he "knew it very well."[33]

Gaspar Antonio's diplomatic acumen enabled his continuing influence in Yucatan and good standing with friars, fellow Mayas, a series of governors, and secular clergymen such as Sánchez de Aguilar. He kept an active cultural life as well, teaching Maya to young clergymen, singing plain chant, and playing the organ. The conquistador Blas Gónzalez credited him with having written many of the sermons still in use in the last decade of the sixteenth century, as Gaspar Antonio gathered testimony supporting his request for a pay increase in 1593.[34] As an author and contributor to other works, he assisted in the production of the map found in the Maní Land Treaty, a Xiu family tree, de Landa's *Relación de las cosas de Yucatán*, and the *Relaciones geograficas*.[35] He authored a now fragmentary manuscript, "Relación de algunas costumbres," preserved in the Archivo General de Indias, which served as the basis for many subsequent, expanded histories (both created with his input and after his death).[36] The life of Gaspar Antonio has fascinated modern-day scholars of Yucatan as well, with many articles and book chapters profiling his biography, though to date no book-length treatment has been written.[37]

Notably, even though he worked as a translator fluent in multiple languages during the same decades as Gaspar Antonio, few scholars are even aware of Alonso de Arévalo. While Gaspar Antonio's biography provides a case study of an Indigenous intellectual who thrived through the turmoil of the conquest and early viceregal era, Arévalo's life history shows how a potentially marginal mestizo parlayed his linguistic and cultural talents into a parallel story of survival and a modicum of success. And while Gaspar Antonio's life exemplifies one of the more successful trajectories of an Indigenous intellectual, Arévalo's better demonstrates the precarity of a more typical intermediary, of a mestizo background with fewer powerful patrons. Overshadowed by Gaspar Antonio, Alonso de Arévalo's less publicized career followed that of his better-known counterpart. The two appear occasionally working in tandem, highlighting in many instances that the two interpreters had an amicable working relationship. The pair worked closely as translators for the *visita* of Dr. don Diego de Palacio. Even while falsely declaring his one-time mentor dead to secure his succession to the post, Arévalo included a previous recommendation from Gaspar Antonio commending his service as a supporting witness to a previous *probanza* from 1586.[38] In his approving testimony, Gaspar Antonio stated that he had known Arévalo for twenty-four years and that he had high regard for his counterpart's translation skills.

Friars, too, called upon Arévalo's talents, but with less appreciation than they showed for Gaspar Antonio. Arévalo worked as a *lengua* for Yucatan's Franciscans, preaching and rooting out Maya underground religion. He boasted that he helped find and confiscate "five thousand idols" alongside the Franciscan fray Pablo Maldonado in Cozumel, an unpaid service.[39] Without specifying dates or superiors, he also asserted that he acted as interpreter for ecclesiastical courts.[40] Such occasional duties on behalf of ecclesiastical authorities likely stemmed from his sporadic displacement from the position of interpreter general.

His ambiguous ancestry also seemed to have hampered Arévalo's career. Though he claimed to have been interpreter general since his first appointment, at least on one occasion he received a pension (*ayuda de costa*) of 110 pesos designated for surviving widows and children of conquistadors during a period in which competitors for the post of interpreter general had displaced him. The record of such payments notes that he was a mestizo.[41] Arévalo acknowledged his illegitimate status, referring to himself as an "hijo natural."[42] This likely prevented him from inheriting an encomienda, as encomenderos needed to marry to keep their encomiendas. Alonso Ruiz de Arévalo, his father, apparently never did and certainly never married the Indigenous mother of his *hijo natural*. Mentions of his father's poverty and his own scattered throughout his *relación de méritos* hint at scarcity that plagued him despite his prestige as a conquistador.[43]

Arévalo never mentioned his mother in the extensive documentation supporting his requests for official appointments and salary increases. Only rarely did his Indigenous connections appear in the documents produced in favor of his appointment, such as when the witness Blas Gónzalez noted that he spoke Indigenous languages so well partly because he had "been raised from his childhood among the natives (*naturales*)."[44] Though racially a mestizo, he relied heavily on Spanish of witnesses to testify on behalf of his petition for reappointment to the post of interpreter and a salary increase. Many of these came from the ranks of conquistadors who accompanied his father. The conquistadors Bartolomé Rojo and Blas Gónzalez both backed his declarations and emphasized the deeds of their companion, his father. Two cabildo members, Juan de Cárdenas, regidor of Valladolid and Juan de Aguilar, regidor of Mérida, also testified in his favor.[45]

By contrast, Gaspar Antonio included mestizos and Mayas among his supporting witnesses as well as a sizeable number of Spaniards, including Blas Gónzalez, who had testified favorably in Arévalo's probanza hearing. The breadth of Gaspar Antonio's impressive support stemmed partly from his fluency in not only Yucatec Maya but also Nahuatl and Latin. The probanza in support of his appointment included supportive testimony from mestizos such as Diego Briceño, son of a conquistador father and Central Mexican mother, don Jorge Xiu, governor of the town of Panabchén, don Pedro Ku, "principal" (or elite) of Homún, and Juan de Estrada (alias Juan Duro), an Indigenous ally of the Spaniards in the conquest of Yucatan.[46] Briceño, who served as *defensor de los naturales*, was the son of an "india mexicana" and a conquistador father.[47] Estrada's self-described origin hints at central Mexican ancestry as well. He appears as an *indio* from the "pueblo de los naboríos," a reference to the Central Mexican allies of the Spaniards in the long conquest of Yucatan. This "pueblo" was adjacent to the Barrio de San Cristóbal, initially settled by Indigenous auxiliaries in Francisco de Montejo's conquest of Yucatan. The most prominent founders came from Central Mexico.[48] Gaspar Antonio's personal life also bolstered his support among central Mexican Indians, the primary inhabitants in the sixteenth century of the *barrios de indios* of San Cristóbal and Santiago. His wife, Francisca Muñoz, was a daughter of a Central Mexican *indio conquistador*, Francisco Muñoz.[49] Few candidates for province-level offices could rely on the backing of Maya, Central Mexican, and mestizo witnesses in their favor. Yet Gaspar also moved comfortably in a Hispanic ambit. He served in positions in which other interpreters rarely worked. He not only translated in the 1583 visita conducted by Dr. Diego García de Palacio but also occasionally served as a witness.[50]

Gaspar Antonio and Arévalo also shared a similarity uncommon in later interpreters as polyglot translators. As already mentioned, Gaspar Antonio spoke, wrote, and read not only Yucatec Maya and Spanish but also Nahuatl and Latin. His skill in the latter language elicited comments from Franciscan supporters and he was often called upon to work on textual translations. For example, in 1607 Gaspar Antonio and Diego de Mora teamed up to translate oral testimony, but Gaspar Antonio translated Maya documents submitted as evidence by the cacique of Yobain, don Juan Pech.[51] Arévalo, too, spoke four languages and wrote in at least two, Yucatec Maya and Spanish. He rarely mentioned his fluency in two other languages, Nahuatl and Chontal, in contrast to Gaspar Antonio, who frequently mentioned his grasp of Nahuatl and Maya.[52] This expansive repertoire of languages served them well in a time when Chontal was still commonplace in the eastern edges of modern-day Campeche and Tabasco, both under the rule of the Mérida-based governors, and many Central Mexican auxiliaries in the conquest settled in Yucatan spoke Nahuatl. No creoles had such linguistic versatility.

Like Gaspar Antonio, Arévalo had patrons from the ranks of the clergy and the royal administrators, starting with his first appointment as the "interpreter of the province" for the governor Lic. Jofre de Loaysa in 1560.[53] The *visitador* Dr. don Diego Palacios hired him as one of three interpreters of the *visita* of 1586. In 1586 the Defensor de los Naturales, Francisco de Palomino, testified favorably to commend Arévalo's skills and experience as interpreter. Arévalo also worked in extirpation campaigns on behalf of Franciscans in remote locations such as Chichimilá, Cozumel, Yaxcabá, Tecoh, and Peto. Based in Valladolid, he emphasized his travels, possibly in contrast to the increasingly immobile Gaspar Antonio, who complained regularly of his injuries from earlier travels beginning in 1581.[54] Reinstated as interpreter general in 1603 by the governor Diego Fernández de Velasco, Arévalo noted that his salary was 170 pesos, less than the 200 pesos paid to his "predecessor," Gaspar Antonio, since 1593.[55] A cédula in 1604 confirmed this appointment, despite the fact that Gaspar Antonio continued to live and translate.

Yet historians and contemporary chroniclers during his lifetime paid more attention to Gaspar Antonio. Did the acclaim, success, and prestige of Gaspar Antonio rankle the mestizo translator and son of a conquistador? Including both the discrepancy in their salaries and misinformation regarding the still-living Gaspar Antonio suggests he did resent the older interpreter at the end of his career. Yet their interactions are complicated.

Gaspar Antonio and Alonso de Arévalo's competition for primacy and recognition appears subdued and genteel compared to other efforts to besmirch and undermine opponents in pursuit of official appointments. Moreover, the two also stand out for their tenacity in retaining the post of interpreter general in the face of growing opposition to Mayas and mestizos holding province-wide positions of power. In their early years, their counterparts were other Mayas and mestizos. Their successors were invariably creoles.

Mestizos, Mayas, and Intensifying Competition

Arévalo's attempts to usurp Gaspar Antonio's position paled in comparison to the heated competition to win official recognition as interpreter general, dependent on the fiat of individual governors. Along with Arévalo, two other mestizos, Diego de Vargas and Antonio Nieto, vied for the appointment. As Arévalo's persistence shows, there was no abrupt shift away from mestizos and Mayas serving as interpreters, in contrast to Caroline Cunill's claim that this change took place due solely to regulation in 1599.[56] Instead, laws selectively enforced against political rivals gradually diminished the ranks of mestizos. Rising anti-mestizo sentiment and deepening distrust of Maya leaders on the part of provincial authorities led to their piecemeal disappearance. Racial politics—tying an enemy's character to their status as mestizo or Maya—combined with legislation to limit the terms of some mestizos, such as Diego de Vargas. Yet others, such as Arévalo and Nieto, continued to serve. Arévalo in particular benefited from general goodwill, in contrast to Vargas.

Unlike Arévalo and Gaspar Antonio, Antonio Nieto's relationship with Gaspar Antonio seems to have had been rather complicated. In one petition for reinstatement, in 1581, Gaspar Antonio complained that the governor, don Guillén de las Casas, had named Antonio Nieto as interpreter in an effort to exclude him from the post.[57] However, officially at least, the outgoing governor—De las Casas's term ended in 1582—only named a second interpreter and did not displace Gaspar Antonio.[58] Even so, the language used in the petition submitted by Gaspar Antonio did not strike such an antagonistic tone as another request for appointment submitted by Marcos Rodríguez. In a petition that sought to oust Nieto, Rodríguez asserted that the two interpreters, whom he did not name though he clearly intended to single out Nieto, abused their position to demand labor, tribute items, and money from the Mayas. The new claimant to the position requested that the Crown issue a real cedula to the effect that neither Mayas nor mestizos ("ningún indio ni mestizo") should act as interpreters. Rodríguez further argued that the interpreters should be sons of *vecinos*, men of confidence, "grandes lenguas" or knowledgeable Maya speakers, and good Christians, implying that Nieto was not.[59] Notably, Gaspar Antonio had interacted with Nieto more cooperatively on earlier occasions, demonstrating that the competition emerged after earlier harmonious relations. For example, in a petition for a pay raise that Gaspar Antonio submitted ten years later in 1580, Antonio Nieto had translated the testimony of a favorable Maya witness, Pedro Ku, as supporting evidence in favor of the claim.[60] Nieto appeared as the "interpreter general of this tribunal," with no challenge from Gaspar Antonio at the time. Evidently, the struggle for official recognition as interpreter general began shortly after.[61]

Indigenous translators continued to work in matters of the church even when the tendency to exclude them from civil legal matters had already become evident. In the 1583 visita of Yucatán undertaken by the *oidor* Dr. Diego García de Palacio, the jurist relied on three interpreters, a Spaniard, Martín Ruiz de Arze (also spelled Darze); a mestizo, Arévalo; and a Maya, Gaspar Antonio.[62] At the same time, Luis Xol, "intérprete de los dichos religiosos," translated on behalf of the Franciscans in Tizimin. His role in collecting tithes on behalf of the friars came under scrutiny in the same judicial review. Elsewhere referred to as a "naguatato de los religiosos," his ongoing translation for the friars indicates that Franciscans continued to rely on their Indigenous legal aides even when no Mayas other than Gaspar Antonio acted as translators in secular legal matters.[63] Xol's role as a local translator on behalf of the Franciscans only surfaced as a result of the *visita*'s investigation into tithes demanded by Franciscan, which the "naguatato" facilitated. Such local intermediaries continued to serve the religious, though with time most Franciscans became fluent in Maya and no longer depended on interpreters such as Xol.

While Franciscans continued to rely on local lenguas, the civil courts relied less on Indigenous interpreters, at least in Yucatan. In the sixteenth century, Yucatan's governors ruled territory that included Chontal Maya speakers to the east and a significant number of Central Mexican auxiliaries whose primary language was Nahuatl. Speakers of these languages suffered a much more precipitous decline in population or were absorbed into the Spanish-speaking urban centers at rates greater than the Yucatec Maya. This rapid decline of Indigenous languages other than Yucatec Maya diminished demand for polyglot translators such as Gaspar Antonio and Alonso de Arévalo and lessened the reliance on multilingual translators. Indeed, while Yucatec Maya prevailed as the leading language of the province, the use of Nahuatl and Chontal Maya declined sharply. Thus, in a century that saw the decrease of linguistic diversity, the growing numbers of bilingual creoles displaced polyglot translators who tended to come from Indigenous backgrounds as interpreters.

Yet, the persistence of Indigenous and mixed-race interpreters in other regions of New Spain shows that the domination of translation by creoles was not replicated elsewhere. In Oaxaca, Michoacán, and Colima, Indigenous individuals, mestizos, and in rare instances, even Afro-Mexicans held official posts as interpreters or translated in situ as "named interpreters" (*intérpretes nombrados*). In Oaxaca, Indigenous nobles worked as official interpreters until at least the end of the seventeenth century.[64] A single family of Indigenous nobles from Pátzcuaro predominated as interpreters in Michoacán until the end of the seventeenth century.[65] In Colima, Indigenous interpreters are largely absent from the record. However, in other ways the seventeenth century saw an increasing diversity among its interpreters compared to the sixteenth, when most interpreters were Spaniards. In the seventeenth century, mestizos, *mulatos*, and one Black interpreter acted as translators.[66] The likeliest explanation for the prevalence of Indigenous interpreters in Oaxaca and Michoacán, in contrast to their apparent absence for the majority of the seventeenth century in Yucatan and Colima, is the ease with which Indigenous translators managed multiple autochthonous languages. In Yucatan, interpreters translated primarily between Yucatec Maya and Spanish and in Colima, between Nahuatl and Spanish. Creoles were likelier able to grasp a high level of literacy and fluency in these two commonly spoken Indigenous languages. Interpreters in Michoacán and Oaxaca, by contrast, often needed to speak, read, and write in multiple Indigenous languages, something that was likelier in the case of Indigenous interpreters.

In Yucatan, the exclusion of mestizos and Mayas from the position of interpreter general occurred over the course of decades, not as a direct result of specific royal decrees. Opposition to mestizos in positions of power throughout Spain's rapidly expanded territory in the Americas accelerated during the second half of the sixteenth century. The decades of the 1560s to the 1590s saw a growing tendency to degrade the legal, professional, and religious status of mestizos. It reached its peak during the 1580s, a high point in a campaign by prominent mestizo activists, especially in the Andes, to counter the increasing restrictions on their career choices with the church and the royal government. Additional restrictions and sumptuary laws prohibited them from carrying weapons. Their legal status went from de facto members of the *república de españoles* to being equated with Afro-

Peruvians of mixed ancestry.[67] Petitions from both advocates of mestizo rights and proponents of race-based restrictions informed the legislation that flowed from Spain. As Adrian Masters demonstrated, in many instances reales cédulas lifted the petitions' language word-for-word. By 1629, according to Antonio de León Pinelo's estimate, the Council of Indies had produced 600 books, 150,000 pages, and 400,000 individual rulings.[68] Contained in this mountain of legislation was a flurry of conflicting decrees, alternately restricting and restoring mestizos' status in the New World.

The disappearance of Mayas and mestizos from the ranks of Yucatan's top interpreters also stemmed from a growing ability and inclination of creoles, American-born Spaniards, to seek employment as interpreters, a stable, well-remunerated, and highly regarded post by the early seventeenth century. More and more creoles fluent in Yucatec Maya qualified for the position as "buenas lenguas." In 1587 Ródriguez, the author of the petition to have Nieto disqualified, opened one sentence with the following line: "que haviendo en esa provinçia españoles personas suficientes que pueden server de tales interpretes" ("since there are in this province sufficient Spaniards who can serve as interpreters").[69] Evidence of bilingual creoles begins to appear in late sixteenth-century documents, though the breadth of their fluency and literacy in Maya expanded gradually over the next century. For example, in testimony gathered against Antonio Rodríguez, a corrupt alcaide of the port of Hocobén, Antonio García recalled a conversation with the Maya residents of Hocobén, Tizimin, and Calotmul regarding their inebriation "en su lengua," or in Maya. A linguistic divide no longer separated all creoles from Mayas.[70]

Increased pay and stability in the position also attracted more bilingual creoles. In Yucatan, the two-hundred-peso salary, the stability of the position, and the prestige that accompanied the title of interpreter general led creoles to successfully pursue the post. Just as Gaspar Antonio had been the last Maya interpreter general, Arévalo was the last individual publicly seen as a mestizo to receive royal recognition as Yucatan's key intermediary. Arévalo's successor, don Manuel de Olivares, was a creole and an encomendero.[71] His petition to receive a salary of two hundred pesos in 1633, a raise from the original hundred-peso salary upheld by Madrid, marked a permanent rise in the profitability of the office of interpreter.[72] A growing number of bilingual creoles combined with the financial benefits of the position led to competition among Spanish-descent Yucatecans for Crown confirmation as interpreters. Mayas and mestizos were effectively shut out. While there may have been interpreters of partial Indigenous descent, they took pains to hide their ancestry and are not recognized as such. From the time of Olivares's appointment to the time of the last interpreter of the colonial period whose position was ended in 1821, creole men exclusively held the post. While the sixteenth century saw two non-Maya women, several Mayas (both paid and forced), mestizos, and conquistadors as translators, such diversity ended with the deaths of Arévalo and Gaspar Antonio in the second decade of the seventeenth century.

Early translators were men and women, Mayas, mestizos, and Spaniards, though by the mid-seventeenth century creole men exclusively held the position of interpreter general. Women who mediated between Maya and Spanish were rare, even in the early years. They disappeared from the documented translators as the major events of the military conquest gave way to the establishment of colonial administration and the growing power of the Franciscans, the monastic order that oversaw a violent and wide-reaching spiritual conquest. Their preference for young men as pupils, usually the sons of Maya elites, and a rigid set of gender norms likely contributed to the emergence of all-male ranks of interpreters, or *lenguas* and *nahuatlatos* as they appear in the documentation of their activities. A century after the conquest, all of the documented interpreters general were creole and men.

The lives these creole men led were, compared to the illustrious life of Gaspar Antonio Chi and the hardships overcome by Alonso de Arévalo, unremarkable. Other than militia service, few attained respectable posts beyond their court appointment as interpreter general. As they focused on criminal and civil cases, none merited mention by Franciscans for their proselytizing efforts. The petitions for higher pay submitted by Arévalo, Gaspar Antonio, Vargas, and Nieto had led to more reliable and higher pay. Combined with the Crown policy establishing greater permanence, this high renumeration led more creoles to seek the job as the province's top translators, displacing the Mayas and mestizos whose petitions, competition, and impressive command of multiple languages created the contours of the interpreters general who translated in Yucatan over the subsequent two centuries of colonial rule.

Notes

1. Arévalo never mentioned his mother but his fluency in Chontal Maya noted by Lic. Jofre de Loaysa in 1560 hints strongly at an Indigenous Chontal mother. Yucatan's interpreters knew Yucatec Maya and on occasion Nahuatl, but Chontal was rare and suggestive of Indigenous parentage. AGI, México 296, "Confirmación de título de intérprete," 1607.

2. AGI, Indiferente 449, L. A1, "Confirmación de título de Alonso de Arévalo," 1607, ff. 151–51v.
3. AGI, México 3048, no. 4, "Diligencias que se hizieron sobre la junta y platicas de algunos indios de que se denunció pareciendo que se alteraban," 1607, ff. 213–17.
4. AGI, México 3048, no. 4, "Diligencias que se hizieron sobre la junta y platicas de algunos indios de que se denunció pareciendo que se alteraban," 1607, f. 214.
5. AGI, México 3048, no. 4, "Diligencias que se hizieron sobre la junta y platicas de algunos indios de que se denunció pareciendo que se alteraban," 1607.
6. AGI, Escribanía de Cámara, 305A, numero 2, pieza 1, "El fiscal con Francisco Cal, Martín Nay, Francisco Pizte y otros indios naturales del pueblo Tecax. . . ." 1610, ff. 147–67v.
7. AGI, México 105A, ramo 4, "Gaspar Antonio Chi de Herrera sobre que no se le quite cierto oficio de intérprete," October 11, 1581. Reproduced in Quezada and Torres Trujillo, *Tres nobles mayas yucatecos*, 53.
8. AGI, México 105B, ramo 4, "Gaspar Antonio interprete general de las provincias de Yucatan y vesino de ellas sobre su ayuda de costa," October 12, 1581. Reproduced in Quezada and Torres Trujillo, *Tres nobles mayas yucatecos*, 55–57.
9. Important works such as Alida Metcalf's *Go-Betweens and the Colonization of Brazil* and Camilla Townsend's *Malintzin's Choices* serve as prime examples of contact-era studies of translation.
10. Two significant works in this vein include José Carlos de la Puente Luna's article "Many Tongues of the King," which offers a brief overview of the Peruvian interpreters from the late sixteenth to the early seventeenth, and Carolina Jurado, "Don Pedro de Dueñas," which provides a case study of the life and career of a seventeenth-century interpreter in Bolivia.
11. Machuca Chávez, *Intérpretes y trasuntos* and Cunill and Testino, *Las lenguas indígenas*.
12. Two articles by Caroline Cunill provide a quick survey of some of the interpreters active in Yucatan during the sixteenth century: "Justicia e interpretación" and "Los intérpretes de Yucatán." Articles and book chapters on Gaspar Antonio Chi include Blom, "Gaspar Antonio Chi"; Hillerkus, "Los méritos y servicios"; Restall, "Gaspar Antonio Chi," 13–31. One dissertation, Cortez's 1995 "Gaspar Antonio Chi and the Xiu Family Tree," focuses on Gaspar Antonio's contributions to early Yucatecan history. Frances Karttunen, *Between Worlds*, also includes a chapter on Gaspar Antonio.
13. Cunill, for example, cites cédulas from 1580, 1588, and 1599 as evidence of a primarily legal basis for closing off access to the top interpreter position to mestizo and Maya candidates. However, the first two cédulas targeted just two individuals for removal, Diego de Vargas and Antonio Nieto. Aspersions to their ancestry made up a small part of the complaints that also targeted their linguistic capability, corrupt practices, low-status employment, and poor treatment of Indigenous subjects, among other criticisms. Cunill, "Los intérpretes de Yucatán," 379.
14. For the most recent examination of such legislation, see Masters, *We, the King*. Karen Graubart used the term "piecemeal" to describe the early efforts at segregation in "Hybrid Thinking," 221.

15. AGI, México 116, R. 4, "Probanza de Antonio Nieto, intérprete de Indios," 1597.
16. AGI, Indiferente General, 1402, "Peticiones y Memoriales—Marcos Rodríguez," 1587.
17. Encinas, *Cedulario indiano*, vol. 4, 7.
18. Encinas, *Cedulario indiano*, vol. 4, 7.
19. Schwaller, *Géneros de Gente*, 87–96.
20. AGI, México 105, "Relación de las ayudas de costa que los gobernadores han dado," 1581.
21. Schwaller, *Géneros de Gente*, 88–90.
22. Masters, "Thousand Invisible Architects," 378–79.
23. Masters, "Thousand Invisible Architects," 381; and Schwaller, *Géneros de Gente*, 51–53.
24. For a discussion of the population estimates for pre-Columbian Yucatan, see García Bernal, *Yucatán*, 28–29. García Bernal estimated the population of Yucatan in 1550, shortly after the completion of the military phase of the conquest, at 232,576.
25. García Bernal, *Yucatán*, 80; and Patch, *Maya and Spaniard*, 22.
26. Schwaller, *Géneros de Gente*, 105–7.
27. Karttunen, *Between Worlds*, 308.
28. "Probanza ad perpetuam Rey e memoriam a pedimento de Gaspar Antonio," AGI, *México*, leg. 104, ramo 3, reproduced in Quezada and Torres Trujillo, *Tres nobles mayas yucatecos*, 43–44, and 48.
29. Restall, "Gaspar Antonio Chi."
30. Hillerkuss, "Los méritos y servicios," 10; Cogolludo, *Historia de Yucathan*, 132.
31. Restall, "Gaspar Antonio Chi," 19.
32. Sánchez de Aguilar, *Informe contra idolorum cultores*, 89v.
33. Cogolludo, *Historia de Yucathan*, 182.
34. "Petición de Gaspar Antonio sobre el pago de su ayuda de costa por el oficio de intérprete general," AGI, *México*, leg. 104, ramo 4, reproduced in Quezada y Torres Trujillo, *Tres nobles Mayas yucatecos*, 65.
35. See Solari, "Circles of Creation"; Cortez, "Gaspar Antonio Chi and the Xiu Family Tree"; and Restall, "Gaspar Antonio Chi," 19.
36. AGI, Mexico 110, "Relación de algunas costumbres," 1582, ff. 78–87.
37. Articles and book chapters on Gaspar Antonio Chi include Blom, "Gaspar Antonio Chi"; Hillerkus, "Los meritos y servicios"; and Restall, "Gaspar Antonio Chi," 13–31. One dissertation, Cortez's 1995 "Gaspar Antonio Chi and the Xiu Family Tree," focuses on Gaspar Antonio's contributions to early Yucatecan history. Karttunen, *Between Worlds*, also includes a chapter on Gaspar Antonio.
38. AGI, México 296, "Confirmación de titulo de intérprete," 1607.
39. AGI, México 296, "Confirmación de titulo de intérprete," 1607.
40. AGI, México 296, "Confirmación de titulo de intérprete," 1607.
41. AGI, México 105, "Relación de las ayudas de costa que los gobernadores han dado," 1581.
42. AGI, México 105, "Relación de las ayudas de costa que los gobernadores han dado," 1581.

43. AGI, México 296, "Confirmación de titulo de intérprete," 1607.
44. AGI, Patronato 69, R. 9, "Información de los méritos y servicios de Alonso Ruiz de Arévalo," 1569. Somewhat contradictorily, another witnesses, the conquistador Bartolomé Rojo stated that the younger Alonso de Arévalo had grown up in the house of Alonso Ruiz de Arévalo, the conquistador, bolstering the younger Alonso's claims to descent from his father.
45. AGI, Patronato 69, R. 9, "Información de los méritos y servicios de Alonso Ruiz de Arévalo," 1569.
46. "Probanza *ad perpetuam Rey e memoriam* a pedimento de Gaspar Antonio va para la real persona y su Consejo de Indias," AGI, *México*, leg. 104, ramo 3, and "Petición de Gaspar Antonio sobre el pago de su ayuda de costa por el oficio de intérprete general," AGI, México 105B, Ramo 4. Reproduced in Quezada and Torres Trujillo, *Tres nobles mayas yucatecos*, 42, 69–77.
47. Quezada y Torres Trujillo, *Tres nobles mayas yucatecos*, 20n83.
48. Chuchiak IV, "Forgotten Allies."
49. AGI, México 105B, ramo 4. Reproduced in Quezada and Torres Trujillo, *Tres nobles mayas yucatecos*, 98.
50. Ortiz Yam and Quezada, *Visita de Diego García de Palacio*, 195.
51. AGI, México 3048, no. 4, "Diligencias que se hizieron sobre la junta y platicas de algunos indios de que se denunció pareciendo que se alteraban," 1607, f. 220.
52. AGI, México 296, "Confirmación de titulo de intérprete," 1607.
53. AGI, México 296, "Confirmación de titulo de intérprete," 1607.
54. AGI, México, 105, ramo 4, "Presentación del interrogatorio de Gaspar Antonio sobre su vejez, enfermedad e indisposiciones," 1581.
55. AGI, México 296, "Confirmación de titulo de intérprete," 1607.
56. Cunill, "Los intérpretes de Yucatán," 372–79.
57. AGI, México 105A, ramo 4, "Gaspar Antonio Chi de Herrera sobre que no se le quite cierto oficio de intérprete," October 11, 1581. Reproduced in Quezada and Torres Trujillo, *Tres nobles mayas yucatecos*, 53.
58. AGI, Indiferente General, 1400, "Peticiones y Memoriales—Antonio Nieto," 1586.
59. AGI, Indiferente General, 1402, "Peticiones y Memoriales—Marcos Rodríguez," 1587.
60. AGI, México 105B, ramo 4, "Petición de Gaspar Antonio sobre el pago de su ayuda de costa por el oficio de intérprete general." Reproduced in Quezada and Torres Trujillo, *Tres nobles mayas yucatecos*, 72.
61. AGI, México 105B, ramo 4, "Petición de Gaspar Antonio sobre el pago de su ayuda de costa por el oficio de intérprete general." Reproduced in Quezada and Torres Trujillo, *Tres nobles mayas yucatecos*, 72.
62. Ortiz Yam and Quezada, *Visita de Diego García de Palacio*, 19. Though Ortíz Yam and Quezada identified Arévalo as a Spaniard, he appears identified as a mestizo and "hijo que dizen ser de conquistador" in a list of recipients of *ayudas de costa*. AGI, México, 105, ramo 3, "Relación de las personas que tienen ayudas de costa" (1581).
63. O'Gorman, "Papeles Relativos a la visita," 430, 438, 447; Ortiz Yam and Quezada, *Visita de Diego García de Palacio*, 119, 124.

64. Yannakakis, *Art of Being In-Between*, 58.
65. Castro Gutiérrez, *Los Tarascos*, 128 and 324.
66. Machuca Chávez, *Intérpretes y trasuntos*, 37–44.
67. Ruan, "Andean Activism," 210–15.
68. Masters, *We, the King*, 12.
69. AGI, Indiferente General 1402, "Peticiones y Memoriales—Marcos Rodríguez," 1587.
70. Ortiz Yam and Quezada, *Visita de Diego García de Palacio*, 181.
71. AGI, Indiferente 453, L.A16, f. 54v., "Real Cédula a Manuel de Olivares para que pueda usar el título de inteprete general de los indios de la provincia de Yucatán," 1633. The information on Olivares's encomienda is found in García Bernal, *Yucatán*, 545.
72. AGI, Indiferente 453, L.A16, f. 54v., "Real Cédula a Manuel de Olivares para que pueda usar el título de interprete general de los indios de la provincia de Yucatán," 1633.

Bibliography

ARCHIVAL SOURCES

Archivo General de Indias (AGI), Seville, Spain.
Sánchez de Aguilar, Pedro. *Informe contra idolorum cultores del obispado de Yucatan*. Madrid, 1639.

PUBLISHED WORKS

Blom, Frans. "Gaspar Antonio Chi, Interpreter." *American Anthropologist* 30, no. 2 (1928): 250–62.
Castro Gutiérrez, Felipe. *Los Tarascos y el Imperio Español, 1600–1740*. Mexico City: Universidad Nacional Autónoma de México, 2004.
Chuchiak, John F., IV. "Forgotten Allies: The Origins and Roles of Native Mesoamerican Auxiliaries and Indios Conquistadores in the Conquest of Yucatan, 1526–1550." In *Indian Conquistadors: Indigenous Allies in the Conquest of Mesoamerica*, edited by Laura E. Matthew and Michel Oudjik, 175–204. Norman: University of Oklahoma Press, 2007.
Cogolludo, Diego López. *Historia de Yucathan*. Madrid: Por Juan Garcia Infanzon, 1688.
Cortez, Constance. "Gaspar Antonio Chi and the Xiu Family Tree." PhD diss., University of California, Los Angeles, 1995.
Cunill, Caroline. "Justicia e interpretación en sociedades plurilingües: El caso de Yucatán en el siglo XVI." *Estudios de Historia Novohispana* 52 (2015): 18–28.
———. "Los intérpretes de Yucatán y la Corona española: Negociación e iniciativas privadas en el Imperio ibérico, siglo XVI." *Colonial Latin American Historical Review* 18, no. 4 (2013): 361–80.
Cunill, Caroline, and Luis Miguel Glave Testino, eds. *Las lenguas indígenas en los tribunales de América Latina: Intérpretes mediación y justicia (Siglos Xvi–Xxi)*. Bogotá: Instituto Colombiano de Antropología e Historia, 2019.

De la Puente Luna, José Carlos. "The Many Tongues of the King: Indigenous Language Interpreters and the Making of the Spanish Empire." *Colonial Latin American Review* 23, no. 2 (2014): 143–70.
Encinas, Diego de, comp. *Cedulario indiano*, 4 vols. Madrid, 1596.
García Bernal, Manuela Cristina. *Yucatán: Población y encomienda bajo los Austrias*. Seville: Escuela de Estudios Hispano-Americanos, 1978.
Graubart, Karen. "Hybrid Thinking: Bringing Postcolonial Theory to Latin American Economic History." In *Postcolonialism Meets Economics*, edited by Eiman O. Zein-Elabdin and S. Charusheela. 215–34. London: Routledge, 2004.
Hillerkuss, Thomas. "Los méritos y servicios de un maya yucateco principal del siglo XVI y la historia de sus probanzas y mercedes." *Estudios de Historia Novohispana* 13 (1993): 9–39.
Jurado, Carolina. "Don Pedro de Dueñas, indio lengua." *Anuario del Archivo y Biblioteca Nacional de Bolivia* 16 (2010): 285–309.
Karttunen, Frances. *Between Worlds: Interpreters, Guides, and Survivors*. New Brunswick NJ: Rutgers University Press, 1994.
Machuca Chávez, Claudia Paulina. *Intérpretes y trasuntos, siglos XVI–XVII: El caso de Colima de la Nueva España*. Colima: Archivo Histórico del Municipio de Colima, 2009.
Masters, Adrian. "A Thousand Invisible Architects: Vassals, the Petition and Response System, and the Creation of Spanish Imperial Caste Legislation." *Hispanic American Historical Review* 98, no. 3 (2018): 377–406.
———. *We, the King: Creating Royal Legislation in the Sixteenth-Century Spanish New World*. Cambridge Latin American Studies, 127. Cambridge: Cambridge University Press, 2023.
Metcalf, Alida. *Go-Betweens and the Colonization of Brazil: 1500–1600*. Austin: University of Texas Press, 2005.
O'Gorman, Edmundo. "Yucatán—Papeles relativos a la visita del Oidor Dr. Diego García de Palacio, año de 1583." *Boletín del Archivo General de la Nación* 11, no. 3 (1940): 72–73.
Ortiz Yam, Inés, and Sergio Quezada, eds. *Visita de Diego García de Palacio a Yucatán, 1583*. Mexico City: UNAM, Instituto de Investigaciones Filológicas, Centro de Estudios Mayas, 2009.
Patch, Robert. *Maya and Spaniard in Yucatan, 1648–1812*. Stanford, CA: Stanford University Press, 1993.
Quezada, Sergio, and Anabel Torres Trujillo. *Tres nobles mayas yucatecos*. Mérida: CONACULTA, 2010.
Restall, Matthew. "Gaspar Antonio Chi: Bridging the Conquest of Yucatan." In *The Human Tradition in Colonial Latin America*, edited by Kenneth J. Andrien, 13–31. Lanham MD: Rowman & Littlefield, 2013.
Ruan, Felipe E. "Andean Activism and the Reformulation of Mestizo Agency and Identity in Early Colonial Peru." *Colonial Latin American Review* 21, no. 2 (2012): 210–15.
Schwaller, Robert F. *Géneros de Gente in Early Colonial Mexico: Defining Racial Difference*. Norman: University of Oklahoma Press, 2016.

Solari, Amara L. "Circles of Creation: The Invention of Maya Cartography in Early Colonial Yucatán." *Art Bulletin* 92, no. 3 (September 2010): 154–68.

Townsend, Camilla. *Malintzin's Choices: An Indian Woman in the Conquest of Mexico.* Albuquerque: University of New Mexico Press, 2006.

Yannakakis, Yanna. *The Art of Being In-Between: Native Intermediaries, Indian Identity, and Local Rule in Colonial Oaxaca.* Durham NC: Duke University Press, 2008.

Misinterpreting for James Wilkinson

From the editors: In the late nineteenth century, James Wilkinson served as a secret agent for Spain, selling information pertaining to U.S. foreign policy and expansionism at a high price. Never identified as a double agent in his lifetime, Wilkinson came close to being exposed on several occasions, including the anecdote below. This story appeared in Andro Linklater's 2010 book An Artist in Treason: The Extraordinary Double Life of General James Wilkinson.

Excerpt from "The Man Who Double-Crossed the Founders"

The real problem for Wilkinson was getting paid for his intelligence, which was the only reason he had become a spy in the first place. Wilkinson was hard pressed to find a way of secretly transporting the loud, unwieldy payments the Spanish sent him—thousands of silver dollars at a time. He tried packing them in casks used for sugar, coffee and rum, but the clinking of the cash made it hard to hide the barrels' valuable contents.

"On one occasion, one of his messengers, who was carrying about 3,000 silver dollars, was murdered by his boatmen," Linklater says. "At that moment, Wilkinson absolutely came to the very edge of being discovered."

The five murderers, all Spanish, took the money and scattered across the Kentucky countryside, but were soon captured and taken before a magistrate. As luck would have it, though, the assassins spoke no English—and Thomas Power, the interpreter the magistrate sent for, was secretly another Spanish spy.

With Power there to translate, the Spaniards explained that the money they had stolen was in fact a payment for information Wilkinson had sold to Spain. But what Power told the magistrate, Linklater recounts, was: "'They just say they're wicked murderers motivated by greed.'"

And just like that, Wilkinson got away.[1]

Notes

1. Andro Linklater, "The Man Who Double-Crossed the Founders," interview by Steve Inskeep, NPR, *Morning Edition*, April 28, 2010, https://www.npr.org/2010/04/28/126363998/the-man-who-double-crossed-the-founders.

2

Captains of Civility

The Indigenous Interpreters of North America Who Attempted
to School Settler Colonists on the Ideals of Civil Community

NICOLE EUSTACE

More than many scholars of Native American and Indigenous studies, specialists of eighteenth-century North America have long recognized that interpreters hold a key to understanding the nature of colonial contact. Records of cross-cultural communications convey a great deal about the character of colonial relations. In 1999, for example, James H. Merrell went so far as to describe "the alchemy of interpretation" as "the very essence of American encounter." Yet, if alchemy implies the successful conversion of lead into gold, it may be instructive to pause over the fact that such efforts at transformation never amounted to more than fantasy—because, in early America, translation often did not fare much better.[1]

According to the *Oxford English Dictionary*, "interpreter" has two primary interrelated but not identical meanings: "one who translates the communications of persons speaking different languages; *spec.* one whose office it is to do so orally in the presence of the persons" and "one who interprets or explains . . . who puts a construction on the meaning or purposes of a person." In the context of cross-cultural encounters between early modern English settler colonists and the Indigenous inhabitants of North America, these meanings were not so much intertwined as snarled in knots. Indigenous interpreters did learn multiple languages and offer themselves as mediators among peoples. Yet, in interactions with Anglo-American settler colonists, they finally succeeded in putting mutually comprehensible "constructions" on the meaning of public utterances only to realize they were operating very much at cross "purposes." Fool's gold indeed.[2]

No matter how much interpreters may have tried to coordinate linguistic terms, they could not integrate oppositional cultural outlooks. Richard White's "middle ground" existed only for ephemeral moments in particular places. More commonly, opposing sides failed to achieve mutual understanding. As Jane T. Merritt explored in depth in a 1998 essay, "Metaphor, Meaning, and Misunderstanding: Language and Power on the Pennsylvania Frontier," a little convenient incomprehension might sustain peace for a time, as when Native peoples and Europeans brought their very different conceptions of fatherhood to their use of that term to define their relations. Yet, ultimately, conflict came anyway, with shared metaphors giving way to Euro-American reliance on polarizing racial rhetoric used in the service of starkly opposed material interests.[3]

Fundamentally, European migrants and the Native inhabitants of North America did not share a common vision of what cross-cultural dialog was intended to accomplish. Native peoples of the eighteenth-century Eastern seaboard regarded translators as moderators, people whose twofold goal was not only to convey the sense of what outside groups sought from encounters but also to create allegiances, new forms of community and shared belonging, among disparate groups of peoples. Whether offering words or proffering gifts, Native translators always sought to act as intermediators as well as interpreters. Yet where Indigenous people approached encounters hoping to achieve a meeting of minds that could create multifaceted alliances, settler colonists came to such gatherings in the mode of negotiators, eager to maximize gain for their own side and to retain their sense of themselves as a separate and superior people. Not only did these dynamics hold in colonies known for their early conflicts, from the first Anglo-Powhatan War in Virginia in 1609 to the Pequot War in Connecticut in 1637, but they also characterized colonies like Pennsylvania, more often studied for their supposedly peaceful early decades.[4]

As scholars including Daniel K. Richter, Collin Calloway, and Ned Blackhawk have recently foregrounded, British settler colonies all began as *land companies*, as speculative ventures in turning Native homelands into the private property of Euro-Americans. Though the English experimented with a wide variety of governmental forms, from royal colonies, to proprietorships, to corporate structures, every colony they founded made the alienation of Indigenous land its organizing principle. Before he ever set foot on the territory he claimed on the basis that "the king of the Country where I live hath given me a great Province therein," William Penn wrote ahead "to the kings of the Indians" to tell them, "I have sent my Commissioners to treat with you about land and a firm league of peace." As Richter particularly reminds us, the "clause about land... roots William Penn... in the everyday politics of the struggle for trade, land, and power." Penn anticipated direct personal profits from the territory he claimed by royal right. His earliest plans for the colony laid out an elaborate system of rents and quitrents that he intended to require settler colonists to pay him and his heirs in perpetuity in exchange for the privilege of living in Pennsylvania and, according to Richard S. Dunn and Mary Dunn, the editors of the William Penn papers, "he expected these payments to be a major source of income." Whereas Native peoples sought to use diplomatic exchanges to breach divisions, European settler colonists sought to define boundaries by claiming property.[5]

William Penn's instructions to his "commissioners" signaled his essential concerns. Not only did he intend for them primarily to "treat about land" but he also urged his commissioners to rely on "honest spies" to find out if "anybody inveighs the Indians not to sell." Penn's goals for diplomacy involved acquiring as much Native land as he could as quickly as possible for as little as possible. No trade mattered so much as the land trade, and even his most fulsome comments on community were little more than flourishes to soften his assertions of sovereignty. In the one treaty that Penn personally signed with Native inhabitants of the Susquehanna River Valley, including people he identified as "the Indians of Connostogoe," Penn declared that "the English Christian inhabitants of the region and the several people of the Nations of Indians" would "forever hereafter be as one head & one heart & live in true Friendship and Amity as one people." Yet he hedged these fair sounding words about cross-cultural unity with a highly significant condition. His "promise" that he and his people would "at all times show themselves to be true Friends and Brothers to all and every of the said Indians" was contingent on "they behaving themselves... and submitting to the laws of this Province in all things." Penn's vision of amity made no room for bilateral relations among peer nations; his hierarchical version of friendship required Native people to relinquish sovereignty and place themselves in positions of submission.[6]

The first Indigenous people to encounter William Penn had recent, intense experience in trying to use diplomacy to dampen conflict and nurture communal ties. Local Native nations included both Algonquian and Iroquoian collectives. Algonquian Lenapes (or Delawares) were key players along with other Algonquian groups, including Shawnee refugees from the Ohio River Valley and Ganawese migrants from Maryland. Iroquoian Susquehannocks, also called the Conestogas after the name of their main settlement, played prominent parts. Though speakers of an Iroquoian language, the Susquehannocks were not members of the Five (later Six) Nations of the Haudenosaunee Confederacy and so remained subject to attack from their distant New York kin until the last quarter of the seventeenth century. As the Susquehannocks shrank, their villages were augmented by newly arriving peoples who soon became interconnected with them through trade and marriage. In addition to multiple different Algonquian groups, these also included new Iroquoian additions from the Seneca and Cayuga nations. Threatened from the north from by peoples of the Great Lakes, menaced from the south by powerful Native groups from below the Potomac, and pushed westward by settler-colonist aggressors everywhere, the peoples of the river valleys of Pennsylvania placed primacy on cross-cultural communication as they sought to fashion new lives together.[7]

Perhaps no single person better embodied the means and aims of Native diplomacy than an Indigenous spokesperson who lived and worked in the Susquehanna River Valley in the first decades of the 1700s, a man whose name—to Anglophone ears—sounded something like "Taquatarensaly." Pennsylvanians recorded at least seven variant spellings of his name, many of which contained the sound /ta/ followed by some variant of the sound /kwa/, including: "Tacuttelence," "Tioquataraghese," "Tagotalessa," and more. Settler colonists never made any reference to the meaning of this name; they were not aware of what specific language it came from any more than they knew to what nation the man belonged. In 1710 they described him as one of "the Seneques Kings," in 1713 as "one of the Chiefs of Conestogo," in 1721 as "a Descendant of the ancient Sasquehannah Indians the old Settlers of these parts, but now reputed as of an Iroquois Descent," and later still, by the 1730s, as a member of the Oneida Nation. Still, even these inexact records of this man's name and origin do offer some suggestive evidence of his identity and his activities. Far from being contradictory, the many tribal affiliations attributed to him may accurately reflect the fact that he could claim membership in more than one Iroquoian group.[8]

By the time that settler colonists in Pennsylvania began to puzzle over their new acquaintance, Taquatarensaly, the Susquehannocks, in particular, had been largely absorbed into the Five Nations of the Haudenosaunee (called the Six Nations after 1722, they were also often referred to as the "Iroquois"). Pennsylvanians understood that Taquatarensaly played an important role as a go-between among Native peoples, but they were at a loss to describe his part precisely. We can start to understand his position by returning to the puzzle of his name with its "Ta" and "Kwa" sounds. According to a seventeenth-century syllabary of the Susquehannock language, the word "Atackqua" meant "shoes." The first two syllables of Taquatarensaly's name correspond closely to this word. Nothing symbolized diplomatic work to Native people like the well-worn moccasins of messengers who devoted themselves to traveling the roads between nations, working to further communications and manage relations. Years later, the significance of what we might call shoe-leather diplomacy remained strong enough that in 1742, an Onondaga member of the Six Nations of the Haudenosaunee praised a translator by saying he "has had a great Deal of Trouble with Us, wore out his Shoes in our Messages." Taquatarensaly likely gained his name because of his work walking between worlds, linking the many disparate peoples of the Susquehanna River Valley in new forms of collectivity.[9]

So difficult did English settler colonists find the effort to say, much less spell, this name that, whenever they met him in council, they generally preferred to refer to him by another moniker: "Captain Civility." Historians have puzzled over why settler colonists would have addressed the Native interpreter this way, variously speculating that doing so could have reflected anything from sarcastic critique to backhanded compliment. Certainly, English settler colonists liked to impose humorous names on those they considered inferior. Enslaved people were often saddled with the names of writers and heroes of classical antiquity, from Cato to Hercules. It's easy enough to imagine some colonial wit in a black frock coat and white silk stockings showing off by deciding to solve the problem of a "savage" man's unpronounceable name by calling him "Civility."[10]

As it turns out, however, settler colonists deserved neither blame nor credit for coining the name. Far from being a casual nickname conferred by colonists, "Captain Civility" was actually a formal title bestowed by Native people. For generations, Susquehannocks used "Civility" not as a personal name but as something more like a professional designation for the person appointed as their ambassador to the English. In the 1660s, a Susquehannock man going by the name of "Civility" succeeded in such cordial negotiations with the governing council of Maryland that it supplied him with guns, lead, and shot. Later, in the 1690s, after a lapse in diplomatic relations, Maryland council members urged a new set of Susquehannock delegates that if they were "inclined to enter into a League with us," they should "make choice of some great man to preside over them as Civility formerly did." By the time a man going by this title stepped forward in Pennsylvania around 1710, the English name "Civility" had been used as an official title by Susquehannock diplomats to the English for half a century or more. Even if the name "Civility" did spark contradictory thoughts of "savagery" among settler colonists, for Susquehannocks and their diverse Native neighbors it evoked a long tradition of inclusive diplomacy.[11]

Settler colonists in Pennsylvania first recorded contact with the man they called "Civility" at the town of Conestoga in May of 1710, where representatives of the Tuscarora Nation, the Seneca Nation, and the Shawnee Nation held a multilateral meeting in the presence of two colonial envoys named John French and Henry Worley. French and Worley had been sent west from Philadelphia by their colony's acting governor, Charles Gookin, to discern the meaning of a certain belt of wampum rumored to carry a war message. Two weeks before, the governor and his council had received intelligence from settler colonists in Gloucester County, New Jersey, saying they had heard not only that "there is a Belt of Wampum Come to Conestogo" but also that "there was a Tomahawk in Red in the belt & that the french with five nations of Indians were designed for War & to fall on some of these Plantations." Concerned by the sheer number of Native people massing at Conestoga—"the meeting being the Greatest that has been known for Twenty Years"—Pennsylvania leaders were determined "to Enquire further of them about the said Belt of Wampum." Imperial rivalry with the French defined the Anglo-American world of the early eighteenth century. Expectations of hostilities with Indigenous peoples were likewise par for the course. Encountering a Native man named "Civility," on the other hand, likely occasioned surprise.[12]

Worley, for one, may have been especially unprepared for such a meeting, having arrived in the first ship of settler colonists with William Penn, charged by King Charles II of England to: "enlarge our English Empire and promote such useful commodities as may be of benefit to us and our dominions as also to reduce the Savage Natives by Gentle and just manners to the Love of civill society and Christian Religion." According to English assumptions, they were the civilized ones, whereas the Indigenous peoples of North America were to be considered "savages" in need of being reduced, that is to say, put in their place beneath the English. In this context, what did it mean for settler colonists to confront a man whose very name defied the binaries Europeans depended on to justify their imperial claims? As Civility stepped forward to greet French and Worley, what critiques of English definitions of civility might he have carried with him? How can we today try to recover the varied historical meanings attached to the word "civility"; to investigate what contemporary interpreters meant when they invoked the word; and to contemplate what a fresh confrontation with the competing understandings of this concept may reveal about the history of North American encounters between settler colonists and the members of the continent's first Nations?[13]

The first time Taquatarensaly was mentioned in Pennsylvania records in 1710, he was identified simply as "Civility," without any modifier at all. But the next time Pennsylvania Council minutes made note of him, in 1712, they offered the information that colonial officials had been visited by "Civility, a War Captain & Chief." In 1713 they called him more simply "one of the chiefs of Conestogoe." He was then described as a "chief" twice more in 1715, as a "captain" accompanying another Indian identified as the Conestoga "chief" in 1716, and as one of multiple "chiefs of the Indians on Susquehanna" in 1717. Was he a chief or was he a war captain? Reflecting colonial incomprehension, in 1718 Pennsylvania record keepers referenced him as "Civility, the present Chief or Captain of the Conestogoe Indians." There could be no doubt about Civility's military bona fides; that same note added that "Civility said, that he with some of the young men had this last spring some inclination to go out to war."[14]

Pennsylvanians' uncertainty about how to describe Taquatarensaly's function stemmed from their basic unfamiliarity with Indigenous ways. As a descendent of the Susquehannock Nation, also known as the "Mingos," Taquatarensaly was heir to a long tradition of Native American diplomacy. Significantly, he did not speak English but, rather, was fluent in multiple Algonquian and Iroquoian tongues. He took up the role of intermediary primarily to enhance ties among neighboring Native nations at a time when interactions with settler colonists had not yet become the most pressing concern for Indigenous communities. Native peoples of the American southeast had a specific title for a man who smoothed relations between peoples by taking up membership in more than one society. Such a man acted simultaneously as a war captain who protected his people and as a spokesman able to intercede for both his own people and for any other peoples who formally adopted him as one of their own. They referred to such people by the title "fanimingo."[15]

English settler colonists had at least a glancing awareness of the term, mentioned in a letter written by an English migrant named Thomas Nairne in 1708. According to Nairne, it was usual for a family in want of protection to choose "some growing man of esteem in the wars" and "claim him for the head of Chief of their family." The man so chosen was addressed thereafter as "chief" and honored with presents. In return, he was "to protect that family and take care of its concerns equally with those of his own." Nairne indicated that an analogous procedure could be used by "two nations at peace" who could designate a fanimingo to go between them. Each was to "chuse these protectors in the other" and, between them, these representatives were "to make up all Breaches between the 2 nations" should any occur. Such a go-between identified equally with his family or nation of origin and with the one that ritually adopted him.[16]

Captain Civility's multiple memberships in the varied Native nations who claimed him; his role as spokesman for a diverse array of Susquehanna River Valley peoples, including a range of Algonquian and Iroquoian groups; and his frequent contacts with European colonial leaders all stemmed from the role he performed in the tradition of the fanimingo. In fact, the word "Mingo" itself *meant* chief. Local Algonquian groups called Iroquoian speakers at Conestoga "Mingos" in recognition of the leadership positions that they had recently assumed in the region. Civility's prominent role as war captain, spokesperson, translator, and go-between for multiple regional peoples—all the duties expected of a "Fanni Mingo"—was one he was positioned to play not only by virtue of his own qualities but also by means of his nation's designation as "Mingos" or chiefs. Although Pennsylvania colonists had no apparent familiarity with the precise term "fanimingo," when they called Taquatarensaly "Civility" they were using a word with much the same meaning: a designated diplomatic figure who took up membership in multiple communities, serving as the living embodiment of civil society.[17]

The original English connotation of "civility" is of "senses relating to citizenship," including "a community of citizens regarded collectively." Seventeenth-century Susquehannock leaders given the title "Civility," who labored both to protect their own people and to create leagues with colonists, were doing nothing if not attempting to create a collective community—one that could encompass both Natives and newcomers. Far from conveying either a backhanded compliment to or a sarcastic critique of so-called savages, then, the title "Civility" may simply have been the best available early seventeenth-century English translation for a unique Native leadership position, one in which a designated protector used ritual relationships to unite disparate peoples.[18]

Taquatarensaly used his position as Captain Civility to urge colonists to adopt just such a unified outlook. On multiple occasions, he made speeches urging them to set aside their competitive and combative impulses in favor of a commitment to cross-cultural harmony. For Native peoples of the Susquehanna River Valley, managing relations meant making a sustained commitment to convening regular meetings, gatherings that included material, emotional, and spiritual components: the sharing of food and goods, the airing and exchange of emotions including condolences for deaths, and the ritual creation of peaceful conditions by actions such as sharing tobacco or presenting strings and belts of wampum.[19]

From their first contacts with Europeans, Native peoples of the mid-Atlantic region had shown strong interest in trading. They regarded the exchange of material goods not only as a means of sharing resources but also as a means of creating civil connections between peoples. In the Susquehanna River region that would come to be called Pennsylvania, in 1640, a Swedish minister created a phrasebook of words in the Susquehannock language that consisted entirely of nouns for food, tools, animals, and trade goods (from *Aanjooza*, "Linen, shirts" offered by the Swedes, to *Skajaano*, "valuables skins or furs, as sable etc." provided by Indians) and verb phrases relating to trade and exchange (from *Skaddanijnu*, "Will you sell or barter something?" to *Kassha schænu*, "Give me that for nothing"). As that last phrase hints, however, Native ideas about exchange differed in essential ways from European assumptions. The phrase supposedly meaning "Give me that for nothing" could better have been translated as "Please demonstrate your generosity and benevolent intentions with a gift." And indeed, words for friendship accounted for four of the seventy-six words or phrases included in the brief vocabulary list: *Generoo*, "Good friend"; *Agændeero*, "We are good friends"; *Chanooro hiss*, "I make much of you"; and *Jihadæaro*, "My particularly good friend." The word *Atackqua* appeared on this list only as the literal translation of the word "shoes," yet, as we have seen, the term actually carried with it strong associations of diplomatic work—a layering of meanings that underscores the extent to which trade ties and community bonds were linked in Native practice. Unlike the motives of personal profit and imperial power driving colonial settlers, Native peoples were interested in establishing relations of reciprocity that would expand their circles of community.[20]

Leaders from the many nations living in and around Conestoga tried to explain to settler colonists how broadly their peoples sought to distribute material riches, the better to create extensive bonds of benevolence between peoples. When asked at one treaty council how they like the diplomatic gifts passed out by Pennsylvania officials, they replied that "not only the Indians that were at Conestogoe . . . but likewise those of the whole Country, were pleased with what then passed, and that the Presents then delivered to them were divided into the smallest parts, that [they] might reach all the Indians everywhere & be read as a Letter." For Indigenous peoples, gifting was a powerful means of communicating. They did everything they could to spread the word of friendship as widely as possible.[21]

Indians called on the analogy of the letter to try to show how sharing goods served a larger purpose. According to Native principles, when two people—or two nations—exchanged gifts, each offered the other a promise to work cooperatively for peace and plenty. Colonists ought to have understand the analogy of the letter. After all, even in the English language, the word "correspondence" could signal more than simply a regular exchange of paper and ink. Mention of a close "correspondence" between two people or things implied a strong similarity or equivalence between them.

When English interpreters translated the Indian word as "letter," instead of using the more capacious term "correspondence," they obscured the fuller meaning of Native gifting. Because of the polyglot nature of the Native community at Conestoga and the limited linguistic skills of settler colonists in the area, translation work usually required a multistep process from Iroquoian tongues to Algonquian ones to English and back again. Colonial traders usually relied exclusively on their knowledge of the Delaware language and so opportunities for subtle but significant shifts in meaning abounded. When Indigenous people said that a gift could be "read as a letter," they meant not only that gifts could convey information but also, more importantly, that, like all "correspondence" they constituted "relations between persons or communities." This was, in fact, a primary definition of the word "correspondence" already very common in English since the seventeenth century. Yet most colonists hardly glanced up from their calculations of profit and loss long enough to consider the Indian approach to gifting.[22]

Colonists' main interest in engaging in trade lay in buying and selling commodities—including human commodities in the form of enslaved Indigenous people—in order to accumulate vast sums of money, not in allocating tokens of material and spiritual harmony as far and wide as possible. At a treaty conference, Taquatarensaly attended in Philadelphia in 1711, he complained that his people "suffered injuries" when they traded with settler colonists, in violation of the fact that "Governor Penn, on his first Coming amongst them, made an agreement with them that they should always live as friends and Brothers and be as one Body." But he could not turn the settler colonists to Native ways of thinking. Officials countered his objections that traders were not generous enough by explaining "in relation to their Complaints of Trade, that they must Consider that the end that all Traders had in view by Buying and Selling was to gain something by it to themselves." Against the mutual good of free distribution, settler colonists set the individual advantage of financial transactions.[23]

The English never wavered in their devotion to the profit motive. At a 1721 conclave at Conestoga, when members of the Five Nations, multiple peoples of the Susquehanna region, and representatives from colonial Pennsylvania all met, the colonial governor told the assembled Native people, who objected to the poor returns they received for their furs, "you must take Care to make the best Bargain you can." After all, he asserted, "every man must take care of himself." Individual opportunity drove the ambitions of Pennsylvania colonists.[24]

At this same conference, colonists recorded, without truly registering, a request made by a representative of the Seneca Nation that "we may now be together as one people." The Senecas preceded this request by presenting a "small parcel of dressed Skins" and followed it by offering "a Bundle of Bear skins." By presenting ritual gifts immediately before and after they spoke, the Seneca representatives made their diplomatic message manifest. In pairing words and goods, they were trying to make something ineffable, that is the feelings that came with unity, into something tangible. Through just such a process of coming together, the members of the Five Nations of the Haudenosaunee had managed to contain conflict among themselves over the last century or more.[25]

However, the assembled Pennsylvanians never considered the joining of peoples that the Senecas proposed. Pennsylvania's representatives steadfastly insisted on sticking to the colonial position, which viewed economic exchanges as a form of competition between opposing peoples. They informed Native peoples repeatedly, "We believe, Those who go into the Woods and spend all their time upon it [should] endeavour to make the best Bargains they can for themselves." That small phrase, "we believe," signaled much about the Pennsylvania perspective. Settler colonists counted themselves as part of a collective "we" that did not include Indigenous peoples. Their sense of themselves as a separate people was defined by their belief system, one in which conducting commerce did not require merging communities.[26]

Settler colonists in Pennsylvania had little appreciation for the role of the Indigenous exchange economy in the creation of civic bonds. Nothing in English legal theory allowed for creating new civil communities by engaging in commerce. That nation's foremost political philosopher, John Locke, declared in his master work, *Two Treatises of Government*, "'Tis not every Compact that puts an end to the state of Nature between Men, but only this one of agreeing together mutually to enter into one Community and make one Body Politick." The creation of governments was the most important foundation of civility as the English understand it: "other Promises, and Compacts, Men may make with one another, and yet still be in the state of Nature." Locke positively denied that commercial ties could ever create civic bonds and he had America in mind when he claimed this. Of course, a bargain was a bargain and was supposed to be honored. But economic links did not make civil connections in English eyes. "The Promises and Bargains for Truck, etc. . . . . between a *Swiss* and an *Indian*, in the Woods of *America*, are binding to them, though they are perfectly in a State of Nature in reference to one another. For Truth and keeping of Faith belong to Men, as Men, and not as Members of Society." Native peoples could and should be honor bound to settler colonists through debt and dependence, but, in the view of England's most advanced theorists, such economic relations by no means implied any sort of civic union.[27]

Nevertheless, the peoples of the Susquehanna region retained the hope that they would bring settler colonists around to their way of understanding the ideal shape of cross-cultural relations, a model in which varied peoples, of myriad Native nations as well as multiple different English colonies, could maintain local autonomy even as they achieved diplomatic unity. At a meeting in 1720, for example, Taquatarensaly again challenged Pennsylvania officials to regard themselves, as William Penn had, as being of "one Body, one Blood, one Heart, and one Head" with Native peoples. And once more, in 1722, he summed up that Penn "made the Two people one flesh." Indigenous peoples had the bones of the story exactly right. The oral history Captain Civility related conformed closely to the written records of William Penn himself. Yet the "flesh" on the bones of each version was markedly different.[28]

Here we come again to matters of metaphors, meanings, and misunderstandings. When Taquatarensaly spoke of being "one flesh" with the English, he meant that as different limbs attached to the same body, their peoples would always act out of shared interest, understanding that an injury to one would harm the whole. He was asking for parity and comity among peoples. When the English used the phrase "one flesh," on the other hand, they were invoking a common way of describing Christian marriage. And, according to English practice, a husband's rule over his wife was unquestioned. Locke believed, in accordance with the traditions of English common law, that once a woman gave her consent to marriage, she was bound in wedlock and obligated to obey her husband. Far from initiating a relationship between equal partners, then, the marriage metaphor only reaffirmed the subordinate position of Native peoples. And indeed, as we have already seen, in the very letter in which Penn pledged to be "one" with the "Indians," he predicated his promise on their submission to his law.[29]

The first time that settler colonists from Pennsylvania met the man they called Captain Civility in 1710, they were investigating rumors of war, trying to decipher the symbols seen on belts of wampum. Yet Taquatarensaly and his fellow diplomats met them not with threats of violence but with calls for safety. In an eight-point message, each one solemnized with the presentation of a separate wampum belt, Captain Civility repeatedly "implored the friendship of the Christians" and requested "on behalf of their children born and those in the womb . . . Room to sport & Play without danger of slavery"; on behalf of young men the "privilege" to hunt "without fear of Death or Slavery"; and on behalf of all Native people, "a Cessation from murdering and taking them." Reports of armed conflict being instigated by Indigenous people against Pennsylvania's settler colonists proved unfounded in 1710, but the enumerated depredations being committed by colonial settlers and slavers were all too real. Tensions mounted decade by decade as the greed of settler colonists grew exponentially along with their population.[30]

Far from trade relations leading to some form of confederacy linking Indigenous peoples and settler colonists in civil society, the rewards of commerce and the riches of Native soil motivated wave after wave of Europeans to make ever greater depredations against Native lands and lives. Settler colonists continued to arrive in astounding numbers for another half century, until finally, in 1764, Pennsylvanians' simmering racism against the Indigenous people they were displacing exploded into a genocidal race riot that resulted in the mass murder of the final surviving members of the Native community at Conestoga.[31]

For all that Native peoples made effective use of the "one body" metaphor introduced by John Locke and invoked by William Penn, they never implied a desire to be incorporated into a British-controlled empire in which political bonds would fix them in a subordinate role. To the contrary, they tried across decades to educate settler colonists on the possibilities of a more flexible form of civil community, one continuously renewed and recreated through trade and ritual diplomacy. They were alive to the possibilities of something like dual sovereignty, a system in which Native peoples could retain their rights even as they created civil connections with newcomers. As they attempted again and again to convey these ideals to the settler colonists, Indigenous interpreters' repeated statements created a remarkably detailed picture of their ideas and values. Reading the translations of their many speeches today, their collective meaning seems abundantly clear. If Native spokespeople failed to get their message across, it was not because of any inherent linguistic limitations on either side. Ultimately, although Taquatarensaly and his fellow Indigenous translators found the words to explain their highest ideals of civility, they could not overcome the barriers to achieving complete and accurate interpretations of fundamentally incommensurate worldviews.[32]

Notes

1. Merrell, *Into the American Woods*, 32. And see Richter, "Cultural Brokers and Intercultural Politics"; Karttunen, *Between Worlds*. For more recent work, see Harvey and Rivett, "Colonial-Indigenous Language Encounters in North America."
2. *Oxford English Dictionary*, s.v. "interpreter, n., sense 2.b", and s.v. "interpreter, n., sense 1.b," accessed September 2023, https://doi.org/10.1093/oed/4949543585.

As Jane H. Hill notes, cautioning against trying to express Indigenous concepts in European words, "particular ways of speaking express some angle on the world." Therefore, "not only do we need to explore the richly detailed specifics of each site where knowledge is shaped and deployed, we must consider the long histories through which these specificities developed and continue to change." See Hill, "Native American Knowledges, Native American Epistemologies," 321 and 320.

3. Merritt, "Metaphor, Meaning, and Misunderstanding." More recent scholars have continued to cast the work of interpretation as a contest for power. As Matt Cohen observes, "communications systems in the early settlement [era] . . . were both occasions for and sites of contest for control over social and economic power because they offered individuals alternative and little-understood ways to gain agency across cultural and linguistic divides." See Cohen, *Networked Wilderness*, 2.

4. On the inapplicability of the "middle ground" construct in early Pennsylvania, see Barr, "Did Pennsylvania Have a Middle Ground?"

5. See Richter, *Trade, Land, Power*, 137; Calloway, *Indian World of George Washington*; Blackhawk, *Rediscovery of America*; Penn, "To the Kings of the Indians," in Dunn and Dunn, *Papers of William Penn* (hereafter cited as PWP), vol. 2, 127–29. On quitrents, see: Dunn and Dunn, PWP, vol. 3, 679.

6. Penn, "To . . . My Commissioners," September 30, 1681, Dunn and Dunn, PWP, vol. 2, 118–21; Penn, "Articles of Agreement with the Susquehanna Indians," April 23, 1701, in Dunn and Dunn, PWP, vol. 4, 51–53. Ana Schwartz argues for recognizing the peril inherent in settler-colonists' hierarchical vision of "sovereign amity." See Schwartz, *Unmoored*, 201–4.

7. Schutt, *Peoples of the River Valleys*. On alliances between the Lenape and the Susquehannocks see Soderlund, *Lenape Country*, 141. On relations with the Shawnee, see Warren, *Worlds the Shawnees Made*, 147–53.

8. Versions of Civility's native name were recorded as follows: "Tagodrancy," July 23, 1712; "Taghuttalese," June 22, 1715; "Tagotelessah," July 30, 1716, in "At a Council held at Philadelpia., ye 22nd of June, 1715;" and "At a Council held at Philadelpia., ye 30th of July, 1716," in *Minutes of the Provincial Council of Pennsylvania* (hereafter cited as MPCP), vol. 2, 553, 603, 613; and "Tagotelessah," July 15, 1717; "Tagotalessa," June 16, 1718; "Tagoleless," July 16, 1720; "Tacuttelence," May 4, 1722; "Taquatarensaly," May 26, 1728, and May 26, 1729; and "Tioquataraghese," August 1, 1735, in MPCP, vol. 3, 45, 102–3, 163, 310, 361, and 598.

9. "Atackqua, *shoes*," in Holm, *Vocabulary of Susquehannock*, 19; MPCP, vol. 4, 581. On Susquehannock absorption into the Haudenosaunee, see Kruer, *Time of Anarchy*.

10. On the imposition of classical names on enslaved people, see Burnard, "Slave Naming Patterns," 335–36. Merrell raises but rejects the possibility that the name recognized Taquatarensaly's "polished colonial manners." See Merrell, *Into the American Woods*, 59.

11. See Minutes for July 28, 1663, in Archives of Maryland, *Proceedings of the Council of Maryland 1636–1667*, 486, and Minutes for April 11, 1693, in Archives of Maryland, *Proceedings of the Council of Maryland 1687/8–1693*, 518. On other men named

"Civility" in seventeenth-century Maryland, see Hanna, *Wilderness Trail*, 80–81. See also Kent, *Susquehanna's Indians*, 62. In like manner, the Indians referred to every Pennsylvania governor as "Onas." An Iroquois word meaning "feather" or "quill," the honorific began as a pun on William Penn's name (as in quill pen) but is now used by area Indians as the generic title for whoever occupies the Pennsylvania governor's office.

12. "Report of Coll. Ffrench & Henry Worley" in "At a Council held at Philadia., the 16th of June, 1710;" quotations from "At a Council held at Philadia, ye 14th April, 1710," in MPCP, vol. 3, 511 and 509.
13. See "William Blathwayt's Draft of the Charter of Pennsylvania" [February 24, 1681], in Dunn and Dunn, *PWP*, vol. 2, 63–77, 66. The Dunns note that this language is identical to that of the final text of the charter. Henry Worley's presence on the ship *Welcome*, which first carried William Penn to North America, has been documented by an association of descendants of the ships passengers at "The *Welcome* Society," accessed September 14, 2023, https://www.welcomesociety.org/passengers-on-1683-ships.html.
14. MPCP, vol. 2, 553, 565, 603, and 613; MPCP, vol. 3, 15, 45, 80, and 310.
15. For findings on wider spread of the Native practice of appointing "Squirrel Kings" beyond the Choctaw and Chickasaw, see Piker, *Okfuskee*, 23 and 214n14 and see St. John, "Inventing Guardianship," 366.
16. See Nairne, *Nairne's Muskhogean Journals*, as cited in Galloway, "'Chief Who Is Your Father,'" 360–61.
17. On the Native practice of appointing "Squirrel Kings" beyond the Choctaw and Chickasaw, see Piker, *Okfuskee*, 23 and 214n14 and see St. John, "Inventing Guardianship," 366.
18. *Oxford English Dictionary Online*, s.v. "Civility, n.," accessed February 6, 2018, http://www.oed.com.proxy.library.nyu.edu/view/Entry/33581?redirectedFrom=civility.
19. On ritual gifts as an element of condolence ceremonies and other community rites, see Richter, *Ordeal of the Longhouse*, 40; and see Hall Jr., *Zamumo's Gifts*.
20. See Johannes Campanius, "Vocabulary of the Minque Language," in Holm, *Vocabulary of Susquehannock*, 158–59.
21. MPCP, vol. 3, 362.
22. See *Oxford English Dictionary Online*, s.v. "Correspondence, n." defined as "1, the action or fact of corresponding, or answering to each other in fitness or mutual adaptation, congruity, harmony, agreement" and definition "2a., relation of agreement, similarity, or analogy"; "3, Concordant or sympathetic response. *Obsolete* (last citation dated 1680)"; and "4. Relation between persons or communities; usually qualified as *good, friendly, fair, ill, etc., Obsolete* (Very common in 17th c.)." On Iroquois ritual diplomatic efforts to ensure "good correspondence and understanding between people," see Parmenter, *Edge of the Woods*, xlvii.
23. MPCP, vol. 3, 556 On native slavery, see Gallay, *Indian Slave Trade*. On commodities vs. gifts, see Hall Jr., *Zamumo's Gifts*, 13.

24. MPCP, vol. 3, 129.
25. "Ghesaont" of the "Sinnekaes Nation," MPCP, vol. 3, 124–25. On ritual gift exchange and the resulting atmosphere of "an emotional climate of peace," see Richter, *Ordeal of the Longhouse*, 40.
26. MPCP, vol. 3, 129.
27. Locke first published this work in 1690. The 1713 edition, published closest to the time of the Cartlidge case, is quoted; Locke, *Two Treatises of Government*, 190.
28. "July the 12th 1720," in MPCP, vol. 3, 93; Penn, "Articles of Agreement with the Susquehannah Indians," April 23, 1701, PWP, vol. 4, 49–55, 51.
29. On Locke, see Eustace, *Passion Is the Gale*, 148–49, and 527n83.
30. "Report of Coll. Ffrench & Henry Worley," June 16, 1710, MPCP, vol. 2, 511–12.
31. On the "Paxton Boys" and their genocidal attack on the remaining Native community members at Conestoga, see Blackhawk, *Rediscovery of America*, 163–69.
32. On Indian concerns over sovereignty and justice, see Smolenski, "Death of Sawantaeny," 118 and 121–22.

Bibliography

Archives of Maryland. *Proceedings of the Council of Maryland 1636–1667*. Edited by William Hand Browne. Baltimore: Maryland Historical Society, 1885.

Archives of Maryland. *Proceedings of the Council of Maryland 1687/8–1693*. Edited by William Hand Browne. Baltimore: Maryland Historical Society, 1890.

Barr, Daniel P. "Did Pennsylvania Have a Middle Ground? Examining Indian-White Relations on the Eighteenth-Century Pennsylvania Frontier." *Pennsylvania Magazine of History and Biography* 136, no. 4 (2012): 337–63.

Blackhawk, Ned. *The Rediscovery of America: Native Peoples and the Unmaking of U.S. History*. New Haven: Yale University Press, 2023.

Burnard, Trevor. "Slave Naming Patterns: Onomastics and the Taxonomy of Race in Eighteenth-Century Jamaica." *Journal of Interdisciplinary History* 31, no. 3 (2001): 325–46.

Calloway, Colin Gordon. *The Indian World of George Washington: The First President, the First Americans, and the Birth of the Nation*. Oxford: Oxford University Press, 2018.

Cohen, Matt. *The Networked Wilderness: Communicating in Early New England*. Minneapolis: University of Minnesota Press, 2009.

Dunn, Richard S., and Mary Maples Dunn, eds. *The Papers of William Penn*. Vol. 2, *1680–1684*. Philadelphia: University of Pennsylvania Press, 1982.

———. *The Papers of William Penn*. Vol. 3, *1685–1700*. Philadelphia: University of Pennsylvania Press, 1986.

———. *The Papers of William Penn*. Vol. 4, *1701–1718*. Philadelphia: University of Pennsylvania Press, 1987.

Eustace, Nicole. *Passion Is the Gale: Emotion, Power, and the Coming of the American Revolution*. Chapel Hill: University of North Carolina Press, 2008.

Gallay, Alan. *The Indian Slave Trade: The Rise of the English Empire in the American South*. New Haven: Yale University Press, 2008.

Galloway, Patricia. "'The Chief Who Is Your Father'." In *Powhatan's Mantle: Indians in the Colonial Southeast*, edited by Gregory A. Waselkov, Peter H. Wood, And Tom Hatley, 345–70. Lincoln: University of Nebraska Press, 2006.

Hall, Joseph M., Jr. *Zamumo's Gifts: Indian-European Exchange in the Colonial Southeast*. Philadelphia: University of Pennsylvania Press, 2012.

Hanna, Charles A. *The Wilderness Trail*. New York: Putnam, 1911.

Harvey, Sean P., and Sarah Rivett. "Colonial-Indigenous Language Encounters in North America and the Intellectual History of the Atlantic World." *Early American Studies* 15, no. 3 (2017): 442–73.

Hill, Jane H. "Native American Knowledges, Native American Epistemologies: Native American Languages as Evidence." In *Native Studies Keywords*, edited by Michelle Raheja, Andrea Smith, and Stephanie Nohelani Teves, 319–38. Tucson: University of Arizona Press, 2015.

Holm, Thomas Campanius. *A Vocabulary of Susquehannock*. Translated by Peter Stephen Du Ponceau and edited by Claudio R. Salvucci. Merchantville NJ: Evolution Publishing, 2007.

Karttunen, Frances E. *Between Worlds: Interpreters, Guides, and Survivors*. New Brunswick NJ: Rutgers University Press, 1994.

Kent, Barry C. *Susquehanna's Indians*. Harrisburg: Pennsylvania Historical and Museum Commission, 1993.

Kruer, Matthew. *Time of Anarchy: Indigenous Power and the Crisis of Colonialism in Early America*. Cambridge MA: Harvard University Press, 2022.

Locke, John. *Two Treatises of Government*. London: John Churchill, 1713.

Merrell, James H. *Into the American Woods: Negotiators on the Pennsylvania Frontier*. New York: W. W. Norton, 1999.

Merritt, Jane T. "Metaphor, Meaning, and Misunderstanding: Language and Power on the Pennsylvania Frontier." In *Contact Points: American Frontiers from the Mohawk Valley to the Mississippi, 1750–1830*, edited by Andrew Cayton and Fredrika J. Teute, 60–87. Chapel Hill: University of North Carolina Press, 1998.

Minutes of the Provincial Council of Pennsylvania. Vols. 2 and 3. Philadelphia: Jo. Severns, 1852.

Minutes of the Provincial Council of Pennsylvania. Vol. 4, *February 7, 1735–36 to October 15, 1745*. Harrisburg: Fenn, 1851.

Parmenter, Jon. *Edge of the Woods: Iroquoia*. Ann Arbor: University of Michigan Press, 2010.

Piker, Joshua Aaron. *Okfuskee: A Creek Town in Colonial America*. Cambridge MA: Harvard University Press, 2009.

Richter, Daniel K. "Cultural Brokers and Intercultural Politics: New York—Iroquois Relations, 1664–1701." *Journal of American History* 75, no. 1 (1988): 40–67.

———. *The Ordeal of the Longhouse: The Peoples of the Iroquois League in the Era of European Colonization*. Chapel Hill: University of North Carolina Press, 1992.

———. *Trade, Land, Power: The Struggle for Eastern North America*. Philadelphia: University of Pennsylvania Press, 2013.
Schutt, Amy C. *Peoples of the River Valleys: The Odyssey of the Delaware Indians*. Philadelphia: University of Pennsylvania Press, 2013.
Schwartz, Ana. *Unmoored: The Search for Sincerity in Colonial America*. Chapel Hill: University of North Carolina Press, 2022.
Smolenski, John. "The Death of Sawantaeny." In *Friends and Enemies in Penn's Woods: Colonists, Indians, and the Racial Construction of Pennsylvania*, edited by William Pencak and Daniel K. Richter, 104–28. University Park: Pennsylvania State University Press, 2004.
Soderlund, Jean R. *Lenape Country: Delaware Valley Society before William Penn*. Philadelphia: University of Pennsylvania Press, 2014.
St. John, Wendy B. "Inventing Guardianship: The Mohegan Indians and Their 'Protectors.'" *New England Quarterly* 72, no. 3 (1999): 362–87.
Warren, Stephen. *The Worlds the Shawnees Made: Migration and Violence in Early America*. Chapel Hill: University of North Carolina Press, 2014.

Maungwudaus Maintains Peace

From the editors: Maungwudaus was a Mississauga/Ojibwa interpreter and born around 1810, likely in Upper Canada. He was converted to Methodist Episcopalian in his teens and later served as an interpreter for the Canadian government on the southeastern coast of Lake Saint Clair. Over the years he befriended the famous American artist and ethnographer George Catlin. Perhaps sensing opportunity, Maungwudaus shifted professions from interpreter and missionary to representative and performer of the Ojibwa. Between 1844 and 1846, Catlin sponsored a portion of a European tour that Maungwudaus organized with his family and other Ojibwa performers. The account below comes from Maungwudaus's published memoir, which he sold at shows throughout the tour.

When we got ready to leave, one of the officers said to us, our ladies would be glad to shake hands with you, and we shook hands with them. Then they were talking amongst themselves; then another officer said to us, "Friends, our ladies think that you do not pay enough respects to them, they desire you to kiss them"; then we kissed them according to our custom on both cheeks. "Why! They have kissed us on our cheeks; what a curious way of kissing this is." Then another officer said to us, "Gentlemen, our pretty squaws are not yet satisfied; they want to be kissed on their mouths." Then we kissed them on their mouths; then there was great shout amongst the English war-chiefs. Say-say-gon, our war-chief, then said in our language to the ladies; "That is all you are good for; as for wives, you are good for nothing." The ladies wanted me to tell them what the war-chief said to them. I then told them that he said he was wishing the officers would invite him very often, that he might again kiss the handsome ladies. Then they said, "Did he? then we will tell our men to invite you again, for we like to be kissed very often; tell him so." They put gold rings on our fingers and gold pins on our breasts, and when we had thanked them for their kindness, we got in our carriage and went to our apartments.[1]

FIG 1. George Henry (Maungwudaus). Digital watercolor by Ricky Hadi, based on "Portrait of Maungwudaus (or Maun-gua-daus alias George Henry)," Library and Archives Canada. Original available at Wikimedia Commons. https://commons.wikimedia.org/w/index.php?curid=75985642.

Notes

1. Maungwudaus, *An Account of the Chippewa Indians, Who Have Been Travelling among the Whites, in the United States, England, Ireland, Scotland, France and Belgium* (Boston: Published by the author, 1848).

3

William Wells... Interpreter?

CAMERON SHRIVER

Interpreters are choke points in a polyglot world. Often imagined as conduits, they frequently serve as lightning rods. William Wells was such an interpreter. He seemed to be everywhere and involved in everything. Born Anglo-American, raised Myaamia (Miami Indian), employed by the United States, raising a Myaamia family—Wells personified a borderland. His ability to interpret language and culture made him critical to U.S. and Myaamia objectives as the eighteenth century transitioned to the nineteenth. If interpreters are meant to be invisible, then Wells did not fit the mold. If interpreters are intended to improve security across cultural divides, he again falls frustratingly short. Wells did much more than translate one person's speech into another language. He was also an agent *employed by the United States* as it first flexed its imperial muscles in the western communities it claimed to control. Wells's interesting life, then, offers a glimpse into the discretionary power of the human agents of empire. Also intimately enmeshed in Myaamia community, Wells was uniquely positioned to *promote Myaamia resistance* to that same empire. These binaries—Anglo-American or Myaamia, advocate of or resister against U.S. federal policies—collapse a complicated reality. At the same time, Wells himself seemed hemmed in by those dichotomous categories—is he one of *us*, or one of *them*?

One might be excused for viewing Wells as walking in "two worlds," a phrase we will return to later. On the one hand, Wells found himself in the midst of profound historical changes. He was the agent of an expansionist empire tasked with transforming Myaamia life until it was no longer Myaamia at all—the people, their polity, and their land would be wholly consumed by the settler state. At the same time, Wells was the mouthpiece of the most prominent Myaamia leader of the era, a man named Mihšihkinaahkwa 'Little Turtle' who stridently pursued a future for his people, violently defended his homeland, and frequently worked against U.S. expansion. Historians have characterized Wells as "caught between his official duties and responsibilities and his close and friendly relations with the Indians."[1] His biographer introduces Wells as "always the man in the middle, moving between two worlds" that were "in mortal conflict with each other."[2] Wells parallels the character studies by James Merrell in his study of the cultural divide of colonial Pennsylvania, in which he argues that intercultural brokers on the Pennsylvania frontier "were firmly anchored on one side of the cultural divide or the other."[3] While Western historians have rightly challenged the frontier concept, fewer have directly engaged with Merrell's reintroduction of the idea that an ineffable cultural divide foreclosed more plural futures. However, while interpreters are bridges between language groups, they are not beset by split personalities. Wells lived in one world. It was and remains a polyglot, changing, complicated place. As a biography of one interpreter, this chapter briefly narrates the forces buffeting William Wells before considering how to describe him and his apparent between-ness.

William Wells was born in 1770 in the Pennsylvania colony. His family moved to Kentucky as part of a mass migration to the region, squatting near modern-day Louisville. As a result of the influx of uninvited newcomers, vicious borderlands warfare beset the region. Soon after, William's mother perished of unknown cause, and his father likely was killed by Myaamia men in 1781. Living with another Anglo family, the thirteen-year-old William was then captured by Delawares and given to a prominent Myaamia leader named Aakaawita 'Porcupine.' Aakaawita and his family raised William, now renamed Eepiihkanita 'Groundnut,' on the lower Kineepikwameekwa Siipiiwi 'Eel River' near its junction with the Waapaahšiki Siipiiwi 'Wabash River.' At some point as a young adult, he married a local Indigenous woman only known to us as 'Nancy.'[4] Americans were getting serious about conquering land north of the Ohio River and sent the U.S. Army north in 1790 and 1791, suffering crushing casualties in each campaign. At the Battle of the Wabash in 1791, the Indigenous confederates reduced the size of the American army by a quarter in the blink of an eye. ("O God, O God," President Washington reputedly exclaimed when informed of the 1791 obliteration).[5] But also in 1791, a smaller cavalry unit sought to neutralize the large Wabash River communities, where Eepiihkanita was living with Nancy and their newborn child. In addition to destroying homes and crops, the Kentucky cavalry captured fifty-two women

FIG 2. William Wells. Digital watercolor by Ricky Hadi, based on a miniature portrait of William Wells, ca. 1812, by an unknown artist. Chicago History Museum Collection.

and children, Wells's spouse and child among them.⁶ As an English speaker, a husband and father to hostages, and son to an important leader, Eepiihkanita joined Aakaawita to parley with the Mihši-maalhsaki 'Americans' on the lower Wabash River. There, he met Samuel Wells, his older brother from his previous life, and subsequently spent a month in Louisville among Anglo-American kin. Coming to the attention of an American envoy, Wells agreed to serve as an interpreter for preliminary peace talks between the Miami- and Kickapoo-speaking communities on the Wabash River and the United States. He earned one dollar per day.⁷

Wells's loyalties would thereafter be open for interpretation. He translated the agreement to release his adopted Myaamia mother, his wife, and his child, resulting in a tearful reunion after about a year of their captivity.⁸ His skill made him valuable. The Americans next promised Wells a hefty sum to travel north, where the full congress of Native leaders was debating whether to continue the war against the Americans. He would enquire as to the acceptable terms of their surrender. Wells told the international Native American and British council that the United States desired peace. Most of the leaders rejected the idea or its messenger, and so Wells spent the next several months in the Miami city of Kiihkayonki.[9] Perhaps at this time, now entering his mid-twenties, he fathered the first of four children with a new partner, Wa-nan-go-peth, and apparently stopped living with his first spouse and child. Wa-nan-go-peth was the daughter of a famous war leader, the primary tactician behind the Indigenous victory at the 1791 Battle of the Wabash, a man named Mihšihkinaahkwa 'Little Turtle.'[10]

As with his adoptive father Aakaawita, Wells's relationship with Mihšihkinaahkwa 'Little Turtle' profoundly affected his life by pulling him into new kin networks. In Myaamiaataweenki, the Miami language, Mihšihkinaahkwa would have referred to Wells as *nilenkwala* 'my son-in-law,' and Wells would have referred to Little Turtle as *nimehšoomakya* 'my father-in-law.'[11] Wells spoke or penned every extant word attributed to Little Turtle. He was an *aalhsaacimwa*, an interpreter, a person who gave a true report of what was said.[12]

Initially, Americans liked Wells and appreciated his enthusiasm. His first American employer described Wells as "a young man of good natural abilities and of an agreable [sic] disposition."[13] Calling Wells "an honest sober man," the frequently un-sober Gen. Anthony Wayne asserted that "he faithfully executed the trust reposed in Him last fall by Genl Putnam—& as faithfully that which was reposed in him by me upon the present occasion!"[14] In preparing for yet another attempted conquest of the Ohio Country, General Wayne formed a small reconnaissance group, naming Wells as its captain.[15] After a successful campaign in 1794, Wayne retained Wells to interpret the surrender, the Treaty of Greenville, in 1795. Mihšihkinaahkwa, making the difficult transition from war leader to delegate, served as a principal orator for the Indigenous parties to the treaty. Immediately after signing the treaty, he requested that his son-in-law be hired as the Fort Wayne interpreter and the government acquiesced.[16]

Wells became the mouthpiece of Mihšihkinaahkwa, a leading figure in Great Lakes geopolitics. Twice in the next four years, Wells accompanied Mihšihkinaahkwa and other chiefs to Philadelphia, the seat of the federal government. Paid for his services as a knowledgeable fixer and interpreter, he signed an oath "to promote to the extent of my power the interest of the United States with the Northwestern Indians."[17] Native leaders asked that Wells "should live among them" because "they think he could be of great service in keeping them in good order and giving them good advice."[18] Wells likewise interpreted between Mihši-hkinaahkwa and the French philosophe the Comte de Volney, who called him "a skillful interpreter." Through Wells's interpretation of biology, geology, geography, and philosophy, Volney came away impressed with Mihšihkinaahkwa, who was now the most prominent leader of the Miami people, comparing him favorably to Rousseau. Over the course of many in-depth conversations, Volney became convinced that Mihšihkinaahkwa saw that Native American ways of life were doomed to change, and that therefore he would promote American civilization as the path forward for his people. Mihšihkinaahkwa probably did not intend to enunciate such a negative view of his nation or their culture. Although we cannot know precisely how, as sentences traveled from Myaamia to English to French, the three men transformed Mihšihkinaahkwa's ideas into quotations that were familiar to the French Enlightenment.[19]

Being an interpreter suited Wells because Wells was a talker. He even talked to animals. The Moravian missionary John Heckewelder (who spoke at least one of the Delaware languages and knew Wells personally) once noticed a young Wells quietly addressing a *mahkwa* 'black bear' he had shot. Wells took issue with the bear's protracted dying. "I told him," Wells explained to the missionary, "that he knew the fortune of war, that one or the other of us must have fallen; that it was his fate to be conquered, and he ought to die like a man, like a hero, and not like an old woman; that if the case had been reversed, and I had fallen into the power of *my enemy*, I would not have disgraced my nation as he did, but would have died with firmness and courage, as becomes a true warrior." As he spoke, Wells occasionally touched the bear's nose with his rifle's ramrod.[20]

Like with the French philosopher Volney's record, we should always critically consider ideas and actions deciphered through languages, cultures, and time. Yet Wells chatting with a bear helps us assess his understanding of a Myaamia worldview. Bears are particularly significant in Myaamia cosmology, seen as among the closest beings to humans.[21] In a similar vein and later in life, Wells penned a short ethnography and history of the Miamis, demonstrating a knowledge of doctoring, rites of passage, deathways, gender relations, and the *miteewioni* or medicine lodge society that was then in decline.[22] And another anecdote indicates Wells's skill. At an international conference in Fort Wayne (Wells's home city and then an Indian agency), assembled Native diplomats held a discovery dance (sometimes called a war dance, and a forerunner to the modern men's traditional genre of powwow). The purpose of this dance was, and is, to tell a story of a particular hunting or war deed through artistic movement. Through the medium of dance, a man might depict himself finding and following tracks, sneaking up, and striking a human or animal adversary by symbolically hitting a central wooden post. On this occasion, Wells sensed danger from a visiting delegation. In the words of a near-contemporary, a "big Indian" danced up to Wells "and spoke in Indian and made demonstrations with his tomahawk that looked dangerous." Wells followed with his own "more vigorous and artistic Indian style." According to the anecdote's author, Wells approached the "big Indian" and "told him that he had killed more Indians than white men, and had killed one that looked just like him, and he believed it was his brother, only much better looking."[23] Even after Wells's reputation waned, his superior admitted that his knowledge of Native American life was "much greater than that of any other person in this country."[24] Whatever his flaws, it seems that he had the linguistic and cultural competence—the fluency—to interpret. That fluency made him both valuable and dangerous.

Hired as the interpreter at Fort Wayne in 1797, Wells lived at the former capital of the most prominent Myaamia band at Kiihkayonki, now renamed in the conquering General Wayne's honor.[25] It was a cosmopolitan entrepôt astride a portage between the Great Lakes and the Mississippi River watershed. Wells was one of (at most) a few people who fluently spoke both Myaamiaataweenki and English, and the only Anglo-American man among them. In 1802 he was promoted to a newly created position, Indian agent of the new Fort Wayne Indian Agency. He was instructed to report intelligence up the chain of command to his superior, the territorial governor of Indiana and superintendent of Indian affairs, William Henry Harrison. Additionally, Wells was to grant trading licenses, distribute annuities, and promote "civilization" as part of the federal government's policy.[26] Having achieved a tenuous peace, the United States began to consider how they might fundamentally transform Native Americans and acquire their land at the same time. Wells became the mouthpiece for that colonial goal, an on-the-ground tool of the American empire.

Almost immediately, Wells's ascent began to falter. If an interpreter's role was to make meanings clear between two languages, Wells failed spectacularly. Rather than aid communication, Wells embodied uncertainty, rumor, and distrust. As he entered his thirties as an Indian agent and key interpreter for father-in-law Mihšihkinaahkwa, an impressive range of regional characters evinced dislike for him. His immediate superior for much of his later career was William Henry Harrison. Himself reporting to the secretary of war, Harrison said that Wells "has so entangled himself in the mazes of his own intrigues that he cannot move without making disclosures that are fatal to him."[27] Wells's rival in the Indian service at

Fort Wayne, John Johnston, frequently maligned him, calling him an "unprincipled bad man."[28] From other quarters, the emerging Shawnee militants, brothers called Tecumseh and the Prophet, disparaged Wells. In 1807, his own star on the rise, Tecumseh addressed the governor of Ohio and Shawnee chief Blue Jacket in a large conference. "Congress has a great many good men," Tecumseh said, looking at Wells. "Let them take away Wells and put one of them here. We hate him."[29] Blue Jacket, also Shawnee but no friend of Tecumseh, elsewhere called Wells "a bad man" who contributed to confusion.[30] The British Indian agent near Detroit told Indigenous delegates that "you all well know that he is a bad man."[31] Even Miami leaders cast doubt on him. Pinšiwa, also called Jean Baptiste Richardville and the most prominent of the young crop of leaders of the emerging Miami Nation, reported that he "was much supprised [sic] to hear" how Wells addressed Miamis in council. In the context of constant treaty frictions that Wells interpreted, Pinšiwa recalled that "Mr. Wells addressed the Miamies and advised them to stick together and keep their right, that he Wells if he was a Miamie would do so."[32] Pinšiwa's characterization—which included the reminder that Wells had taken an oath "to support the Government of the United States"—asserted that Wells was attempting to influence Myaamia foreign policy and simultaneously undercut U.S. land acquisition objectives.[33]

Harrison, Tecumseh, McKee, Johnston, Blue Jacket, Pinšiwa—these were among the most important people in the Northwest, all at odds with one another, yet united in their distrust of Wells. Briefly put, he seemed almost uniquely poor at his job, yet he worked for two decades as an Indian agent and interpreter. He even earned a few pay raises.[34] What should we make of his story?

Here seems a good place to reveal that there is no surefire theory, no smoking gun source, that explains William Wells. The most common contemporary critique of Wells was his self-interest. For example, Wells decided to build the government council house and blacksmith shop "on what is called Wells's place in the inside of his pasture field," a somewhat inconvenient spot for everyone but him because it was across a river from the fort and warehouse.[35] According to his successor, the government-employed carpenter effectively worked for Wells's benefit.[36] "The fact is admitted that he makes more money than any man in the Territory," Governor Harrison wrote. Wells's colleague reported that he made over $6,000 in 1804 ("how he can do this honestly I am at a loss to know").[37] If true, this would have made Wells among the wealthiest people in the region, although his estate was modest at the time of his death.[38] As Wells started writing directly to the U.S. secretary of war—bypassing the chain of command—he dug himself deeper. "I fear that Wells is too attentive to pecuniary considerations," the war secretary said.[39] Days later, the secretary repeated that "I fear that he calculates on making money by supplying the Indians" and "I am satisfied that for several years past, Wells has been very intent on making money."[40] It should be said that the other public agents—Wells's colleagues and detractors among them—also found ways to line their pockets. But for Wells, his ability to bridge the linguistic divide made him more suspicious to U.S. bureaucrats. John Johnston (who would repeat many of the very practices he maligned in Wells) wrote that "owing to his speaking the Indian language, there was scarcely any means of detecting" the scale of his embezzlement.[41] Johnston left unspecified how Wells's ability to speak Indigenous languages camouflaged his apparent fraud.

Interpreting Wells requires understanding his role as an agent of Jeffersonian Indian policy, a changing set of plans to transform Native Americans. Wells was an employee of the U.S. War Department and an agent of its mission. In effect, U.S. policy demanded acquiring Native American territory for fiscal, political, and social imperatives.[42] In theory, this would be accomplished by purchasing supposedly underused Indigenous territories in return for the gift of civilization. The federal government carefully managed Native American economies through a system of trading houses called "factories." Employing agents like Wells, the Department of War intended to convert Native American societies to plow-based agriculturalists. President Thomas Jefferson, as a primary author of the plan, frequently contradicted himself and changed his ideas, while promoting some designs publicly and others privately.[43] (We would not typically say that Jefferson was "between two worlds," even if he was a complicated person.) Mihšihkinaahkwa could, at times, promote tenets of the civilization plan. He frequently visited federal officials on the East Coast, where his statements seemed to agree with American imperial goals of Native American transformation. He lobbied for alcohol prohibition; he signed his share of treaties; he invited Quakers to set up a model farm in Myaamia country.[44]

Of course, Mihšihkinaahkwa's ideas required Wells's interpretation, and this in itself was not a radical idea in Myaamia history. Wells's position and behavior fits the Myaamia role of *kaapia*, which is typically translated as "chief's assistant." Ethnological and linguistic evidence suggests the ideal *kaapia* was a go-between for an *akima* 'chief.' A *kaapia* frequently was tasked with interpreting, carrying and displaying wampum belts, passing pipes, or distributing food equitably to the community at large.[45] As Mihšihkinaahkwa's voice, the caretaker of treaties, and the distributor of annuities, it is easy to see how Wells had competing roles: he worked for Mihšihkinaahkwa *and* William Henry Harrison as those two leaders pursued different national objectives. Wells's reputation rested on the larger interpretation of multivalent and polyglot goals in a region very much up for grabs.

If anything orients us to Wells's true self in this complicated and rapidly changing world, it was his loyalty to his multicultural family. Wells's closeness to Mihšihkinaahkwa, the father of his second wife, caused distrust among many. The two men never contradicted each other in the record. Indeed, it would have been impossible for Mihšihkinaahkwa, who did not speak English and thus spoke through Wells. Prominent Miamis rebuked Wells's behavior (and, as we will see, came to repudiate Mihšihkinaahkwa as well). When Mihšihkinaahkwa sent a somewhat complaining letter to President Jefferson, Wells's rival John Johnston reported that because "the Turtle [Mihšihkinaahkwa] never could have taken up the idea himself, it must have originated elsewhere than in his brain."[46] When Wells expressed that Indigenous communities were unhappy with recent treaties that expropriated a great deal of their land, Harrison questioned the source. "Whether the idea of opposition to those Treaties originated with [Mihšihkinaahkwa 'Little Turtle'] or with Mr. Wells I cannot determine," he wrote, but "the opinions of the one are always the opinions of the other. . . . When Wells speaks of the Miami Nation being of this or that opinion he must be understood as meaning no more than the Turtle and himself."[47] As Wells and Mihšihkinaahkwa pushed back against U.S. imperialism, U.S. imperialists increasingly sidelined both of them.

But even this narrative—characters transitioning from important to peripheral—is too binary an interpretation. For Wells's reputation had multiple peaks and valleys, like a barometer reflecting the success of U.S. objectives from season to season. From a U.S. federal perspective, land acquisition and security were the twin pillars of the early nineteenth century. After the Treaty of Greenville (1795) built a foundation for lasting peace and stability, it only took eight years for the United States to complete the next territorial acquisition by treaty. Treaties of expropriation became the primary focus of the region's Indigenous leaders, Wells, and Indiana governor Harrison in the first decade of the 1800s. Delegates signed treaties in Indiana Territory at a yearly rate. Harrison's career as superintendent of Indian affairs (a position co-occuring with governor of Indiana Territory) rested on his ability to acquire Native American territory. He was good at it. Delawares, Potawatomis, Miamis, and others often complained of his tactics and the low returns for vast swaths of territory. Theoretically, Wells's job was to transmit this dissatisfaction. Harrison's accusation of Wells's "cunning" and "intrigue"—that any Native American displeasure was surely created by Wells himself—shielded

Harrison from closer scrutiny. Harrison could create his own narratives, and perhaps his own truths. He informed both Wells and the War Department that Native Americans were *not really* angry about losing their land. Tipping his hand, Harrison complained that "Capt. Wells has certainly not exerted himself to pacify the Indians who have taken offense at the late Treaties."[48] Understanding his precarious position, Wells conciliated several times and promised to silence Delaware and Miami information.

Wells was important to the other American mission: security. As an American agent, Wells was an intelligence-gatherer. His knowledge of local opinions and news made Wells particularly important after 1807, when war loomed between the United States and Great Britain. In 1807 two developments forbode violence. First, the British HMS *Leopard* seized an American ship. The *Chesapeake-Leopard* affair was the most famous early British impressment, as the British naval vessel attacked, boarded, and searched the U.S. ship for deserters from the Royal Navy. Closer to home, an Indigenous evangelist called the Shawnee Prophet was earning a reputation as a powerful man. Tenskwatawa (the Prophet) and William Henry Harrison would embroil themselves in a holy war.[49]

Wells fanned these flames in his own way, pointing to the Prophet as particularly dangerous to Americans, albeit one he was uniquely able to mitigate. Penning open letters to newspapers, Wells asserted that Native Americans generally were no danger in Ohio or Kentucky.[50] Through official channels, he sought to convince Harrison of an alliance between the Prophet and the British in Canada. Harrison believed him.[51] Wells's value spiked in 1807 and 1808, as he connected the Prophet and the British in a conspiracy against the Americans. Wells asserted his ability to tap into "secret" information networks among Native Americans and their potential British allies just to the north. For example, he offered to "endeavour to git everything out of them and from time to time write you everything that comes to my knowledge."[52] For their part, the Prophet and Tecumseh usually blamed Wells and Little Turtle for spreading misinformation.[53] It is impossible to know from which quarters much of the information emerged. But Wells could monger rumors, and his role as useful informant briefly put him in Harrison's good graces.

Not for long. Harrison could use a scapegoat by 1809. For years, he had played this card. Native folks were angry at Harrison's strong-arm treaty-making, and Harrison wanted an interpreter on his side. In 1805, for example, when Wells reported (with witnesses) a Delaware leader's anger at a treaty negotiated in bad faith by Harrison, Harrison noted that Wells "will go any length and use any means to carry a favorite point and much mischief may ensue from his knowledge of the

Indians."[54] Was Wells inciting disapproval of a treaty? Or, was he relaying information? Shouldn't an interpreter and Indian agent have excellent "knowledge of the Indians"? Be that as it may, Harrison fired Wells. In his place, he recommended an interpreter named Joseph Barron. In Harrison's words, Barron's qualifications included his linguistic skill and that he was "the only interpreter I ever knew who was solely devoted to the interests of the United States, to the exclusion of every sympathy for the Indians which would interfere with his duty. Nine tenths of them preferring the interests of the Indians to that of their employers."[55] Years earlier, Harrison had depicted Wells as "more attached to the Indians than to the people of the United States."[56] In short, Wells's inability or unwillingness to hush Harrison's Indigenous critics trumped his value as an intelligence-gatherer in 1809. As Harrison explained several years later, "the wayward disposition of the man" had gotten him into trouble, but he was good at collecting information in Indian Country.[57] The purpose of an interpreter, at least in Harrison's view, was to accomplish U.S. objectives: acquiring land and relaying intelligence. Wells sat at the center of these policies. He did not defy them completely, but nor did he facilitate them to the satisfaction of his American colleagues.

Wells also operated in his Indigenous geopolitical context. Myaamia politics and economies were bound up in treaty-making, in which Indigenous leaders negotiated the best possible outcomes for what was becoming an inevitable dispossession via dependency on U.S. trade. Myaamia communities were increasingly consolidating in the face of growing imperial threats. Myaamia families and their leaders faced mounting stresses; their decisions were made under conditions of imperial coercion. Myaamia leaders sought to carefully manage imposed changes, sometimes resisting, sometimes cooperating, always attempting to make the best choice in a range of increasingly awful ones.[58] Wells worked between several competing Indigenous futures. On one hand was the idealism of the Shawnee Prophet and Tecumseh. Their spiritually divined plan called for the development of racial consciousness among Native Americans; common land tenure among the various Native nations and ethnic groups; following (to some degree) the spiritual prescriptions of the Prophet; and rejecting both trade and land negotiations with the United States. Nearly all Miamis rejected this, in part because the Shawnee brothers' vision required the Miamis to give up their claim as *most* Indigenous to the Wabash River Valley.[59] The rejection of all things American did not seem tenable to most Myaamiaki.

A more subtle development was a rejection of Mihšihkinaahkwa as the principal Myaamia leader. Myaamia politics had long been based in mostly independent villages. A cadre of chiefs increasingly attempted to isolate the Turtle and his mouthpiece, Wells. This was in motion as early as the late 1790s, when Mihšihkinaahkwa appeared too friendly to missionary efforts to introduce cattle to the Myaamia economy.⁶⁰ By 1805, during a treaty negotiation, influential leaders openly rejected Mihšihkinaahkwa as a national representative.⁶¹ Wells admitted as much two years later, lumping a few Miami and Potawatomi leaders as being left on the outside of "secrets" lower down the Wabash—in the direction of the anti-American Prophetstown—as those chiefs "ought not to know anything about the affairs of the Indians." By 1809 Harrison got the point. He told Miamis that "he perfectly understood and admitted that they the (Mississinway Chiefs) were the real Representatives of the Miami Nation."⁶²

For Mihšihkinaahkwa and his assistant William Wells, leadership crumbled with astonishing speed. Wells's family was no longer in a central role in the Myaamia community, a denouement beginning in 1805 and seemingly completed after the Treaty of Fort Wayne in 1809. Years after his death, rumors began to swirl that Little Turtle was not even *really* a Miami. A Myaamia leader in the 1820s said that the Turtle's mother had been Mahican and his father Báxoje (Iowa). Decades later, Mihšihkinaahkwa's granddaughter (not via Wells) would refute this explicitly, and no further evidence suggests that Mihšihkinaahkwa had non-Myaamia ancestry.⁶³ Mihšihkinaahkwa died at Wells's home in 1812, suffering from gout. Soon, the violence of the War of 1812 finally erupted, and Wells was killed while evacuating his Anglo-American niece and nephew, as well as the other Americans, from Fort Dearborn near Chicago in 1812. He was forty-two. All accounts agree on an unusual detail: that the Potawatomis and Ho-Chunks who attacked the evacuation convoy ate Wells's heart.⁶⁴

Wells's interesting life and spectacular death have made him popular in regional history. Scholars have called Wells "brave and enterprising" and "sagacious and intrepid."⁶⁵ His most recent biographer tells us that "perhaps more than anyone on the frontier, he understood both the Indian and white perspectives" and that "few people, either Indian or white, trusted him."⁶⁶ Historical novelists—much-read ones in the Midwest—frame Wells as the "meddling" antagonist to the region's real hero, Tecumseh.⁶⁷ Historian Richard White asserted that Wells was "a figure as thoroughly a product of the middle ground as any person in the *pays d'en haut*."⁶⁸ Wells is the prototypical go-between and an exemplary misunderstanding-maker. He figures prominently in origin stories of Fort Wayne (as landowner, justice of the peace, Indian agent, and interpreter) and Chicago (as a central character in the 1812 Battle of Fort Dearborn), which explains why Wells Street is a main thoroughfare in both midwestern cities. For the last eight decades, Ohio politicians and their aides have seen Wells depicted in Howard Chandler Christy's giant 1945 oil painting, which hangs adjacent to the Capitol Rotunda in Columbus. In the vignette he stands, larger than life, between Miami chief Little Turtle and American general Anthony Wayne. In this version, he was the key interpreter in the land transfer that paved the way for Ohio statehood.[69]

This transition to U.S. hegemony marked the end of the metaphorical space that Richard White called the *middle ground* and signaled the beginning of an increasingly binary set of theoretical futures. Wells was an agent of American imperialism as it was being invented. He interpreted it. Focused on security and nascent state building, the U.S. government tasked agents and interpreters like Wells with facilitating the dispossession of Native Americans. Wells's life coincided with profound changes in American and Native American life. It was chaotic, and so are the traces that Wells left us to interpret.

Binaries are useful in making sense of what was a confusing reality. The literature not only suggests a settler and an Indigenous world but frequently points to Native American leaders as either working with, or against, settler colonialism. Treaty chiefs, accommodationists, and other more pejorative categorizations: How do we understand folks like Mihšihkinaahkwa who signed their x-marks, assenting to changes in circumstances not of their own making? For that matter, what do we do with Native nations themselves incorporated into the U.S. empire? Mihšihkinaahkwa (via Wells) purportedly told the French philosopher Volney that white folks "spread like oil on a blanket; we melt like snow before the sun. If things do not greatly change, the red men will disappear very shortly."[70] As the historian Ned Blackhawk has written, "once adaptation becomes synonymous with assimilation, change over time—the commonplace definition of history—becomes a death knell. The more things change, the greater the loss."[71] Still, adapting to new technologies, politics, and economies, Myaamia people did not lose themselves. Mihšihkinaahkwa (or Wells) promoted neither assimilation nor rejection, but what Myaamia historian George Ironstrack has dubbed the "Third Path of adaptive resistance," of embracing change in order to control it. Ironstrack also helps us consider multiethnicity when he asserts that "if you can learn the language, kinship networks, and the responsibilities of each group, then it is possible to belong to all of the communities that your family connects you to."[72] If U.S. hegemony offered a binary—replacing savagery with civilization—Wells's choices suggest a more plural history of change and family connections.

One of those changes was this: In 1810, few Myaamia people spoke English. In 1910, only four Myaamia people *did not* speak English.[73] (One of them was

Kiilhsoohkwa, Mihšihkinaahkwa's granddaughter, who recalled brushing his hair as a very young girl.) This transition to English was unprecedented in Myaamia experience, which since the beginning had been multilingual. English-language interpreters became an obsolete relic of a Myaamia past. As a result of English dominance, Myaamia people began to separate the past as a different world to their present. An outgrowth of the civilization versus primitivism framework at the foundation of American policy in Wells's era, allotment and boarding schools would similarly seek to end Native American power and culture. As Carl Schurz put it in 1881, Native people faced "this stern alternative: extermination or civilization."[74] The two worlds were asymmetrical. Indigeneity (glossed as primitivism) was the past, civilization the future. English-language dominance would slowly come to characterize Myaamia life until Myaamiaataweenki was no longer conversationally spoken by the 1960s.[75] Of course, the larger context of U.S. oppression forced this change. But Myaamia people adopted the change as their own personal decisions. Myaamia elder Eugene Brown put it this way: "I asked my mom, I asked her 'why didn't you teach us the language' and she said 'you live in a white man's world. That is not going to do you any good.'"[76] Brown's mother attended Haskell Institute, a boarding school for Native Americans. Sharon Burkybile, a granddaughter of a Chilocco and Carlisle Indian School survivor asserted that this decision to stop intergenerational language transfer was because elders "were shielding us from the unpleasant things about our past."[77] Mildred Walker, a survivor of Seneca Indian School, published her experience for the tribal newspaper in the late 1990s. Her schooling, she thought, allowed for the "transition to the white man's world." But she was sure to highlight the cost, including cultural shame and damaged identity. "This loss of self image has left the Indian, generations later, still struggling to join these two separate selves."[78] Mildred Walker was a revered person, remembered for her humor, her power, her cultural knowledge—when she spoke, everybody listened. She did not have a split personality. She was a full human being living in a complicated world.

Vine Deloria Jr. shouted his disillusionment with the concept that Native Americans struggled "BETWEEN TWO WORLDS." In the 1970s, anthropologists and the mainstream generally saw Native Americans as neither authentic Indians of the past, nor modern individuals of the present.[79] The incompatibility of supposed Indian and Western thought-worlds, according to "between two worlds" theorists, was liable to create what we might label cultural schizophrenics. Language became a marker of these worlds, and Wells was among the first bilingual Myaamia-English speakers (he also spoke Potawatomi) and produced a family of

Myaamiaataweenki-English speakers. Although Wells's reputation suffered in the larger Myaamia community, his own children remembered him more fondly. They called him "papa" in letters in the wake of his death.[80] His daughter named one of her sons William Wells. Some of the family joined with the deported Miami Nation to Kansas in the 1840s and continued as enrolled in the Miami Nation. Wells's grandson, a Myaamia enrolled citizen, even served as an interpreter in the 1860s.[81] Others in the family had moved with their Anglo-American husbands and avoided deportation—these children had been sent away from the potential violence at the beginning of the War of 1812 for schooling in Kentucky. Not included on the rolls of the Miami Nation, this part of the family was forced to petition for membership in the mid and late nineteenth century.[82] Their petitions highlighted Little Turtle's esteem and Wells's significance. They focused particularly on the Treaty of Greenville in 1795 as the most significant moment of the two men's careers and largely ignored both the war years preceding it and the controversies characterizing their ancestors' later years. Wells's grandchildren asserted that due to "his profound knowledge of Indian character and language [and] intimate acquaintance with the various tribes, he exercised an extended influence, and was enabled to render commendable service in the performance of important duties" preceding and during the Treaty of Greenville. The descendants "cannot forbear," they wrote, "to *briefly* allude, with Mingled pride and pleasure, to the *historical Career*, praiseworthy Efforts, and able assistance rendered, by their illustrious ancestors," Wells and Little Turtle. In this telling, the duo "by their foresight, efforts, and influence, were largely instrumental in the construction and adoption of the wise terms and *beneficent* conditions formed in the covenants and stipulations" found in the Greenville Treaty.[83] "We are proud of our Indian (Little Turtle) blood, and of our Capt. Wells blood," said James Wolcott, one of William Wells's grandsons in the late nineteenth century. "We try to keep up the customs of our ancestors."[84]

Two worlds? Not in reality. In fact, Wells's descendants are actively working against this framework. In the 1990s Wells's descendant Daryl Baldwin would be a key catalyst in the reclamation of the Myaamia language. "It's that whole notion of 'walking in two worlds,' which I completely don't agree with," he said when discussing language learning. Instead, he asserts, people can have different backgrounds and meaningfully belong to multiple communities.[85] The changes never stop, he said, nor does the struggle against polarization. In that way, "We're not them, but we're an extension of them."[86] Wells's seventh great-grandson is an interpreter of a sort: he works at the forefront of a small group who can speak English *and* Myaamiaataweenki and is a language teacher for the Miami Tribe of Oklahoma. The Miami Nation today is a descendant of the centralizing polity interpreted by Wells, and it still seeks to strengthen itself by building relationships with allied communities, maintaining a cohesive foreign policy, and finding solutions to the problems of colonization.

If Wells bridged two competing worlds, it was on this axis: American policymakers increasingly sought to engineer the disappearance of Native Americans, while Native Americans counter-engineered their own futures. No wonder folks had mixed feelings on Wells. He interpreted destruction and creation.

One would be hard-pressed to find a more suitable vessel through which to narrate the violence of conquest and the functioning of Jeffersonian Indian policy. But it is more difficult to understand how he shaped those changes. Was he an active historical agent? That was his title, after all: Indian agent. Was he an interpreter? That was his other title, one that suggests a less assertive, if no less important, role. Should we understand his actions as a *kaapia*, chief's assistant? Wells served as part of a system that intended to transmit information between the United States government and Indigenous families. Many of those government agents and Indigenous families considered him poor in this job. Too interested in profits; too tied to his father-in-law's aspirations for an emerging Miami Nation; too partial. Wells was tasked with a difficult job. He held competing roles: interpreter and a U.S. agent. In reality, he often served as a Myaamia agent (or agent of one Myaamia leader). His superiors obviously expected him to convince and to enquire, to persuade and to probe—these are not expectations of modern interpreters. More universally, Wells illuminates a truth. Any attempt to systematize interpretation relies on human decisions. Not only that, Wells experienced his own world and may not have recognized himself as existing in-between. Language and even the historical record are too complicated—too open to interpretation—for seamless translation.

Notes

The author would like to acknowledge the help of many people in interpreting William Wells over the years, including most prominently Daryl Baldwin, George Ironstrack, and Paul Mapp.

1. Thornbrough, *Letter Book of the Indian Agency at Fort Wayne*, 14.
2. Heath, *William Wells*, xi.
3. Merrell, *Into the American Woods*, 37. Critiques of the two worlds trope include Deloria Jr., *Custer Died for Your Sins*, 86; Chaat Smith, *Everything You Know about*

Indians Is Wrong, 34–35; Buss and Genetin-Pilawa, *Beyond Two Worlds*.
4. Wade, "Notes on the Wabash River," 289.
5. Calloway, *Victory with No Name*; Irving, *Life of George Washington*, vol. 5, 108.
6. "List of Indian Prisoners," June 1, 1791, *American State Papers, Indian Affairs*, vol. 1, 133.
7. Hutton, "William Wells," 188–90; Rufus Putnam to Henry Knox, July 14, 1792, in Buell, *Memoirs of Rufus Putnam*, 296.
8. Heckewelder, "Narrative," 45.
9. Wayne to Knox, September 17, 1793, in Knopf, *Anthony Wayne*, 272–73; Instructions to Mr. Wells, October 7, 1792, in Buell, *Memoirs of Rufus Putnam*, 370; Edmunds, "'Nothing Has Been Effected,'" 25; Putnam to Henry Knox, October 9, 1792, in Buell, *Memoirs of Rufus Putnam*, 381. Wells was the "young man" reported at the Glaize, in "Extract of a Letter from the Glaize dated 5th of January, 1793," in Cruikshank, *Correspondence of Lieut. Governor John Graves Simcoe*, vol. 1, 282–83.
10. Carter, *Little Turtle*, 103. The Battle of the Wabash is detailed in Calloway, *Victory with No Name*. The name Wa-nan-go-peth is poorly understood today. Unlike many Myaamia names, as of this writing there is no standardized modern orthography of her name. David Costa, Jarrid Baldwin, Hunter Thompson Lockwood, and Daryl Baldwin email thread with the author, January 29–31, 2025.
11. Costa, "Kinship Terminology of the Miami-Illinois Language," 39, 43–44.
12. Thanks to Hunter Thompson Lockwood and David Costa for helping me understand the cultural weight of the word.
13. Putnam to Knox, July 14, 1792 in Buell, *Memoirs of Rufus Putnam*, 296.
14. Wayne to Knox, September 17, 1793, in Knopf, "Western Campaign," 300.
15. Hutton, "William Wells," 193–94. Wells's activities are suggested in "Subsistence account of William Wells from 13 Sept 93 to 30 June," Northwest History Collection, Indiana State Library, https://images.indianahistory.org/digital/collection/onwt/id/911/rec/1; "The United States in account with William Wells, Interpreter," 1793–95, Northwest History Collection, Indiana State Library, https://images.indianahistory.org/digital/collection/onwt/id/916/rec/2.
16. 7 Stat., 49; "At a private conference, on the 12th August, with the Miamies, Eel River, and Kickapoo Indians," *American State Papers, Indian Affairs*, vol. 1, 483; Ironstrack, "The Treaty of Greenville (1795), Part 1."
17. "Philadelphia, December 9, 1796," Northwest History Collection, Indiana State Library, https://images.indianahistory.org/digital/collection/onwt/id/1739/rec/4.
18. Speech of Soldier, 1796, quoted in Heath, *William Wells*, 239.
19. Volney, *View of the Soil*, 354–87.
20. Heckewelder, *History, Manners, and Customs*, 255–56.
21. This is the author's observation as a participant in Myaamia community and intellectual life and is supported by related cultures such as the Cree. For example, one anthropologist wrote of Mistassini Cree hunters, "prior to the killing the hunter talks to the bear, and it is believed that the animal understands." Tanner, *Bringing Home Animals*, 146.

22. William Wells, "The Manners, and Customs of the North Western Indians," ca. 1811, Indian Documents, Fort Wayne manuscript, 1811–12, Chicago Historical Society.
23. The anecdote was remembered by the wife of Fort Wayne's surgeon, Abraham Edwards, and told to her son, Alexander H. Edwards, born in Fort Wayne in 1807. Alexander Edwards related the story directly in Wentworth, *Early Chicago*, 54–57. It is possible that the event occurred in May of 1812, when many Kickapoos and Ho-Chunks, as well as Tecumseh, were conferencing in the region, and Wells's performance would have been recalled in contrast to the naive new agent, Benjamin Stickney. Wells detailed the performance of this genre of dance in "The Manners, and Customs of the North Western Indians."
24. Harrison to Dearborn, quoted in Heath, *William Wells*, 334.
25. Henry Dearborn to Thomas Pasteur, June 4, 1802, in Carter, *Territorial Papers*, vol. 7, 52.
26. Harrison's career in Indian policy as ably explained in Owens, *Mr. Jefferson's Hammer*.
27. Harrison to Dearborn, July 10, 1805, in Esarey, *Messages and Letters*, vol. 1, 147.
28. Johnston to Eustis, July 1, 1812, Letters Received, Office of the Secretary of War, RG 107, M221, reel 24, NARA, Washington DC.
29. Quoted in Sugden, *Tecumseh*, 6.
30. Quoted in Sugden, *Tecumseh*, 162.
31. Alexander McKee speech to Indigenous delegates near Detroit, November, 1804, in Esarey, *Messages and Letters*, vol. 1, 112.
32. John Gibson and Vigo to Harrison, July 6, 1805, in Esarey, *Messages and Letters*, vol. 1, 145.
33. Wells's frictions with Myaamia leaders and the Shawnee Prophet has been fruitfully explored in Bottiger, *Borderland of Fear*, 48–53, 89–91, and Bickers, "Who Speaks in the Name of the Miami Nation?" 73–77.
34. Dearborn to Wells, January 19, 1804, in Carter, *Territorial Papers*, vol. 7, 168; Harrison to Eustis, April 23, 1811, in Esarey, *Messages and Letters*, vol. 1, 508.
35. John Johnston to John Smith, April 15, 1809, in Thornbrough, *Letter Book*, 44–45.
36. John Johnston to William Eustis, April 15, 1809, in Thornbrough, *Letter Book*, 37.
37. Harrison to Dearborn, July 10, 1805, in Esarey, *Messages and Letters*, vol. 1, 147–49.
38. Jefferson County KY will books, 784–1833, will book 1:252, Kentucky Probate Records, digitized from the University of Kentucky Libraries by FamilySearch International, https://www.familysearch.org/ark:/61903/3:1:3QS7-89LJ-59G2?lang=en&i=138.
39. Dearborn to Harrison, February 20, 1808, in Esarey, *Messages and Letters*, vol. 1, 285.
40. Dearborn to Johnston, March 1808, in Thornbrough, *Letter Book*, 21.
41. Johnston to Eustis, July 1, 1812, Letters Received, Office of the Secretary of War, RG 107, M221, reel 24, NARA, Washington DC.
42. Blaakman, *Speculation Nation*.
43. Nichols, *Engines of Diplomacy*; Sheehan, *Seeds of Extinction*.
44. Carter, *Little Turtle*; Daggar, *Cultivating Empire*. For Little Turtle on the agricul-

tural transformation, see Volney, *View of the Soil and Climate*, 357–58, 375–76; on prohibition, "Sketches of Indian Chiefs in the West," Hinde Papers Draper Manuscripts 31Y; and "Extract of a Talk Delivered by the Little Turtle to the President of the United States," January 4, 1802, *American State Papers, Indian Affairs*, vol. 1, 655.

45. Trowbridge, *Meearmeear Traditions*, 13–19, Albert Gatschet field notes, file 236, NAA MS 2108; Dunn, *Indiana and Indianans*, 43.
46. Johnston to Harrison, February 28, 1806, in Carter, *Territorial Papers*, vol. 7, 344.
47. Harrison to Henry Dearborn, March 3, 1803, in Esarey, *Messages and Letters*, vol. 1, 76–78.
48. Harrison to Dearborn, March 3, 1803, in Esarey, *Messages and Letters*, vol. 1, 76. For Wells submitting to Harrison's wishes, see Harrison to Dearborn, August 10, 1805, in Esarey, *Messages and Letters*, vol. 1, 161. This complex landscape of truth-making is explained in Bottiger, *Borderland of Fear*.
49. Jortner, *Gods of Prophetstown*.
50. "Lexington, (Ken.) August 2," *City Gazette* (Charleston SC), August 26, 1806; "By the Mails Cincinnati, (Ohio), October 19 Fort Wayne," reprinted in *Spooner's Vermont Journal*, December 21, 1807.
51. Harrison to Dearborn, July 11, 1807, in Esarey, *Messages and Letters*, vol. 1, 222; Wells to Harrison, August 20, 1807, in Esarey, *Messages and Letters*, vol. 1, 239–40; Harrison to Dearborn, September 5, 1807, in Esarey, *Messages and Letters*, vol. 1, 248; Wells to Harrison, July 30, 1812, William Wells Papers, Chicago Historical Society.
52. Wells to Harrison, August 20, 1807, in Esarey, *Messages and Letters*, vol. 1, 243.
53. For example, Johnston to Eustis, July 1, 1812, Letters Received, Office of the Secretary of War, RG 107, M221, reel 24, NARA, Washington DC.
54. Harrison to Dearborn, April 26 1805, in Esarey, *Messages and Letters*, vol. 1, 125.
55. Harrison to Eustis, December 3, 1809, in Esarey, *Messages and Letters*, vol. 1, 395.
56. John Gibson and Vigo to Harrison, July 6 1805, in Esarey, *Messages and Letters*, vol. 1, 146.
57. Harrison to Eustis July 8, 1812, in Esarey, *Messages and Letters*, vol. 2, 67–70.
58. "Adaptive resistance" is frequently used in Myaamia historical circles, as taken from archaeologist Ben Secunda's focus on Potawatomis; Secunda, "To Cede or Seed?" Cooperation without submission is a similar idea developed among Hopis and enunciated in Richland, *Cooperation without Submission*. My thinking on the dynamics of treaty-making in particular draws from Lyons, *X-Marks*.
59. This dynamic is handled in Bottiger, *Borderland of Fear*.
60. Harrison to Thomas Jefferson, June 18, 1805, in Carter, *Territorial Papers*, vol. 7, 294.
61. "Minutes of a Council held at Fort Wayne on the 21st day of June 1805," in Esarey, *Messages and Letters*, vol. 1, 139; Harrison to Jefferson, June 18, 1805, in Carter, *Territorial Papers*, vol. 7, 294.
62. Wells to Harrison, August 20, 1807, in Esarey, *Messages and Letters*, vol. 1, 239–40; Harrison's report on the treaty of 1809, in Esarey, *Messages and Letters*, vol. 1, 366.
63. Bickers, "Who Speaks in the Name of the Miami Nation?" 81; Trowbridge, *Meearmeear Traditions*, 87; Kaler and Maring, *History of Whitley County*, 80.

64. Carter, *Little Turtle*, 233.
65. Owens, *Mr. Jefferson's Hammer*, 21 ("brave and enterprising"); Young, *Little Turtle*, 82.
66. Heath, *William Wells*, 3.
67. See, for example, Thom, *Panther in the Sky*; Eckert, *Frontiersmen*; Eckert, *Sorrow in Our Heart*, 573 ("meddling").
68. White, *Middle Ground*, 500–501.
69. Ohio Statehouse website, Statehouse Ohio Videos, accessed February 12, 2023, https://www.ohiostatehouse.org/galleries/media/capitol-ohio-113-treaty-of-greenville-126979.
70. Volney, *View of the Climate and the Soil*, 385. Note that this concept agreed with the general Enlightenment consensus of the age, and helped to support Volney's preexisting mission to collect Native American language data because "in a few ages, the *red men* will probably perish forever," 424.
71. Blackhawk, *Violence over the Land*, 4.
72. Ironstrack, "The Mihši-maalhsa Wars, Part 1;" Ironstrack, "nahi meehtohseeniwinki," 182.
73. Rinehart, "Miami Indian Language Shift," 198.
74. Schurz, "Present Aspects of the Indian Problem," 47.
75. Baldwin, "Miami Language Reclamation," 11; Leonard and Shoemaker, "'I Heart This Camp,'" 186–209; Baldwin and Costa, "Myaamiaataweenki," 553–70.
76. Eugene Brown interview with George Ironstrack, December 11, 2008, Myaamia Center Archive.
77. Sharon Burkybile interview, in *Always a People*, 42–45. More evidence for this shift is in Stewart Rafert interview with Eva Bossley and Swan Hunter, 1978, Stewart Rafert interview with Oliver Godfroy, August 7, 1977, copy in Myaamia Center Archive; Rose Carver interview, T-0307, September 9, 1968, DDC; Sharon Burkybile interview, June 1996, Miami Oral History Interviews, Collection HC 2, box 1, MHMA. For language shift for the Myaamia-speaking communities, see Rinehart, "Miami Indian Language Shift," 216.
78. Mildred Walker, "My Experience at Seneca Indian School," box 1, folder 1, M. Walker MS 5, MHMA.
79. Deloria Jr., *Custer Died for Your Sins*, 79–86; see also Raibmon, *Authentic Indians*, 7.
80. Roberts, "William Wells," 6.
81. 10 Stats., 1093, June 5, 1854; Hunter, "Continued Movement between Indiana and the Miami Reservation."
82. Peter Blystone to Anne Blystone, December 30, 1854; Peter and Anne Blystone to Smith and Mary Gilbert, March 2, 1868, box 2 folder 1, LWC.
83. Memorial Statement and Exhibit, ca. 1880s, LWC.
84. Wentworth, *Early Chicago*, 46.
85. Leonard, "Miami Language Reclamation in the Home," 109.
86. Daryl Baldwin, personal communication with the author, May 17, 2024.

Bibliography

ARCHIVAL SOURCES

Chicago Historical Society.
DDC. Doris Duke Collection of American Indian Oral History, Western History Collections, University of Oklahoma. Norman.
Draper Manuscripts. Microfilm. Wisconsin Historical Society. Madison.
Jefferson County, Kentucky Court House. Will Books, 1784–1833.
Letters Received, Office of the Secretary of War. Record Group 107, Records of the Office of the Secretary of War. National Archives and Records Administration, Washington DC.
LWC. Lambillotte-Willard Collection of Turtle-Wells Family Papers. Myaamia Collection, Walter Havighurst Special Collections and University Archives, Miami University, Oxford OH.
MHMA. Myaamia Heritage Museum and Archive, Miami OK.
Myaamia Center Archive. Miami University, Oxford OH.
NAA. National Anthropological Archives. Smithsonian Institution. Washington DC.
Northwest History Collection, Indiana State Library. Indianapolis.

PUBLISHED WORKS

Always a People: Oral Histories of Contemporary Woodland Indians. Collected by Rita Kohn and W. Lynwood Montell. Bloomington: Indiana University Press, 1997.
American State Papers, Documents, Legislative, and Executive, of the Congress of the United States, Class II, Indian Affairs. Edited by Matthew St. Clair Clarke and Walter Lowrie. 2 vols. Washington DC: Gales and Seaton, 1832–34.
Baldwin, Daryl. "Miami Language Reclamation: From Ground Zero." *Center for Writing Speaker Series*, University of Minnesota, no. 24 (2003): 1–21.
Baldwin, Daryl, and David J. Costa. "Myaamiaataweenki: Revitalization of a Sleeping Language." In *The Oxford Handbook of Endangered Languages*, edited by Kenneth L. Rehg and Lyle Campbell, 553–70. New York: Oxford University Press, 2018.
Bickers, John. "Who Speaks in the Name of the Miami Nation?" In *Settling Ohio: First Peoples and Beyond*, edited by Timothy G. Anderson and Brian Schoen, 64–97. Athens: Ohio University Press, 2023.
Blaakman, Michael A. *Speculation Nation: Land Mania in the Revolutionary American Republic*. Philadelphia: University of Pennsylvania Press, 2023.
Blackhawk, Ned. *Violence over the Land: Indians and Empires in the Early American West*. Cambridge MA: Harvard University Press, 2006.
Bottiger, Patrick. *The Borderland of Fear: Vincennes, Prophetstown, and the Invasion of the Miami Homeland*. Lincoln: University of Nebraska Press, 2016.
Buell, Rowena, ed. *The Memoirs of Rufus Putnam, and Certain Official Papers and Correspondence*. New York: Houghton, Mifflin, 1903.
Buss, James Joseph, and C. Joseph Genetin-Pilawa, eds. *Beyond Two Worlds: Critical Con-

versations on Language and Power in Native North America. Albany: State University of New York Press, 2014.

Calloway, Colin G. *The Victory with No Name: The Native American Defeat of the First American Army*. New York: Oxford University Press, 2015.

Carter, Clarence Edwin., comp. *The Territorial Papers of the United States*, 27 vols. Washington DC: Government Printing Office, 1934–62.

Carter, Harvey Lewis. *The Life and Times of Little Turtle: First Sagamore of the Wabash*. Chicago: University of Illinois Press, 1987.

Chaat Smith, Paul. *Everything You Know about Indians Is Wrong*. Minneapolis: University of Minnesota Press, 2009.

Costa, David J. "The Kinship Terminology of the Miami-Illinois Language." *Anthropological Linguistics* 41, no. 1 (1999): 28–53.

Cruikshank, Ernest A., ed. *The Correspondence of Lieut. Governor John Graves Simcoe, with Allied Documents Relating to His Administration of the Government of Upper Canada*. 5 vols. Toronto: University of Toronto Press, 1923–31.

Daggar, Lori J. *Cultivating Empire: Capitalism, Philanthropy, and the Negotiation of American Imperialism in Indian Country*. Philadelphia: University of Pennsylvania Press, 2022.

Deloria, Vine, Jr. *Custer Died for Your Sins: An Indian Manifesto*. New York: Macmillan, 1969.

Dunn, Jacob Piatt. *Indiana and Indianans*. Chicago: American Historical Society, 1919.

Eckert, Allan W. *The Frontiersmen: A Narrative*. Ashland KY: Jesse Stuart Foundation, 1967.

———. *A Sorrow in Our Heart: The Life of Tecumseh*. New York: Bantam, 1992.

Edmunds, R. David. "'Nothing Has Been Effected': The Vincennes Treaty of 1792." *Indiana Magazine of History* 74, no. 1 (1978): 23–35.

Esarey, Logan, ed. *Messages and Letters of William Henry Harrison*. 2 vols. Indianapolis: Indiana Historical Commission, 1922.

Heath, William. *William Wells and the Struggle for the Old Northwest*. Norman: University of Oklahoma Press, 2015.

Heckewelder, John. *History, Manners, and Customs of the Indian Nations Who Once Inhabited Pennsylvania and the Neighbouring States*. Rev. ed. Philadelphia: Historical Society of Pennsylvania, 1881.

———. "Narrative of John Heckewelder's Journey to the Wabash in 1792 (continued)." *Pennsylvania Magazine of History and Biography* 12, no. 1 (1888): 34–54.

Hunter, Diane. "Continued Movement between Indiana and the Miami Reservation." *Aacimotaatiiyankwi* community blog, December 3, 2021. https://aacimotaatiiyankwi.org/2021/12/03/continued-movement-between-indiana-and-the-miami-reservation/.

Hutton, Paul A. "William Wells: Frontier Scout and Indian Agent." *Indiana Magazine of History* 74, no. 3 (1978): 183–222.

Ironstrack, George. "The Mihši-maalhsa Wars, Part 1." *Aacimotaatiiyankwi* community blog, January 10, 2014. https://aacimotaatiiyankwi.org/2014/01/10/the-mihsi-maalhsa-wars-part-1/.

———. "nahi meehtohseeniwinki: iilinweeyankwi neehi iši meehtohseeniwiyankwi aatotamankwa 'To Live Well: Our Language and Our Lives.'" In Buss and Genetin-Pilawa, *Beyond Two Worlds*, 181–208.

———. "The Treaty of Greenville (1795), Part 1." *Aacimotaatiiyankwi* community blog, October 3, 2016. https://aacimotaatiiyankwi.org/2016/10/03/the-treaty-of-greenville-1795-part-1/.

Irving, Washington. *Life of George Washington*. 5 vols. New York: Putnam, 1855–59.

Jortner, Adam. *The Gods of Prophetstown: The Battle of Tippecanoe and the Holy War for the American Frontier*. New York: Oxford University Press, 2012.

Kaler, Samuel P., and Richard H. Maring, *History of Whitley County, Indiana*. B. F. Bowen, 1907.

Knopf, Richard C., ed. *Anthony Wayne: A Name in Arms*. Pittsburgh: University of Pittsburgh Press, 1959.

———. "The Western Campaign: The Wayne-Knox Correspondence, 1793–1794." *Pennsylvania Magazine of History and Biography* 78, no. 3 (1954): 298–341.

Leonard, Wesley Y. "Miami Language Reclamation in the Home: A Case Study." PhD diss., University of California, Berkeley, 2007.

Leonard, Wesley Y., and Scott M. Shoemaker. "'I Heart This Camp': Participant Perspectives within the Story of Miami Youth Camps." In *Papers of the Fortieth Annual Algonquian Conference*, edited by Karl S. Hele and J. Randolph Valentine, 186–209. Albany: State University of New York Press, 2008.

Lyons, Scott Richard. *X-Marks: Native Signatures of Assent*. Minneapolis: University of Minnesota Press, 2010.

Merrell, James. *Into the American Woods: Negotiators on the Pennsylvania Frontier*. New York: Norton, 1999.

Nichols, David Andrew. *Engines of Diplomacy: Indian Trading Factories and the Negotiation of American Empire*. Chapel Hill: University of North Carolina Press, 2016.

Owens, Robert M. *Mr. Jefferson's Hammer: William Henry Harrison and the Origins of American Indian Policy*. Norman: University of Oklahoma Press, 2007.

Raibmon, Paige. *Authentic Indians: Episodes of Encounter from the Late-Nineteenth-Century Northwest Coast*. Durham NC: Duke University Press, 2005.

Richland, Justin B. *Cooperation without Submission: Indigenous Jurisdictions in Native Nation-US Engagements*. Chicago: University of Chicago Press, 2021.

Rinehart, Melissa A. "Miami Indian Language Shift and Recovery, Volume 1." PhD diss., Michigan State University, 2006.

Roberts, Bessie Keeran. "William Wells, a Legend in the Councils of Two Nations." *Old Fort News* 17 (1954): 5–10.

Schurz, Carl. "Present Aspects of the Indian Problem." Reprinted in *North American Review*, 258, no. 4 (1973): 45–54.

Secunda, Ben W. "To Cede or Seed? Risk and Identity among the Woodland Potawatomi during the Removal Period." *Midcontinental Journal of Archaeology* 31, no. 1 (2006): 57–88.

Sheehan, Bernard. *Seeds of Extinction: Jeffersonian Philanthropy and the American Indian*. Chapel Hill: University of North Carolina Press, 1974.

Sugden, John. *Tecumseh: A Life*. New York: Henry Holt, 1997.
Tanner, Adrian. *Bringing Home Animals: Religious Ideology and the Mode of Production of the Mistassini Cree Hunters*. Social and Economic Studies no. 23, Institute of Social and Economic Research, Memorial University of Newfoundland, 1979.
Thom, James Alexander. *Panther in the Sky*. New York: Ballantine Books, 1989.
Thornbrough, Gayle, ed. *Letter Book of the Indian Agency at Fort Wayne, 1809–1815*. Indianapolis: Indiana Historical Society, 1961.
Trowbridge, Charles Christopher. *Meearmeear Traditions*. Ann Arbor: University of Michigan Press, 1938.
Volney, Constantin François de Chasseboeuf, comte de. *A View of the Soil and Climate of the United States of America: With Supplementary Remarks upon Florida; on the French Colonies on the Mississippi and Ohio, and in Canada; and on the Aboriginal tribes of America*. Edited by C. B. Brown. Philadelphia: J. Conrad, 1804.
Wade, John. "Notes on the Wabash River in 1795." Edited by Dwight L. Smith. *Indiana Magazine of History* 50, no. 3 (1954): 277–90.
Wentworth, John. *Early Chicago: Fort Dearborn, An Address*. Chicago: Fergus Printing, 1881.
White, Richard. *The Middle Ground: Indians, Empires, and Republics in the Great Lakes Region, 1650–1815*. New York: Cambridge University Press, 1991.
Young, Calvin M. *Little Turtle, the Great Chief of the Miami Indian Nation*. Greenville OH: Calvin Young, 1917.

Ma-Son-Ne John Simpson Smith

From the editors: John Simpson Smith's life in the western borderlands spanned from the fur-trader years of the early 1800s to the Indian Wars of the 1860s. Smith was an active trader and interpreter, enmeshed in the polyglot world at Bent's Fort. He was married to Na-to-mah (Cheyenne), and he spoke Cheyenne, Arapaho, and Blackfoot, among other languages. Though the intercultural marriage between Smith and Na-to-mah afforded many opportunities in the earlier West, their location on a widening racial gap proved costly when Chivington's soldiers killed their son, Jack, as a "half-breed" during the Sand Creek Massacre (1864). The excerpt below, capturing the humor and pleasures of Smith's earlier life, comes via Lewis Garrard, whose travels in the West during the 1840s relied on Smith's interpretive skills.

Wah-To-Yah and The Taos Trail

Smith was strange in some respects; his peculiar adaptation to surrounding circumstances, and perceptive faculties, enabled him to pick up a little knowledge of everything, and to show it off much to his own credit—an unaccountable composition of goodness and evil, cleverness and meanness, caution and recklessness. I used to look at him with astonishment, and wonder if he was not the devil incognito. He and I often sang hymns, and a look, more sanctimonious, meek, at-peace-with-mankind than in his countenance could nowhere be found. At other times he *sacre*-ed in French *caraho*-ed in Spanish-Mexican, interpolated with *Thunder strike you* in Cheyenne, or, at others, he genuinely and emphatically *damned* in American.

I had a backgammon board, brought from St. Louis. Smith kept the squaws of the lodge "chunking" up the fire, to give light for us; and "deuce ace," "double sixes," were, probably for the first time, heard in the Cheyenne village. We played for hours, interrupted occasionally by a squaw with a robe to trade; then having attended to her wants, we would resume the board. The Indians laughed at us, saying *"ten-o-wast"*—What is it?—which we explained to the best of our ability. My books, backgammon board, paper and pencil, were great novelties to the [Indians], who would attentively examine them, look at me, shake their heads, and, after a sober pause, and sometimes with a puzzled expression of features, exclaim, "*Mah-ke-o-nih-ma-son-ne*," "Big Wolf's foolish." So it was! everything beyond their comprehension, was *ma-son-ne*.

Smith's voice was capable of some little harmonious modulation, and we used to sing, "The Days When We Went Gipsying," "The Mellow Horn," "The Minstrel's Returned from the War," and other antiquated melodies, interspersed with hymns, and our own crude airs and compositions, making the lodge resound, to the infinite amusement of the squaws and children, and sometimes calling forth contemptuous "*Ve-heo mah-son-nes* (white men are fools)" from the ridiculously solemn old men. Frequently, when executing a song in our very best manner, the village dogs chimed in with their original and touching music, forcing us to acknowledge ourselves beaten, in fair fight, and to withdraw, leaving them undisputed masters of the field; our only consolation was in the idea that they, being Indian dogs, were incapable of appreciating our efforts.

It would be superfluous in me to dilate on the changes effected in the way of empires, republics, arts, sciences, and religion, during the past eighteen hundred and forty-six years. All know these historical facts; and, as John Smith and myself are but heroes in our own small way, and as historians are so obtuse to a sense of justice, as to omit mentioning the hardy souls—the forerunners of civilization—who waste dear life among the [Indians], teaching them the pure English language (to say nothing of the robes we had to take from them), I shall have to be, to rescue our names from the depths of oblivion, narrator for both, to apprise everyone of our occupation and whereabouts on New Year's day.[1]

Notes

1. Lewis H. Garrard, *Wah-To-Yah and The Taos Trail*, ed. Walter S. Campbell (Oklahoma City: Harlow, 1927 [1850]), 65–66, 93.

PART 2

ALONG THE BORDERS OF CONSOLIDATING POWER

4

Translating Slavery

ALICE BAUMGARTNER

In the summer of 2013, I was in Mexico City, doing research at Archivo Histórico de la Secretaría de Relaciones Exteriores. The reading room was in the basement, with fluorescent lights and a dozen or so chairs arranged behind a large, U-shaped table. I was just beginning to research what would become my dissertation, and I spent hours pulling drawers from the card catalogue that spanned one of the walls of the reading room. I was looking for any documents relating to enslaved people who escaped from the United States to Mexico in the nineteenth century, and while rifling through the cards with keywords like "NEGROS" and "ESCLAVITUD," I found records relating to a freedman named Burrill Daniel, who appeared before the U.S.-Mexico Claims Commission in 1870, demanding 125,000 pesos for having been held in bondage in Mexico since 1865, when he was forced by his enslaver to march from Arkansas to Mexico and then sold into debt peonage to pay for the cost of his own abduction.[1]

At the heart of Burrill Daniel's case was a question of translation. To what extent was debt peonage in Mexico the same as chattel slavery in the United States? The over two hundred pages of testimonies taken by Mexican officials in the case did not provide an easy answer: Burrill Daniel claimed that being forced to pay off a debt he did not willingly assume was the same as slavery, but his wife, Mariana, insisted that she was free. The various definitions of slavery, put forward by activists and scholars over the past century, could not determine which view of these two views was correct. Defining slavery (as the League of Nations put it in 1926) as "the status or condition of a person over whom any or all the powers attaching to the right of ownership are exercised" confirmed Mariana's perspective: she and

Burrill were not, technically speaking, property. But if the defining feature of slavery was instead the "permanent, violent domination of natally alienated and generally dishonored people," as the historian Orlando Peterson famously suggested, then Burrill was right to believe that he remained in bondage.[2] Who was right? In my dissertation and later my book, I hedged, suggesting how "his claim shows that even within the black community, even within the same family, African Americans disputed the meaning of freedom."[3]

One of the first academic reviews of the book, which appeared on the website Black Perspectives, took me to task for this "problematic section concerning gender and free labor after the Civil War." The reviewer pointed out the need for "a deeper, nuanced explanation that demonstrates the complexity of post-emancipation life and the challenges that formerly enslaved people faced, including in places like Mexico, where they could supposedly enjoy their freedom."[4] The reviewer was right, and I decided to return to Burrill Daniel's case. Nearly a decade after I had come across his claim, I went back to the testimonies that I had found in the Archivo Histórico de la Secretaría de Relaciones Exteriores. During the pandemic, I hired a research assistant to photograph the over six hundred pages about this case in the archives of the U.S.-Mexico Claims Commission at the National Archives in College Park. I decided to expand the couple of pages in my book about Burrill Daniel's claim into an article.[5]

As I was finishing that article, I attended the symposium at the University of Miami at Ohio about translation and interpretation. I had written a draft of a paper about another case brought before the U.S.-Mexico Claims Commission, which hinged upon the translation of the Spanish verb "dejar." But as I listened to the other presentations that weekend, I found myself thinking about translation and interpretation in Daniel's case: the literal translation of "slavery" and "debt peonage" in his testimony; the legal interpretation of these two labor systems by the U.S.-Mexico Claims Commission, and the historical interpretation that I was trying to carry out over a hundred and fifty years later as a historian.

Thinking about the case across these three registers helped me to see how this long-forgotten case might shift how we think about emancipation in North America. The Thirteenth Amendment has received much less attention than the other Reconstruction amendments, with historians frequently noting how it "almost immediately fell into disuse."[6] This observation holds true for federal courts. (One of the few cases involving slavery and the Thirteenth Amendment was heard in the Maryland circuit court in 1867, when Elizabeth Turner, a young

Black woman who had been apprenticed to her former enslaver, sued for—and won—her freedom.[7]) But dozens of other freedom seekers presented their cases to the nearest federal official: consuls, Freedmen's Bureau agents, provost marshals, military commanders, Indian agents, and justices of the peace.[8]

These freedom suits had lasting consequences, for they pushed federal officials to take a more expansive view of what slavery was and what the Thirteenth Amendment had actually abolished.[9] On June 9, 1865, President Andrew Johnson issued an executive order ordering the liberation of Indians who "had been seized and reduced into Slavery," because he had received reports from New Mexico and California of Indigenous captivity.[10] A year later, Congress passed a law that prohibited the "kidnapping or carrying away any person for the purpose of selling them into involuntary servitude," again on the basis of "verbal communications" that a "system of kidnapping" had developed in Texas, Louisiana, and Mississippi.[11] On January 3, 1867, Senator Charles Sumner recommended that the Judiciary Committee investigate "if any further legislation is needed to prevent the enslavement of Indians in New Mexico or any system of peonage there," because he had received reports from Special Indian Agent J. K. Graves that "this pernicious system of slavery still exists to an alarming extent."[12] Congress abolished peonage three months later.[13]

The framework of "translation" can help us to understand why this expansive interpretation of the Thirteenth Amendment has been overlooked. The enslaved people who claimed their freedom under these laws did not apply to federal courts, where their cases would have been publicized in newspapers or written about in formal opinions. More common was the case of Burrill Daniel or the "half-breed named Evanoff" who, in 1870, told Jefferson C. Davis, the commander of the District of Alaska, via an interpreter that the Sitka Indians had enslaved him. (General Davis told Evanoff that he was "a free man" and ordered his Sitka enslaver to emancipate him or face arrest.[14]) In the same way that other contributors have shown how translation was not always the exclusive purview of trained professionals, these cases remind us how that nonjudicial actors also contributed to constitutional interpretation.[15] Their suits were remarkably successful: an Indian agent or army officer could grant freedom and enforce it faster and more cheaply than any court. But these suits, filed across multiple federal agencies and dispersed across North America, also dulled the impact of their radical interpretations and obscured the ways that slavery continued long after abolition.

Burrill Daniel's Claim before the U.S.-Mexico Claims Commission

Born into slavery in 1832, Burrill Daniel was around thirty-eight years old when he presented his case to an agent of the U.S.-Mexico Claims Commission in Chihuahua: former New Mexico territorial governor Robert Byington Mitchell.[16] In his testimony, Daniel explained that he and his family had been owned by Colonel Joel M. Bryant, a Confederate guerrilla who had made a name for himself launching raids in Missouri, Arkansas, and Indian Territory.[17] At the end of the war, Bryant forced Daniel and his family from Indian Territory to Chihuahua, Mexico. Claiming that his former slaves owed him for the costs of their journey, Bryant opened "a true slave market" to sell their debts and, by extension, their labor.[18] According to Daniel, the United States consul in Chihuahua City, Charles Moye, purchased two girls, Amanda and Amalia, as well as a mixed-race woman named Rany Tam Willoughby. Governor Luis Terrazas of Chihuahua, who had long participated in the Indigenous slave trade in Mexico, bought Daniel and his family for 113 pesos.[19]

Soon after his debts were transferred to Governor Terrazas, Daniel escaped from his new employer's hacienda. Arrested and thrown into jail, Daniel faced a criminal tribunal. He tried to explain that "he was made free in the United States," but the judge stated that "he was now in Mexico, and the present proceeding was in accordance with the laws of the Republic," likely the laws governing labor contracts, which forced debtors to pay off what they owed.[20] But why didn't the judge question the legitimacy of Daniel's debts? Perhaps he, like Terrazas, was complicit in Indigenous slavery, or perhaps he believed that all contracts were sacrosanct. Another possibility is that Daniel had no interpreter or an inadequate one, making it difficult if not impossible for him to make his case. Chastened, Daniel returned to Governor Terrazas's hacienda. For four years, he "was the faithful and the hardworking slave of the Governor." In November of 1869, Daniel's debts were transferred to Don Jacobo Hamburg, a merchant of the city, for two hundred pesos.[21]

For his work, Daniel received wages—often, a marker of freedom—but he insisted that he was held in slavery: what little he earned paid down a debt he did not legitimately owe. As his lawyer put it in 1870, the claim that "he and his family were indebted to said Bryant for being abducted and kidnapped from their native country to a foreign country and for expenses of said abduction and kidnapping is a fraud upon its face, and is alike an insult to justice and common sense."[22] But the argument that Burrill Daniel should not have to repay an unjust debt threatened to undermine other institutions besides slavery.

In the late fall of 1870, Mexico's Secretaría de Relaciones Exteriores began an investigation into Daniel's claim, which exposed how dangerous this argument was. Mexican authorities interviewed Daniel's wife and two sons; his employer, Jacobo Hamburg, and a number of other German-born businessmen in Chihuahua City; the current U.S. consul in Chihuahua City, Charles Moye, and his predecessor, Reuben Creel; and a Cherokee freedman named Tomás who had made the journey to Mexico along with the Daniel family. The witnesses acknowledged that Bryant and the other rebels who accompanied him clearly intended to hold their formerly enslaved people in bondage. Tomás testified that he had come to Mexico, along with the Daniel family. Tomás, who was fifteen at the time, explained that he and the other enslaved people who marched to Mexico did so because "they did not know that the American government had liberated them."[23] Reuben Creel, a Kentucky-born merchant, who served as a soldier in the U.S.-Mexico War, and as U.S. consul in Chihuahua City during the U.S. Civil War, also testified that Colonel Bryant made the Daniel family "work without their consent and without paying them."[24]

Nevertheless, the witnesses denied that Bryant had opened a slave market outside of Chihuahua City. Henry Muller, a German-born businessman living in Chihuahua, testified that he had seen Colonel Bryant sell "some horses to the French and also livestock to various people, but that it was absolutely false that Bryant put slaves up for sale, nor did he believe that it would have been permitted in case he tried to do it."[25] Consul Charles Moye explained that he had hired a woman named Amalia as a cook, paying her five pesos a month, until her brother asked her to join him in El Paso, Texas.[26] He denied having held Amalia as a slave: he had not purchased her; she received wages for her labor; and she left his service when she pleased. Even Daniel's son, sixteen-year-old Luis Daniel, testified that Colonel Bryant had never opened a slave market in Chihuahua City.[27]

Why didn't Bryant's pretensions of mastery call into question the legitimacy of the debts that his slaves supposedly owed? Some of them were no doubt trying to justify their own participation in Bryant's "slave market." Others might have tailored their responses to match the implicit or explicit desires of the officials interviewing them. But these statements also reflected a more general respect for contracts, even those signed under duress. As Senator Juan de Dios Cañedo of Jalisco argued in 1827, disorder would reign "in a country of conquest like ours, if we were to plunder on the pretext of the initial acquisition having been unjust."[28] If the government reversed Daniel's debt because it was unjust, what contract in Mexico would be legal?

The witnesses emphasized that Daniel was treated like other workers. Creel, the U.S. consul, testified that he had "never known that these Blacks [had] been mistreated by Mexicans." At the Terrazas's hacienda, the Daniel family received "the same salary as the other Mexican peons and the same treatment."[29] The German businessman Henry Muller agreed. Burrill Daniel earned what was customary and was treated fairly. Daniel understood that he worked "as a free man" because Muller had told him "various times" that "he could leave when he wanted, to work wherever suited him."

The reason that Daniel "never managed to acquire enough to satisfy the needs of his family" was not that he had been forced to pay off a debt he should not have owed but because he was "quite lazy," and few employers were willing to hire him because "it was known that he put little effort in his work."[30] Jacobo Hamburg agreed: although he provided Burrill and his wife, Mariana, with clothing and paid them each eight pesos a month, he testified that Burrill did not fulfill his duties, and their children moved from job to job in Chihuahua City, using what they earned to repay the two hundred pesos that their parents owed him.[31] From their perspective, Burrill Daniel's poverty owed to laziness—a commonplace and deeply racist charge, shared among reformers across North America, who feared that people of African descent would not work unless forced.

The argument that Daniel should not have to pay back debts he had never agreed to assume threatened not only the foundations of capitalism but also the institution of marriage, as was made clear in the testimony of Burrill Daniel's wife, who was described by Francis Blaisdell, a nurseryman and insurance agent who knew her in Chihuahua, as "an earnest active colored woman, as smart a woman as could be found in 500."[32] On November 19, 1870, when she arrived to give her deposition, she explained that her name was Doña Mariana. Asked for a family name, she stated that she had none. ("Expresó no tener otro nombre.") This simple, unassuming statement of fact was a quiet but forceful denial. She was neither Mariana Bryant, after her former enslaver, nor Mariana Daniel, after her husband, who, she testified, had escaped to Texas earlier that fall, leaving her with his debts and the responsibility for their children.

Mariana testified that after arriving in Mexico, she had taken her children to Chihuahua City to escape Bryant's cruel treatment. Bryant found her after bribing someone with six pesos to tell him where she was. Mariana and her husband—this is the first mention of Burrill Daniel—told Bryant that "they were free and did not want to continue in his service." They worked out the amount that Bryant "would charge them for food and additional costs of their journey to Mexico" and then went to work with Don Luis Terrazas. Mariana insisted that she was not held in slavery in Mexico. She and her family received "their salary and rations like all of the other servants." According to her testimony, "she has always considered herself free, and is free up to the present moment."[33]

In her recorded testimony, Mariana hardly mentioned her husband. From her perspective, he might not have seemed worth mentioning. Burrill Daniel did not defend her or their children from Bryant's mistreatment. Nor did he decide to escape to Chihuahua City: she did. Mariana first mentioned her husband when she explains how she—and, suddenly, Burrill—refused to return to Bryant's service.[34] That she invokes her husband at the moment she claimed her freedom might not be mere coincidence. During the U.S. Civil War, Congress yoked the freedom of Black women to the status of their husbands. Beginning with the Militia Act of 1862, which protected the wives and children of enslaved men who fled disloyal owners for Union lines, legislation established, as Tera Hunter puts it, "masculine conceptions of freedom and citizenship."[35] At a time when marriage or motherhood were often the only routes to freedom, it is no surprise that Mariana would mention Burrill, at the moment in her testimony where she refused to return to Bryant's service. If Burrill was free, then so was she.

Burrill's usefulness, however, proved short-lived. According to Mariana, she and her husband negotiated *their* obligations with Bryant, but while working for Jacobo Hamburg, she found her salary deducted to pay *his* debt, as if to suggest that she had long repaid their joint obligation, while her husband continued to accumulate more. In some respects, Mariana's testimony confirmed her husband's claims that he could not provide for his family. But she explained his failure in different terms. Mariana denied that she and her family remained in bondage. She did not fault Governor Luis Terrazas or Consul Charles Moye or Jacobo Hamburg, as Burrill did. Instead she blamed her husband, whose name she refused to take but whose debts she was forced, as his wife, to work to repay. While insisting that she was free, she described an arrangement in which she did not, in fact, control her own labor. For Mariana, this was marriage, not slavery.

To a remarkable degree, both Mariana and Burrill realized their distinct notions of freedom. Although the Claims Commission would take years to decide his case, and the Mexican courts did not protect him from the abuses of Jacobo Hamburg, in the meantime, Burrill won a measure of freedom by escaping to Texas. Meanwhile, Mariana secured a different kind of freedom. With Burrill in

Texas, she liberated herself, at least momentarily, from the bonds of marriage. In two different countries, seeking out two distinct understandings of freedom, they awaited the decision of the U.S.-Mexico Claims Commission.

Burrill Daniel's Claim before the U.S.-Mexico Commission

Burrill Daniel's claim was among the 1,017 cases filed by American citizens before the U.S.-Mexico Claims Commission. Since 1848 the U.S. Legation in Mexico City had forwarded hundreds of such complaints to the State Department in Washington DC. Secretary of State William Seward complained in the midst of the Civil War, "I find the archives here full of complaints against the Mexican government for violations of contracts and spoliations and cruelties practiced against American citizens."[36] But it was only on July 4, 1868, that Mexico and the United States signed a treaty establishing a commission to adjudicate these claims.[37]

According to the treaty, the claims were to be "impartially and carefully examined by the Commissioners" and decided "to the best of their judgement according to public law, justice, and equity."[38] This was easier said than done. J. Hubley Ashton, one of the agents of the United States before the commission, summarized the difficulties in 1876, as follows: "The transactions involved in them had occurred principally in the territory of the Mexican Republic, where the evidence both for the claimants and the defendant governments was chiefly to be obtained. The proofs were to be taken in two languages, those adduced by the Mexican government being wholly in the Spanish language, and when presented they were to be translated into English for the use of the commission."[39]

The statements taken, transcribed, and translated for Burrill Daniel's case revolved around the question of whether he and his family were enslaved. But for the commissioners, this question was secondary. The opening briefs in the case revolved around two different questions. The first was whether Governor Terrazas acted in a public or private capacity when he assumed Burrill Daniel's supposed debts. The diplomat Caleb Cushing, who represented the Mexican government, argued that Governor Terrazas was not acting *as governor* when hiring laborers to work on his hacienda.[40] Robert Mitchell countered that the governor was acting in his public capacity because "there can be no doubt that he used his official position to secure such service and labor." After all, "no private citizen could arrest and confine an American citizen by the military authority of the republic ... without some pretence [sic] of power as a public functionary."[41]

The second question was whether the U.S.-Mexico Claims Commission had jurisdiction over a case that could have—and should have—been raised first before the Mexican courts. Cushing insisted that slavery had been abolished in Mexico, and as such, Burrill Daniel "had a perfect remedy under the laws of Mexico to obtain his freedom" and "was bound to pursue this remedy" before appealing to the Claims Commission.[42] Mitchell scoffed at Cushing's argument. "It is not a reasonable presumption that an American citizen restrained of his liberty in a foreign country, ignorant of the language and of its laws, and without any opportunity being afforded him of making his complaints to his own government or to the higher tribunals of the Republic of Mexico, could be held to the strict technical rule applied by the Honorable Counsel representing the Mexican Government."[43] Cushing, however, remained unconvinced. "If the petitioner could present his claim here, why could he not have presented it to the Mexican Courts?" he asked. The reason was that this was a "case of *hired labor*, which must have been a lawful and proper one."[44]

Daniel's case divided the U.S.-Mexico Claims Commission. William Henry Wadsworth, the representative of the United States, ruled in favor of Burrill Daniel, despite having voted against the Thirteenth Amendment in 1865. "Here was a poor colored man run out of the United States by his pretended owner, taken a prisoner to Chihuahua & sold into Slavery to the Governor of that State & kept in slavery for years & with his family still held there." Governor Terrazas of Chihuahua was responsible, and Wadsworth recommended an "ample indemnity" of ten thousand dollars.[45] The Mexican commissioner, Manuel Maria de Zamacona, disagreed. "The fact alleged by this claimant is morally impossible in Mexico," because slavery had been abolished in Mexico. Burrill Daniel had been held in debt peonage, not chattel slavery, and whatever injustice he endured would be subject to civil or criminal courts, not the U.S. Mexico-Claims Commission.[46]

Since the commissioners of Mexico and the United States disagreed about their ruling, Burrill Daniel's case was sent to the umpire, the minister of the United Kingdom to the United States, Edward Thornton. Thornton surmised that Burrill Daniel had admitted to being indebted to Colonel Bryant in order to "get rid of him as a master," seemingly suggesting that the contract was voluntary. Since "both the claimant and his family worked for wages," the umpire concluded that they "were to all intents and purposes free." Thornton agreed with Mitchell's assessment that "an uneducated man . . . under the watchful eye of his Master" would not have been able to sue before a Mexican court. But he suggested nonetheless that "any one of his friends or countrymen" could have "easily taken such steps as were necessary to have him produced in Court and to have his wrongs redressed if those wrongs really existed."[47] On March 16, 1876, over six years after Burrill Daniel testified before the U.S.-Mexico Claims Commission, Thornton dismissed his case, awarding no damages.

Why would that umpire, the British minister to the United States, have decided against Burrill Daniel? Thornton represented the British government, which had abolished slavery across its empire in 1833 and sought to eradicate indentured servitude in the decade or so that followed. But, as historian Jonathon Conolly has demonstrated, "new forms of social-scientific thinking reshaped conceptions of free labor at mid-century, transforming indenture from an unnatural scandal into a mutually beneficent form of development."[48] Convinced that workers would only work under compulsion, Britons saw indenture as an urgent corrective to the supposed failures of emancipation. By the time that Edward Thornton dismissed Burrill Daniel's case, a similar transformation was underway in the United States. The expansive definition of slavery, which included indentured servitude, debt bondage, and Indigenous captivity—a definition that enslaved people themselves helped to forge—was being narrowed to chattel slavery alone.

As difficult as it was for freedpeople to secure a measure of freedom in the United States, it was even more so for those whose enslavers had forced them to move to Mexico, Cuba, and Brazil. Burrill Daniel was far from U.S. federal officials who might have understood that whatever wages he earned were being used to pay a debt that he did not owe.[49] Although he used his vernacular knowledge of the different legal systems in Mexico and the United States to make strategic, situationally contingent claims for freedom, the venues available to him were less likely to recognize his claim. Without adequate interpretation in Mexican courts, Daniel could not make his case clearly and convincingly. Appealing to the U.S.-Mexico Claims Commission lessened those issues of translation. At the same time, the mandate of the commission meant that it would decide Daniel's case not only on its merits but in terms of the liability of the Mexican government. The need to translate between languages and legal systems seemed to make it more unlikely that Burrill Daniel would be understood.

Refusing to Translate: The Historian's Role

Burrill Daniel's claim is categorized in the records of the U.S.-Mexico Claims Commission as a case of "unlawful arrest and imprisonment of claimant and family." This is the same category that was used to describe the very different claims of

Jesus M. Ainsa, who was arrested for his involvement in Henry A. Crabb's filibustering expedition, and George L. Macmanus, a Confederate sympathizer who was detained for refusing to pay a forced loan to the Mexican government.[50] Ironically, the circumstances that made it harder for Burrill Daniel to win his case also made it easier for me to find: the fact that his claim spanned two countries and two languages meant that it would be filed in two different archives, with two different cataloguing systems. I would never have ordered Burrill Daniel's case file, if the card catalogue at the Archivo Histórico de la Secretaría de Relaciones Exteriores in Mexico City had categorized it as "unlawful arrest."

Historians interrogate and historicize categories, while also being beholden to them: these are the keywords we search for on databases and in card catalogues, and the terms by which we define our own work. Like the case of William Wells in the preceding chapter, Burrill Daniel's claim defies easy categorization. Outliers such as these force us to reconsider the familiar terms that we use. I had come across hundreds of freedom suits from before and during the Civil War, but never one from after. (Indeed, Loren Schweninger's pathbreaking Race and Slavery Petitions Project, which has collected 2,023 freedom suits from across the South, ends in 1865.) I had assumed that such claims were nonexistent because they were unnecessary. Most of the scholarship that I had read stated that after the Confederate surrender, "most planters conceded slavery's legal demise."[51] Even scholars who acknowledge the deep commitment to slavery and white supremacy conclude that "inevitably, reality impinged upon old ideas."[52]

Burrill Daniel's case pointed to a much more complicated story about the end of slavery, both as an institution and as a word. Colonel Bryant did not concede slavery's demise: he fled to Mexico to avoid complying with the terms of the Emancipation Proclamation. In Chihuahua, he found that he could not hold the Daniel family in bondage as he had in the pre–Civil War United States. The local authorities did not support his property rights. The U.S. consul in Chihuahua City, Ruben Creel, reportedly sent a servant to the Daniel family to inform that "no one had the authority of a master over them."[53] If Colonel Bryant did try to sell his slaves, as Daniel testified, he received far less than the asking price of four thousand pesos. Bryant's previously unassailable prerogative to sell enslaved people as property had evaporated. And yet not all of his prerogatives were gone: he sold Daniel's supposed debts for 113 pesos, forcing him and his family into a labor arrangement to which they had not voluntarily agreed.

Burrill Daniel argued that this situation amounted to slavery, and I was fascinated by the way that he made sense of this question. The Thirteenth Amendment

Translating Slavery 99

had shattered the institution of slavery, and everyone—freedpeople, their former enslavers, U.S. soldiers, even Mexican judges—was trying to figure out what to make of the pieces. If coercive labor practices existed on a continuum, with slavery at one extreme, where would the line be drawn between what was legal and what was not?

As I thought about that question, I started to wonder whether there might be other post-emancipation freedom suits. These freedom suits were not easy to find, interspersed among court files, military records, and reports addressed to the Office of Indian Affairs. They included a habeas corpus petition from Maria País de Silva, of Albuquerque, New Mexico, who invoked the language of the Thirteenth Amendment to free her son José from "involuntary servitude" because of "a Debt claimed to be due from your Petitioner."[54] I found another case from Sitka, Alaska, in 1871, in which a seventeen-year-old Haida boy named Jim claimed to be held in slavery among the Sitka Indians. The military officer who heard the case freed Jim and ordered that "such punishment will be dealt to these Indians as will make them and the people of their tribe know that they cannot enslave the unfortunate."[55]

As I looked through court files, military records, and Indian Agent reports, I found dozens of freedom suits, which told a very different story about how the Thirteenth Amendment was understood and enforced. Far from being "ignored" or "interpreted narrowly," the amendment was being used in radical and expansive ways in military posts, consular offices, Freedmen's Bureau offices, and local courts across North America. Why do we not know about the expansive vision of the Thirteenth Amendment? This is, at its heart, an issue of translation. Freedom suits were heard by the Freedmen's Bureau, the U.S. Army, the Office of Indian Affairs, and the Department of State. The divided and dispersed nature of federal power made it easier to ignore the extent to which slavery continued after emancipation, at the same time as it limited how a policy implemented by one agency would affect the others.

The law also helped to recategorize slavery. As legal anthropologist Elizabeth Mertz has argued, legal language is "social transformative," because it "constantly effects a translation of people in their roles (plaintiff, defendant) and actions into their legal categories (tort, breach of contract)."[56] Freedom suits like Burrill Daniel's were conceptually dangerous, because they threatened to expose the similarities between slave and free labor. But by the 1870s, the features of slavery that had once been used to invoke the Thirteenth Amendment were being described in other terms. The whippings that freedpeople were dealt were described as "battery" or "assault." When they worked for no wages, they became complainants in suits to recover debts.[57] This shift resulted, at least in part, from the strategic decisions of freedom seekers themselves. Eighteenth- and nineteenth-century freedom suits established a legal precedent that denied damages or back pay to illegally held slaves.[58] As a result, post-emancipation freedom seekers were more likely to receive some form of compensation if they sued for breach of contract. The defining characteristics of slavery did not disappear, but the word itself seemed to.[59]

What word, then, should historians use to describe Burrill Daniel? Was he an enslaved person, a freedman, or a debt peon? I keep thinking about what standard has been used to decide the question of Daniel's status. Burrill and Mariana could compare their experiences in Mexico and the United States, arriving at two different conclusions. The umpire of the U.S.-Mexico Claims Commission read the case file against what he understood of public law—an understanding that was shaped by his own conceptions of free labor. How should we, as historians, decide? By applying the standards of our time or his? The interpretations of Burrill or his wife, Mariana?

In each attempt to write about Burrill Daniel's case, I have approached my own role as a historian—an interpreter of the past—differently. In *South to Freedom*, I resisted the desire to comment on Burrill's and Mariana's testimony, instead using their statements to narrate a coherent account of what had happened to them. I tried to make myself invisible, masking the decisions that I was making to make sense of the case's conflicting testimonies. In the article that I wrote a few years later about the case, I gave up trying to tell a coherent story: instead, I tried to let the witnesses speak for themselves, inserting myself only to provide some broader context for their statements. I never wrote in the first person, and I never thought to articulate my own questions about the case. I had seen my work as an academic historian as professional translators see theirs—in the words of Norman Shapiro, "like a pane of glass . . . it should never call attention to itself."[60]

After workshopping this paper with the participants from the symposium, I was advised to include myself more in the story. In the months that followed, I found myself thinking about Lawrence Venuti's point that "the effect of transparency conceals the numerous conditions under which the translation is made, starting with the translator's crucial intervention."[61] As I rewrote the essay, trying to make my own role more visible, I found an answer to the question that has made me return to this case so often. I had never been able to make sense of Burrill and Mariana's conflicting testimonies, but this approach helped me to see that there was no way to translate what they experienced into terms like "slavery" or "freedom" because those categories were themselves in the process of being reconstructed in the wake of emancipation. Interpreting the past, I realized, sometimes means refusing to translate.

Notes

1. Niblo, "United States-Mexican Claims Commission," 101–22. For more on the Claims Commission, see McClendon, "Weil and La Abra Claims against Mexico," 31–54; Sepulveda, "Sobre reclamaciones de norteamericanos a México," 180–206; and Paulsen, "Fraud, Honor, and Trade," 175–90.
2. Lenski, "Framing the Question," 50.
3. Baumgartner, *South to Freedom*, 227–50.
4. Parker, "Runaway Slaves to Mexico."
5. Baumgartner, "Burrill Daniel's Claim," 80–106.
6. Foner, *Second Founding*.
7. One of the few cases involving slavery and the Thirteenth Amendment was heard in the Maryland circuit court in 1867, when Elizabeth Turner, a young Black woman who had been apprenticed to her former enslaver, sued for—and won—her freedom. See Hyman, *Reconstruction Justice*, 123–39.
8. For some examples of these freedom suits, see Head to Evans; Kelly to Huntington; Romero to Delgado; Ward to Norton.
9. Balkin and Levinson, "Dangerous Thirteenth Amendment."
10. Order of Andrew Johnson.
11. Hamilton, "Legislative and Judicial History," 182; Rothman, *Beyond Freedom's Reach*, 178–79.
12. Report of Special Agent J. K. Graves, in Bogy, *Report of the Commissioner of Indian Affairs*, 133.
13. Peonage Abolition Act. For more on this act, see Tsesis, *Thirteenth Amendment*, 55; Smith, "Emancipating Peons, Excluding Coolies," 46–76; Murphy, "Reconstruction in New Mexico," 103; Kiser, *Coast-to-Coast Empire*, 122.
14. "From the Sitka (Alaska Territory) Times: Slavery in Alaska," *Milwaukee Daily Sentinel*, January 28, 1870, 3.
15. Legal historians have conceded this point. See Kramer, *People Themselves*; Tushnet, *Taking the Constitution Away from the Courts*; Yoo, *Powers of War and Peace*.
16. Moye to Fish; "Sketch of General Robert B. Mitchell," 632–37; Murphy, "Reconstruction in New Mexico," 99–115.
17. "American Citizens Enslaved in Mexico," *New York Tribune*, March 30, 1870. For more on guerrilla warfare in Arkansas, see Sutherland, "Guerrillas: The Real War in Arkansas," 148.
18. Burrill Daniel's testimony.
19. Perez to Secretaría de Relaciones Exteriores; Conrad, *Apache Diaspora*, 226.
20. Burrill Daniel's testimony.

21. Perez to Secretaría de Relaciones Exteriores.
22. Burrill Daniel's testimony.
23. Testimony of Tomás, RG 76, NARA-CP 37–40.
24. Testimony of Tomás, RG 76, NARA-CP, f. 44–45.
25. Testimony of Henry Muller, RG 76, NARA-CP, f. 51.
26. Testimony of Charles Moye, November 22, 1870, RG 76, NARA-CP, f. 61.
27. Testimony of Luis Daniel, RG 76, NARA-CP, f. 34–35.
28. "Camara de Senadores, Sesión del día 17 de enero," no. 1316, *El Sol*, January 22, 1827, 1–2.
29. "Camara de Senadores, Sesión del día 17 de enero," no. 1316, *El Sol*, January 22, 1827, f. 48.
30. Testimony of Henry Muller, RG 76, NARA-CP, f. 52–53.
31. Testimony of Jacobo Hamburg, RG 76, NARA-CP, f. 28–30.
32. Blaisdale deposition.
33. Blaisdale deposition. For more on the experience of freedwomen, see Glymph, *Out of the House of Bondage*, 137–226.
34. Jones, *Labor of Love, Labor of Sorrow*, 59; Brimmer, *Claiming Union Widowhood*.
35. Hunter, *Bound in Wedlock*, 167.
36. Seward to Corwin, "Claims on the Part of the Citizens," 13.
37. Niblo, "United States-Mexican Claims Commission of 1868," 101–22.
38. "Claims on the Part of the Citizens," 12.
39. "Claims on the Part of the Citizens," 14.
40. Cushing, opening brief.
41. Mitchell, reply to the opening brief.
42. Cushing, opening brief.
43. Mitchell, reply to the opening brief.
44. Cushing, reply to claimants' arguments.
45. Wadsworth opinion.
46. Zamacona opinion.
47. Thornton, decision of umpire.
48. Connolly, "Indentured Labor Migration and the Meaning of Emancipation," 85–120.
49. Cole to Mills.
50. "Claims on the Part of the Citizens," 24, 25.
51. Rodrigue, *Reconstruction in the Cane Fields*, 64.
52. Roark, *Masters without Slaves*, 161.
53. Roark, *Masters without Slaves*, f. 46.
54. Petition of Maria Pais de Silva.
55. Report in the cases of An-cut-achin.
56. Mertz, "Linguistic Ideology and Praxis," 149–62.
57. *Small v. Schlosser*.
58. This legal precedent was established when slavery was legal, in cases where enslaved people claimed to be unlawfully held in bondage. See *Adelle v. Beauregard*, 1 Mart.

La. 183, Fall 1810, in Catterall, *Judicial Cases*, vol. 3, 447; *Phillis v. Gentin, 9 La. 208*, March 1836, in Catterall, *Judicial Cases*, vol. 3, 447; *Francois v Lobrano*, 10 Rob. La. 450, April 1845, in Catterall, *Judicial Cases*, vol. 3, 569; *Eugenie v. Preval et al.*, 2 La.An. 180, February 1847, in Catterall, *Judicial Cases*, vol. 3, 580.

59. Americans did go into hysterics about "white slavery" and "coolie slavery" but these agglutinative terms were seen then as distinct from chattel slavery in the South.
60. Venuti, *Translator's Invisibility*, epigraph to chap. 1.
61. Venuti, *Translator's Invisibility*, chap. 1.

Bibliography

ARCHIVAL SOURCES

A. C. Small v. Henry E. Schlosser, Justice Court of Pheonix, case 32, box 1, SG 8, RG 107, Arizona State Library, Archives, and Public Records.

Blaisdale, Francis. Deposition taken before District Court of El Paso, at the solicitation of Burrill Daniel, February 28, 1870, docket 683, U.S.-Mexico Claims Commission, RG 76, National Records and Archives Association, College Park.

Burrill Daniel's testimony, n.d. Docket 683, U.S.-Mexico Claims Commission, RG 76, National Archives and Records Administration, College Park.

Cole, Nathan, to Lt S.M. Mills, 9th Inf, November 17, 1866, encl. in Charles Gilbert, to O.D. Green, AAG, Dept of Arkansas, December 10, 1866, box 1, entry 269, Letters Received, Department of Arkansas, RG 393, National Archives, Washington DC (NARA-DC).

Cushing, Caleb. Opening brief of the Mexican Republic, October 14, 1870, docket 683, U.S.-Mexico Claims Commission, RG 76, NARA-CP.

Cushing, Caleb. Reply to claimants' arguments against exceptions, n.d., docket 683, U.S.-Mexico Claims Commission, RG 76, NARA-CP.

Head, Lafayette, Conejos Agency, C.T., to Hon John Evans, July 17, 1865, f. 629–631, roll 552, Letters Received by the Office of Indian Affairs, New Mexico Superintendency.

Johnson, Andrew. Order, June 9, 1865, f. 759, roll 552, Letters Received by the Office of Indian Affairs, New Mexico Superintendency.

Kelly, William, Capt 1st Cav. Oregon Volunteers, Commanding Fort Klamath, Oregon, to J.W.P. Huntington, April 7, 1865, Records of the Oregon Superintendency of Indian Affairs, Letters Received, roll 21, f. 460.

Mitchell, R. B. Reply to the opening brief and motion to dismiss made by the Counsel for the Mexican Government, November 12, 1870, docket 683, U.S.-Mexico Claims Commission, RG 76, NARA-CP.

Moye, Carlos, to Fish. February 15, 1870, Consular Despatches from Chihuahua, reel 1.

Peonage Abolition Act, 42 U.S. Code § 1994.

Perez, Antonio, to Secretaría de Relaciones Exteriores. May 17, 1870, exp. 2, leg. 228, Archivo de la Embajada Mexicana en los Estados Unidos de America, Archivo Histórico de la Secretaría de Relaciones Exteriores.

Petition of Maria Pais de Silva. November 9, 1866, folder Habeas Corpus, 1862–89, District Court Bernalillo County, box 001, Miscellaneous Records, Records of the United States Territorial and New Mexico District Courts for Bernalillo County, New Mexico State Records Commission and Archive.

Report in the cases of An-cut-achin, Jack-Mi-Kan and In-Kat-Seen, Sitka Indians, Permits, Decisions, Etc. July 20, 1871, Post of Sitka, entry 434–10, RG 393 (Part V), NARA-DC.

Romero, Toribio, to Felipe Delgado. April 25, 1866, f. 235, roll 7, Records of the New Mexico Superintendency.

Seward to Corwin, April 6, 1862. "Claims on the Part of the Citizens of the United States and Mexico," Senate Ex. Do. No. 31, 44th Congress, 2nd Session. Washington DC: Government Printing Office, 1877.

Thornton, Edward. Decision of Umpire, March 16, 1876, docket 683, U.S.-Mexico Claims Commission, RG 76, NARA-CP.

Wadsworth, W. H. Opinion, June 3, 1875, docket 683, U.S.-Mexico Claims Commission, RG 76, NARA-CP.

Ward to Norton, August 5, 1867, reel 552, Letters Received by the Office of Indian Affairs, New Mexico Superintendency.

Zamacona, Manuel Maria de. Opinion, June 3, 1875, docket 683, U.S.-Mexico Claims Commission, RG 76, NARA-CP.

PUBLISHED WORKS

Balkin, Jack M., and Sanford Levinson. "The Dangerous Thirteenth Amendment." *Columbia Law Review* 112 (2012): 1459–99.

Baumgartner, Alice L. "Burrill Daniel's Claim: A Freedom Seeker in the U.S.-Mexico Borderlands, 1865–70." *Southwestern Historical Quarterly* (2023): 80–106.

———. *South to Freedom: Runaway Slaves to Mexico and the Road to the Civil War*. New York: Basic Books, 2020.

Bogy, L. V. *Report of the Commissioner of Indian Affairs*. Washington DC: GPO, 1866.

Brimmer, Brandi Clay. *Claiming Union Widowhood: Race, Respectability, and Poverty in the Post-Emancipation South*. Durham NC: Duke University Press, 2020.

Catterall, Helen Tunnicliff, ed. *Judicial Cases concerning American Slavery and the Negro*. 5 vols. Washington DC: Carnegie Institution of Washington, 1932.

Connolly, Jonathan. "Indentured Labor Migration and the Meaning of Emancipation: Free Trade, Race, and Labour in British Public Debate, 1838–1860." *Past and Present* no. 238 (February 2018): 85–120.

Conrad, Paul. *The Apache Diaspora: Four Centuries of Displacement and Survival*. Philadelphia: University of Pennsylvania Press, 2021.

Foner, Eric. *The Second Founding: How the Civil War and Reconstruction Remade the Constitution*. New York: Norton, 2019.

Glymph, Thavolia. *Out of the House of Bondage: The Transformation of the Plantation Household*. Cambridge UK: Cambridge University Press, 2003.

Hamilton, Howard Devon. "The Legislative and Judicial History of the Thirteenth Amendment." PhD diss., University of Illinois at Urbana-Champaign, 1950.

Hunter, Tera. *Bound in Wedlock: Slave and Free Black Marriage in the Nineteenth Century*. Cambridge MA: Harvard University Press, 2017.

Hyman, Harold. *The Reconstruction Justice of Salmon P. Chase: In Re Turner and Texas V. White*. Lawrence: University Press of Kansas, 1997.

Jones, Jacqueline. *Labor of Love, Labor of Sorrow: Black Women, Work, and Family From Slavery to the Present*. New York: Basic Books, 1985.

Kiser, William. *Coast-to-Coast Empire: Manifest Destiny and the New Mexico Borderland*. Norman: University of Oklahoma Press, 2018.

Kramer, Larry. *The People Themselves: Popular Constitutionalism and Judicial Review*. Oxford: Oxford University Press, 2004.

Lenski, Noel. "Framing the Question: What Is a Slave Society." In *What Is a Slave Society? The Practice of Slavery in Global Perspective*, edited by Noel Lenski and Catherine M. Cameron, 15–58. Cambridge UK: Cambridge University Press, 2018.

McClendon, R. Earl. "The Weil and La Abra Claims against Mexico." *Hispanic American Historical Review* 19, no. 1 (1939): 31–54.

Mertz, Elizabeth. "Linguistic Ideology and Praxis in U.S. Law School Classrooms." In *Language Ideologies: Practice and Theory*, edited by Bambi B. Schieffelin, Kathryn A. Woolard, and Paul V. Kroskrity, 149–62. New York: Oxford University Press, 1996.

Murphy, Lawrence R. "Reconstruction in New Mexico." *New Mexico Historical Review* 42 (1968): 99–115.

Niblo, Stephen R. "The United States-Mexican Claims Commission of 1868." *New Mexico Historical Review* 50, no. 2 (1975): 101–22.

Parker, Nakia D. "Runaway Slaves to Mexico and the Road to the Civil War." *Black Perspectives*, January 28, 2021. https://www.aaihs.org/runaway-slaves-to-mexico-and-the-road-to-the-civil-war/.

Paulsen, George E. "Fraud, Honor, and Trade: The United States-Mexico Dispute over the Claim of La Abra Company, 1875–1902." *Pacific Historical Review* 52, no. 2 (1983): 175–90.

Roark, James L. *Masters without Slaves: Southern Planters in the Civil War and Reconstruction*. New York: Norton, 1974.

Rodrigue, John C. *Reconstruction in the Cane Fields: From Slavery to Free Labor in Louisiana's Sugar Parishes, 1862–1880*. Baton Rouge: LSU Press, 2001.

Rothman, Adam. *Beyond Freedom's Reach: A Kidnapping in the Twilight of Slavery*. Cambridge MA: Harvard University Press, 2015.

Sepulveda, César. "Sobre reclamaciones de norteamericanos a México." *Historia Mexicana* 11, no. 2 (1961): 180–206.

"Sketch of the Career of General Robert B. Mitchell." *Kansas Historical Collection* 16 (1923–24): 632–37.

Smith, Stacey, L. "Emancipating Peons, Excluding Coolies: Reconstructing Coercion in the American West." In *The World the Civil War Made*, edited by Gregory P. Downs and Kate Masur, 46–74. Chapel Hill: North Carolina University Press, 2015.

Sutherland, Daniel E. "Guerrillas: The Real War in Arkansas." In *Civil War Arkansas: Beyond Battles and Leaders*, edited by Anne J. Bailey and Daniel E. Sutherland, 133–54. Fayetteville: University of Arkansas Press, 2000.

Tsesis, Alexander. *The Thirteenth Amendment and American Freedom: A Legal History*. New York: NYU Press, 2004.

Tushnet, Mark. *Taking the Constitution Away from the Courts*. Princeton NJ: Princeton University Press, 1999.

Venuti, Lawrence. *The Translator's Invisibility: A History of Translation*. New York: Routledge, 1995.

Yoo, John. *The Powers of War and Peace*. Chicago: University of Chicago Press, 2005.

Jeffrey Deroine, Freedman and Ioway Interpreter

From the editors: Interpreters abound on the margins of images and texts of the American West. Below is the example of Jeffrey Deroine, or "Doraway," a man born into slavery and purchased out of it, who often traded among the Ioway in the early nineteenth century. He knew George Catlin well and accompanied a group of Ioway to tour England in 1844 and 1845. This was done in part to raise funds for the dispossessed peoples, who hoped to make earnings off of the successes of Catlin's European shows.

Excerpt from "Slave, Trader, Interpreter, and World Traveler"

It is perhaps not surprising that Catlin rarely mentioned Deroine in his three hundred-page account of the Ioways' travels in Europe. While this lack of information is disappointing, we might infer that it meant that Deroine approached the trip with a degree of worldly sophistication that made him unremarkable in the writer's eye. After all, Catlin's book was almost exclusively devoted to the Ioways' often humorous and sometimes insightful reactions to the unfamiliar European environment. Had Deroine played the role of the unsophisticated hayseed in the great cities of Europe, Catlin most likely would have exaggerated it for comic effect. Instead, Catlin noted that Deroine was, in fact, an experienced traveler whom he had previously encountered in such places as St. Louis and New York City. While the opportunity to travel no doubt came as part of Deroine's employment with the Office of Indian Affairs, it, like his status as a free man, gave him an uncommon place among African Americans in antebellum America.[1]

FIG 3. Jeffrey Deroine. Digital watercolor by Ricky Hadi, based on William Harvey Miner, *The Iowa* (Cedar Rapids: Torch Press, 1911).

Notes

1. Greg Olson, "Slave, Trader, Interpreter, and World Traveler: The Remarkable Story of Jeffrey Deroine," *Missouri Historical Review* 107, no. 4 (2013): 227.

5

The Interpreter Generation

Boarding School Survivors, Euro-American Scholars, and Chiricahua Apache History in the Twentieth Century

PAUL CONRAD

A box of old documents sits on a wood desk in the reading room of a university library. I'm seated in a matching chair, my shoes pressing against padded blue carpet as I sift through the box's contents: the personal papers of an Apache man stored in those of the Euro-American woman who collected them. "Why is this here?" I keep wondering. There's a playful postcard from a sister to her middle-aged brother—"be a good boy, Sammy;" a faded advertisement for a prosthetic leg; a notice of a past-due car payment; a letter from New Mexico with news for relatives in Oklahoma.[1]

Why were these documents entrusted to her? Do the relatives know where they are now? I think about how inaccessible they are to the community, while also feeling thankful to have found them here: precious crumbs from the past to help me piece together someone's life and the world in which they lived. I also feel a weight of responsibility when I visit reading rooms like this one. To develop an interpretation of people and their role in history—from letters, postcards, bills, contracts—is no small or straightforward task, especially when they come from different communities and backgrounds than my own.[2]

Three pieces from the past.

The first, a letter: historian Eve Ball writes to her friend Angie Debo about "Sammy," or Samuel Kenoi, an Apache interpreter. Kenoi "might be a liar," she claims, but some of his stories seem "too circumstantial to be manufactured."[3]

The second: anthropologist Morris Opler writes, "If anything questionable is going on in the Southwest, you can depend on these worthies to get involved." Opler shares his unfiltered view of Eve Ball and her assistant with a colleague. Opler, who had relied on Kenoi as a key interpreter for his fieldwork, apparently had not found him to be a liar.[4]

A third, from a typewritten manuscript: "That fellow is crazy... Oh, he's a bad one!" writes Kenoi. "You go along with him and the first thing you know he does you dirt." Sam dismisses a fellow Chiricahua named Asa Daklugie, whose stories and personal records Ball relied upon for her books.[5]

These snippets divulge a world of liars and haters all around, it seems, but also one of fascinating and sometimes admirable human beings.

This is a story of four intertwined lives: those of two Chiricahua Apaches—Sam Kenoi and Asa Daklugie—and two white American scholars they assisted, Eve Ball and Morris Opler. It's also a story about interpreters and their historical impact. Every time and place needs people who can translate words from one language to another or explain matters of importance across a cultural divide. But the expectations placed on interpreters and the nature of their work also change over time.[6]

The four protagonists of this chapter were part of a uniquely influential "interpreter generation" in the American West in the twentieth century. In previous generations, Indigenous and colonial communities alike often relied on outsiders to interpret for them, including former captives with limited fluency in two or more languages. U.S. Army officer Charles Gatewood succinctly summarized this interpretive era: "There was no white man, or red either, in all the country who could interpret reliably from Indian to English . . . misunderstandings arose frequently, sometimes leading to series complications [and] ridiculous results."[7]

A new era of interpreting began in the late nineteenth century. The separation of Native youths from their kin on reservations as they were sent to attend boarding schools was traumatic and deadly. But an unintended consequence of colonial education was the return of survivors to their people, to put their new English language skills to use. They translated in courtrooms, churches, and for tribal business meetings. They ascended to leadership positions in which they conveyed community perspectives to reservation agents and U.S. politicians. They drew upon their knowledge of U.S. bureaucracy and racism in efforts to improve their peoples' futures.[8]

Boarding school survivors also worked with a different type of interpreter that emerged during this period: white Americans interested in studying Native cultures. This fascination was fueled by the very destructiveness of U.S. settler colonialism, which led to an urgent if mistaken sense in the late nineteenth and early twentieth centuries that Native cultures needed to be documented before they vanished altogether. Though they were not translators in the same sense as Kenoi and Daklugie, Opler and Ball became influential interpreters nonetheless: as exponents of Apache culture and history within academia and to the public.[9]

Their publications present quite distinct perspectives on Chiricahua history and culture. In charting the lifecycle of a traditional Chiricahua person in *The Apache Lifeway* (1941), Opler challenged the emphasis on Apache raiding and violence current in the United States at the time. His focus on daily life humanized Apaches and made it clear that there was much more to their history and culture than the feats of men in war. Ball's major publications—*In the Days of Victorio* (1972) and *Indeh: An Apache Odyssey* (1980)—reflected decades of work collecting the oral histories of Chiricahua Apaches. This was controversial, especially among historians, given the preference in the discipline of history for archival research. Though her methods were innovative, the focus of her books was traditional—on Apache stories about warfare with the United States in the late nineteenth century. This focus likely owed to Ball's own interests and, importantly, to the perceived interests of her audience.[10]

These influential publications would not have been possible without the Chiricahua informants who assisted Opler and Ball. Yet historians have mostly overlooked the relationship between Chiricahua Apaches and the Euro-American scholars for whom they interpreted. In the case of Opler, this may be because of the way he wrote his informants out of *An Apache Lifeway*, quoting from them only anonymously. It's primarily by visiting his personal papers that one can see how reliant he was on Sam Kenoi and several others of his generation to interpret for him and help to explain Apache language and concepts to him.[11]

Ball's works present the reverse problem. She took significant literary license, adding details and even inventing passages wholesale. This was known at the time and has been pointed out again since. Yet historians still quote from Ball's texts as if they present the literal speech of the Apaches whose oral histories she collected. In part because historians are anxious to present Native voices, they have too readily dismissed Ball's role in shaping them.[12]

A focus on these four people's stories helps us better understand interpreters and their historical impact in the North American West and beyond. The impact of interpreters was significant in day-to-day life, in diplomacy and activism, but also—as is my primary focus here—in shaping the transmission of historical and cultural knowledge. Examining the relationship between Chiricahua interpreters and scholars helps us better understand Chiricahua Apache history in the twentieth century, which has received relatively little study in part because of the decisions of the scholars discussed here. It also serves as a reminder to scholars today to reflect on the influential role we play as interpreters in our own right.[13]

Roots of the Interpreter Generation

The historical homelands of the Chiricahua Apaches stretched down the mountain spines of what we now call Arizona and New Mexico into Sonora and Chihuahua. As with many Indigenous tribal names, both "Chiricahua" and "Apache" were exonyms, terms originally ascribed to them by outsiders. The broadest name for themselves in their own language is the term "Ndé," or "the people." Though Ndé groups interacted, intermarried, and allied strategically at times to pursue shared interests, they did not constitute one nation in the past or present. They recognized finer political distinctions based on kinship and place of residence. Those that came to be known as "Chiricahuas" in the twentieth century, for example, originally recognized at least four distinct bands: the Chokonen, Chihene, Nedni, and Bedonkohe.[14]

Asa Daklugie and Sam Kenoi were both born in the mid-1870s, amid Ndé struggles against U.S. settler colonialism. Daklugie's name means "forced his way through," and he was the son of Ishkey and Juh (from the Bedonkohe and Nedni bands). He was a nephew of Geronimo. Kenoi was also Nedni, son of Tsaltaykoo and David Fatty. Kenoi claimed to not remember his Apache name (at least in conversations with outsiders), and the name he went by was one he chose for himself as a youth. It was not unusual for Apaches to take multiple names over the course of their lives—both in their own language and in Spanish or English.[15]

Though Daklugie and Kenoi shared ancestry and knew each other well, they did not share the same perspectives on Apache history or culture. The divisions between them (and within their broader community) were informed by their childhoods. They were born during the period of President Ulysses S. Grant's so-called peace policy. At the core of this policy was the creation of reservations for Apache and other Native peoples. Through savvy diplomacy, Apache groups sought and briefly achieved the creation of reservations in their own homelands. But the existence of such reservations for most Apache groups proved fleeting. For the U.S. government, bureaucratic efficiency and a desire to keep more lands for white settlement led officials to forcibly remove most Apaches, including Chiricahuas, to the San Carlos and Fort Apache reservation in Arizona in the mid-1870s.[16]

The saga of Chiricahua-U.S. relations in subsequent years is well-known: raids, skirmishes, battles, and flights across borders; the stuff of Western films. This period was important also, though, for the key divisions it solidified within the Chiricahua Apache community. The choice was difficult: live in exile on the land of other Natives at San Carlos; or try to survive as fugitives in the mountains in the United States or Mexico. Most Chiricahuas chose reservation life by the early 1880s, in part because they had grown tired of the loss of kin to death or captivity when they traveled beyond the reservation. Some Chiricahua Apache men even aided the United States as scouts in tracking down those like Geronimo and Chihuahua who continued exercising mobility and raiding.[17]

Many in Sam Kenoi's extended family chose this path, while relatives of Daklugie like Geronimo continued to travel into Mexico. For Daklugie, it was Geronimo who had chosen the manly path, while others were cowards to appease or assist white Americans. For Kenoi, it was Geronimo who had proven selfish and cowardly, because his actions had brought so much pain and suffering to Apache people. Kenoi described this division as one between the "loyal and faithful" or "scout" Indians and the "bandits." For his own part, Daklugie appropriated the characterization: "I'm not only an Apache, I'm Nednhi. And we were the worst of the lot!" Or at least that is what Eve Ball reported he said to her.[18]

After Geronimo's surrender in 1886, the United States rounded up almost all Chiricahuas as prisoners of war and interned them in Florida, then Alabama, and ultimately in Oklahoma. A twenty-seven-year period as POWs coincided with the early years of the U.S. off-reservation boarding school system. Apache youths already exiled from their homelands experienced a second displacement—from their interned kin to attend schools like Carlisle Indian Industrial School (Pennsylvania) and Hampton Institute (Virginia). Daklugie was shipped to Carlisle years before Kenoi in one of the first forced migrations in 1886 when Chiricahuas were interned at Fort Marion, Florida. Kenoi wouldn't go to Carlisle until later when he was about twenty-five years old in 1899. Kenoi's colonial schooling and education in English began at the school established briefly at Fort Marion and then at the military reserve where Chiricahuas were subsequently interned at Mt. Vernon Barracks, Alabama. Why Kenoi was not sent away to Carlisle at the same time as Daklugie isn't clear from extant records or Apache oral histories. But his experience was not a total outlier. As historian Sarah Whitt has emphasized, it was not unusual for Natives in their twenties or even early thirties to be shipped off to attend boarding schools, including married couples.[19]

Though Daklugie spent a longer time in Pennsylvania, the education both men received was similar: a regimented, discipline-focused regime that drew from the military background of its founders like Richard Pratt. In addition to basic academic skills, such as reading and writing in English, the curriculum of Carlisle also reflected the racial and gender ideologies of the era. For boys and men, this meant education in blacksmithing, construction, machining, and farming. For girls and women, this meant a focus on domestic tasks such as sewing, laundering, and baking.[20]

The education Natives received went beyond classroom learning and practical skills as well. Because most youths spent significant time in the outing system, in which they were placed to labor in white households, they also learned about white American culture and racism while away from home. It was while on a placement in Bucks County, Pennsylvania, for example, that Kenoi recalled learning the concept of "white boy country." Though he wanted to visit other Native boys at neighboring farms, any white boys he came across would "take after [him] and fight," which made such travel difficult. Kenoi brought this lesson about white supremacy back with him to the West.[21]

The lessons Daklugie took away from Carlisle also appear to have been different than policymakers intended. First and foremost, like Kenoi, he chose to return to and advocate for Apache communities rather than integrate into white society. "I was educated purposely to help my people and I have helped them a great deal," Eve Ball reported Daklugie told her.[22]

Chiricahua Interpreters and Euro-American Scholars

After their boarding school experiences, each took up varied roles as interpreters. Daklugie's best-known interpreting role was for Stephen M. Barrett for the collection of Geronimo's autobiography. He also interpreted for the Dutch Reformed Church at Fort Sill, Oklahoma, aiding staff with routine business. Later, he interpreted for Father Albert Braun, a Franciscan priest assigned to the Mescalero Reservation as a missionary in 1916, at least until Braun learned enough to be able to give sermons in broken Apache.[23]

Sam Kenoi's most important employment as an interpreter came after the United States finally released the Chiricahuas from prisoner of war status in 1913. They were given the choice of staying in Oklahoma and accepting farm tracts or joining Mescalero Apaches on their reservation in New Mexico. Kenoi chose to go to Mescalero, where he was paid by the reservation agent to interpret in Santa Fe for court cases and other legal affairs involving the reservation in the late 1910s.[24]

These men's work as interpreters for day-to-day community affairs illustrates one key historical impact of this interpreter generation within and beyond their communities. I intend to write more about this in a book I am writing after I visit more reading rooms and have more conversations with descendants. What is clear to me already, however, is that day-to-day interpreting helped prepare boarding school survivors like Daklugie and Kenoi to serve as informants for outsiders interested in Apache history and culture. Through their daily work for wages, each gained a reputation as someone with the linguistic skills and cross-cultural knowledge needed to be able to translate between Apache and English and to explain concepts across the cultural divide. Each brought with them their unique perspectives, Kenoi as a descendant of scouts and Daklugie as a part of the group that identified with the so-called bandits like Geronimo.[25]

Kenoi and Daklugie—and the Euro-American scholars they assisted—stepped into a longer tradition of Chiricahua Apache interpreting that warrants explanation here. For Chiricahuas, a good interpreter was someone with sufficient mastery of languages to be able to convey words between them accurately, which was not always a given before the twentieth century. Yet a good interpreter was also someone with sufficient knowledge of speaker and audience to be able to do so persuasively. *Ilts'á idits'agí*—interpreter, he who hears/understands. Achieving understanding often meant being able to select an especially effective analogy or metaphor in the second (or third) language, blurring the lines between translator and spokesperson or diplomat. For this reason, some Chiricahua leaders were known to use a favored interpreter because of their persuasive skill, even when they were perfectly competent in the language of their audience themselves.[26]

Daklugie began interpreting for outsiders—including white American scholars—earlier in his life than Kenoi. He was hired by S. M. Barrett to help in the creation of Geronimo's autobiography in October 1905, when he and other Chiricahuas were still interned at Fort Sill, Oklahoma. Barrett was a superintendent of schools in Lawton, Oklahoma, and was interested in building a reputation for himself as a scholar of Indian affairs. He sensed opportunity in publishing Geronimo's side of the story given Geronimo's fame and his own proximity to the Chiricahua community at Fort Sill. For his part, Geronimo was a savvy businessman and likely saw an appeal in further burgeoning and monetizing his own fame while presenting his point of view in the process. He and his relatives like Daklugie were also keen to pressure the United States to release them from POW status and allow them to return to homelands in the Southwest.[27]

Geronimo was picky about his choice of interpreters, and he had expressed to U.S. officials that interpreters (especially *bad* ones) were responsible for many of the problems he had faced over time in his dealings with outsiders. Geronimo's choice of a trusted relative with proven skills to interpret for him was thus a fitting one. In his work on Geronimo's autobiography, Daklugie appears to have interpreted in a Chiricahua Apache way: faithful to the message of the speaker while taking rhetorical license to appeal to the intended audience. Eve Ball later claimed, for example, that Daklugie did not include everything Geronimo wanted him to "for fear that if he did so this book would be withheld from publication."[28] The anthropologist Morris Opler also viewed Daklugie's influence as significant. In correspondence with the historian Angie Debo, he explained to her that he had never met anyone as untrustworthy as Daklugie and warned against her use of the text in preparing her biography of Geronimo. Yet Opler's view was undoubtedly shaded by the views of those of his key informants like Kenoi and the scout faction of Chiricahuas. In my assessment, there is little reason to believe that Daklugie was not faithful to Geronimo's perspective, even if he may have omitted passages and selected the English words, metaphors, and rhetorical flourishes that shape the feel of the text.[29]

There is also ample reason to believe that Barrett's presentation of Daklugie's translations was faithful. He put them to paper during his meetings with Daklugie and Geronimo, and he added his own commentary and explanations via footnotes. Eve Ball later reported that Daklugie was pleased with the autobiography overall. According to her recollection of his interviews with her, he told her that, "what Barrett changed to suit himself we could not prevent." He added, "but he didn't change much . . . Geronimo wanted that book printed and so did I."[30]

The arguments presented in Geronimo's autobiography—about the treachery of Mexicans (and to a lesser extent, Americans) and the valor and martial skill of Apache men—significantly influenced the writing of Apache history in the twentieth century. It reinforced interest in the so-called Apache campaigns of the late nineteenth century and importantly, framed Apaches who resisted settlement on reservations as brave, true Apaches. Geronimo—with Daklugie's key assistance—did not shy away from presenting Apache violence: "I have killed many Mexicans; I do not know how many, for frequently I did not count them," for example. Importantly, however, the text frames this violence as a response to treachery and mistreatment. In this way, Geronimo and Daklugie were significantly responsible for the rehabilitation of Geronimo and Chiricahuas more broadly, from bandits to freedom fighters in the eyes of the U.S. public.[31]

FIG 4. Asa Daklugie. Digital watercolor by Ricky Hadi, based on a photograph of Geronimo and Asa Daklugie, n.d., The Gateway to Oklahoma History, https://gateway.okhistory.org; crediting Oklahoma Historical Society.

Daklugie would later reinforce these ideas about Apache history and culture when he agreed to collaborate with Eve Ball. Ball was a teacher turned writer who had moved to Ruidoso, New Mexico (near the Mescalero reservation) in 1942, just after Opler had published *An Apache Lifeway*. She got to know Apaches and began encouraging them to tell her their stories. Ball noted that it took four years to get Asa Daklugie to talk to her, but after many visits with his wife Ramona and daughter Maude, she was finally successful in getting him to sit down for a series of interviews in the mid-1950s. She transcribed these at the time in shorthand. Eventually, Ball amassed a significant body of oral histories from Daklugie and others of his generation that she kept in filing cabinets in her Ruidoso home.[32]

Though the publication process was fraught—owing to challenges with publishers and her own health—Ball published two influential texts that present Apache oral histories and her own historical research: *In the Days of Victorio* (1972) and *Indeh: An Apache Odyssey* (1980). While each book is presented as containing verbatim or little edited accounts of informants like Daklugie, comparison between transcripts in her personal papers and the published texts reveals significant authorship on the part of Ball—not simply in editing or word choice. The writer Sherry Robinson, who subsequently drew from some of Ball's previously unpublished oral histories in her book *Apache Voices*, notes succinctly that Ball's style—"first person and somewhat fictionalized"—was "problematic." My own consultation of Ball's personal papers and correspondence confirms and builds upon Robinson's analysis. Ball may have been faithful to her informants' larger ideas about Apache history and culture, but she moved fluidly between the roles of editor and author in the way she presented them.[33]

Ball's first book, *In the Days of Victorio*, is illustrative of her process. It is presented as the autobiographical account of James Kaywaykla, a Chiricahua Apache and boarding school survivor of the same generation as Daklugie and Kenoi. Kaywaykla was among the group of Chiricahuas who had stayed in Oklahoma after being released from POW status and accepted farm tracts (allotments) instead of joining Mescaleros on their reservation. He met Ball in the mid-1950s when he was visiting Mescalero for summer feast days—the major annual festival at Mescalero that coincides with the traditional puberty ceremony for girls. He stayed at least one other time while visiting Mescalero in late 1955 at her home. They agreed to work together on a book about his life and stories and began a long correspondence that continued until his death in 1963.[34]

In the Days of Victorio credits Kaywaykla as "narrator," but Ball drew from the larger body of Apache oral histories she had collected by the early 1960s as well as her own historical research in crafting it. The process was at least somewhat collaborative, but correspondence between the Kaywaykla and Ball reveals her dominant role. In November 1955, for example, Kaywaykla wrote Ball from Apache, Oklahoma, to complain that "some of the statement should be corrected or be retold so as to get it right" in the latest chapter draft she had sent. Though her response to him is not extant in her papers, his concerns apparently continued in the coming months.[35] In response to another draft chapter, Kaywaykla explained that some of what Ball was crediting to him was information that he knew little about. "Am sending back to you the copys [sic]," he wrote in February 1956 while explaining that they contained a lot of details from "way back before my time which I know nothing about."[36] The back-and-forth continued periodically for several years. When the manuscript was nearing completion, Kaywaykla asked her to send it to him so he could read it over. She responded with frustration and condescension, noting that he had spent a month at her home for the purpose of making corrections. "I know you do not understand," she wrote, "but I have quoted from many people . . . most of the material is taken from history written by officers or put into military reports . . . there is no necessity for your having the manuscript." Rather than allowing further revisions, she threatened to simply remove his name from the book. "If the book goes to press under the title I have selected," she wrote, "I am willing to pay you as promised. If you do not want your name used, there is no reason for you receiving anything for it." Ball and Kaywaykla eventually reconciled, and he wrote her thanking her for their friendship before his death the next year. But their correspondence leaves no doubt that Ball, not Kaywaykla, was the primary narrator of *In the Days of Victorio*.[37]

Ball's subsequent book, which the preface pitched as "Daklugie's book . . . not his alone, but largely his," also evinces her significant role in interpreting Apache oral histories. At first glance, *Indeh: An Apache Odyssey* does suggest greater care on the part of Ball in distinguishing between her words and those of her informants like Daklugie. At the suggestion of historian friends, especially Angie Debo, she wrote herself into the text, describing the setting of her conversations with Apaches like Daklugie and quoting from them instead of presenting a simple first-person narrative in their voices as she had in her previous book.[38] Comparison of Ball's records in her papers at BYU with the published version of *Indeh* suggest that her approach didn't actually change much, however. A typed transcript following Ball's shorthand notes of an interview with Daklugie contains the following testimony credited to him, for example: "I went to Carlisle when I was about fifteen. 124 Apaches lie in the cemetary [*sic*] at Carlisle Barracks. Ramona went at the same time—five girls and four boys. We were going up from the South and there was a big snowstorm in Virginia; we were from Arizona."[39] The published account is significantly different, as Ball expanded the original short paragraph into two pages. Among other new details is romance: Daklugie sees Ramona (his future wife) on the platform "tall and beautiful" and describes feeling a desire to protect her. The snowstorm remains but is embellished with a story of the train getting stuck and fears among the children about what would happen if the snow didn't melt quickly. "If the food should give out," Daklugie says, "who would be eaten first? The Apache children, of course."[40]

I've struggled with how to think about Ball and her work. On the one hand, there is much to criticize. The scholar in me finds it frustrating, for example, to have to travel to Provo, Utah, and consult her records to get closer to the actual words of her informants. And though she clearly gained Chiricahuas' trust—enough for some to give their personal papers to her—her relationship with informants was also at times problematic, as her threats to remove James Kaywaykla's name as author of *In the Days of Victorio* reveal. Yet conversations with a Chiricahua Apache descendant have also weighed into my thinking about Ball. Highlighting his own positive view of Ball, and those of others in the community, Sigfried Second-Jumper explained to me that her books are still seen as "like the Bible" on the reservation. First and foremost, Jumper noted, they are among few published works on Apaches that centered their oral histories and made them narrators of their own past. Ball is seen as having been true to their larger perspectives on Apache history by those whose stories she claimed to tell.[41]

The key arguments about Chiricahua Apache history and culture credited to Daklugie do conform with what he wrote and said elsewhere. For example, Ball reports that Daklugie critiqued U.S. treatment of Apaches as "extermination" and noted that while he had not heard the word "genocide" before, it seemed a fitting one. She quotes Daklugie as speaking fondly of Geronimo, describing how he respected him "above all living men . . . the embodiment of the Apache spirit, of the fighting Chiricahua." What emerges from *Indeh: An Apache Odyssey* is Daklugie's pride in Chiricahuas' resistance, independence, and survival that fits with his life and activism documented elsewhere: from his lobbying for Chiricahuas to be released from POW status, to his work as chairman of the tribal business committee, to his activism seeking reparations from the U.S. government.[42]

The relationship between Ball and her informants shows the important influence that bilingual boarding school survivors like Asa Daklugie had on outsiders' perspectives of Chiricahua culture and history in the twentieth century. Yet making sense of these oral histories also requires taking seriously Ball's role as interpreter as well. This role was multifaceted. She made choices about whose voices to include or exclude. Though she interviewed Sam Kenoi, for example, and even collected his personal records, she did not quote him in her publications, perhaps because of the animosity between him and supporters of Geronimo whose perspectives she favored like Daklugie. At times, Ball interpreted in a Chiricahua Apache way, taking rhetorical license to convey her informants' testimony in a manner that would be persuasive and compelling while staying close to their actual words. She often moved into the role of author or storyteller herself, though, such as by inventing details and dialogue. In the end, this analysis suggests that anyone using her books to present Apache voices must make Ball visible as interpreter and

FIG 5. Samuel Kenoi. Digital watercolor by Ricky Hadi, based on a photograph taken by Harry Hoijer in the 1930s, Morris Edward Opler Papers, Cornell Library Special Collections, box 37, folder 14.

author. "As Eve Ball stated that Daklugie had told her" may be a clunky phrase, but it is more accurate than alternatives like "as Daklugie said," unless a quote has been verified in Ball's shorthand notes at BYU.[43]

The relationship between Sam Kenoi and Morris Opler provides another example of the power of this "Interpreter Generation" in shaping cross-cultural knowledge and understandings. Kenoi's role in informing outsiders' understandings of Apache history and culture is less well-known than Daklugie's, in part because of the distinct approach of the scholar each assisted. If Ball sought to minimize her own authorship by crediting her books to Chiricahuas, Opler in many ways did the reverse: presenting Chiricahua culture and history in an expert authoritative voice and quoting from Apache informants anonymously.[44]

122 *Along the Borders*

Kenoi's historical and historiographical influence was nonetheless significant. He came from a less prominent family than Daklugie and was not seen as a *nantan* ("chief" or "spokesperson") in the same way as Daklugie was throughout much of his life. Yet Kenoi drew upon one of his key skills—his commanding power of writing in English—to lobby for his community in ways that gained him leadership positions over time. He waged campaigns against corrupt reservation officials, not hesitating to craft petitions to the commissioner of Indian Affairs himself if needed. He helped organize efforts to obtain payments to Chiricahuas from tribal resources and funds that white officials had mismanaged. And he also helped lead a campaign to gain Chiricahua Apaches compensation for their twenty-seven years as prisoners of war by lobbying congressman and senators in Oklahoma and New Mexico to introduce bills in Congress on their behalf. While this effort failed in the 1930s, it eventually developed into a claim before the Indian Claims Commission that ended in a substantial payment to Chiricahua Apaches in the early 1970s.[45]

Such work as an advocate, go-between, and interpreter helped bring Kenoi to the attention of Morris Edward Opler. Opler first visited Mescalero as part of a team of anthropologists in 1931 to conduct fieldwork, gather oral histories, and study traditional Chiricahua culture while individuals from the pre-reservation era were still alive. Kenoi and another Chiricahua, Dan Nicholas, were Opler's most important interpreters, taking him to see elders who did not speak English and translating on their behalf. Kenoi, the older of the two, was also an especially important informant himself, helping Opler to understand Chiricahua kinship terms and concepts, explaining historical places of residence and lifeways, and more. In fact, his name is among the most common to appear in Opler's voluminous field notebooks housed in his papers at Cornell.[46]

Key to Opler's relationship with his informants was his gathering of their life stories. Over the course of his stays at Mescalero in the 1930s, Opler collected lengthy oral histories from both Sam Kenoi and Dan Nicholas. He used the collection of their autobiographies as a means of building trust, spending further time with them and asking them more questions to clarify information they had helped him gather from Chiricahua elders. In the end, the autobiographical manuscript of Kenoi totaled more than seven hundred pages.[47]

Kenoi's perspective on Chiricahua Apache history—as evident in both his autobiographical manuscript and personal correspondence—was twofold. First, he emphasized the fact that the majority of Chiricahuas had been peacefully residing on their Arizona reservation during Geronimo's so-called outbreaks. Second, he noted that despite this, the United States had treacherously exiled all Chiricahuas. In fact, his assessment of U.S.-Native relations was stark—that he had known nothing but wrongs and mistreatment. And yet at the same time, he blamed Geronimo and his faction for the experience of Chiricahuas as much as he did the United States: "These people, these Chiricahua Indians, who lived at Fort Apache peacefully, and the scouts who helped the army to run down Geronimo's band, were taken to prison for what Geronimo had done."[48]

Kenoi's perspectives are apparent in Opler's scholarship. *An Apache Lifeway* (1941) remains one of the most cited ethnographic texts on Chiricahuas more than eighty years after it was first published.[49] Like his key informant, Opler highlighted daily and community life and religious and spiritual traditions rather than raiding and warfare. As Opler explained, "I have wanted the average Chiricahua to be an intelligible and sympathetic figure, not in the sense that the reader approves or disapproves all his ideas and actions, but in the sense that the reader understands what he has become in terms of what he has experienced." In varied chapters covering topics ranging from childhood and medicinal practices to agriculture and the supernatural, raiding and warfare occupy relatively little space—twenty pages or so, in a more than four-hundred-page book.[50]

Kenoi's power to influence Opler's presentation of Apache history and culture nonetheless had limits. While he was key to shaping the information Opler was able to collect and his views on Apache culture—including as a translator for older Chiricahuas that Opler interviewed—Opler exercised significant power in choosing what content to include or exclude in his publications. Opler, for example, limited his readers' knowledge of twentieth-century Apache history by choosing not to relay in his publications the content Kenoi had shared with him about this period, the focus of hundreds of pages of Kenoi's oral history. More than fifty years after Kenoi and Nicholas first shared their stories with Opler, they remained mostly unpublished. "While I am eager to get to the preparation of the Chiricahua autobiographies . . . they shall have to wait their turn," he wrote to an interested publisher in 1985.[51]

Opler's decision-making reflects the tradition of cultural anthropology in which he had been trained. He and his generation of peers had sought to understand and record Indigenous cultures before they were changed by settlement on U.S.-run reservations, and before understandings of the pre-conquest period was lost. While he felt fondly about his informants as people, he viewed their own way of life as too altered to represent the original, traditional Apache culture he was interested in documenting, and thus lacking in "scientific value."[52]

Opler's role as scholar and interpreter of Apache culture was complex, though for different reasons than that of Eve Ball. I have long admired the depth of his research, a view that has only further solidified as I've paged through his voluminous ethnographic field notes as well as the far-ranging archival research in his personal papers at Cornell University. His scholarship contrasts with that of Ball, who focused on compelling presentation and storytelling at the expense of accuracy. Indeed, Opler looked down on Ball personally for this reason, mixing elitism with a bit of misogyny in seeing her work as little worth his time. But Opler was also problematic in his own ways: the fact that the autobiographical narratives his informants spent so long relaying to him were mostly left to languish in his filing cabinets; the fact that he visited and corresponded with them little after his fieldwork in the 1930s ended. Opler later regretted this, writing upon learning of Dan Nicholas's death that he "felt guilty . . . I always thought I would get back soon to see him, but wars, foreign work, sickness—something always interfered."[53]

Yet if Opler's published works obscured the ideas and work of his informants like Kenoi, he did carry forward what he had learned from them, even if not always in his publications. Perhaps most influential for the Chiricahua community was his instrumental work as an expert for their case before the Indian Claims Commission in the 1950s and 1960s. This commission was founded after World War II to hear disputes against the U.S. government by tribal nations, such as those that Daklugie and Kenoi had been presenting to politicians and reservation agents for years. The attorneys working for Chiricahuas smartly hired Opler to be an expert witness. In the evidence he helped gather, and in his testimony at trial, he showed his skills as a scholar, but he also stepped into the role of skilled interpreter in the Chiricahua tradition. He made persuasive arguments, including under cross-examination at trial, that drew from his archival research and fieldwork but also at times stretched the evidence to convince his audience—non-Native judges—that the United States had wronged Chiricahuas and that they deserved compensation. The $15 million settlement Chiricahuas received for the taking of their reservations without compensation was among the largest of any tribal nation. Opler expressed pride in the result in a letter to the tribal chairman at Mescalero, Wendel Chino, in 1969. He said he had been told his testimony was influential, but he expressed gratitude to his friends and interpreters Dan Nicholas and Sam Kenoi who had "helped me get started in my work in the right way." They were the ones who deserved "much of the credit," he explained.[54]

Conclusion

A new generation of interpreters emerged in the American West beginning in the late nineteenth and early twentieth centuries. Boarding school survivors like Asa Daklugie and Sam Kenoi played an important role in the daily life of their communities after they returned home, translating for monolingual elders and rising to leadership positions due to their facility in English and knowledge of U.S. bureaucracy. The role of this interpreter generation in terms of daily life and activism warrants further attention, as does Chiricahua Apache history in the twentieth century more generally.

Boarding school survivors also became translators and informants for another type of interpreter that emerged during this period: the Euro-American scholars like Ball and Opler who sought to document and understand Apache culture before it was irrevocably changed. The relationship between them has received little attention by scholars of Apache history, even as it deeply shaped the transmission of cultural and historical knowledge we continue to rely upon. On the one hand, Opler and Ball were reliant on Chiricahua Apache informants—and the divisions between them—in ways that have not been adequately appreciated. It is helpful to read their works with Chiricahua factionalism in mind: Opler, "the scout" and Ball, "the bandit." Yet Opler's and Ball's roles as interpreters also were significant, especially their decisions about what to include or exclude and how to present what their informants had shared with them. Ball often took the Chirichaua tradition of interpreter as persuasive speaker too far—inventing rather than faithfully presenting the oral histories of her Apache friends and informants. Opler, in contrast, presented evidence from his informants' stories faithfully in his publications but minimized their role by not quoting them by name and by not publishing their oral histories that dealt with life after U.S. conquest.[55]

In the end, thinking about these four and their intertwined lives has often made me reflect on my own role as a historian in the present. It is impossible to get everything right: to translate every word with the right nuance, to describe the meaning of things in clear and compelling writing, to maintain faithfully the relationships that have made our work possible. This past generation of interpreters illustrates the power that our interpretive decisions have for better or worse: to reflect faithfully the perspectives of those we are writing about, or to distort or silence them. May we exercise this power with care.

Notes

1. This vignette draws from material in the Eve Ball Papers, box 6.
2. For a succinct overview of discussions around archives and Indigenous peoples see Christen, "Opening Archives," 185–210.
3. Angie Debo to Eve Ball, February 9, 1972, Ball Papers, box 25.
4. Morris Edward Opler to John N. Drayton, September 3, 1983, Opler Papers, box 36, folder 26.
5. "Autobiography of a Chiricahua Apache (Sam Kenoi)," Opler Papers, box 36, folders 1–7, p. 603. Hereafter cited as "Kenoi autobiography, p. #."
6. As noted in the intro to this volume, there is a significant literature on the role of interpreters and go-betweens in the context of colonialism, but surprisingly little scholarship has focused systematically on the role of the interpreter in the history of the North American West. For a recent exception that has influenced my thinking, see Hyde, *Born of Lakes and Plains*.
7. Quote, with commas added for readability, is from Gatewood and Kraft, *Lt. Charles Gatewood*, 42. Though not the primary focus of most historians' analysis, mention of interpreters and the challenges of cross-cultural communication in the period before the twentieth century is ubiquitous. See, for example, Calloway, *One Vast Winter Count*; Hyde, *Empires, Nations, and Families*.
8. The focus on the role of interpreters is my own, but for cogent overviews of this period in U.S. and Native history more broadly see Blackhawk, *Rediscovery of America*, especially 329–407; Truett, *Heartbeat of Wounded Knee*; Prucha, *Great Father*, 152–97.
9. For the history of anthropology in this era see especially Bruchac, *Savage Kin*; Sackman, *Wild Men*.
10. Opler published extensively on Apache peoples, but his most-cited work is *An Apache Life-Way*. For Eve Ball and her life and work see Robinson and Ball, *Apache Voices*; Kaywaykla and Ball, *In the Days of Victorio*; Ball, *Indeh*.
11. He briefly mentions his interpreters in the introduction to *Apache Life-Way* as follows: "John Allard, Samuel E. Kenoi, and Daniel Nicholas acted as interpreters as well as informants, and their interest and help far exceeded the ordinary requirements of their task," but in the text quotes from these and other informants are anonymized.
12. For a discussion of Ball's writing process, see Robinson and Ball, *Apache Voices*, xi–xiv, 203–20. Ball's approach to oral histories was also a subject in correspondence with her historian friends. See especially her letters exchanged with Angie Debo in Ball Papers, box 25. Google Scholar reveals 113 citations for *Indeh* and 140 for *In the Days of Victorio*. Works quoting directly from her oral histories range from specialized monographs on Apache history to broader texts on the U.S. Indian boarding school system and U.S.-Native relations.
13. The relative lack of study of Chiricahua Apache history in the twentieth century

resonates with David Truett's insights about the focus of non-Natives on pre-1890 Native history in *The Heartbeat of Wounded Knee*. Scholars that have charted Chiricahua history after Geronimo's surrender have focused primarily on their period of internment as prisoners of war. See, for example, Turcheneske Jr., *Chiricahua Apache Prisoners of War*. An exception is Lieder and Page, *Wild Justice*.

14. Conrad, *Apache Diaspora*, 4–5.
15. Delgadillo and Perrett, *From Fort Marion to Fort Sill*, 60–62 [Daklugie] and 149–51 [Kenoi]. For Kenoi's name selection see Conrad, *Apache Diaspora*, 274. See also Vignette #5 regarding changing names in this collection.
16. The best overview of this period in Apache history is Sweeney, *From Cochise to Geronimo*. See also White, *Republic for Which It Stands*, 290–94.
17. Conrad, *Apache Diaspora*, 209–48.
18. For Chiricahua factionalism see Kenoi autobiography, 700–704; Daklugie quote in Ball, *Indeh*, xx.
19. For Chiricahua experiences at Carlisle see Conrad, *Apache Diaspora*, 271–79; Delgadillo and Perrett, *From Fort Marion to Fort Sill*. For adults at boarding school see Whitt, "An Ordinary Case of Discipline." See also records accessible online at the Carlisle Indian School Digital Resource Center: https://carlisleindian.dickinson.edu/.
20. Adams, *Education for Extinction*.
21. Conrad, *Apache Diaspora*, 271–79 [quote on 277]. My analysis of Carlisle's outing system builds from Whalen, *Native Students at Work*.
22. Undated transcript of Daklugie oral history in Ball Papers, box 5, folder 2. My sense of Daklugie and his work also draws from the broader collection of Daklugie's papers and correspondence in Ball's papers, as well as the records of the Mescalero agency from the 1920s and 1930s I've consulted at the National Archives.
23. Ball, *Indeh*, 310. See also "Mr. and Mrs. Asa Daklugie," *El Paso Times* [undated], ca. 1955 from context in Ball Papers, box 5, folder 2.
24. Kenoi autobiography, 472–73.
25. My thinking on who tends to occupy the role of interpreter and go-betweens draws from Yannakakis, *Art of Being In-Between*, especially 1–32.
26. For Apache word for interpreters and glosses of it see Bray, ed., *Western Apache-English Dictionary*, 150, 373. For interpreters in Chiricahua Apache history see Sweeney, ed., *Making Peace with Cochise*, especially 93; Hutton, *Apache Wars*, especially 163–72, 200–205; Sweeney, *From Cochise to Geronimo*; Shapard, *Chief Loco*, 193.
27. Huizar-Hernández, "The Real Geronimo Got Away." See also Debo, *Geronimo*, especially 388–91; Geronimo and Barrett, *Geronimo's Story of His Life*; Utley, *Geronimo*.
28. Handwritten note by Eve Ball on typewritten document, "Bibliography," in Ball Papers, box 2, folder 2.
29. For Barrett's process see Huizar-Hernández, "'The Real Geronimo got Away." For Opler's view see Angie Debo to Morris Opler, 31 August 1972, Opler Papers, box 37, folder 5.
30. For Asa Daklugie's perspective, as recorded by Ball, see *Indeh*, 12. Her notes related to these interviews mostly align in sentiment with what she printed in her book, though

not word-for-word. See Ball papers, box 5, folder 2, especially transcript [undated], "Asa Daklugie," which begins "I and my friends were not rounded up with Geronimo." On Geronimo's autobiography, he is quoted in her notes as stating "I interpreted Geronimo's life most of [it] in book. What he ewanted [*sic*] to tell; but he was not telling everything. He could not sit still while he was telling the story."

31. For historiographical (and public) shifts on Geronimo, see Utley, *Geronimo*, especially intro. See also Kemper, "'Geronimo'!". Quote from Geronimo and Barrett, *Geronimo's Story of His Life*, 68.
32. For Eve Ball and her life and work see Robinson and Ball, *Apache Voices*; Kaywaykla and Ball, *In the Days of Victorio*; Ball, Henn, and Sanchez, *Indeh*. See also "Biographical History" in http://archives.lib.byu.edu/repositories/14/resources/1570.
33. Robinson and Ball, *Apache Voices*, 12, 212–19 [quote on 12]. Robinson presents many key concerns about Ball's methods in her book, but she is not always as direct in her explanations as I think is warranted, in part due to her understandable admiration for Ball's longtime relationship with her Apache informants.
34. James Kaywaykla to Eve Ball, January 4, 1956, Ball Papers, box 5, folder 19. See also Kaywaykla and Ball, *In the Days of Victorio*, ix–xv; Delgadillo and Perrett, *From Fort Marion to Fort Sill*, 146–47.
35. James Kaywaykla to Eve Ball, November 22, 1955, Ball Papers, box 5, folder 19.
36. Kaywaykla to Ball, February 10, 1956, Ball Papers, box 5, folder 19.
37. Ball to Kaywaykla, March 17, 1962, Ball Papers, box 5, folder 19. See also Robinson and Ball, *Apache Voices*, 212–19.
38. Ball, *Indeh*, xiii–xvi.
39. Typescript of interview of Asa Daklugie by Eve Ball, August 10, 1954, Ball Papers, box 5, folder 1.
40. Ball, *Indeh*, 141.
41. Personal communication with Sigfried R. Second-Jumper, February 10, 2023. Note that while Robinson published new and corrected accounts in *Apache Voices*, it is not entirely clear from her text whether she did so solely from typed transcripts extant in Ball's papers, or from the original shorthand notes. I, unfortunately, do not read shorthand but intend to investigate this issue further as my research continues.
42. Ball, *Indeh*, 78, 134. I am researching Asa Daklugie's broader life and work as part of a longer book project on the "Interpreter Generation." My sense of him is based in part on that research, including voluminous records of his time in tribal leadership extant at the National Archives, record group 75, Central Classified Files, Mescalero, 1907–39.
43. Her extensive material on Sam Kenoi, including an interview with him, is in Ball Papers, box 2 and box 6. Ball, like other interpreters, should be revealed rather than hidden in scholarly writing.
44. In doing so, he was not unusual for his generation of scholars. For further context on this generation of anthropologists see especially Bruchac, *Savage Kin*.
45. This overview of his life draws from Kenoi autobiography; Kenoi correspondence in Ball Papers, boxes 2 and 6; and Mescalero agency records in NARA, record group 75, Central Classified Files, Mescalero, 1907–39.

46. Opler, *An Apache Lifeway*, 6–9. For notes showing Kenoi's importance to Opler's work, see for example "Sam Kenoi Materials 1932," in Opler Papers, box 36, folder 9.
47. Handwritten versions of Kenoi's and Nicholas's life histories are extant in Opler papers, box 48, folders 6 and 9. These correspond well with typed versions of the narratives in box 35, folder 15 and box 36, folders 2–7 that Opler likely prepared decades later when he had a renewed interest in getting them published. He discusses his interest in seeing them published before his death in the 1980s in Opler Papers, box 124. The autobiographies long remained almost entirely unpublished other than a short portion of Kenoi's account of the campaign to capture in Geronimo originally published in the *New Mexico Historical Review* in 1938. See "A Chiricahua Apache's Account." Recently, portions of Kenoi and Nicholas' narratives related to their experience of boarding school have been published in Krupat, *From the Boarding Schools*.
48. Kenoi autobiography, especially 293–95, 339 [quote on 294].
49. Google Scholar reveals 459 citations for *An Apache Life-Way*, including many from recent decades.
50. Opler, *An Apache Life-Way*, 7 and 290–307 [quote on 7].
51. Morris Opler to Raymond J. Demallie and Douglas R. Parks, July 11, 1985, Opler Papers, box 124, folder 2.
52. See, for example, an undated note about the scientific value of the narratives that begins "In my opinion the chief value," in Opler Papers, box 35, folder 4. Opler did express his intention in *An Apache Life-Way* to publish on Apaches' "current condition" in planned future books. He did eventually publish, autobiographical narrative of Charlie Smith, a Mescalero he had met while doing his fieldwork in the 1930s that deals significantly with the cultural changes of the twentieth century. The autobiographies of his Chiricahua informants remained mostly unpublished, however. See Opler, *Apache Odyssey*.
53. For condescension toward Ball, see Morris Edward Opler to John N. Drayton, September 3, 1983, Opler Papers, box 36, folder 26. For regrets about losing touch with informants see Morris Opler to Wendel Chino, March 14, 1969, Opler Papers, box 37, folder 15.
54. Opler to Chino, March 14, 1969. For Apache ICC Cases see Lieder and Jake Page, *Wild Justice*.
55. My analysis of these scholars of Chiricahua Apache history is indebted to and extends some of the insights of Bruchac, *Savage Kin*, to the context of Apache/Ndé studies.

Bibliography

ARCHIVAL SOURCES

Eve Ball papers; MSS 3096; 20th Century Western and Mormon Manuscripts; L. Tom Perry Special Collections, Harold B. Lee Library, Brigham Young University.

Morris Edward Opler papers; #14-25-3238; Division of Rare and Manuscript Collections, Cornell University Library.

National Archives and Records Administration, Washington DC; record group 75, Central Classified Files, Mescalero, 1907–39.

PUBLISHED WORKS

Adams, David Wallace. *Education for Extinction: American Indians and the Boarding School Experience, 1875–1928*. Lawrence: University Press of Kansas, 1995.

Ball, Eve. *Indeh: An Apache Odyssey*. Norman: University of Oklahoma Press, 1988.

Blackhawk, Ned. *The Rediscovery of America: Native Peoples and the Unmaking of U.S. History*. New Haven: Yale University Press, 2023.

Bray, Dorothy, ed. *Western Apache-English Dictionary: A Community-Generated Bilingual Dictionary*. Tempe AZ: Bilingual Press, 1998.

Bruchac, Margaret M. *Savage Kin: Indigenous Informants and American Anthropologists*. Tucson: University of Arizona Press, 2018.

Calloway, Colin. *One Vast Winter Count: The Native American West before Lewis and Clark*. Lincoln: University of Nebraska Press, 2003.

Christen, Kimberly. "Opening Archives: Respectful Repatriation." *American Archivist* 74, no. 1 (2011): 185–210.

Conrad, Paul. *The Apache Diaspora: Four Centuries of Displacement and Survival*. Philadelphia: University of Pennsylvania Press, 2021.

Debo, Angie. *Geronimo: The Man, His Time, His Place*. Norman: University of Oklahoma Press, 1976.

Delgadillo, Alicia, and Miriam A. Perrett. *From Fort Marion to Fort Sill: A Documentary History of the Chiricahua Apache Prisoners of War, 1886–1913*. Lincoln: University of Nebraska Press, 2013.

Gatewood, Charles B., and Louis Kraft. *Lt. Charles Gatewood and His Apache Wars Memoir*. Lincoln: University of Nebraska Press, 2005.

Geronimo, and S. M. Barrett. *Geronimo's Story of His Life*. Bowie MD: Heritage Books, 1990.

Huizar-Hernández, Anita. "'The Real Geronimo Got Away': Eluding Expectations in Geronimo: His Own Story; Autobiography of a Great Patriot Warrior." *Studies in American Indian Literature* 29, no. 2 (2017): 49–70.

Hyde, Anne. *Born of Lakes and Plains: Mixed Descent Peoples and the Making of the American West*. New York: W. W. Norton, 2022.

———. *Empires, Nations, and Families: A History of the North American West, 1800–1860*. Lincoln: University of Nebraska Press, 2011.

Hutton, Paul Andrew. *The Apache Wars: The Hunt for Geronimo, the Apache Kid, and the Captive Boy Who Started the Longest War in American History*. New York: Broadway Books, 2016.

Kaywaykla, James, and Eve Ball. *In the Days of Victorio; Recollections of a Warm Springs Apache*. Tucson: University of Arizona Press, 1972.

Kemper, Kevin R. "'Geronimo'! The Ideologies of Colonial and Indigenous Masculinities in Historical and Contemporary Representations about Apache Men." *Wicazo Sa Review* 29, no. 2 (2014): 39–62.

Krupat, Arnold. *From the Boarding Schools: Apache Indian Students Speak*. Lincoln: University of Nebraska Press, 2023.

Lieder, Michael, and Jake Page. *Wild Justice: The People of Geronimo vs. the United States*. New York: Random House, 1997.

Opler, Morris Edward. *An Apache Life-Way: The Economic, Social, & Religious Institutions of the Chiricahua Indians*. Reprint ed. Lincoln: Bison Books, 1996.

———. *Apache Odyssey: A Journey Between Two Worlds*. Lincoln: University of Nebraska Press, 2002.

———. "A Chiricahua Apache's Account of the Geronimo Campaign of 1886." *Journal of Arizona History* 27, no. 1 (1986): 71–90.

Prucha, Paul. *The Great Father: The United States Government and the American Indians*, abr. ed. Lincoln: University of Nebraska Press, 1984.

Robinson, Sherry, and Eve Ball. *Apache Voices: Their Stories of Survival as Told to Eve Ball*. Albuquerque: University of New Mexico Press, 2000.

Sackman, Douglas Cazaux. *Wild Men: Ishi and Kroeber in the Wilderness of Modern America*. Oxford: Oxford University Press, 2010.

Shapard, Bud. *Chief Loco: Apache Peacemaker*. Norman: University of Oklahoma Press, 2010.

Sweeney, Edwin R. *From Cochise to Geronimo: The Chiricahua Apaches, 1874–1886*. Norman: University of Oklahoma Press, 2010.

Sweeney, Edwin R., ed. *Making Peace with Cochise*. Norman: University of Oklahoma Press, 1997.

Truett, David. *The Heartbeat of Wounded Knee: Native American from 1890 to the Present*. New York: Riverhead Books, 2019.

Turcheneske, John, Jr. *The Chiricahua Apache Prisoners of War: Fort Sill, 1894–1914*. Denver: University Press of Colorado, 1996.

Utley, Robert. *Geronimo*. New Haven: Yale University Press, 2012.

Whalen, Kevin. *Native Students at Work: American Indian Labor and Sherman Institute's Outing Program, 1900–1945*. Seattle: University of Washington Press, 2018.

White, Richard. *The Republic for Which It Stands: The United States during Reconstruction and the Gilded Age, 1865–1896*. New York: Oxford University Press, 2017.

Whitt, Sarah. "'An Ordinary Case of Discipline': Deputizing White Americans and Punishing Indian Men at the Carlisle Indian Industrial School, 1900–1918." *Western Historical Quarterly* 54, no. 1 (2023): 51–70.

Yannakakis, Yanna. *The Art of Being In-Between: Native Intermediaries, Indian Identity, and Local Rule in Colonial Oaxaca*. Durham: Duke University Press, 2008.

Changing Names

From the editors: The following selections from an article written by Frank Terry, then "superintendent of U.S. Boarding School for Crow Indians, Montana," lays out the precarity of cultural interpretation when assigning new names to Indigenous peoples. Note the intention behind this practice: to make names and families traceable to the U.S. government for purposes of allotment, i.e., record-keeping and tracking private property. In this, one can sense the cultural losses related to something as rudimentary—yet tremendously complex—as interpreting a single name.

"Naming the Indians"

This system of nomenclature the government of the United States in its dealings with the Indian tribes has aimed to establish among them as one means the better to fit them for the privileges and advantages of American citizenship; and that this is a wise and humane act on the part of the government cannot be gainsaid. The Indian Department has continually urged this matter upon its agents, superintendents, and other workers "in the field." The command to give names to the Indians and to establish the same as far as possible by continuous use has been a part of the "Rules and Regulations" for years past. Hon. Thomas J. Morgan, during his incumbency of the office of Commissioner of Indian Affairs, issued the following circular letter, which I quote in its entirety, as it clearly and forcefully sets forth the government's view of the matter:

DEPARTMENT OF THE INTERIOR,
OFFICE OF INDIAN AFFAIRS,
Washington DC, March 19, 1890.

To Indian Agents and Superintendents of Schools:

As allotment work progresses it appears that some care must be exercised in regard to preserving among Indians family names. When Indians become citizens of the United States, under the allotment act, the inheritance of property will be governed by the laws of the respective states, and it will cause needless confusion and doubtless considerable ultimate loss to the Indians if no attempt is made to have the different members of the family known by the same family name on the records and by general reputation. Among other customs of the white people it is becoming important that Indians adopt that in regard to names.

There seems, however, no good reason for continuing a custom which has prevailed to a considerable extent of substituting English for Indian names, especially when different members of the same family are named with no regard to the family surname. Doubtless, in many cases, the Indian name is difficult to pronounce and to remember; but in many other cases the Indian word is as short and euphonious as the English word that is substituted, while, other things being equal, the fact that it is an Indian name makes it a better one.

For convenience, as English "Christian name" may be given and the Indian name be retained as a surname. If the Indian name is unusually long and difficult, it may perhaps be arbitrarily shortened.

The practice of calling Indians by the English translation of their Indian names also seems to me unadvisable. The names thus obtained are usually awkward and uncouth and such as the children when they grow older will dislike to retain.

In any event the habit of adopting sobriquets given to Indians, such as "Tobacco," "Mogul," "Tom," "Pete," etc., by which they become generally known, is unfortunate and should be discontinued. It degrades the Indian, and as he or his children gain in education and culture they will be annoyed by a designation which has been fastened upon them and of which they cannot rid themselves without difficulty.

Hereafter in submitting to this office, for approval, names of Indian employees to be appointed as policemen, judges, teamsters, laborers, etc., all nicknames must be discarded and effort made to ascertain and adopt the actual names or such as should be permanent designations. The names decided upon must be made well known to the respective Indians and the importance of retaining such names must be fully explained to them. I am aware that this will involve some expenditure of time and trouble, but no more than will be warranted by the importance of the matter in the near future.

Of course, sudden change cannot be made in Indian nomenclature; but if agents and school superintendents will systematically endeavor, so far as practicable, to have children and wives known by the names of the fathers and husbands, very great improvement in this respect will be brought about within a few years.

Respectfully,
T. J. Morgan, Commissioner

RULES NOT OBEYED.

One can contemplate only with pain the extent to which these reasonable requirements of the Indian Office have been disregarded by trusted servants in the field. While some have made earnest efforts to carry out the wishes of the Department in this particular, others have treated the matter as one of little or no concern. In many cases no attempt seems ever to have been made to systematize the names of the Indians, and in many others where such attempt was made the correct names, for want of attention on the part of officers in charge, have been forgotten or permitted to fall into disuse. I direct attention to the records of allotments of lands among the members of the several Indian tribes as proofs that officials intrusted [sic] by the Indian Department with the carrying out of its instructions on this subject have been so derelict in this duty that the Indian people, even those who have made the best advances in civilization, are to-day a very poorly named race. In many cases long, unpronounceable Indian names have been retained, in others Indian names have been translated into English with the most unsatisfactory results, "vulgar or otherwise offensive sobriquets" have been countenanced, and a list is produced which should have no place upon record, local or national.

"DON'T KNOW."

A funny little incident is reported from the Apache reservation in Arizona. An Indian policeman rode up to the government school and delivered a little boy to the superintendent. "What's his name?" inquired the superintendent. "Des-to-dah," replied the Indian in Federal blue, as he rode away. "Destodah," mused the superintendent. "Queer name, ain't it? 'Max' will fit him very nicely for a 'first name.'" So the little fellow was duly christened "Max Destodah." It turned out, however, that *des-to-dah* was the Indian word for "don't know." The policeman had simply said he didn't know what the boy's name was. It further turned out that Max was one of four brothers in the same school, no two of whom had the same surname....

Translations of Indian names, as a rule, have been unsatisfactory, though there are exceptions. The case is reported from the Pawnee reservation, Oklahoma, of an Indian name Coo-rux ruh-rah-ruk-koo. He was commonly called Afraid-of-a-bear. The literal interpretation of his name, as given to me, is "fearing a bear that is wild." With this interpretation the agent proceeded to call the Indian Fearing B. Wilde; not a bad arrangement, if he had made a success of it. But he did not, for the allotment was finally made to the Indian's native name. But such names as Flying eagle, Pipe-chief, Crazy-horse, Yellow bonnet, Afraid-of-his-enemy, Walk-in-the-water, Rain-in-the-face, Bull-all-the-time, Keeps-his-head-above-water, No-hair-on-his-tail, Bob-tail-wolf-No. 3, Kills-the-one-with-the-blue-mark-in-the-centre-of-the-chin, are ridiculous and should not be perpetuated. Such names are uncouth, un-American, and uncivilized.

The plan resorted to in some quarters of discarding the Indian names altogether and fitting the Indians out with names that are purely English has not worked well, for those selected in many cases are names illustrious in American history, and this has caused the Indians to become the butt of many a vulgar joke. William Penn, Fitzhugh Lee, David B. Hill and William Shakespeare are policemen at the Shoshone Agency, Wyoming. Only a short while ago it was reported that on an Indian reservation in New Mexico William Breckenridge arrested John G. Carlisle for being drunken and disorderly. It would no doubt surprise the reader, and no less so our Honorable Secretary of the Navy, should I say that I have seen George Washington, John Quincy Adams, Franklin Pierce, Rip Van Winkle, Allen G. Thurman and Hillary Herbert engaged together in a game of shinney.

I have said that one contemplates this with pain. One is astonished that [Indian agents] supposed to be intelligent, earnest and honest should treat a matter so grave with such exceeding unconcern—that men intrusted [*sic*] with the weal of this dependent and confiding people, familiar as these men were with civilized methods, knowing that the subject was of great moment, should commit, or stand idly by and allow committed, this careless trifling with the nomenclature of a great race like the aborigines of this Continent.[1]

Notes

1. Frank Terry, "Naming the Indians," *Review of Reviews*, March 1897, 301–7.

6

Diplomacy in the Aftermath of Pancho Villa's Raid

Consul Antonio Landín in Columbus, 1917–1920

BRANDON MORGAN

On the morning of September 16, 1917, residents of Columbus, New Mexico, noticed that the Mexican flag had been raised above the consular agency. Despite the fact that consulates often fly the flags of their respective nations, particularly on significant holidays, Columbus residents chafed at the sight of the Mexican colors flying in their town. They quickly complained to the village trustees and to Antonio Landín, the Mexican consular agent.

Landín was relatively new to his post, having arrived the previous month. He surely understood the reasons for local fury over the public raising of the flag on Mexico's Independence Day, but he also understood what was at stake. His was the unenviable task of protecting the rights and reasserting the place of Mexicans in the town that General Francisco "Pancho" Villa had ransacked a little over a year earlier. To Landín, flying the flag represented a significant, if symbolic, early step toward rebuilding trust between the American and Mexican communities in the border town.

When local authorities ordered Landín to lower the flag immediately, he refused, ensuring instead that the flag remained in place until 6:00 p.m. that evening, the close of business. For his efforts, he received the commendation of his superiors at the Consulate General in El Paso. More importantly, he set the tone for a two-year tenure in Columbus that eventually saw the formation of a Club

Patriótica for the Colonia Mexicana (as locals referred to the local Mexican community), which in turn restarted public celebrations of Mexican Independence Day in collaboration with the people in Palomas, just across the international border.[1]

Yet, despite the positive outcomes of his service in Columbus, Landín did not always enjoy the confidence of the very people he was assigned to serve. As was the case across the Southwest in the early twentieth century, those belonging to the diaspora, or *México de Afuera*, sought to celebrate their heritage and maintain their culture while living in the United States. Many planned to return home after building up savings, but, for most, a return to Mexico on their own terms was impractical. Mexicans who had never migrated to *el norte* often considered México de Afuera in a dismissive or expressly negative light. Members of the consular service sometimes possessed such attitudes about Mexicans living in the United States as well, and many used their posts to further their own political and economic ambitions.[2]

The precarities of Mexican residents in places like Columbus were complicated further by regular cross-border migrations. People like Reysedel Gómez, a prominent member of the Colonia Mexicana and who later headed the *Junta Colonizadora Palomas*, maintained one foot in each nation. Gómez had served as the *jefe político* in La Ascensión, Chihuahua, prior to his residency in Columbus. The Columbus Colonia Mexicana was aptly named in that it wasn't quite a diaspora; it was a group of Mexicans who maintained regular ties to their home communities while forging their place in a North American community.

Although Landín did promote the rights of Mexican people in Columbus, his work seems to have resonated more strongly with the white American population than with the Colonia Mexicana. Mexican residents of the area recognized the ways that he leveraged his post in the promotion of his own ambitions, sometimes at the expense of their interests.

Antonio Landín: Interpreter or Interpretee?

Two years after the controversial flag raising, Antonio Landín fled Columbus in the early hours of October 23, 1919. His assistant consul, Leopóldo López, only received word of his flight and resignation the following day via telegram from El Paso. Why did a consular agent with such a strong record resign his post in the middle of the night? What conditions would have pushed him to abandon his post before his tenure had ended? Fragmentary evidence from Landín's personnel file and contemporary newspapers shed some light, but these are questions that lack definitive answers.

On one hand, documents in his personnel file, held in the Archivo Historico Génaro Estrada of the Secretaría de Relaciones Exteriores in Mexico City, provide a window into his consular work from his perspective and that of some of his superiors. On the other, reporting in borderlands newspapers, particularly the *Columbus Courier*, *Deming Headlight*, and *Deming Graphic*, offers some hints about how the white, English-speaking population viewed him and his initiatives.

In attempting to discover, understand, and recount Landín's story, my role as an interpreter of historical figures and events has been brought into sharp relief. When I first encountered Landín's story in the archive, I tended to view him in a heroic light. I had read widely on the histories of the Lower Mimbres Valley, and I understood the violence and discrimination against Mexican people that only intensified following Villa's raid. Landín faced a herculean task and, in addition to the accomplishments laid out above, in 1919 he played an instrumental role in abolishing racist housing covenants that would have denied housing to Mexican and African American residents in Columbus neighborhoods.

Yet, as I continued to read his personnel file in the context of contemporary accounts in the *Columbus Courier* and regional newspapers, I discovered the story of an embattled consul who failed to gain the trust of the communities he was assigned to represent. I began to be more cognizant of my own role as an interpreter of the past, as Limerick and Offenburger emphasize in the introduction to this volume. And, similar to Baumgartner's realization that thinking across the different registers of how historical actors understood their situations and how we as historians interpret and translate those historical moments, refocusing on Landín with my own interpretive role at the forefront pushed me to consider his story anew. Newspaper accounts paint a picture of a consul who found himself on the wrong side of a partisan divide when a new president came to power in Mexico City at the end of the Mexican Revolution. *La Prensa* in San Antonio, Texas, forged a connection with several Colonias Mexicanas across the Southwest, including the one in Columbus. Along with El Paso's *La República*, it reveals the partisan divisions that defined Landín's tenure in Columbus. Although Landín may have been placed in the role of cultural broker or bridge, the Colonia Mexicana didn't necessarily accept him as such.

Local and regional English-language newspapers give the impression of a consul tightly connected to the local Mexican population, and who regularly participated in community initiatives, including Red Cross drives to fund the North

American World War I effort. Less than a year following the September 16 flag controversy, Landín received the support of several prominent Columbus residents when he again flew the Mexican colors at the consular office on July 4, 1918. This time, prominent residents like Lee Riggs "explained to the curious that it was proper." Mayor J. R. Blair publicly shared a letter that he received from Landín in which the consul explained that his actions had been taken "in accordance with the Treaty of Friendship and Commerce that exists between Mexico and the United States as a matter of courtesy to this Country in its Glorious Day."[3]

Shifting attitudes, as well as Landín's concerted campaign to present positive images of Mexico and its people to counter the derogatory photos and films that dominated in the United States in 1918, suggest that he had done much to gain the respect and trust of locals. Additionally, Landín was recorded as having attended local weddings, celebrations, and social events. He gave from his own funds to aid the restoration of the Columbus Catholic church. In 1919 he spearheaded the formation of a Club Patriotica that renewed the joint participation of residents of Columbus and Palomas in celebration of September 16. And, perhaps most significantly, he worked with the village mayor and trustees to prevent a local construction company from implementing a racist housing covenant that would have prevented the sale of new homes to Black and Mexican-heritage residents of Columbus.

The first half of his 186-page personnel file seems to echo and augment such interpretations of Landín's service in Columbus. In addition to the items mentioned in the press, he emphasized a 1918 episode in which he traveled to Deming to rescue six Mexicans and a Spanish citizen from impressment into the U.S. military.

A few details about his personal background come into focus in the pages of his file, as well. When he began his consular service at Columbus in August of 1917, he had recently been assigned as an agent of the Mexican Secret Service in Calexico, California, where he stepped in for an absentee consul. He was young, only twenty-six years old. He spoke both Spanish and English and was not married.

In petitions for leave in 1918 and the spring of 1919, the former to travel to Deming and the latter to visit his ailing father, Landín requested that Leopoldo G. López, the Secret Service agent assigned to Columbus, take charge of the consular agency in his stead. In 1918 the Secretaría de Relaciones Exteriores did not find López an acceptable substitute, but the following year it did. López's name often accompanied Landín's in the regional press's reporting on the Colonia Mexicana, along with other Columbus locals such as Juan Favela, Génaro Forzan, Reydesel Gómez, and Juan Carreón.

López had arrived in Columbus around the same time as Landín in 1917. He was a native of León, Guanajuato. Both were appointees of Venustiano Carranza's government. Although North Americans seemed to view them as close collaborators, Landín's personnel file indicates that they were often at odds. Sometime early in their two-year tenure, López had discovered that Landín was involved with a contraband operation involving minted gold and silver Mexican coinage. He also witnessed Landín's involvement in a plot to smuggle twelve hundred head of cattle to the Ojitos hacienda near Janos in Chihuahua. Landín apparently looked the other way when the cattle were transported but then participated in a scheme by which he split the proceeds of the fine assessed against the Ojitos operation when a coconspirator confessed to authorities.

López informed Andrés G. García, then both the general consul and visitador general in El Paso, of what he had learned about Landín's involvement in the shady activities. To his surprise, García seemed bothered by his report but then thanked him for his honesty and for carrying out his duty to the Mexican government. Only later, López learned that García was also participating in the contraband coinage scheme. According to López, from that point forward, "they made sure to harass me for what they considered to be a bad action."[4]

The conflict between López and Landín matters because it sheds some light onto the estrangement between the consular agent and the Colonia Mexicana in Columbus, and it illustrates the divergent perspectives about Landín's consular work held by the English-speaking population and Mexican-heritage Columbusites. Ideally, I would love to read the words of the leading figures of the Colonia Mexicana who weren't connected to Landín (there were a few), but I have not yet located any such records. Instead, I've relied on clues from the press, particularly the *Columbus Courier*, and Landín's own personnel file to trace out the complexities of his relationship with Mexicans in his zone.

The Context in Columbus

On the surface, Landín's tenure in Columbus appears to have been exemplary. Given the recent history of the locale, his was no small task. Just over a year before he arrived, Pancho Villa had led his infamous raid that left eighteen Americans dead and cost the lives of over one hundred of his own men. Despite later oral history accounts that suggested little animosity between the white and Mexican-heritage population after the raid, contemporary records show that Columbus sought vengeance against captured *villistas* and Mexican locals alike in the hours and days following the attack. Several villistas were summarily executed within hours of the raid. Most outraged survivors made no distinction between the group of villistas who had assaulted Columbus and the general populace of Mexican-heritage people who inhabited the New Mexico–Chihuahua border region. In a letter to his sister, former *Columbus Courier* editor Perrow G. Moseley remarked, "Most of our local Mexicans have been made to leave and many of them have died very unnatural deaths since the battle. Our people are very bitter and the soldiers are letting them (our people) do pretty much as they please—all the Mexican Prisoners were taken out of camp and turned loose—our citizens were informed of what was to be done and shot them as they were turned loose."[5]

Along with many Columbusites, Colonel Herbert Slocum, commanding officer of the Thirteenth Cavalry at Columbus who received much criticism for his inability to prevent the raid, believed that local Mexican residents had supported the attack and perhaps aided the villistas. Several Mexican inhabitants of Columbus were charged with espionage and arrested. In the case of Pedro Sánchez, the evidence against him consisted only of his possession of a pair of binoculars. Based on similarly thin evidence, Slocum gave a group of alleged spies and coconspirators until sundown on the evening after the raid to evacuate the town and "most have not been heard from since," according to military investigator E. B. Stone. Stone also reported that an elderly man named Hidado Vavel failed to leave town. Stone recounted that the night following the raid, Vavel "was seen in the brush about 1/2 mile from camp here by the sentries who ordered him to halt; instead of halting, the old man kept running; the sentries shot him down and killed him." By another account, "local old-timers" spoke in hushed voices, "saying that many of the wounded villistas were murdered after fighting. Some were said to be relieved of their suffering by having their heads slammed against wagon wheels." Genáro Forzán, the cashier for the Palomas Land and Cattle Company, left town with his wife "thinking it was best for him not to remain while feeling was running intensely against Mexicans."[6]

In the same issue that chronicled the triumphal entry into Mexico of "Old Glory" at the head of the Pershing Punitive Expedition, the *Deming Graphic* reported that a man named Alfredo Aragón had worked for weeks in one of the Columbus hotels as a cover to aid and abet the villistas during the raid. According to the short blurb in the paper, Aragón was a "Mexican Spy" who "had an Elks' badge and a United States army uniform" as evidence of his role in the attack. Despite such evidence, he was only suspected of working with Villa and his fate was not reported.[7]

Although this violent and xenophobic treatment of Mexicans became less overt over the ensuing months, military support for General Pershing's Punitive Expedition from Camp Furlong meant that memories of the raid remained fresh. The military presence decreased but persisted following Pershing's return in February 1917, and it wasn't long before Columbus leaders found that agents of the Phelps Dodge company and law enforcement from Bisbee, Arizona, had "deported" about twelve hundred striking miners to the desert just west of town.

When news of the arrival of the Bisbee deportees reached Columbus, the response was broadly humanitarian. Many deportees were associated with the Industrial Workers of the World (I.W.W.) labor movement, but large numbers were not. In the context of recent U.S. involvement in World War I, Bisbee officials deemed the socialist Wobblies and the majority Mexican and Slavic workers a menace to the U.S. war effort. Of course, to the executives of the Phelps Dodge Company, the strike was a direct threat to the company's bottom line.[8]

Although some people in the area took issue with the idea that the Phelps Dodge Company and Bisbee community leaders would think to exile the strikers to their doorstep, most sympathized with the plight of the deportees. The masthead of the July 13 *Columbus Courier* proclaimed, "Striking Miners Are More Welcome Here than Would be 1200 Cochise County, Arizona, Corporation Deputies."[9] Editor G. E. Parks ran a column on the front page titled "Reserve Judgment in the Case of the IWWs"; Parks's efforts to convince his readership that the deportees posed no threat suggest that, perhaps, some Columbusites did not share his perspective. Yet, when investigator Fred Fornoff made his report to New Mexico governor Washington E. Lindsay about the situation on August 12, he characterized relations between the town and the deportees as calm. By his account, "No alarm is felt by level headed citizens here. The mayor believes that the question will resolve itself in a little while," a conclusion that Fornoff shared. Colonel Sickel, the commanding officer at Camp Furlong who oversaw the rations of food, water, and clothing that were supplied to the refugees, agreed.[10]

A few of the refugees remained in Columbus for as many as three months, although most left by mid-September. During their time there, relations reached cordial levels. By mid-August the refugees "mingled to a small extent" with the people of the town, as well as with the soldiers at Camp Furlong. When the main body of them left, many crossing the border into Mexico, the *Courier*'s new editor, J. B. Smith quipped that "their vacation so pleasantly spent in Columbus at the expense of Uncle Sam, has come to an end." Like a few of the other town leaders, his patience with the group had run somewhat thin. Even those most disposed to help the deportees due to their poor treatment at the hands of Sheriff Wheeler and Phelps Dodge executives commented that the group's presence was an imposition to Columbus. Worse, animosities toward Mexicans had not faded that much since the Villa raid. As historian Samuel Truett has emphasized, "generally forgotten is that the largest foreign group that was dumped into the desert that day was from Mexico."[11]

It is no surprise, then, that a special Mexican Consular Agency was established in Columbus in August 1917. Landín worked to ensure that the remaining Bisbee refugees received sufficient rations and fair treatment by local authorities and residents. Support from residents like G. E. Parks, Lee Riggs, and mayor and member of the Townsite Company's board J. R. Blair was indispensable. Landín worked with the Secretaría de Relaciones Exteriores to provide resettlement in northern Mexico for those who wanted it. Many deportees took the Mexican government up on its offer, although those with families, who numbered between 150 and 250 depending on the count, worked to return home to Bisbee.[12]

Within this context, Landín's raising of the Mexican flag in September 1917 received its harsh backlash, demonstrating that charity toward the strikers did not necessarily indicate goodwill toward Mexicans. Additionally, Venustiano Carranza's leadership as the First Chief of the Revolution and then as de facto president of Mexico shaped Landín's tenure in Columbus. As early as 1914, Carranza reorganized the diplomatic corps. He ousted Huerta appointees and made plans to leverage the foreign service, particularly Mexican representatives in the United States, to push back against negative reporting on Mexico in general, and on Carranza's leadership in particular. Along with their charge to promote commerce, "protect transient or resident Mexicans," and "defend the good name of the Republic," Carranza ordered consuls to "conduct 'minute investigations' of anti-Carranza stories printed in U.S. newspapers."[13]

Carranza's brand of diplomacy emphasized propaganda. Although Columbus was unique as the only U.S. border town to have been directly attacked by a Mexican revolutionary force, consuls stationed along the western border expressed outrage at the ways in which Mexican people were portrayed in photo and film across the Southwest. The Mexican consul in Tucson protested widely distributed "films which depicted Mexicans abusing women and children."[14] In line with the efforts of other Carranza appointees, Landín initiated a campaign to combat negative images of Mexican people in photos and films in town sometime near the beginning of 1918. Rather than directly speak out against such representations of Mexicans, he invited locals to an annex of the consulate to screen films that demonstrated the daily realities of life in Mexico. His effort reached as far as Deming and surrounding towns in his zone.

Landín even went so far as to censure the importation of films and photos that presented Mexicans in a denigrating light. As he returned to Columbus from a trip to Mexico City in January 1918, he noticed that American travelers on the train brought photos and other paraphernalia that presented negative aspects of life in Mexico. Although his report does not provide specifics about the "vistas denigrantes," he called on Laredo customs agents to detain the train and confiscate the various photos and other items in the Americans' possession. The customs officials complied and, by his own account, Landín himself collected the offending items from the passengers. He also reported that the agents confiscated a large sum of gold coins that a group of travelers had attempted to smuggle into the United States without paying their customs fees.[15]

A column on the front page of the September 20, 1918, *Columbus Courier* described Landín's propaganda effort in the context of a Mexican Independence Day celebration that had been held at the consulate. The article's description and tone provide a window into the relationship, and the distance, between the English-speaking population of Columbus and the Colonia Mexicana. Significantly, near the beginning of the column the author noted that "it is impossible to give an idea as to the program carried out for it was all in Spanish, but anyone could enjoy the speaking even if not one word of it could be understood." The article identified the major Mexican participants on the program, including "Genaro Forzan, Jr., A. Landin, the consul, [Leopoldo] Lopez, [Reysedel] Gomez, and others." Although this seemed to be an important moment for the Colonia Mexicana, the ties to the English-speaking Americans in attendance were tenuous at best. This was not only because they didn't understand Spanish, but because of commentary such as, "The people were generally surprised to note the talent among the Mexican people," in discussing the music and dancing. Such commentary, coupled with the efforts to create a place myth centered on white, Protestant values, hearkened back to a gulf between Anglo Americans and Mexicans that had existed in Columbus even before Villa's raid.[16]

Landín made two of his greatest achievements in 1919: he was instrumental in successfully challenging a racist housing covenant in a new Columbus housing development and his efforts resulted in the formation of the Club Patriotica that brought together people of Mexican heritage in and around Columbus to celebrate Mexican independence. Real estate developers Prewitt & Pender had inserted the language, "No lot contained in this tract shall be sold to Mexicans or colored people within one year from date."[17] Landín brought the issue to the attention of Mayor J. R. Blair and the village trustees, who unanimously condemned the move and required the company to remove the covenant from its contracts of sale. And, although the celebration of Mexico's independence day occurred at the consulate in 1918, by various accounts in the *Columbus Courier* and even in San Antonio's *La Prensa*, the 1919 celebrations were at a larger scale under the guidance of the Club Patriotica.[18] Festivities took place in both Columbus and Palomas, and, unlike the 1918 commemorations, reports mentioned the presence of Timotea Fontes de Landín, the consul's wife.

Interpreting the Fragments

When I read the sources on Landín for my dissertation and then book project, my focus was less on his personal story and more on how his actions impacted Columbus and the surrounding areas. I was fascinated by the fact that the Villa raid and Venustiano Carranza's rise to power seemed to have inspired the decision to install a consular agent in Columbus, when the Mexican consulate had previously been located in Deming, New Mexico. The narrative that I found in the archive showed that the Carrancista government took seriously the situation along the rural border and that Landín, a young novice to the diplomatic corps, rose to the occasion. For those reasons, I originally considered him as something of a hero, and my interpretation of his actions in Columbus was admittedly one-dimensional. His story is also one of a bureaucrat leveraging his position for personal benefit, and it shows how changes in national leadership on the heels of the Mexican Revolution impacted the diplomatic corps.

Once I began investigating the question of why Landín fled his post in the middle of the night, only to be reassigned to El Salvador and to then lose his post in the diplomatic service altogether, I realized that records identified him as single when he arrived in Columbus and, as married by July 1919.[19] Yet, there was no report of a wedding in the social columns of the *Columbus Courier*. All of a sudden, seemingly, Landín was a married man.

This small wrinkle didn't concern me at first. As I returned to reframe Landín as an interpreter or cultural bridge for the symposium that resulted in this volume, however, I dug deeper into the question of his sudden abandonment of his post and found that members of Columbus's Colonia Mexicana held suspicions of improprieties around his marriage. In the wake of his resignation, López, Reysedel Gómez, and a few others, filed claims with the consular agency that

Landín had never officially or legally married the woman he claimed to be his wife. They claimed that when Timotea had appeared at a dance in Casas Grandes, Chihuahua, with Landín shortly after their purported marriage in Hermosillo, Sonora, those in attendance recognized her as the "beloved of a Carrancista general."[20] When they reportedly contacted the judge in Hermosillo to inquire about records of the matrimony, he told them that "not only had Landín not contracted any marriage whatsoever, but I have never met anyone named Landín."[21] These members of Columbus's Colonia Mexicana challenged Landín's standing as consul, claiming that he was making a joke of polite society. Notably, none of them attempted to gain Timotea's perspective or offer her any support. She appears in their arguments against Landín as a prop to challenge his position.

After Landín fled Columbus on October 23, 1919, neither he nor his accusers mentioned her again. When the partisan El Paso *La República* reported on November 5, 1919, that "the Carrancista consul from Columbus was forced from his post due to violations of American laws," Timotea's name was not cited. Instead, the paper reported that Landín was expelled from the town because he had violated the Mann Act "by bringing to that town a woman that was not his wife for immoral ends."[22] The charge of violating the Mann Act does not appear in either Landín's personnel file or in the pages of the *Columbus Courier*.

Landín's accusers may have had political motives and it appears that they exaggerated the accusations against him. Although Landín took care not to directly comment on politics during his time in El Paso in November and December 1919, the *El Paso Herald* recorded his statement that "Ygnacio Bonillas, civilian candidate for the presidency, appears to be well liked by the people."[23] Bonillas was Venustiano Carranza's hand-picked successor and at that time, General Alvaro Obregón had openly challenged his bid for the presidency. The political rift between Obregón and Carranza that marked the end of the violent phase of the Mexican Revolution and that ended in Carranza's death seemed to also be at the heart of Landín's troubles. In his report outlining the claims of the Colonia Mexicana, López emphasized his support for Obregón's new government (the report was filed in December 1920 after the general had become Mexico's president). The revolutionary affiliation of the other members of the Colonia Mexicana is less clear; some may even have been villistas given their roots in La Ascensión, a Villa stronghold that today prides itself on being the site where the Dorados were organized.[24] People with those political leanings would have opposed the continued presence of a Carrancista as consul.

After a bureaucratic back and forth with the Secretaría de Relaciones Exteriores, Landín received a new post in San Salvador. In that capacity, however, he became outspoken in his opposition to Obregón. He sent telegrams and letters to Mexico City officials stating his view that Obregón had usurped the rightful place of Carranza and his heir at the head of the Mexican state. Based on those actions, the Secretaría terminated his post in El Salvador on August 1, 1920, citing in private the idea that his opinions could "create a scandal." He spent the next few years petitioning the department for his official service record so that he could use it for "political purposes," though it remains unclear what those purposes were.[25]

Conclusion

Landín's stint with the Mexican consular service was a flashpoint in the history of the village of Columbus, New Mexico, and it provides a historical example of the difficult task of acting as a cultural interpreter or bridge at a highly partisan moment during the Mexican Revolution. Landín's story also underscores the reality that historical actors are imperfect human beings who look out for their own best interests. As a historian who has worked with the set of evidence relating to Landín and the broader histories of Columbus, Palomas, and the U.S.-Mexico borderlands during the Mexican Revolution, his story has given me space to reflect on how I respond to archival documentation. I still remember opening Landín's file in July 2012 in the basement reading room in the Archivo Genaro Estrada at the Secretaría de Relaciones Exteriores in Mexico City and finding a colorful, fold-out broadside flier for the September 16, 1919, Mexican Independence celebration. It was among the first pages in the expediente and was printed in red and green ink on a white background. I took three separate photographs just to be sure that I would have a clear and usable remembrance of that page.

I also allowed that experience to shape the way I worked through the rest of the file.

As I revisited Landín's expediente for this symposium, thinking of him as an interpreter, I read him differently. The story that was most relevant to my book project was the one that emphasized his successes as a cultural mediator. At that time, I wasn't looking to understand him as a three-dimensional human being, but as one among many actors and voices in Columbus. Landín himself became the center of my analysis when I began to consider him as a cultural bridge, and I found him to be an inexperienced young man who used his consular position to enrich himself and to attempt to promote the agenda of the Mexican state under Venustiano Carranza.

These things are all true, as is the reality that Landín served as a cultural bridge at a crucial moment in the history of the rural U.S.-Mexico borderlands. He certainly accomplished much during his tenure as consular agent by defending the flag, serving the Bisbee "deportees," challenging negative images of Mexican people in film, restoring a Club Patriotica in Columbus, and defeating a racist housing covenant.

I don't think that I'm saying anything particularly groundbreaking in laying out my interpretive choices. Every historian makes similar decisions as they craft their analyses and narratives about the past. As professional historians, however, we don't often name the ways in which we work. Examining the actions of an imperfect cultural interpreter along the U.S.-Mexico border pushed me to think more deeply about my role as an interpreter, and perhaps even a translator, of the past.

Notes

1. The account of Landín's refusal to lower the flag is mentioned several times in his personnel file, specifically: Informe de Antonio Landin al Servicio Consular Mexicano, December 29, 1917, ASRE Landín. There is no record of attempts to forcibly remove the banner or of the necessity of Landín standing guard.
2. In the 1890s the Mexican Consul in Deming, New Mexico, Salvador Malliefert, used his position to secure thousands of acres of newly declared terrenos baldíos in northwestern Chihuahua. See *Deming Headlight*, February 28, 1891; Romney, *Mormon Colonies in Mexico*, 63–64; and "Memorandum de M. Fernández, Secretaría de Fomento," February 23, 1891, and "Letter from M. Azpiroz, Sección Consular," February 24, 1891, tomo 398, ASRE AEMEU. For an overview of the ways that people within and without Mexico view those in México de Afuera, see Hernández, *Mexican American Colonization*, introduction.
3. Informe de Antonio Landin al Secretario de Relaciones Exteriores, August 21, 1920, ASRE Landín; and *Columbus Courier*, July 5, 1918.
4. Informe de Leopoldo López al Secretario de Relaciones Exteriores, December 4, 1920, ASRE Landín. Original: "procuraron hostilizarme por aquello que reputaron ellos como una mala acción."
5. "Columbus Editor Writes Letter Home," P. G. Mosely to Mrs. M. R. Huffman, March 13, 1916, binder 3, Dean Archive. Mosely turned the *Courier* over to G. E. Parks in September 1914; see *Columbus Courier*, September 4, 1914. After a battle with tuberculosis, Mosely died a few weeks after the Villa raid. For an overview of the raid and the various questions it has generated for contemporaries and historians alike, see Katz, *Life and Times*, 550–70.

6. Welsome, *General and the Jaguar*, loc. 2235–74; *Columbus Courier*, March 24, 1916. Notably, New Mexico senator Albert B. Fall led the critique of Slocum, as evidenced in his scathing editorial published in the *New York Times* on March 19, 1916.
7. *Deming Graphic*, March 17, 1916.
8. Benton-Cohen, *Borderline Americans*, 1–3, and chap. 7, quote on p. 3; Truett, *Fugitive Landscapes*, 174–76; and "IWW Wobblies" binder, Dean Archive.
9. *Columbus Courier*, July 13, 1917.
10. In a letter to Governor Washington E. Lindsey of New Mexico dated August 12, 1917, Fred Fornoff also mentioned that two Columbus residents, "Jack London and a Mr. Callen," traveled to Fort Bliss where they petitioned General Bell to send extra troops to defend Columbus against the refugees. General Bell rebuked them for making the request and sent them back home. Lindsey Papers.
11. Truett, *Fugitive Landscapes*, 174; and *Columbus Courier*, September 21, 1917.
12. For the varying counts, see Benton-Cohen, *Borderline Americans*, 3; Report on the Deportees, August 1917, Lindsey Papers.
13. Duties listed in the 1902 "Reglamento del Cuerpo Consular, *Guia Diplomática y Consular*," cited in Gómez Quiñones, "Piedras Contra la Luna," 496; for Carranza's reorganization of the diplomatic corps, see Richmond, *Venustiano Carranza's Nationalist Struggle*, 190–91.
14. Richmond, *Carranza's Nationalist Struggle*, 190.
15. Informe de Antonio Landín al Secretario de Relaciones Exteriores, August 21, 1920, ASRE Landín.
16. Morgan, *Raid and Reconciliation*, 11–12, and chap. 5.
17. Resolutions of the Columbus Mayor and Village Trustees, 1919, ASRE Landín.
18. *La Prensa* (San Antonio), September 24, 2019; *Columbus Courier*, September 19, 1919.
19. *Columbus Courier*, July 11, 1919.
20. Informe de Leopoldo G. López, December 4, 1920, ASRE Landín.
21. Informe de Leopoldo G. López, December 4, 1920, ASRE Landín.
22. *La República* (El Paso), November 5, 1919. The Mann Act was also known as the "White-Slave Traffic Act of 1910." The law drew on the Commerce Clause to criminalize the transportation of "any woman or girl for the purpose of prostitution or debauchery, or for any other immoral purpose." In application, the law had racist overtones and it was most often used to prosecute consensual premarital or interracial relationships. See "Mann Act," Cornell Law School Legal Information Institute, accessed September 28, 2023, https://www.law.cornell.edu/wex/mann_act.
23. *El Paso Herald*, December 17, 1919.
24. For the Obregón-Carranza rift, see Gonzales, *Mexican Revolution*, 178–80. For more on La Ascensión as the birthplace of the Dorados, see Ramírez Tafoya, *Ascensión antes y después*.
25. Constancia de servicio, no. 01045, February 3, 1922, ASRE Landín.

Bibliography

ARCHIVAL SOURCES

ASRE Landín. Expediente de Antonio Landín, 3-19-40, Expedientes Personales, Archivo Histórico Genaro Estrada, Secretaría de Relaciones Exteriores, Mexico City.

ASRE AEMEU. Archivo Embajada de México en los Estados Unidos Americanos, Archivo Histórico Genaro Estrada, Secretaría de Relaciones Exteriores, Mexico City.

Dean Archive. Personal Archive of Richard R. Dean, President of the Columbus Historical Society, Columbus, New Mexico.

Lindsey Papers. Papers of Governor Washington E. Lindsey, Question of Deportation of IWWs from Bisbee, Arizona, to Columbus, New Mexico, 1917, box 9, folder 180. New Mexico State Records Center and Archives, Santa Fe.

PUBLISHED WORKS

Benton-Cohen, Katherine. *Borderline Americans: Racial Division and Labor in the Arizona Borderlands*. Cambridge MA: Harvard University Press, 2009.

Gómez Quiñones, Juan. "Piedras Contra la Luna, México en Aztlán y Aztlán en México: Chicano-Mexican Relations and the Mexican Consulates, 1900–1920," in *Contemporary Mexico: Papers of the IV International Congress of Mexican History*, edited by James W. Wilkie, Michael C. Meyer, and Edna Monzón de Wilkie, 494–528. Berkeley: University of California Press, 1976.

Gonzales, Michael J. *The Mexican Revolution, 1910–1940*. Albuquerque: University of New Mexico Press, 2002.

Hernández, José Angel. *Mexican American Colonization during the Nineteenth Century: A History of the U.S.-Mexico Borderlands*. New York: Cambridge University Press, 2012.

Katz, Friedrich. *The Life and Times of Pancho Villa*. Stanford: Stanford University Press: 1998.

Morgan, Brandon. *Raid and Reconciliation: Pancho Villa, Modernization, and Violence in the U.S.-Mexico Borderlands*. Lincoln: University of Nebraska Press, 2024.

Ramírez Tafoya, Ramón. *Ascensión antes y después de la revolución*. Chihuahua, Chihuahua: Instituto Chihuahuense de Cultura, 2011.

Richmond, Douglas. *Venustiano Carranza's Nationalist Struggle, 1893–1920*. Lincoln: University of Nebraska Press, 1983.

Romney, Thomas Cottam. *The Mormon Colonies in Mexico*. 1938. Reprint, Salt Lake City: University of Utah Press, 2005.

Truett, Samuel. *Fugitive Landscapes: The Forgotten History of the U.S.-Mexico Borderlands*. New Haven: Yale University Press, 2006.

Welsome, Eileen. *The General and the Jaguar: Pershing's Hunt for Pancho Villa, a True Story of Revolution and Revenge*. New York: Little, Brown, 2006.

John Collier

NO HANDS RAISED

Excerpt from "Minutes of a Meeting Held at Miami"

MR. COLLIER: I will pause here and find out whether everybody or nearly everybody understands English and whether there are a good many who do not understand English. Will those who do not understand English so indicate by raising their hand. (*No hands raised.*) Are there any here who need an interpreter? (*No hands raised.*) That is good. It will save us hours of time. Now to explain the reason for the Wheeler-Howard Bill—

LADY IN AUDIENCE: I don't think these Indians understood your question.

MR. COLLIER: Will somebody translate my question? I want to know how many Indians there are here who don't understand English. I think there are a good many Osages who don't understand English.

MR. GRIFFITH: I think all the Quapaws here understand English.

Henry Tallchief interprets to the Osages.[1]

Notes

1. "Minutes of a Meeting Held at Miami, Oklahoma, March 24th, 1934 by Commissioner of Indian Affairs Collier to Discuss the Wheeler-Howard Indian Rights Bill with the Indians of the Quapaw and Osage Jurisdictions," 330–31, https://www.google.com/books/edition/The_Indian_Reorganization_Act/sGDSWgdM8ucC?hl=en&gbpv=1&bsq=tallchief.

7

Interpreters of Diné dóó Gáamalii Oral Histories

FARINA KING

On a summer afternoon, in 2008, when my husband and I were living with my aunt, Phyllis, in Iyanbito, we started to walk around the rolling red dirt hills and gazed at the towering buttes and mesas covered with sagebrush, juniper, and various wiry grasses.[1] In Diné bizaad, the Navajo language, *ayánni bitó* refers to "buffalo's water" or "buffalo springs," which are the English translations for Iyanbito.[2] I have never seen buffalos in Iyanbito, but there are some waterways associated with the new Puerco River nearby that pass through the community even if they are thin and often mostly dry in the arid climate. Diné use the phrase *jiní*, meaning "they say," to recite the people's history, emphasizing its significance. There was a time when people could see the buffalo that would arrive in herds to drink "at a watering hole located east of the present chapter site," *jiní*.[3] Some Diné of the area such as a chapter president, Steven Arviso, "remembers seeing them [the buffalo]" as he returned home from school in Gallup.[4]

A variety of stories about the origins of buffalos, which became the namesake of the region with their presence between the 1960s and 1995, include a train derailment and an escape from Gallup's Intertribal Ceremonial buffalo riding competition, but a consensus remains out of reach.[5] Every place in Diné Bikéyah, Navajo land, has a name and stories embedded to the landscape. Many places like Iyanbito emphasize water, because *Tó éí iiná át'é*, or "water is life," and communities grow around water. Interpreters are the storytellers who not only translate such names and terms but also make conscious decisions about the stories that they want to tell and why. The work of interpreters is often messy, because they are like artists who mold their new forms out of clay and other materials that already stand on their own. But narrative creations enable new understandings. The creations also leave layers and tracks. As Diné witnessed buffalo in the area, where some of my relatives dwell, they started to call the place "Ayánni bitó," and then after increasingly more Diné started to learn and interpret Diné bizaad for English speakers, many now call the community "Iyanbito." Of the years that I have visited family in Iyanbito, I have wondered how many buffalos my own relatives have seen since living there. Even if they have not seen any buffalo, they continue to call the place Iyanbito and will continue to do so, maybe until another person and event reinterprets the land.

My interpretations of the land, people, and language are shaped by my own positionality and the questions and communities that link me to these stories, this past. As a young woman raised by Latter-day Saint converts, my Diné father and white mother, I started to ask what everyday teachings of the Church of Jesus Christ of Latter-day Saints mean to my Diné kin. My father dedicated his life to American Indian health, working many years in Diné Bikéyah, Navajo lands, with healthcare and public health administration, while also upholding his faith in the church. Diné relate to land through language on a spiritual level.[6] But what happens when the sense of spirituality changes with the introduction of different religious interpretations, text, and terms? As language is considered sacred, how do ideas and terminologies of the sacred translate between Diné bizaad and English through the late twentieth century into the early twenty-first? This chapter delves into some cases and examples of Diné interpreters who shape such transitions and directions of meanings.

Diné engaged with Christianity during their earliest exchanges with Europeans, dating to the sixteenth century. While different forms and practices of Christianity have affected Diné for generations, Latter-day Saint missionaries did not come in larger numbers until the late twentieth century, especially in the 1970s. By the 1990s, thousands of Diné had joined the Church of Jesus Christ of Latter-day Saints, constituting nearly a quarter of the total Diné population.[7] In my 2023 book, *Diné dóó Gáamalii*, I trace the growth of the church and Mormonism among Diné in that period, focusing on Diné Latter-day Saint perspectives and experiences.[8] Drawing from this research, I want to highlight the significance of Diné interpreters in the exchanges and dynamics that characterized and formed Diné dóó Gáamalii (Navajo Latter-day Saint) communities.

This chapter is only a window into broader areas that require more analysis, such as the vast work of Diné interpreters and translators who created Latter-day

Saint missionary training materials in the late twentieth century. A team translated parts of the Book of Mormon into Diné bizaad by 1980. Some Diné interpreters and translators work for the church during general conferences, when high church leaders address the world with what they claim to be revelation and guidance.[9]

A Diné linguist, translator, and interpreter, Clayton Long has been part of an effort to complete the translation of the entire Book of Mormon, *Naaltsoos Mormon Wolyéhígíí*, in Diné bizaad. Long made a vow to translate the Book of Mormon because he believes that the book is "sealed" to his mother, grandmother, grandfather, and ancestors, who only spoke Diné bizaad. Clayton explains, "I made a decision that someday I want to translate this book for my mother and for my father . . . The Second Coming is coming. We have only scratched the surface on translation. The Lord wants (the Book of Mormon) in every language."[10] He also emphasizes that languages live through scriptures, and he hopes that Diné bizaad will live on through the Book of Mormon.[11]

Since there were only certain passages of the Book of Mormon previously translated, Long and Charlotta Lacy began to finish the translation in 2019. They developed a full first draft by 2022 and submitted it to an "ecclesiastical review committee" with the hope that the full text of the scriptures would soon become available. Lacy articulates the significance of Diné bizaad to her people, specifically relating to language in the sense of spirituality and religion: "We are spoken to in our mother language, we really feel the love, peace, hope and harmony. All those words come to not only our minds but also to our hearts. And I feel that some of the words that we use, it has a different feeling when we say it in English, compared to when we say it in Navajo."[12] Speaking and expressing themselves in Diné bizaad with access to church teachings forms the basis of Diné dóó Gáamalii identities. Indeed, some Diné interpreters, as converts and believers themselves, were instrumental in making the Church of Jesus Christ of Latter-day Saints one of the most influential churches in the Navajo Nation by the late twentieth and early twenty-first centuries.[13]

The term *Gáamalii* first impressed upon me in Iyanbito on the day that my husband and I were walking around the area. Iyanbito was the place and site of my first deepest memory of the term that interpreters formed by conveying the concept of and identifying "Mormons." As we passed the hogans and scattered houses on our walk in Iyanbito, some Diné neighbors pointed with their lips at my husband and shouted, "Gáamalii!" Maybe they envisioned my husband, a blonde and blue-eyed Bilagáana, wearing a white shirt, necktie, and dress pants like the missionaries. He actually went on a mission for the church when he was nineteen years old, as expected of Latter-day Saint young men.[14] My husband is both Gáamalii dóó Bilagáana, Latter-day Saint, and white American. But Diné would only call him Gáamalii, because they emphasize a difference between general white Americans and Latter-day Saints, who are commonly and historically known as "Mormons."

During the late 1940s and 1950s, linguists Robert W. Young and Morgan William worked with Diné elders such as Hastiin Biyo' Łání Yée Biye' to record their histories, especially in the Diné community of Ramah at the crossroads of Diné, Pueblo, and white settler-colonizer, specifically Latter-day Saint, convergences in what became known as New Mexico.[15] In Ramah and later other parts of Diné Bikéyah, they noted how Diné distinguished white Latter-day Saints from other whites through the terms *Gáamalii* and *Máamalii*, which they assumed were Diné forms of pronouncing "Mormon."[16]

I often wondered about the origins of Gáamalii and what it means in Diné bizaad. My father who speaks Diné bizaad as his mother tongue did not know if Gáamalii meant anything other than "Mormon" to Diné, and other fluent speakers responded in a similar way to my question. The roots of the Diné word puzzled them.

During the 2023 annual conference of the Native American and Indigenous Studies Association, in Tkaronto, I talked with a Diné scholar and ethnomusicologist, Renata Yazzie, who shared with me her grandfather's story about the word Gáamalii, and she consented to me repeating it. Yazzie asked if I knew the meaning of "Gáamalii," and I explained how I could not find anything else other than the work of Young and Morgan with Diné elders that describe it as a Diné adaption of "Mormon." She has a family history with the Reformed Church and Presbyterian background, and her research focuses on Christian Diné hymns and music.[17]

Her grandfather told her that there were Mormon missionaries trying to proselytize to a Diné elderly man who did not speak English, and the missionaries did not understand and could not communicate in Diné bizaad. The elderly man knew that the missionaries were Mormon, which Diné pronounced as "Máamalii." He wanted the missionaries to leave him alone, so he shouted at them: "Go, Máamalii!" or "Get, Máamalii!" Together, the words blurred and sounded like "Gáa-Máalii." Other Diné heard of this story and started to say "Gáamalii" ever since to refer to Mormons. It does not matter if the story happened exactly as it was told, because it is meaningful and telling. Some Diné believe it, and it reveals how Diné have viewed Mormons as pests. The grandfather who told the story was a religious and spiritual leader, especially among Diné Christians of the Presbyterian faith. Renata grew up affiliated with the Reformed Church, which is the same church in Rehoboth where many of my family live and have some connection with it.

In the same conference panel where I met Yazzie, titled "Aural Resuscitations: Breathing Life into Our Songs, Oral Histories, and Knowledges," Unangax̂ scholar Haliehana Alag̃um Ayagaa Stepetin caught my attention with her reference to "translation as violence."[18] An African studies scholar, Elana Jefferson-Tatum, addresses the "violence of translation" in her 2015 article, calling out how Euro-centric translations "privilege Western and Christian normative social standards over local ideologies."[19] Focusing on Dahomean society and European colonial narratives and translations of violence, Jefferson-Tatum explains that the European colonizer "narratives tell us more about the colonial ideology of othering than about the moral and social parameters of Dahomean society. Colonial narratives—extensions of a 'know and conquer' imperialist agenda—resulted in the signification and control of African bodies."[20] In the context of Diné experiences, English translations, specifically those of a Latter-day Saint framework, change meanings and have the potential of causing harm. The interpreter directs and carries out the translation, which could cause damage instead of bridge-building and connecting as many scholars portray interpreters' work.[21] While interpreters know their aims, they may not realize the full impacts of their actions, such as the violence of translation that can be intergenerational and enduring.

During the second half of the twentieth century, under the leadership of Spencer W. Kimball, the Church of Jesus Christ of Latter-day Saints developed extensive programs for Native Americans that especially spread among Diné. Since most Diné did not attend schools until after World War II, generations such as that of my father knew Diné bizaad as their first language and their parents may have not spoken or learned English. Diné culture, language, and spiritual ways of life surrounded my father's generation, even though he also went to a boarding school that sought to erase and suppress such aspects of Diné identity. My father was one of many Diné who knew and embraced Diné teachings of *hózhǫ́*, a central teaching and ideal of beauty, harmony, and happiness, although he converted and joined the church. Under Kimball's supervision and leadership, the church developed an intricate American Indian Program, including "Lamanite" (or American Indian) missions such as the Southwest Indian Mission, Lamanite congregations, Indian seminaries, the Indian Student Placement Program, and the BYU Indian Education Program. Kimball's legacy has continued to shape the identity of Diné dóó Gáamalii, while they have also faced different challenges and experiences in the generations after his leadership.[22]

Only a few scholars have contributed to understanding Mormonism among Native Americans in the twentieth century and even fewer have addressed experiences of Mormonism on the level of specific Native Nations and peoples. Among the many diverse Indigenous peoples in the Americas, there are many cultures and languages, reflecting the multiple ways that concepts of church teachings can be perceived and understood in various contexts. In her work, Elise Boxer addresses overarching questions and brings a central framework to understanding Mormon-Indigenous relations by applying decolonizing methodologies to the study of Mormonism, which has undeniable roots among Indigenous peoples.[23] The Book of Mormon, the foundational text of Mormonism, noted in its original introduction that the book was "written to the Lamanites" and then identified American Indians as the descendants of Lamanites.[24] Indeed, many Latter-day Saints, including the church's founder, Joseph Smith Jr., claimed that Native Americans were the posterity of the Lamanites—an ancient civilization of Israelites that came to the Americas where they lived in cycles of prosperity, war, and destruction with other peoples that branched from the Israel family of a prophet named Lehi, all described and traced in the Book of Mormon.[25] Unsurprisingly in this context, members of the church often equated all Native Americans with "Lamanites." Some scholars such as Thomas Murphy pioneered what has become known as Lamanite studies or critical Indigenous Mormon studies, which other scholars such as Hokulani Aikau, Elise Boxer, Angelo Baca, Arcia Tecun, and Hemoperekei Simon have expanded upon by using a critical Indigenous studies lens to unpack and emphasize Indigenous experiences and perspectives of Mormonism.[26] These scholars foremostly point out the forms of colonialism that white Latter-day Saints used to control and dispossess Indigenous peoples, specifically Native Americans, Indigenous Pacific Islanders such as Native Hawaiians and Māori peoples, and Indigenous peoples of the Americas considered Latiné (or Latinx). Murphy in particular questioned the general Mormon beliefs that equated Native Americans with Lamanites.[27] The church has since moved away from widely using the term "Lamanite" to refer to Native Americans or any living people by the early twenty-first century.[28]

For those seeking to understand Diné-specific Latter-day Saint experiences, there is even less scholarship and dialogue, and it is often scattered.[29] Robert McPherson is a historian who has worked primarily with Diné communities in southeastern Utah through oral histories and a variety of primary sources such as archival documents. He coauthored a book to share the autobiography of a Diné Latter-day Saint named Jim Dandy. McPherson and Dandy collaborated with Sarah E. Burak to write *Navajo Tradition, Mormon Life*, which underscores what the authors framed as a kind "syncretism" in Dandy's life as he sought balance of Diné and Latter-day Saint spiritual ways of life.[30] Another scholar, Steve Pavlik, also addresses ideas of syncretism among Diné and Christian beliefs.[31] He points out that "Mormonism allows [young Diné] a dual identity" as they "become acculturated to white society, yet feel the need to also maintain an Indian identity."[32]

Syncretism refers to how Diné dóó Gáamalii draw from both Diné ancestral teachings and Latter-day Saint teachings, but such a framework implies that their faith is not a cohesive whole but rather consists of potentially incongruent pieces of several faiths. For some Diné dóó Gáamalii, as this chapter introduces, their faith is whole and interwoven, even when others including those from respective Diné and Latter-day Saint communities might perceive them otherwise. Conversion is a closely related concept, signifying how people not only join the church but also sense "turning their hearts" and believing in a faith that changes them. Many Diné dóó Gáamalii identify as converts, but there can be different perspectives of conversion and converts. While Latter-day Saints seek "converts" to teach and baptize, many Diné worry about losing their ancestral spiritual ways. When they join the church, they might assume the title of "convert," but at least for some, such as Jim Dandy, they are not rejecting their Diné spirituality but adding another layer to it—as part of multiple or multifaceted religious identities.

Dandy was an interpreter in his own right, who described to McPherson and Burak along with the public readers of his book Diné ancestral teachings and terms that he perceived as a Diné Latter-day Saint convert. He was born into a family and home immersed in Diné bizaad and Diné lifeways. Missionaries and later educational programs introduced and taught him not only English but the meanings of Latter-day Saint terms.[33] Dandy participated in the Indian Student Placement Program, known as "Placement," that the church established to arrange for baptized Latter-day Saint youth to live and attend public schools with Latter-day Saint families off Native American reservations. Similar to Indian boarding schools, the Placement program emphasized teaching English and curriculum designed for assimilation to white American society. Unlike Indian boarding schools, Latter-day Saint church officials designed Placement to prioritize an immersive experience in a Latter-day Saint family that upheld principles of the church.[34] To church officials and organizers, teaching the secular school curriculum of language and other subjects was not as important as inculcating Latter-day

Saint Native American youth in church teachings and values. As youth like Dandy joined the Placement program, some later became interpreters for the church by returning to their Diné communities and navigating different worlds.[35]

Diné Interpreters before Placement

Although thousands of Diné participated in the Placement program after it started in the 1950s, prior to this period only a few Diné decided to join the church and served as interpreters and advocates for the church.[36] One of these converts, Ruth Polacca, articulated her testimony about her faith: "We Navajo people know the true gospel of our forefathers are told by our Latter-day Saint missionaries. Our goal is to bring unto the Lamanites more missionaries which is to build character ... and knowledge of the Lord."[37] In 1948, while seeking to recuperate and heal from his serious medical conditions, an apostle of the church at the time named Spencer W. Kimball wanted to stay by the Polacca family on the Navajo reservation in their home of Crystal, New Mexico.[38] Ruth Polacca and her husband, Howela, became long-lasting friends with Kimball, and they actively proselytized for the church in Diné Bikéyah. In a 1950 district conference on the reservation in Toadlena, New Mexico, Polacca drew connections between the Book of Mormon and Diné teachings that "the Lord would in His own due time reveal his words to our people."[39] She believed that Latter-day Saint missionaries conveyed to her people the full truth foreseen by her ancestors.

Clyde Beyal is one of the few named Diné interpreters, as most of them remain unnamed or difficult to trace in records. They helped make recordings that the white missionaries and those who did not speak Diné bizaad, such as Pacific Islander and other diverse missionaries, would then play at meetings to introduce the church teachings to Diné populations in Diné Bikéyah.[40] Little is known about Diné interpreters such as Beyal, who laid the foundations for Latter-day Saint missions after World War II. They paved the way for translation work in the "Lamanite Era" that Kimball spearheaded. Kimball was called as an apostle in the church in 1943 and later became the president of the church between 1973 and 1985.

Ruth Polacca carried the name of her grandfather who was known historically as an interpreter, Jesus Arviso. Kimball directly interviewed Ruth Jesus Arviso Polacca in Gallup, New Mexico, in 1953, creating an oral history that the church archives preserve. I had never heard of a church apostle, president, or prophet being an oral historian before, interviewing a Native American to record the histories of Indigenous peoples.

Polacca shared stories of her grandparents, who survived the Long Walk when the U.S. military violently removed Diné from their ancestral homelands. Her grandmother told her that many Diné "died from starvation" and suffered while forced to stay four years at Fort Sumner, known as the "Land of Suffering" or Hwééłdi to Diné.[41] Her grandfather Jesus Arviso became known as a guide to the U.S. military and an interpreter in the negotiations that led to the Treaty of 1868, which set the terms for Diné to return to their homelands within the Four Sacred Mountains from their internment at Hwééłdi.[42] He was not considered born as Diné but was of Hispanic lineage and raised and married into Diné families, spending the bulk of his life with Diné. Arviso told Polacca that the U.S. government "promised the Navajo people that they will come back on the reservation and give them a place to live and take their children and educate them."[43]

In the interview with Polacca, Kimball expressed his admiration of Ruth and Howela Polacca as "two of the finest people that I've ever known." He continued to tell her that "you have a fine family and I love you for your strength and your fortitude and for your courage. You're about the first members of the Church in this area."[44] Polacca had worked for the church for about fourteen years at the time of their interview. Kimball asked Polacca questions to understand Diné culture, such as the meaning of names and naming. Polacca told him that Diné women "are named after the warriors" and that Diné are "supposed to keep [certain names] sacred."[45] Kimball knew that Polacca had been through the Latter-day Saint temple, and he asked her if she knew of any "old legends" or traditions that "seem to correspond in some degree with the temple ordinance."[46] Polacca confirmed that "in each room [of the temple] I can see the things that correspond with our Indian tradition," and she discusses these similarities with Kimball. Although they spoke directly to each other in English, Polacca served as a kind of interpreter for the Latter-day Saint apostle and prophet who did not know the ceremonies, practices, and language of Diné but wanted to understand possible connections.

A church leader and convert of the church from Germany, Dieter F. Uchtdorf, was a part of the First Presidency of the church when he said, "We members of this church speak many languages, and we come from many cultures, but we share the same blessings of the gospel. This is truly a universal church, with members spread across the nations of the earth proclaiming the universal message of the gospel of Jesus Christ to all, irrespective of language, race, or ethnic roots."[47] These ideas of universalism have stirred some debates, with sensitivities over how terms and teachings of the church are upheld. Māori scholar Gina Colvin, for example, is wary of a "Mormon culture," which seeks to homogenize a sense of being "Mormon" or Latter-day Saint as conforming to white American cultural practices and interpretations.⁴⁸

Diverse Diné Latter-day Saint Interpretations

Some Diné Latter-day Saints have tried to meet the expectations of predominantly white American church leaders and members, even at the expense of their culture and language. As bishop of the Window Rock Ward in the Navajo Nation during the 1990s Arnold Yazzie explained:

> There are some older people . . . they would like to hear instructions in the Navajo language, to be taught in Navajo in the Church standards, the gospel. . . . We had one brother teaching a class that was making a lot of references back to Navajo things, Navajo religion. People were getting confused, so we had to put a stop to that. . . . He was using too much of that, as opposed to teaching what we are instructed to teach from the manuals and using the scriptures. . . . It was interesting, but at the same time, the Church doesn't say to present your lessons that way.⁴⁹

In his comments, Yazzie differentiated between two manifestations of Diné cultural traditions among Diné congregations. To him, Diné bizaad is a part of culture that Diné Latter-day Saints can guard and encourage. But Yazzie then pinpointed how an inappropriate use of Diné culture occurs when Diné Latter-day Saints compare and combine components of Diné cosmology with Latter-day Saint teachings. He based these judgments on the expectations and instructions of church officials. Some Diné have embraced Latter-day Saint teachings as a way to liberation; for example, Diné scholar Moroni Benally claims that the Book of Mormon has been not only a tool of colonialism but also a tool for decolonization and resistance among Diné.⁵⁰ It is through the practice of translation and interpretation that Diné have applied the scriptures and religious teachings for their needs and purposes.

As one Diné Latter-day Saint, Wallace Brown, asserts, "Knowing that what I know about the traditional and cultural teachings of the Diné, if the Diné people knew for sure the ceremonials, the songs, and the prayers for real, they would understand that that was the only way that our people could preserve the teachings and prophecies that were going to come to pass."⁵¹ Echoing Ruth Polacca's testimony from previous decades, Brown views the church as setting the path to fulfill Diné ancestral teachings and prophecies. Another Diné Latter-day Saint, Ruby Whitesinger Benally, also referred to the connections between Diné and Latter-day Saint ceremonies, emphasizing the spiritual power of Diné bizaad. Hearing and speaking Diné bizaad in phrases such as "Diyin ayóó'ánhó'nínígíí, ba'áłchíní niidlíinii, doo béézhdoot'ą́ą́' át'ée da" ("Our Father in Heaven's love for us, His children, surpasses by far our ability to comprehend"), for example, would mean more to her than in the English language.[52]

Diné dóó Gáamalii Interpreters and Nanabah Bia Begay

In the case study that follows, I focus on a recorded oral history between three Gáamalii, or Latter-day Saints, to illuminate the complex dynamics and what sometimes is misunderstood in translation with Diné dóó Gáamalii interpreters. The three Gáamalii come from different lenses and positions: one was a church historian and employee; another a bilingual Diné Latter-day Saint; and the third a monolingual Diné bizaad–speaking Latter-day Saint elder. This section presents personal reflections and a discourse with my father, Phillip L. Smith, who has helped me to interpret Diné dóó Gáamalii oral histories. We worked together to interpret a special archival source, an oral history of a monolingual Diné convert, that the church historians recorded and hold in the special collections and archives of the Church Library in Salt Lake City, Utah. These reflections offer insights into research with Native American Latter-day Saints and the need for serious consideration of interpreters.

My father's first language is Diné bizaad, but I did not start to learn the language until I was in college. I continue to study and try to learn Diné bizaad. Along with other relatives, my father has been a major resource to me in my research and understandings of Diné bizaad and culture. While I was conducting research for my book, *Diné dóó Gáamalii*, I came across a unique oral history in the Church History Library. Matthew Heiss, a church employee and historian for the Church History Department, directed me to the source when we were discussing the oral histories that he recorded in the Navajo Nation from the 1990s. He told me that one of his most impressive experiences on the reservation was when he interviewed a Diné elder with the assistance of an interpreter.

A mentor, Jessie Embry, who had written extensively about Latter-day Saint history and worked especially with diverse LDS oral histories, introduced me to Heiss. In the course of his travels throughout the world recording oral histories for the church, Heiss recorded dozens of oral histories in the Navajo Nation between

1991 and 1997. He visited the Navajo Nation, specifically areas that were part of newly formed Latter-day Saint "stakes" (a large congregational unit comparable to a diocese) in Chinle and Tuba City respectively. Part of his task was to record oral histories of Latter-day Saints who contributed to the institutional development and leadership of the church in those regions. Heiss remembered the controversy and negative media attention on the church around the time, in 1989, when Latter-day Saint officials excommunicated one of the first Native American general authorities of the church, George P. Lee, who was a Diné man from the Navajo reservation.

After years of serving in the church as a missionary and leader, Lee publicly criticized church leaders in the late 1980s, claiming that they were guilty of a "silent, subtle scriptural and spiritual slaughter" of the "Lamanites" (referring to Native Americans).[53] Lee apostatized, seeking to open and lead his own religious movement based in the Navajo Nation.[54] Heiss noted that the church suddenly dedicated stakes on the reservation, following only a few years after Lee's excommunication. He wondered how the controversy affected Diné Latter-day Saints on the reservation and elsewhere.[55]

In *Diné dóó Gáamalii*, I refer to sixteen of the oral histories he facilitated throughout the Navajo Nation during the 1990s, primarily in the western region in areas such as Chinle, Window Rock, and Kayenta. Heiss received support for planning his oral history visits and recruiting interviewees from local church leaders of the new stakes, such as President Edward W. McCombs and his wife Ruth Ann McCombs of the Chinle Stake. McCombs referred Heiss to church auxiliaries and leaders in the region, but he insisted that Heiss meet and interview an elderly woman in the community of Many Farms near Chinle—the newly selected stake center in the Navajo Nation. He also arranged for an interpreter from the local Diné congregation, Helena Yellowhair, whom Heiss did not have enough time to meet before the interview. Heiss normally tries to meet with interpreters before the scheduled interview, and he also prefers to conduct an oral history of the interpreter as well. In the context of this oral history, he did not follow either of those typical parts of his protocol.

In 1997 Heiss interviewed Nanabah Bia Begay, who was estimated to be about ninety-three years old at the time, in Many Farms, Navajo Nation, with Helena Yellowhair as a Diné interpreter. I first reviewed the transcript of the interview in the Church History Library. I realized that the transcript did not include any of the discourse in Diné bizaad. Only a conversation between Heiss and Yellowhair appeared in the transcript. Knowing and studying several languages, I knew that translation changes much of the meanings, and so I felt the need to listen to the interview recording that preserved the original discourse with all English and Diné bizaad parts. In interviews with interpreters, multiple conversations occur.

Heiss remembers how Nanabah "dressed to the nines," wearing a long purple velvet skirt with a beautiful turquoise belt. "She just looked absolutely amazing," and "she put on her finest," which "set the tone" to Heiss.[56] He had traveled the world, interviewing thousands, but this oral history impressed him because he had never met someone like Nanabah before. He noticed her many wrinkles and realized that he was meeting someone who was over ninety years old with real connections to another era and place. He hoped that the interpreter would not "get in his way" of understanding and connecting with her. He knew little about Yellowhair, but he could tell that she knew Nanabah. They did not seem to be direct relatives but were familiar with each other, probably from going to church together. Heiss assumes that the stake president McCombs arranged for Yellowhair to interpret for him, but he does not recall all the details since the interview was over twenty years ago in 1997.

Begay and her oral history stood out to Heiss, because she was the only Diné Latter-day Saint that he interviewed who was a monolingual Diné elder in Diné bizaad. Of over one hundred oral histories with Native American Latter-day Saints that either the Charles Redd Center for Western Studies at Brigham Young University or the Church History Department sponsored, primarily with Diné Latter-day Saints conducted between the 1990s and 2000s, Nanabah Bia Begay's oral history is the only one I know of that focuses on a Diné bizaad monolingual oral history narrator (or interviewee).[57]

From my research with Diné oral histories of the Doris Duke project, I found it common for interviews with Diné elders who spoke only Diné bizaad to be accessible in the archives exclusively through an interpreter's English translation. In my first book, *The Earth Memory Compass*, for example, I introduce a source featuring a Diné elder called Hopi-Hopi whom a Diné oral historian and interpreter, Tom Ration, interviewed for the Doris Duke Collection of American Indian Oral History in 1969. The transcripts of the interview are only in English, whereas the oral history reveals that Hopi-Hopi did not speak English. The methodology and translation process of the oral history is opaque. Some researchers might access the English translation of the oral history and not ask about the original recording in Diné bizaad. I traveled to the Center for Southwest Research in New Mexico to access the oral history recording to see if I could hear the original words in Diné bizaad of Hopi-Hopi. When I accessed and listened to the recording, I could only hear a deep voice rattling in English, matching the words of the transcript. I assumed

FIG 6. Helena Yellowhair. Digital watercolor by Ricky Hadi, based on a photograph of, and courtesy of, Helena Yellowhair, posted on Facebook, 2024.

it was Tom Ration speaking out loud and recording his translations of what the elder had said, but I could not find any definitive description of this process.

Was it Tom Ration's voice on the recording? Was the Diné elder Hopi-Hopi's voice recorded at all? When I realized that I could not hear or know what Hopi-Hopi had actually said in Diné bizaad, I felt that a key part of the source was missing from the archives.[58] This experience shaped my approach to learning about Nanabah Begay's oral history in the Church Library. When I accessed Begay's oral history transcript, the entire transcript was written in English, representing a conversation between Heiss and Yellowhair without any of the actual words in Diné bizaad of the featured oral history narrator, Nanabah Begay.

Interpreters of Diné dóó Gáamalii 167

Traveling to the church archives in Salt Lake City, I requested to listen to the audio recording of the interview to see if there was a situation similar to Hopi-Hopi's interview. The audio recording included the voice of Nanabah Begay and her words in Diné bizaad. Since I was beginning to learn the language, I relied on my father's assistance to translate the audio recording and to help me understand Helena Yellowhair as an interpreter. My father's positionality as a Diné Latter-day Saint convert shaped his own interpretations of the exchange, which I recognize and try to point out. This process reveals a kaleidoscope of interpretations and perspectives that might reflect each other but with changing patterns and dynamics. While more questions remain such as understanding who Yellowhair and Begay actually were more fully, here I concentrate on this short oral history as a window into their lives and backgrounds. I can hypothesize and share possibilities of their backgrounds, but they are gestures toward understanding what Yellowhair and Begay's contemporaries experienced as well as what they themselves might have directly experienced, too.

In this oral history, there were two main exchanges: one between Yellowhair and Heiss, conducted in English, and another between Yellowhair and Begay, conducted in Diné bizaad. The audiotape and transcript preserve little of the nonverbal communication between the three individuals. Initially, for my own research purposes, I asked my father to go to the archives and listen to the tape that was only available there, so that he could transcribe the Diné bizaad discourse for me. My father did not have enough time in the archives to transcribe the Diné bizaad parts, so I then arranged with the Church Library to allow us more time and access to the recording to transcribe the Diné bizaad discourse of the interview. I offered to provide this revised transcript to the library, which I did about a year after receiving access to the recording.

Over the course of several months, my father listened carefully to the recordings and transcribed everything, including the Diné bizaad portion. He then provided his own translation of the Diné bizaad discourse. The revised transcript preserves Begay's words in Diné bizaad, and it allows one to see how interviews with interpreters can follow two distinct conversations and directions: one between the interpreter and the interviewer and the other between the interpreter and the interviewee. In the case of Begay's oral history and interview, I learn how Diné describe their membership and experience in the church using their language and the worldviews contained in it—the language that connects them to their ancestors since time immemorial. As I highlight certain excerpts from the oral history, I navigate the interpretations of the moment in the past, specifically, the context of 1997 during the interview, and my own and my father's interpretations.

Heiss begins the oral history with basic questions, getting to know Nanabah Begay and her background. Heiss knew little about the interpreter, Yellowhair, but the oral history reveals as much about her as about Nanabah Begay. Yellowhair did not demonstrate a kind of professional interpreter training or approach, but she showed an effort to help by addressing what she thought that Heiss expected or wanted to hear as an employee of the church.

In one example, in the following excerpt of the transcript based on my father's work with the oral history audiotape, Heiss asks a question referring to how Begay attends and participates in Latter-day Saint ceremonies in the temple:

MATTHEW HEISS: And, tell me how you feel about going to the temple, and what you feel in your heart in the temple?

HELENA YELLOWHAIR: 'Ako 'ałnanidago la'. Háálá nt'éé łe, nijei' biyi dóó háálá la nt'éé łe? Niłni.

PHILLIP SMITH'S TRANSLATION: Well, when you go there [to the temple], how is your heart and how are you? He said.

NANABAH BEGAY: Yá'át'ééh. Jó shijei' 'eí bił hózhǫ́. 'Ako' 'eí kwe'é 'eí shikéé baa dahaas'ą́ąnígíí 'eí 'ąąn' nlei' 'azee' 'ał'i'nígí sha'yéé' nit'i'go 'ako, 'ako shił tadi'aash. 'Akéédę́ę́ nili'. Salena wolyé. 'Eí ts'ídá 'alaa'ho' nahali, jó 'ako tadóó bee nizaadi nagha'. Dóó yá'á'shóó da', na'ash. Bilagáana yił sik'é'.

SMITH'S TRANSLATION: Good. My heart is happy. But here, my foot has problems, but they are taking care of it at the hospital, where she takes me around (my youngest daughter). Her name is Salena. She is most active. She lives far away. It is difficult where they are. She is married to a white.

YELLOWHAIR: She said her youngest daughter, named Salena who is . . . aah, . . . married to a white, says she lives . . .[59]

[Yellowhair then asks the following question in Diné bizaad to Begay] Haidi' bighan? Háádíísh bighan? [Where does she live?]

BEGAY: Sal Laa [Salt Lake City, Utah].

YELLOWHAIR: In Salt Lake. She lives in Salt Lake some place . . . and she takes her to the temple, and she says she feels really good about the temple and really happy about it. And she is thankful that her daughter is able to take her to over there.[60]

Smith's translation reveals that Begay may have misunderstood the questions as interpreted by Yellowhair. Begay explained that her heart was in good health, but her body suffers in other areas such as her foot. To Heiss, Yellowhair did not mention Begay's reference to her health and how her daughter takes her to the hospital. Instead, Yellowhair alters Begay's message to convey that her daughter Salena takes Begay to the temple. Entrance and work in the temple are one of the greatest honors and ceremonial practices for Latter-day Saints, which is why Yellowhair tries to direct the interpretations to Latter-day Saint ideas about the temple. Interpretation is a difficult task, especially when interpreters must work quickly and directly as Yellowhair did. However, the reader wonders if Begay really had the opportunity to express her feelings and describe her experience of going to the temple because of miscommunication. Yellowhair was also a member of the church, and she seems to intentionally offer the responses that she expects Heiss would want to hear as a church employee. My father is also Diné dóó Gáamalii, which made me realize that he brought his own lens as a second interpreter and translator of the recording and conversation. But he was not present in person with Begay like Yellowhair, and he could not affect the conversation by that presence and nonverbal communication (all that the transcript and audio recording do not capture).

Heiss begins to ask questions comparable to Kimball's inquiries with Polacca about possible similarities between Latter-day Saint temple practices and Diné ceremonies:

> HEISS: Does what you learn in the temple, aaahmm . . . , correspond to the Navajo belief?
>
> YELLOWHAIR: Díídi 'nlei' sodizin bahoghan nisini'yá hádą́ą́' la'—t'áá ni' Diné' béé 'ól'í'nígíí' díí Diné binahaghá' 'at'é'ígíí béé ałchi'i'. Ninanil. Niłni háléé' yit'áo t'á' áálhééhól't'é' lá' ní'.
>
> SMITH'S TRANSLATION: When you went to the Church (temple), did you compare it to the Navajo religion? He said. How are they similar? He said.
>
> BEGAY: 'Aoo', jó' eí', eí' 'ako't'é'. 'Ei' Diné binahghá' 'ado kwo'dóó. Tá'dídíín da' 'eí' dóó bee nizh'ííd da.
>
> SMITH'S TRANSLATION: Yes, well, it, it is like that. The Navajo Religion and here. The Sacred Corn Pollen and others, I just don't bother with it.[61]
>
> YELLOWHAIR: Jó', nlei tádíín' niya' háádę́ę́, nlei temple 'adi', 'eí' Hozhǫ́' k'é'gó táhó'dígís' naha'linígíí 'at'áo 'eí' nlei' éé dahaltééh dóó 'ado 'at'é'ígíí 'eí' ła hait'áo táásh 'akót'é' nahalin?

170 *Along the Borders*

SMITH'S TRANSLATION: Well, when you went to the temple, there like the Blessing Way washing and like the dressings; and how they are . . . how do they look?

BEGAY: 'Aoo'. 'Akot'é'. 'Aoo'. T'áá'í'yíz'shíí, t'aa'í'yíz'shíí yá'át'ééh. Akot'é'gó' shił tadi'aash. 'Aoo, jó 'ako' daat'éégó nidahwindłah. 'Ako' díí 'eí' hoł beedahozinígíí 'eí' shika' 'áándá'jíl'wó' dóó.

SMITH'S TRANSLATION: Yes, it is like that. Yes. I really like it. I like it. She takes me around like that. Well, it is where it is difficult; therefore, those who know, should be helping me.

YELLOWHAIR: She said she put "my Navajo Tradition stuff back, and I don't bother it to this day because I like the temple."

As in the earlier example, this part of the transcript reveals differences in the interpretations that Yellowhair provides Heiss. My father's translations also present a particular context, which emphasizes the significance of transcribing the actual Diné bizaad discourse between Yellowhair and Begay. My father translated "Diné binahaghá,'" for example, as "Navajo Religion" (that he capitalized). Diné consider "nahaghá" as ritual. Diné did not traditionally have a concept for "religion" but used terms to convey ways of life. In the context of Yellowhair and Begay's conversation, they referred to "Diné binahaghá'" as religion (or at least Yellowhair meant to do so). This example shows how Yellowhair and Begay engaged in a separate dialogue by discussing different Diné rituals and concepts, such as "Tá'dídíín" (Corn Pollen), that do not appear in the original English only transcript.[62] Diné have communicated with Diyin Dine'é, Holy People, with Tádídíín as a "conduit" since time immemorial.[63] Heiss was left out of the discussions concerning the Sacred Corn Pollen and Blessingway references. The revised and translated transcript with Diné bizaad parts reveals how Diné dóó Gáamalii share thoughts with each other about the correlations between Diné traditional ways of life and the Latter-day Saint practices and teachings.

Despite some of the misinterpretations and multiple conversations in the interview, Begay was able to express in her own language of Diné bizaad her decision to prepare and enter the temple, representing dedication to the Latter-day Saint faith. Yellowhair asked her, "'Ako'. Háá'nit'é łe, 'akoo ałnanidáágó? [Well, how are you when you go there?]" Begay answered, "'Ako'. Shijéí 'eíya' yá'át'ééh. Shinits'ikéés nlei' yá'át'ééh [Well, my heart is good. My mind/thinking is good]."[64] I wonder why Begay could refer to her "heart" being good at that moment, when she thinks specifically about the temple, as compared to the first time that Yellowhair tried to ask her how her "heart" was when talking more broadly about the church and faith.

In the oral history, which I recognize as a form of dialogue, understandings grow and take new directions with interpretations flowing like a waterfall. Maybe it took more time for Begay to understand what Yellowhorse and Heiss were asking her and seeking to learn about her perspective and experience in the church. The words needed to continue to flow and converge into a common understanding. While Begay could recognize connections between Diné and Latter-day Saint lifeways as the second example indicates, she chose to follow Latter-day Saint teachings with "a good heart and mind" as a Diné elderly woman.[65] These cases also illustrate the power of interpreters in recording history, particularly Diné dóó Gáamalii history, as interpreters generate the sources that historians trace to draft and tell narratives of the past.

At the end of the oral history with Nanabah Begay, Heiss asks her to "bear her testimony." Before Yellowhair interprets the request for Begay, she describes how "Sister Begay" gave her testimony in church after a trip to the Mesa temple and how a temple worker who "saw Sister Begay at the temple" was also present and stood up to share her testimony. On the first Sunday of the month, Latter-day Saint congregations open the pulpit to anyone who wants to talk about their faith in Jesus Christ and the church teachings in a practice known as a "fast and testimony meeting."[66] Yellowhair remembers hearing the testimonies of Begay and the temple worker and that "there was a spiritual moment for her to feel the spirit there."[67]

Yellowhair said the following to Begay to encourage her to respond to Heiss and his request to hear her testimony of the church: "Diyiin yadahanii'go [they are praising the Holy Spirit in reference to people in church]—shi' 'ei' t'aa'aani 'at'e' nisin [truthfulness or real], dii nlei 'ata' alna' naashdah [returning] daniigo, la 'ako' daniile' [as for me, I know this is true when I return there such as church/temple/holy places] . . . niish 'ako'teego la hadii'dzi [What about you? Would you say the same thing]? Nilni [He said]?"[68]

My father, who assisted me with these translations, explained that literal translations do not make sense in Diné bizaad if a person tries to translate sentence by sentence or thought by thought. The translation does not match word for word. Because of these dynamics of translation, Yellowhair was bearing her testimony and asking if Nanbah Begay can say the same about her testimony. Although little is recorded about Yellowhair and her story in any known church archives, Yellowhair expresses her own faith in the church in between the lines and her interpretations for Heiss and Begay. Yellowhair understood Heiss and his purpose to record faith-promoting stories and experiences in the oral history, and she assumed the role as an interpreter to provide such a narrative.

Begay responded to Yellowhair's question and efforts to evoke her testimony in a way that Yellowhair probably did not expect, since her response was not testimony-building or affirming: "Begay: 'Ei' 'eiya' adin [I have none], nlei 'aadi' ei' dooda [No, I don't have anything. There is nothing there]. Jo [So] bilagáana 'eiya [those white people], jo nlei nahi' di t'eiya', dikwiishi nahai' [however many years] yeedaa 'akw'e'e' hasdzii' [how many years since the white people spoke]. T'aa' nahi' 'aji'—Chinili [They came one time to Chinli]. 'Ei' t'eiya taala'i'di 'adi' datsi' 'ako'dza' [I think it happened that way]."

Maybe Begay was trying to understand when the church became true, or maybe she was trying to say that she did not believe initially in the church but later her testimony formed. Yellowhair continued to prompt her: "Jo, hait'ao banitsi'ni-keez [Then *how* did you come to think about it]? Nilni. 'Ako.'" Yellowhair clarified the question further by asking, "'Eish diyiin ni'igii, 'ei' diish 'ako'tao hani'dziih nilnigo datsi' kodi yee ninil' halni' le? [Then, how did this thing that is holy come into your thoughts?]"

After these series of prompts and clarifications, Begay responds: "'Aoo. 'Akot'e... T'aahadee' 'i't'ego nt'ei' 'akot'e' doo ndzil niliigo doo 'ako't'e' [It was like that]. T'aa'nahol'go t'aa'aanii 'akwi' hashdzii'. 'Aoo. 'Ako' t'aa'anii yá'át'ééh [It was good to know it was true]. 'Iidaa' koji' dine' binahagha' [Navajo rituals/singing/worship/ceremony] ei', ei' bits'aniya [walking in the sense that a person was once with it but is separating from it] diniid [I walked away]."[69]

In Diné bizaad, my father notes that "the only way you move from something [as expressed in the language] is walking away from it." He also interpreted Begay's usage of "walking away" from Diné ancestral spiritual practices as a way of her conveying that "she didn't need it anymore."

From these last exchanges recorded in the oral history, Yellowhair interprets Begay for Heiss in the following: "She said she does have a testimony and that she... Just what I told you. When she came back from the temple, she bear her testimony. She said that when she bears her testimony to the people, and told them that I am now over here and... the traditional ways is behind me, past."[70] The oral history recording wraps up soon after this point. Begay explains that she is having a hard time with hearing, and she wishes that she could speak and understand more English while Heiss also apologizes for not being able to speak Navajo and wishes that he could speak it. Begay's frustration with her poor hearing might also

Interpreters of Diné dóó Gáamalii

help account for some of the miscommunication with Yellowhair. Maybe Begay could not fully hear the questions even if spoken in Diné bizaad.

The oral history interview ended earlier than most interviews that Heiss conducts, because Begay had livestock, specifically, sheep to take care of and was worried about them during their conversation. Heiss noticed that Yellowhair and Begay arrived and left together, assuming that Yellowhair most likely drove Begay to their meeting. Thus, he did not have an opportunity to interview Yellowhair as part of the Chinle stake oral histories. Heiss could tell when Begay suddenly became anxious during the interview, and Yellowhair explained Begay's need to care for her livestock. None of this exchange was recorded in the oral history, which Heiss later recounted to me in 2023.[71]

While Heiss felt honored and amazed to meet and hear Nanabah Begay, his oral history with Begay also recorded an exchange between two Diné Latter-day Saints that Yellowhair directed as an interpreter. Heiss did not realize that Begay's oral history reveals as much about Yellowhair, especially when the Diné bizaad parts of the interviews are transcribed and translated. Even as my father helped me with the translations, his positionality as a Diné Latter-day Saint shaped how he was reading and understanding the exchange. The precise meanings and what each person understood from the conversation may always be fleeting to grasp, but the processes of interpretation and translation with Diné dóó Gáamalii reveal what they want to reaffirm—that Diné can also be Latter-day Saints.

"Diné nishłį!" / "I Am Navajo!"

While my father assists me with interpreting and understanding Diné Latter-day Saint language and oral histories, his own story as a devout Diné dóó Gáamalii has shaped my work. My paternal grandfather banished my father from the family and home, after he joined the church. Soon after that traumatic rupture, my father accepted a call to serve in the LDS Southwest Indian Mission that encompassed Diné Bikéyah. While on his mission, he received a message that his father was dying. His mission president granted him permission to see his father in the hospital. My grandfather and father reconciled during their hospital visit, as my grandfather apologized to my father for their last encounter. That was the last time they saw each other. My father returned to his mission, and my grandfather passed away soon after their visit.[72]

My father believed and would bear testimony of his faith in the church before this experience with my grandfather, but this story has become an integral part of his conversion and identity as Diné dóó Gáamalii. One time I heard him share this experience with a group of Latter-day Saint Native American youth in the Franklin Second Ward of Provo, a Native American congregation, around 2012. The Franklin Second Ward is one of the few Native American congregational units that remain since the Kimball era and includes numerous Diné members. He told the youth how his family derided him for joining the church, claiming that he was no longer Diné. He exclaimed to the youth that while being Latter-day Saint, "I am Navajo! I am Navajo through and through!" Diné Latter-day Saints draw upon their personal experiences, memories, heritage, and Diné bizaad to live and express their spirituality. Internal fractions have persisted among Diné as to what direction and forms of change are permissible to define their people and future. Diné bizaad and sacred teachings, however, are interwoven into the fabric of Diné dóó Gáamalii identity, and Diné interpreters have shaped these meanings and identity through generations.

Notes

1. See Allison and Ashcroft, "New Mexico Range Plants"; and "Selected Plants of Navajo Rangelands."
2. "Iyanbito: Ayánni bitó (buffalo's water)—Eastern Agency"; and Cindy Yurth, "Where the Buffalo Roamed: After Tough Times, Little Iyanbito Is Poised to Grow," *Navajo Times*, May 23, 2013, https://navajotimes.com/news/chapters/052313iya.php.
3. "Iyanbito: Ayánni bitó (buffalo's water)—Eastern Agency."
4. Yurth, "Where the Buffalo Roamed."
5. Yurth, "Where the Buffalo Roamed."
6. Lee, *Nihikéyah*. Lee and the contributing authors delve into the diverse perspectives of Diné about their land with the common underpinnings of Diné language and spirituality.
7. Pavlik, "Of Saints and Lamanites," 21.
8. King, *Diné dóó Gáamalii*.
9. Martinich, "LDS Outreach among the Navajo."
10. Clayton Long cited in Joshua Rust, "Navajo Translators and Experts Work to Complete Standard Works," *BYU Universe*, June 5, 2023, https://universe.byu.edu/2023/06/05/navajo-translators-and-experts-work-to-complete-standard-works/#:~:text=Clayton%20long%20and%20charlotta%20lacy,the%20first%20draft%20in%202022.
11. Clayton Long, "Translation of the Book of Mormon into the Navajo Language," *BYU Universe*, YouTube video, posted on May 1, 2023, accessed September 30, 2023, https://youtu.be/f6nic0vdgd0?si=liubz6m4ua3o8dj2.

12. Charlotta Lacy cited in Rust, "Navajo Translators and Experts."
13. Fernanda Santos, "Some Find Path to Navajo Roots through Mormon Church," *New York Times*, October 30, 2013, https://www.nytimes.com/2013/10/31/us/for-some-the-path-to-navajo-values-weaves-through-the-mormon-church.html#:~:text=In%20a%20land%20troubled%20by,churches%20around%20it%20have%20struggled. Santos notes that membership in the Tuba City Stake (a regional cluster of Latter-day Saint congregations on the Navajo reservation) "has increased by 25 percent since 2008."
14. As of 2023 the officials of the Church of Jesus Christ of Latter-day Saints insist on using the full name of the church. Instead of always writing the full name of the church, I will use the term "church" to refer to it. Although the church currently avoids using "Mormon" as an identification, I will sometimes use the term "Mormon" based on historical references and other citations including what people say in quotes. The church also prefers Latter-day Saint as an adjective instead of "Mormon" or "LDS," but I use these different terms depending on the context and point in the chapter.
15. Note that Robert W. Young is a controversial figure for his translation and linguistic work in the Navajo Nation that continued to support the Americanization of Diné people, including their language. See Peery, "New Deal Navajo Linguistics."
16. Biyé, Young, and Morgan, *Ramah Navahos*, ii. It is also important to note that scholars have disproportionately studied the Diné community of Ramah, making unsubstantiated generalizations about Diné from throughout the Navajo Nation. Diné communities vary in their use of language and ways of life. See Bahr, "Multiplying Glimpses, Gleaning Genres," 57.
17. Yazzie, "Jesus Woodláájí Sin."
18. Learn more about Haliehana Alaĝum Ayagaa Stepetin and her work on her official website, "About," Haliehana Stepetin, accessed online June 8, 2023, https://www.haliehana.com; Stepetin, "Unangam Qaqamiiĝuu [Unangax̂ Subsistence] Cosmologies."
19. Jefferson-Tatum, "Violence of Translation," 279.
20. Jefferson-Tatum, "Violence of Translation," 310.
21. Scholars have depicted Native American women especially in this light as "intermediary," or a kind of bridge and connector. See Jager, *Malinche, Pocahontas, and Sacagawea*; Hebard, *Sacagawea*; and Nelson, *Interpreters with Lewis and Clark*.
22. Kimball also surrounded himself with people who supported and helped to drive his initiatives, such as the Indian Committee that he formed and Golden Buchanan and Clarence Bishop who were among facilitators and influencers of the Indian Student Placement Program. See Garrett, *Making Lamanites*, 77.
23. Boxer, "'This Is the Place!'"; and Boxer, "Book of Mormon as Mormon Settler Colonialism," 4.
24. Carrie A. Moore, "Debate Renewed with Change in Book of Mormon Introduction," *Deseret News*, November 8, 2007, https://www.deseret.com/2007/11/8/20052445/debate-renewed-with-change-in-book-of-mormon-introduction.

25. Mauss, *All Abraham's Children*, 50; and Boxer, "Book of Mormon as Mormon Settler Colonialism," 5.
26. See Boxer, "Book of Mormon as Mormon Settler Colonialism"; Murphy, "Other Mormon Histories"; Murphy, "Imagining Lamanites"; Thayne, "Blood of Father Lehi"; Mauss, *All Abraham's Children*, 10; Aikau, *A Chosen People, a Promised Land*; Newton, *Tiki and Temple*; Parker, "Queso y gusanos"; Pulido, *Spiritual Evolution of Margarito Bautista*; Tecun, "A Divine Rebellion," 1; Simon, "Hoea Te Waka ki Uta"; Garrett, "Disentangling Binaries and the Rise of Lamanite Studies"; King, "Indigenizing Mormonisms"; and "Indigenous Perspectives on the Meanings of 'Lamanite.'"
27. Murphy, "Lamanite Genesis, Genealogy, and Genetics."
28. See also Duffy, "Use of 'Lamanite' in Official LDS Discourse."
29. Diné scholar Moroni Benally wrote an article about Native American Latter-day Saints but did not focus as much on Diné Latter-day Saint experiences specifically. See Benally, "Decolonizing the Blossoming."
30. McPherson, Dandy, and Burak, *Navajo Tradition, Mormon Life*.
31. Pavlik, "Navajo Christianity," 43.
32. Pavlik, "Of Saints and Lamanites," 26.
33. McPherson, Dandy, and Burak, *Navajo Tradition, Mormon Life*, 49.
34. To learn more about the Placement program, see Garrett, *Making Lamanites*, 2016.
35. McPherson, Dandy, and Burak, *Navajo Tradition, Mormon Life*, 49.
36. See Garrett, *Making Lamanites*, 2. Garrett estimates "some fifty thousand students (mostly Navajo)" participated in the Placement program for one or more school years.
37. "Ruth Polacca Testimony," Lucy Guymon Bloomfield, Correspondence, 1905–81, MS 13266, box 3, folders 21–22, Church History Library. Polacca used the term "Lamanites" to refer to Native Americans.
38. King, *Diné dóó Gáamalii*, 20.
39. Ruth Polacca, District Conference, Toadlena, New Mexico, September 9–10, 1950, MS 13266 box 3 folder 22, Church History Library; and see King, *Diné dóó Gáamalii*, 20. The capitalization of "His" comes directly from the text.
40. See King, *Diné dóó Gáamalii*, 69 and 57. On page 57, I refer to church documents that mention how "educated natives" were "interpreters and part-time missionaries"; and King, "Aloha in Diné Bikéyah," 163.
41. Ruth Polacca, interview by Spencer W. Kimball, Gallup, New Mexico, June 14, 1953, oral history transcript, MS 3878, Church History Library, 2.
42. Hardin-Burrola, Sarath, and Rosebrough, *Legendary Locals of Gallup, New Mexico*, 15; and Taylor, *Navajo Scouts during the Apache Wars*.
43. Polacca, interview, 4.
44. Polacca, interview, 11.
45. Polacca, interview, 5.
46. Polacca interview, 6.
47. Uchtdorf, "Heeding the Voice of the Prophets."

48. See Colvin, "A Maori Mormon Testimony"; and Colvin, "Introduction."
49. Arnold Yazzie, interview by Michael Landon, April 26, 1997, Window Rock, Arizona, OH 1649, Church History Library, 22–23.
50. Benally, "Decolonizing the Blossoming," 74.
51. Wallace Brown cited in King, *Diné dóó Gáamalii*, 191.
52. Ruby Whitesinger Benally cited in King, *Diné dóó Gáamalii*, 194.
53. George P. Lee papers [photocopies], 1989, ACCN 1112, Special Collections, J. Willard Marriott Library, University of Utah; see also https://archiveswest.orbiscascade.org/ark:80444/xv61599#:~:text=George%20p.%20lee%20is%20a,of%20racism%20toward%20native%20americans.
54. See King, *Diné dóó Gáamalii*, note 90 on 265.
55. Matthew Heiss, (phone) interview by Farina King, September 26, 2023, notes in the author's possession, used with permission.
56. Heiss, interview.
57. Oral historians primarily refer to interviewees as oral history narrators in recent years. See "Narrator," in Glossary of the Oral History Association.
58. Hopi-Hopi interview by Tom Ration cited in King, *Earth Memory Compass*, 2.
59. My father, Phillip L. Smith, notes the verbal pauses in his transcription of the oral history audio recording, which most transcripts delete.
60. Phillip L. Smith transcription and translation of Nanabah Bia Begay, interviewed by Matthew Heiss, interpreted by Helena Yellowhair, April 27, 1997, Many Farms, Navajo Nation, AZ, OH 1645, Church History Library, tape recording and transcript. Phillip Smith retranslated the Diné bizaad parts of the oral history tape recording in 2013.
61. I retain the capitalization of my father's translations of the transcript.
62. Tádídíín is another common spelling for Corn Pollen in Diné bizaad. Spellings and accents vary in written forms of Diné bizaad.
63. "Tádídíín," Navajo Word of the Day, accessed September 30, 2023, https://navajowotd.com/word/tadidiin/.
64. Nanabah Bia Begay, interviewed by Matthew Heiss, interpreted by Helena Yellowhair, April 27, 1997, Many Farms, Arizona, LDS Church Archives, tape recording and transcript. Phillip Smith re-translated the Diné bizaad parts of the interview tape recording in 2013.
65. King, *Diné dóó Gáamalii*, 195.
66. Church leaders and protocols also encourage Latter-day Saints to fast on the first Sunday of the month.
67. Yellowhair in Nanabah Begay oral history. In this part of the oral history, I think that Yellowhair is referring to the temple worker who felt the "spirit" (or was touched) by how Nanabah Begay spoke at the pulpit, sharing her testimony. Begay inspired the (unnamed) temple worker to share her testimony at the pulpit too.
68. This excerpt does not include proper accents and diacritical markings, which needs to be added. My father did not have a Diné bizaad keyboard, so he wrote his transla-

tions by hand and included the accents on the handwritten form that I submitted to the Church History Library. I do not include the full English translations for space in certain parts of the manuscript.

69. Begay oral history.
70. Yellowhair in Begay, oral history.
71. Heiss, interview.
72. King, *Diné dóó Gáamalii*, 19.

Bibliography

ARCHIVAL SOURCES

Church History Library, The Church of Jesus Christ of Latter-day Saints, Salt Lake City, Utah.
    Ruth Polacca, District Conference, Toadlena, New Mexico, September 9–10, 1950. MS 13266 box 3, folder 22.
    Ruth Polacca, interview by Spencer W. Kimball, Gallup, New Mexico, June 14, 1953. Oral history transcript, MS 3878, Church History Library, 2.
    "Ruth Polacca Testimony." In Lucy Guymon Bloomfield, Correspondence, 1905–81, MS 13266, box 3, folders 21–22.
    Yazzie, Arnold. Interview by Michael Landon, April 26, 1997, Window Rock AZ. OH 1649, Church History Library, 22–23.
LDS Church Archives. Nanabah Bia Begay, interviewed by Matthew Heiss, interpreted by Helena Yellowhair, April 27, 1997, Many Farms, Arizona, tape recording and transcript. Phillip Smith retranslated the Diné bizaad parts of the interview tape recording in 2013.
Special Collections, J. Willard Marriott Library, University of Utah. George P. Lee papers [photocopies], 1989, ACCN 1112.. https://archiveswest.orbiscascade.org/ark:80444/xv61599#:~:text=George%20p.%20lee%20is%20a,of%20racism%20toward%20native%20americans.

PUBLISHED WORKS

Aikau, Hokulani. *A Chosen People, a Promised Land: Mormonism and Race in Hawai'i*. Minneapolis: University of Minnesota Press, 2012.
Allison, Christopher D., and Nick Ashcroft. "New Mexico Range Plants," New Mexico State University, June 8, 2023. https://pubs.nmsu.edu/_circulars/cr374_lg.pdf.
Bahr, Howard M. "Multiplying Glimpses, Gleaning Genres: A Multidisciplinary Approach to the Study of Change among Navajo Peoples." *Human Organization* 53, no. 1 (1994): 55–73.
Benally, Moroni. "Decolonizing the Blossoming: Indigenous People's Faith in a Colonizing Church." *Dialogue: A Journal of Mormon Thought* 50, no. 4 (2017): 71–78.
Biyé, Hastiin Biyo' Łání Yéę, Robert W. Young, and William Morgan. *The Ramah Navahos: Tł'ohchiníjí diné kéédahat'ilnii baa hane'*. Washington DC: U.S. Department of

Interior, 1949.

Boxer, Elise. "The Book of Mormon as Mormon Settler Colonialism." In Hafen and Rensink, *Essays on American Indian and Mormon History*, 3–22.

——. "'This Is the Place!': Disrupting Mormon Settler Colonialism." In Colvin and Brooks, *Decolonizing Mormonism*, 77–100.

Colvin, Gina. "Introduction: Theorizing Mormon Race Scholarship." *Journal of Mormon History* 41, no. 3 (2015): 11–21.

——. "A Maori Mormon Testimony." In Colvin and Brooks, *Decolonizing Mormonism*, 27–46.

Colvin, Gina, and Joanna Brooks, eds. *Decolonizing Mormonism: Approaching a Postcolonial Zion*. Salt Lake City: University of Utah Press, 2018.

Duffy, John-Charles. "The Use of 'Lamanite' in Official LDS Discourse." *Journal of Mormon History* 34, no. 1 (2008): 118–67.

Garrett, Matthew. "Disentangling Binaries and the Rise of Lamanite Studies." *Religion Compass* 12, no. 11 (2018).

——. *Making Lamanites: Mormons, Native Americans, and the Indian Student Placement Program, 1947–2000*. Salt Lake City: University of Utah Press, 2016.

Hafen, Jane, and Brenda W. Rensink, eds. *Essays on American Indian and Mormon History*. Salt Lake City: University of Utah Press, 2019.

Hardin-Burrola, Elizabeth, Carol Sarath, and Bob Rosebrough. *Legendary Locals of Gallup, New Mexico*. Charleston SC: Legendary Locals, Arcadia Publishing, 2017.

Hebard, Grace Raymond. *Sacagawea: Guide and Interpreter of Lewis and Clark*. Mineola NY: Dover, 2002.

"Indigenous Perspectives on the Meanings of 'Lamanite.'" Workshop organized by Farina King and Michael Kaulana Ing, April 2023, Claremont Graduate University. Recordings available online. https://mormonstudies.cgu.edu/annual-mormon-studies-conference-indigenous-perspectives-on-the-meaning-of-lamanite/.

"Iyanbito: Ayánni bitó (buffalo's water)—Eastern Agency." *Navajo Nation Wind* website, Navajo Nation Division of Community Development. Accessed June 8, 2023. https://navajoprofile.wind.enavajo.org/Chapter/Iyanbito.

Jager, Rebecca Kay. *Malinche, Pocahontas, and Sacagawea: Indian Women as Cultural Intermediaries and National Symbols*. Norman: University of Oklahoma Press, 2015.

Jefferson-Tatum, Elana. "The Violence of Translation: An Indigenous World-Sense and the Western 'Prostitution' of Dahomean Bodies." *Journal of African Religions* 3, no. 3 (2015): 279–324.

King, Farina. "Aloha in Diné Bikéyah: Mormon Hawaiians and Navajos, 1949 to 1990." In Hafen and Rensink, *Essays on American Indian and Mormon History*, 161–82.

——. *Diné dóó Gáamalii: Navajo Latter-day Saint Experiences in the Twentieth Century*. Lawrence: University Press of Kansas, 2023.

——. *The Earth Memory Compass: Diné Landscapes and Education in the Twentieth Century*. Lawrence: University Press of Kansas, 2018.

——. "Indigenizing Mormonisms." *Mormon Studies Review* 6 (2019): 1–16.

Lee, Lloyd L., ed. *Nihikéyah: Navajo Homeland*. Tucson: University of Arizona Press,

2023.

Martinich, Matt. "LDS Outreach among the Navajo." *Cumorah.com*, August 2012. https://www.cumorah.com/articles/caseStudies/7/327/lds-outreach-among-the-navajo.

Mauss, Armand L. *All Abraham's Children: Changing Mormon Conceptions of Race and Lineage*. Champaign: University of Illinois Press, 2003.

McPherson, Robert S., Jim Dandy, and Sarah E. Burak. *Navajo Tradition, Mormon Life: The Autobiography and Teachings of Jim Dandy*. Salt Lake City: University of Utah Press, 2012.

Murphy, Thomas. "Lamanite Genesis, Genealogy, and Genetics." In *American Apocrypha: Essays on the Book of Mormon*, edited by Dan Vogel and Brent Metcalfe, 47–77. Salt Lake City: Signature, 2002.

Murphy, Thomas W. "Imagining Lamanites: Native Americans and the Book of Mormon." PhD diss., University of Washington, 2003.

———. "Other Mormon Histories: Lamanite Subjectivity in Mexico." *Journal of Mormon History* 26, no. 2 (2000): 179–213.

"Narrator." In *Glossary of the Oral History Association*. Accessed September 25, 2023. https://oralhistory.org/narrator/#:~:text=While%20there%20are%20many%20possible,merely%20"living%20human%20subjects.

Nelson, Dale W. *Interpreters with Lewis and Clark: The Story of Sacagawea and Toussaint Charbonneau*. College Station: University of North Texas Press, 2003.

Newton, Marjorie. *Tiki and Temple: The Mormon Mission in New Zealand, 1854–1958*. Draper UT: Greg Kofford Books, 2012.

Parker, Stuart. "Queso y gusanos: The Cosmos of Indigenous Mormon Intellectual Margarito Bautista." In *Just South of Zion: The Mormons in Mexico and Its Borderlands*, edited by Jason H. Dormady and Jared M. Tamez, 111–30. Albuquerque: University of New Mexico Press, 2015.

Pavlik, Steve. "Navajo Christianity: Historical Origins and Modern Trends." *Wicazo Sa Review* 12, no. 2 (1997): 43–58.

———. "Of Saints and Lamanites: An Analysis of Navajo Mormonism." *Wicazo Sa Review* 8, no. 1 (1992): 21–30.

Peery, Char. "New Deal Navajo Linguistics: Language Ideology and Political Transformation." *Language and Communication* 32, no. 2 (2012): 114–23.

Pulido, Elisa Eastwood. *The Spiritual Evolution of Margarito Bautista: Mexican Mormon Evangelizer, Polygamist Dissident, and Utopian Founder, 1878–1961*. New York: Oxford University Press, 2020.

"Selected Plants of Navajo Rangelands." New Mexico State University website, 2018. https://navajorange.nmsu.edu.

Simon, Hemopereki. "Hoea Te Waka ki Uta: Critical Kaupapa Māori Research and Mormon Studies Moving Forward." *New Sociology: Journal of Critical Praxis* 3, no. 1 (2022).

Stepetin, Haliehana. "Unangam Qaqamiiĝuu [Unangax̂ Subsistence] Cosmologies: Protocols of Sustainability, or Ways of Being Unangax̂." PhD diss., University of

California, Davis, 2023.

Taylor, John Lewis. *Navajo Scouts During the Apache Wars*. Mount Pleasant SC: Arcadia, 2010.

Thayne, Stanley. "The Blood of Father Lehi: Indigenous Americans and the Book of Mormon." PhD diss., University of North Carolina, 2016.

Tecun, Arcia [Daniel Hernandez]. "A Divine Rebellion: Indigenous Sacraments among Global 'Lamanites.'" *Religions* 12, no. 280 (2021).

Uchtdorf, Dieter F. "Heeding the Voice of the Prophets." July 2008. https://www.churchofjesuschrist.org/study/liahona/2008/07/heeding-the-voice-of-the-prophets?lang=eng.

Yazzie, Renata. "Jesus Woodláájí Sin: Sounding a Self-Determined Navajo Christian Church." Master's thesis, University of New Mexico, 2022.

Rough Interpretations

Note from the editors: In the following excerpt from Mark Twain's novel Roughing It *(1872), Buck Fanshaw has passed away, and his good friend Scotty Briggs was tasked with planning the funeral. His exchange with the local minister parodies the miscommunications between classes (mine workers and clergy) and regions (West and East).*

Excerpt from Roughing It

Prodigious preparations were made for the funeral. All the vehicles in town were hired, all the saloons put in mourning, all the municipal and fire-company flags hung at half-mast, and all the firemen ordered to muster in uniform and bring their machines duly draped in black. Now—let us remark in parenthesis—as all the peoples of the earth had representative adventurers in the Silverland, and as each adventurer had brought the slang of his nation or his locality with him, the combination made the slang of Nevada the richest and the most infinitely varied and copious that had ever existed anywhere in the world, perhaps, except in the mines of California in the "early days." Slang was the language of Nevada. It was hard to preach a sermon without it, and be understood. Such phrases as "You bet!" "Oh, no, I reckon not!" "No Irish need apply," and a hundred others, became so common as to fall from the lips of a speaker unconsciously—and very often when they did not touch the subject under discussion and consequently failed to mean anything.

After Buck Fanshaw's inquest, a meeting of the short-haired brotherhood was held, for nothing can be done on the Pacific coast without a public meeting and an expression of sentiment. Regretful resolutions were passed and various committees appointed; among others, a committee of one was deputed to call on the minister, a fragile, gentle, spiritual new fledgling from an Eastern theological seminary, and as yet unacquainted with the ways of the mines. The committeeman, "Scotty" Briggs, made his visit; and in after days it was worth something to hear the minister tell about it. Scotty was a stalwart rough, whose customary suit, when on weighty official business, like committee work, was a fire helmet, flaming red flannel shirt, patent leather belt with spanner and revolver attached, coat hung over arm, and pants stuffed into boot tops. He formed something of a contrast to the pale theological student. It is fair to say of Scotty, however, in passing, that he had a warm heart, and a strong love for his friends, and never entered into a quarrel when he could reasonably keep out of it. Indeed, it was commonly said that whenever one of Scotty's fights was investigated, it always turned out that it had originally been no affair of his, but that out of native good-heartedness he had dropped in of his own accord to help the man who was getting the worst of it. He and Buck Fanshaw were bosom friends, for years, and had often taken adventurous "pot-luck" together. On one occasion, they had thrown off their coats and taken the weaker side in a fight among strangers, and after gaining a hard-earned victory, turned and found that the men they were helping had deserted early, and not only that, but had stolen their coats and made off with them! But to return to Scotty's visit to the minister. He was on a sorrowful mission, now, and his face was the picture of woe. Being admitted to the presence he sat down before the clergyman, placed his fire-hat on an unfinished manuscript sermon under the minister's nose, took from it a red silk handkerchief, wiped his brow and heaved a sigh of dismal impressiveness, explanatory of his business.

He choked, and even shed tears; but with an effort he mastered his voice and said in lugubrious tones:

"Are you the duck that runs the gospel-mill next door?"

"Am I the—pardon me, I believe I do not understand?"

With another sigh and a half-sob, Scotty rejoined:

"Why you see we are in a bit of trouble, and the boys thought maybe you would give us a lift, if we'd tackle you—that is, if I've got the rights of it and you are the head clerk of the doxology-works next door."

"I am the shepherd in charge of the flock whose fold is next door."

"The which?"

"The spiritual adviser of the little company of believers whose sanctuary adjoins these premises."

Scotty scratched his head, reflected a moment, and then said:

"You ruther hold over me, pard. I reckon I can't call that hand. Ante and pass the buck."

"How? I beg pardon. What did I understand you to say?"

"Well, you've ruther got the bulge on me. Or maybe we've both got the bulge, somehow. You don't smoke me and I don't smoke you. You see, one of the boys has passed in his checks and we want to give him a good send-off, and so the thing I'm on now is to roust out somebody to jerk a little chin-music for us and waltz him through handsome."

"My friend, I seem to grow more and more bewildered. Your observations are wholly incomprehensible to me. Cannot you simplify them in some way? At first I thought perhaps I understood you, but I grope now. Would it not expedite matters if you restricted yourself to categorical statements of fact unencumbered with obstructing accumulations of metaphor and allegory?"

Another pause, and more reflection. Then, said Scotty:

"I'll have to pass, I judge."

"How?"

"You've raised me out, pard."

"I still fail to catch your meaning."

"Why, that last lead of yourn is too many for me—that's the idea. I can't neither-trump nor follow suit."

The clergyman sank back in his chair perplexed. Scotty leaned his head on his hand and gave himself up to thought.

Presently his face came up, sorrowful but confident.

"I've got it now, so's you can savvy," he said. "What we want is a gospel-sharp. See?"

"A what?"

"Gospel-sharp. Parson."

"Oh! Why did you not say so before? I am a clergyman—a parson."

"Now you talk! You see my blind and straddle it like a man. Put it there!"— extending a brawny paw, which closed over the minister's small hand and gave it a shake indicative of fraternal sympathy and fervent gratification.

"Now we're all right, pard. Let's start fresh. Don't you mind my snuffling a little—becuz we're in a power of trouble. You see, one of the boys has gone up the flume—"

"Gone where?"

"Up the flume—throwed up the sponge, you understand."

"Thrown up the sponge?"

"Yes—kicked the bucket—"

"Ah—has departed to that mysterious country from whose bourne no traveler returns."

"Return! I reckon not. Why pard, he's dead!"

"Yes, I understand."

"Oh, you do? Well I thought maybe you might be getting tangled some more. Yes, you see he's dead again—"

"Again? Why, has he ever been dead before?"

"Dead before? No! Do you reckon a man has got as many lives as a cat? But you bet you he's awful dead now, poor old boy, and I wish I'd never seen this day. I don't want no better friend than Buck Fanshaw. I knowed him by the back; and when I know a man and like him, I freeze to him—you hear me. Take him all round, pard, there never was a bullier man in the mines. No man ever knowed Buck Fanshaw to go back on a friend. But it's all up, you know, it's all up. It ain't no use. They've scooped him."

"Scooped him?"

"Yes—death has. Well, well, well, we've got to give him up. Yes indeed. It's a kind of a hard world, after all, ain't it? But pard, he was a rustler! You ought to seen him get started once. He was a bully boy with a glass eye! Just spit in his face and give him room according to his strength, and it was just beautiful to see him peel and go in. He was the worst son of a thief that ever drawed breath. Pard, he was on it! He was on it bigger than an Injun!"

"On it? On what?"

"On the shoot. On the shoulder. On the fight, you understand. He didn't give a continental for any body. Beg your pardon, friend, for coming so near saying a cuss-word—but you see I'm on an awful strain, in this palaver, on account of having to cramp down and draw everything so mild. But we've got to give him up. There ain't any getting around that, I don't reckon. Now if we can get you to help plant him—"

"Preach the funeral discourse? Assist at the obsequies?"

"Obs'quies is good. Yes. That's it—that's our little game. We are going to get the thing up regardless, you know. He was always nifty himself, and so you bet you his funeral ain't going to be no slouch—solid silver door-plate on his coffin, six plumes on the hearse, and a n***** on the box in a biled shirt and a plug hat—how's that for high? And we'll take care of you, pard. We'll fix you all right. There'll be a kerridge for you; and whatever you want, you just 'scape out and we'll 'tend to it. We've got a shebang fixed up for you to stand behind, in No. 1's house, and don't you be afraid. Just go in and toot your horn, if you don't sell a clam. Put Buck through as bully as you can, pard, for anybody that knowed him will tell you that he was one of the whitest men that was ever in the mines. You can't draw it too strong. He never could stand it to see things going wrong. He's done more to make this town quiet and peaceable than any man in it. I've seen him lick four [Mexicans] in eleven minutes, myself. If a thing wanted regulating, he warn't a man to go browsing around after somebody to do it, but he would prance in and regulate it himself. He warn't a Catholic. Scasely. He was down on 'em. His word was, 'No Irish need apply!' But it didn't make no difference about that when it came down to what a man's rights was—and so, when some roughs jumped the Catholic boneyard and started in to stake out town-lots in it he went for 'em! And he cleaned 'em, too! I was there, pard, and I seen it myself."

"That was very well indeed—at least the impulse was—whether the act was strictly defensible or not. Had deceased any religious convictions? That is to say, did he feel a dependence upon, or acknowledge allegiance to a higher power?"

More reflection.

"I reckon you've stumped me again, pard. Could you say it over once more, and say it slow?"

"Well, to simplify it somewhat, was he, or rather had he ever been connected with any organization sequestered from secular concerns and devoted to self-sacrifice in the interests of morality?"

"All down but nine—set 'em up on the other alley, pard."

"What did I understand you to say?"

"Why, you're most too many for me, you know. When you get in with your left I hunt grass every time. Every time you draw, you fill; but I don't seem to have any luck. Lets have a new deal."

"How? Begin again?"

"That's it."

"Very well. Was he a good man, and—"

"There—I see that; don't put up another chip till I look at my hand. A good man, says you? Pard, it ain't no name for it. He was the best man that ever—pard, you would have doted on that man. He could lam any galoot of his inches in America. It was him that put down the riot last election before it got a start; and everybody said he was the only man that could have done it. He waltzed in with a spanner in one hand and a trumpet in the other, and sent fourteen men home on a shutter in less than three minutes. He had that riot all broke up and prevented nice before anybody ever got a chance to strike a blow. He was always for peace, and he would have peace—he could not stand disturbances. Pard, he was a great loss to this town. It would please the boys if you could chip in something like that and do him justice. Here once when the Micks got to throwing stones through the Methodis' Sunday school windows, Buck Fanshaw, all of his own notion, shut up his saloon and took a couple of six-shooters and mounted guard over the Sunday school. Says he, 'No Irish need apply!' And they didn't. He was the bulliest man in the mountains, pard! He could run faster, jump higher, hit harder, and hold more tangle-foot whisky without spilling it than any man in seventeen counties. Put that in, pard—it'll please the boys more than anything you could say. And you can say, pard, that he never shook his mother."

"Never shook his mother?"

"That's it—any of the boys will tell you so."

"Well, but why should he shake her?"

"That's what I say—but some people does."

"Not people of any repute?"

"Well, some that averages pretty so-so."

"In my opinion the man that would offer personal violence to his own mother, ought to—"

"Cheese it, pard; you've banked your ball clean outside the string. What I was a drivin' at, was, that he never throwed off on his mother—don't you see? No indeedy. He give her a house to live in, and town lots, and plenty of money; and he looked after her and took care of her all the time; and when she was down with the small-pox I'm d——d if he didn't set up nights and nuss her himself! Beg your pardon for saying it, but it hopped out too quick for yours truly.

"You've treated me like a gentleman, pard, and I ain't the man to hurt your feelings intentional. I think you're white. I think you're a square man, pard. I like you, and I'll lick any man that don't. I'll lick him till he can't tell himself from a last year's corpse! Put it there!" [Another fraternal hand-shake—and exit.][1]

Notes

1. Mark Twain, *Roughing It* (1872; Project Gutenberg, 2004), http://www.gutenberg.org/ebooks/3177.

PART 3

INTERPRETING IN PRACTICE

8

"Do You Solemnly Swear to Interpret Accurately and Without Bias?"

Professional Court Interpreting in the Twentieth and Twenty-First Centuries

TAYLOR COZZENS

"ALL RISE!"

The bailiff's voice reverberates throughout the courtroom as everyone hastens to stand. The judge in her long robes steps up to the bench. "Thank you," she says. "You may be seated."

From my seat in the public galley, I watch the attorneys at the bar tables put away their iPhones and pull out their paperwork. I sit down, waiting to work at one of my first jobs as a certified courtroom interpreter in central Oklahoma. As the judge begins calling the docket, I listen for the case to which I have been assigned and watch to see which attorneys will be covering it. When she calls it out, I stand again, along with two attorneys.

"State present, your honor," responds a lawyer at the prosecutor's table.

"Defendant present, your honor," adds another, standing beside a man wearing an orange prison uniform.

"Interpreter present, your honor," I say.

By and by, the proceedings begin. The alleged crime in this case is robbery of a large metal sink and some building materials from a convenience store that the new owners are renovating in downtown Oklahoma City. These owners, a well-dressed Pakistani couple, have come to testify in the proceedings, along with one of their construction workers who witnessed the theft. Although the owners speak English proficiently, the Latino worker does not. The only way he can testify is by means of an interpreter—me, in this case. Standing beside him on the witness stand, I interpret his story into English: from his pickup, he observed the defendant slip through two metal studs and then drag the sink out to the curb; he watched the defendant struggle to load the sink into the trunk of his car; he noted how the trunk would not close completely with the sink inside, so the defendant had to secure the trunk door with twine; finally, he testifies that he started his own vehicle and followed the defendant's car long enough to take pictures of the license plate and get a sense of where the defendant was heading. After three rounds of questions from the attorneys (direct examination, cross examination, and redirect), the witness steps down, and my job concludes.

In U.S. courtrooms, non-English speakers regularly appear as witnesses, victims, and defendants. When they do, none of the proceedings—bail hearings, arraignments, preliminary hearings, depositions, guilty pleas, trials, etc.—can go forward without interpreters. While studying history over the past five years, I have moonlighted as a Spanish-English interpreter.[1] This experience has given me a balanced and, at times, conflicted perspective on the history of interpreters. On one hand, I understand the traditional scholarly criticism of interpreters as agents of colonizers or imperialists; on the other, I believe firmly in their potential to help diverse societies function fairly by facilitating communication across cultural and linguistic borders.

History certainly furnishes examples of interpreters who serve mainly as agents of colonizers. In writing about British colonization of India, Gayatri Spivak cites Thomas Babington Macaulay's 1835 call for "a class [of] interpreters... Indian in blood and colour, but English in taste, in opinions, in morals, and in intellect." Such interpreters, Spivak argues, catalyze cultural subordination.[2] As another example, scholar Shaden M. Tageldin, in her work on the French and British colonization of Egypt, treats the art of translation as inherently deceptive. According to Tageldin, the language brokering that the colonizers oversaw constituted "translational seduction," even the "copulation of the colonizer and the colonized." In her view, translation beguiles the colonized, allowing them to feel attraction for the colonizer who is culturally violating them.[3] For an example of interpretation and imperialism from twentieth-century U.S. history, scholars could cite the career of Vernon Walters, a talented interpreter, military officer, and administrator who employed his linguistic skills throughout much of the Cold

War in the service of the State Department, White House, and CIA, often facilitating their perverse alliances with Latin American dictators.[4]

While colonizers and imperialists have no doubt relied on interpreters to achieve their designs, scholars' emphasis on this reliance often omits the perspectives of the interpreters themselves, including the difficult, sometimes dangerous or coerced, circumstances in which they work. In their own role as interpreters of the past, historians of colonial Latin America have helped lead the way among scholars in considering intermediaries' perspectives, as well as the many ways beyond colonial subjugation that their decisions have shaped societies.[5] In colonial Mexico, for example, Nancy Farriss has examined the efforts of Dominican friars to learn Indigenous languages, concluding that these efforts contributed to the evolution of a hybrid culture that exists to this day.[6] Similarly, Yanna Yannakakis has explored the role of mixed-race legal intermediaries in a later period of Spanish colonialism. As agents unto themselves, these "lynchpin[s]" of colonial society "negotiated, brokered, and played decisive roles in changing the local societies in which they lived."[7] Moving back to the twentieth century, a counterpoint to the work of Vernon Walters in Latin America is the role of Mexican American general Marc Cisneros in the U.S. invasion of Panama in the late 1980s. Although Cisneros was clearly loyal to the U.S. military and committed to its mission in Panama, he repeatedly used his language skills to talk with—and, at times, talk down—Panamanian soldiers and civilians, preferring dialogue over shootouts.[8]

Even with a focus on interpreters' agency and perspectives, many scholars still return to the question of power dynamics and, specifically, the role of interpreters in facilitating imperialism. Whose interests, in other words, does the work of interpreters usually serve? In his study of friars in colonial Mexico, William Taylor argues convincingly that these intermediaries had the potential to "oppose, as well as support, [state] power."[9] At the same time, as Alida Metcalf points out, colonizers usually have more resources to pay, employ, and secure the loyalty of interpreters. "In historical settings," she writes, "go-betweens can be neutral mediators, but in fact they rarely are. They are almost always loyal to (and paid by) one side or another."[10]

In the history of the American West, the U.S. government and military have undoubtedly played the role of a conquering, colonizing nation.[11] For generations, as Cam Shriver's study of William Wells in this volume suggests, government authorities expected bilingual Indian agents and other hired interpreters to use their skills in favor of U.S. expansion (see chapter 3). In later cases, such as the "interpreter generation" of boarding school attendees that Paul Conrad discusses, bilingual members of Native American nations sought mainly to serve their own communities (see chapter 5). Other intermediaries, such as Antonio Landín in 1917 New Mexico or Graciela Vrieze and Pom Kavan in Storm Lake, Iowa seven decades later, seem sincerely committed, at least for the most part, to improving relations between speakers of different languages in situations of significant social uneasiness (see chapters 6 and 9). At other times, interpreters' only real loyalty seems to be to themselves (see chapter 1). In short, interpreters in Western history have played many roles and had many loyalties.[12] Ultimately, however, many did contribute to colonization As Andrew Offenburger writes, "wherever goes empire, so go interpreters" (chapter 9). Farina King adds that in the process of settler colonialism, even well-intentioned interpreters can unwittingly "cause damage instead of bridge-building" (chapter 7).

How, then, did the United States come to a point in the late twentieth century when non-English speakers in courtrooms, clinics, and other institutions began to request interpreters and expect the government to provide them? One important answer is the civil rights movement, which marks a crucial turning point in the history of interpreters. The movement made authorities more aware of minorities and their needs, including the need to reduce language barriers so that these individuals could participate more equally in U.S. institutions. This awareness led to significant efforts to find, train, and fund professional interpreters for the courts and, later, for hospitals and schools.

Gramscian scholars could argue that such efforts represent merely a concession designed to preserve the hegemony of the ever-imperial U.S. government.[13] Yet many interpreters and linguistic minorities would beg to differ. When an immigrant from El Salvador hurts his back in a landscaping job and must explain in detail what happened so that a doctor can decide whether insurance will cover the surgery or the condition was "preexisting," is it in the individual's best interest to have an interpreter, or is the interpreter merely reinforcing hegemonic relationships? When a ten-year-old immigrant from Mexico is sexually abused by the friend of a relative and must appear in court to formally identify the perpetrator, does she deserve an interpreter? When an immigrant from Guatemala is assaulted in her mobile home by a burglar and must later explain before a judge exactly what happened, does it help her to have an interpreter? If the assailant is also a monolingual Spanish speaker, does he deserve to understand the criminal proceedings as would an English speaker in his position? Or even when a construction worker witnesses the robbery of a metal sink, does the interpretation of his testimony make society more or less just? In my experience, linguistic minorities in such cases not only want interpreters, they consider state-funded interpretation services a fundamental right.

The history of court interpreting in the twentieth century is not so much a history of imperialism as it is a history of civil rights. Notably, this history is concentrated, to an extent, in the U.S. West where large percentages of state populations have been Spanish speakers. In his study *America's West*, historian David Wrobel argues that the West in the first half of the twentieth century led the rest of the nation in many social movements and intellectual trends.[14] In a similar way, the West in later decades helped lead the United States in the process of interpreter professionalization. While this process remains incomplete in many parts of the country, the developing role of professional courtroom interpreters from the 1970s onward represents one of the most significant institutional efforts of the past century to recognize and honor the rights of linguistic minorities.

In the history of the U.S. courts, the absence of interpreters—not their presence—has most often reinforced state power and social injustice. As interpreting scholars Roseann Dueñas González, Victoria Vásquez, and Holly Mikkelson have argued, throughout most of the twentieth century court authorities responded to language barriers by deeming interpreters unnecessary or by grabbing the first bilingual (or marginally bilingual) person available and asking for an interpretation of only the most salient portions of a dialogue. Attorneys, police officers, family members, and others often ended up in this position, regardless of their skills or their interests. In these situations, there was no sense of ethics or standards of professional practice. As a result, language barriers often persisted and, in turn, denied full access to the legal system to countless citizens with limited English.[15]

To illustrate the potential consequences of limited or biased interpretation services, no story is as effective as that of Mexican immigrant Gregorio Cortez. In 1901 the sheriff of Karnes County, Texas, W. T. Morris, paid a visit to the home of Cortez and his brother, Romaldo, to inquire about a stolen horse. To interpret his questions, Morris had brought along his deputy, Boone Choate. Choate, however, proved grossly unqualified. As historian Américo Paredes records, when the sheriff arrived and asked to speak with Gregorio, Romaldo, who was already outside, let his brother know by calling out, *Te quieren*, which in this context would mean, "somebody wants to talk to you." But Choate, assuming that Cortez was guilty, took these two words to mean "they have come for you" and shared his personal suspicions with the sheriff.

From this point onward, the interpretation—and the situation—went downhill. When the sheriff asked Cortez if he had traded a horse, Cortez explained that he had not traded a horse (*caballo*) but a mare (*yegua*). Choate, however, did not know the word *yegua*, so he omitted the idea altogether and led the sheriff to believe that Cortez was simply saying untruthfully that he had not traded a horse. Morris then crossed the fence into Cortez's property and, through Choate, told Gregorio and Romaldo that he was going to arrest them. As the sheriff approached, Cortez said something, which Paredes estimates was "You can't arrest me for nothing" but which Choate interpreted as "No man can arrest me." This interpretation gave Morris the impression that the Cortez brothers were going to resist. "In the next few seconds," as Paredes explains, Romaldo, who was unarmed, moved to intervene between the sheriff and his brother. "Morris [then] shot Romaldo Cortez, shot at Gregorio and missed, and was in turn shot by Gregorio." Both Romaldo and Morris soon died from their wounds. Cortez fled, and one of the largest manhunts in the history of Texas ensued, followed by another fatal encounter, this one with a posse.[16]

While the story of Gregorio Cortez provides a dramatic example of the consequences of interpreter bias and incompetence, it is not an isolated case. In Paredes's words, "if one goes over court records, investigations of claims, and other documents concerning relations between Mexicans and Anglo-Texans, one finds that jail sentences, decisions on claims, and even the 'facts' of history have often been based on statements by men who have qualified as experts on Mexican affairs without even knowing the Spanish language." Speaking of the Cortez case specifically, Paredes adds, "Boone Choate, perhaps through no fault of his own, was one of these men. A number of people might not have died had Choate either known more Spanish or known enough to know what he did not know."[17] As Paredes suggests, the problem of authorities such as Morris and Choate was not just their ignorance of the language but also their enormous condescension toward the communities that they could not understand. Arrogance, as well as ignorance, relegated countless Spanish speakers to the fringes of the U.S. legal system.

Exclusion of linguistic minorities from the U.S. system of justice remained the norm throughout much of the twentieth century. Dueñas González, Vásquez, and Mikkelson mark the 1907 case *Perovich v. United States* as an important precedent in which U.S. courts adopted "a casual attitude and even a marked reluctance to provide interpreters for defendants" in trial courts.[18] In this case, authorities in Alaska convicted Vuco Perovich, a young immigrant from Montenegro, of homicide near the city of Fairbanks. Since Perovich was not a native English speaker, the question of interpretation came up, but the federal judges who reviewed the case ruled that the matter of interpretation was outside their purview. "Whether or not the appointment of an interpreter is necessary," they wrote, "is within the sound discretion of the trial court."[19]

Although this decision made up a relatively minor part of the Perovich case, the ramifications for U.S. case law were extensive. The federal government had essentially turned a blind eye to the problem of language barriers in U.S. courts, which meant that trial court judges and other local authorities could get away with doing very little or even enforcing a de facto policy that said, in essence, "This is America; we speak English here." Dueñas Gonzalez and her coauthors note several cases from the 1920s through the 1970s in which courts carried out "perfunctory examinations of a defendant's English," such as quick Yes-No quizzes, and deemed interpreters unnecessary, although defendants were clearly unprepared for "the complex register of English used in the courtroom."[20]

Court authorities' reluctance to provide qualified interpreters—or sometimes any interpreter at all—deprived countless people of justice and, as scholar Doris Sommer has written, helped reinforce the nation's social hierarchies. In her study of continued racial discrimination in the courts, she writes, "blind and deaf, but not dumb, the country's courts continue to promulgate rules that resent intrusive minorities, as if discouraging [people of color] from expecting real equity were a guarantee of white privilege and property."[21] As Sommer's work suggests, the U.S. courtroom symbolizes the nation's promise of justice for all, yet if court authorities fail to provide interpreters, many minorities cannot seek legal redress for injustices they face, nor do they have equal footing in any conflict involving English speakers. They remain, in Sommer's words, "virtually indefensible 'outsiders.'"[22]

While the U.S. courts continued to minimize the importance of accurate interpretation, the nations of Europe set an important standard for court interpreting in the Nuremberg trials of 1945–46. Of course, the context of Nuremberg differed markedly from that of the American West, yet the trial highlighted several principles of court interpreting that U.S. authorities would eventually embrace. For one, qualified interpreters were just as necessary for prosecutors as they were for defendants. As historian Francesca Gaiba has explained, in Nuremberg the Allies implemented simultaneous interpretation in German, French, Russian, and English—a significant linguistic and logistical feat for the day—in order to hear testimony from numerous victims and witnesses about war crimes. At the same time, the defendants relied heavily on interpreters. "Of course I want counsel," Hermann Göring famously declared. "But it is even more important to have a good interpreter."[23] For both sides, the trials could not go forward without interpreters.

Additionally, Nuremberg helped set professional and ethical standards regarding neutrality, conflicts of interest, and interpreter inconspicuousness. In multilingual Europe, some of these standards already existed, but the Nuremberg experience reinforced them.[24] For example, Gaiba notes, when some interpreters purposely omitted Nazi witnesses' descriptions of work camps or their derogatory language about Jews because the language was hard to repeat, "they had to be replaced, because their behavior was compromising the impact of such testimony on the trial." As Alfred Steer, head of the Translation Division in Nuremberg, told the interpreters, "It is *your* responsibility to give an accurate and complete translation, even if it *isn't* in harmony with your ideas."[25] This standard of accuracy makes Boone Choate's omissions, meaning changes, and interjections of his own thoughts look pitiful as well as criminal.

Nuremberg also set a new standard of peaceful bilateral relations made possible through professional interpreters. Successful language brokering at these trials helped lead to the permanent use of staff interpreters at the United Nations and, in time, other multilateral organizations, including the European Union and the International Court of Justice.[26] In his study of violence and world history, Harvard psychologist Steven Pinker marks the creation and operation of these organizations as one important step in a long process of decreasing world violence.[27] Professional interpreters and standardized interpretation practices underpin the daily functions of these organizations. Granted, these institutions are different from the U.S. courts, but in the United States, too, some authorities eventually realized the correlation between qualified interpreters and fair, peaceful interactions between speakers of different languages.[28]

In the United States, the civil rights movement helped foster, in many institutions, a greater awareness of the marginalization of linguistic minorities, and court authorities began taking steps to reduce the problem. The first court case that affirmed defendants' right to interpreters occurred in New York in 1970. Three years earlier, a jury had convicted Rogelio Nieves Negrón, a Puerto Rican immigrant working as a potato packer, of murder, and a judge sentenced him to at least twenty years of prison. The problem with the trial, however, was that Negrón spoke no English, and court authorities provided an interpreter only when they needed to interrogate him. For most of the trial, Negrón did not understand what anyone was saying.

Regardless of guilt, Negrón later argued that the language barrier had undermined his right to participate in his own defense. The district and circuit judges agreed. For defendants with limited English, they ruled, the normal rights to consult counsel and confront witness logically implied a "derivative right" to a qualified interpreter. As the judges further explained, Negron's right to hear and question the English-speaking witnesses against him "necessitated that he hear more than the babble of their voices." If necessary, they added, the interpreter "is to be supplied at state expense." As one law review noted, the Negrón case became the first court decision to render a trial constitutionally infirm because of inadequate interpretation services. "It is ... difficult to comprehend," the review added, "why a right as basic to our system as [the right to an interpreter] has not previously been subject to judicial scrutiny."[29]

Importantly, the judges specified the need for the state to fund interpretation services not because they wanted interpreters to favor the state but mainly because low-income defendants, such as Negrón, who could not afford private attorneys, could not afford private interpreters either. The right to court-appointed attorneys or public defenders had been established in the sixth amendment of the U.S. Constitution: "In all criminal prosecutions, the accused shall enjoy the right to a speedy and public trial ... and to have the Assistance of Counsel for his defense."[30] The Negrón ruling made a case that the accused had a similar right to an interpreter if needed.

In some states, the fight against exclusion in the courts gained momentum from the fight against exclusion of linguistic minorities in schools. In the late 1960s legal aid agencies as well as parents of schoolchildren in states such as Texas, Colorado, California, and New York began protesting the practice of placing minority children in special education classes because English was their second language.[31] One prominent California case, *Diana v. Board of Education*, preceded reform in the courts. Representing the plaintiffs in the case was the California Rural Legal Assistance (CRLA), a poverty law agency from the Johnson era under the direction of Cruz Reynoso, a skilled civil rights attorney whose parents had been farmworkers. In 1970 Mexican American parents in Soledad spoke with CRLA staff about the local school board's practice of placing farmworker children in special education classes. Further investigation revealed that thousands of children throughout the state had received the same treatment because they performed poorly on the all-English Stanford-Binet Intelligent Test.[32] The evidence lampooned public education administrators. As observer Mary Ellen Leary wrote, school districts were using the test to "cull [minority] children out of mainstream education" and effectively ruin their futures. "No one pretends children illiterate in the classroom language are not a problem," she continued. "The horror lies in how that problem has been met in the past."[33]

The CRLA, which had a history of using bold lawsuits against government institutions, acted decisively by suing the California Board of Education on behalf of several Mexican American children, including Diana, the plaintiff for whom the case was named.[34] In preparing their case, CRLA attorneys pointed out that with a little language help these children were perfectly capable of keeping up in their classes. They also argued that placement in special education programs not only denied these children their education but also subjected them to verbal abuse from their peers. As the research revealed, "one [child] bore the nickname 'Mentally Ill Manuel.'"[35] The Department of Education quickly reached a settlement with the plaintiffs and began developing "culturally relevant" placement tests for children with limited English. Soon, it moved thousands of children back to regular classes and provided some funds for schools to help them catch up.[36]

In the wake of this case, civil rights advocates in California moved the fight against exclusion from the classroom to the courtroom. In 1973 the Judicial Council of California began investigating the language needs of citizens in the courts.[37] The next year, the state legislature amended article 1, section 14 of the California Constitution to read, "A person unable to understand English who is charged with a crime has a right to an interpreter throughout the proceedings."[38] While the amendment, like the Negrón ruling, represented an important milestone, court authorities were not prepared to provide interpreters. Implementation would require a process of its own.

Meanwhile, courts in other western states were also discussing the fundamental right to court interpreters. In 1974 an Arizona jury found José Natividad, a farmworker who was out of a job, guilty of transportation of marijuana and possession of the drug for sale, and the court sentenced him to prison for several years. Natividad, however, appealed the verdict, arguing that the court denied his Fourteenth Amendment right to due process by failing to inform him of his right to a court-appointed interpreter. In this case the right existed; at issue was authorities' full observance of the right. Instead of providing—or at least offering to provide—an interpreter throughout the proceedings, they found an interpreter for Natividad only when he took the stand. As in the Negrón case, they used an interpreter mainly to prosecute Natividad, but they did not provide one to help him defend himself or to understand simply what was going on. In cases such as these, interpretation did indeed favor the state. In response, Natividad rightly argued that without an interpreter he could not exercise his rights to confront witnesses, to assist in the preparation of his defense, and to be represented by competent counsel.[39]

Natividad won the appeal, and the justices of the Arizona Supreme Court remanded the case for a hearing to determine Natividad's need for an interpreter. "It is axiomatic," wrote the justices, "that an indigent defendant who is unable to speak and understand the English language should be afforded the right to have the trial proceedings translated into his native language in order to participate effectively in his own defense." The justices also refuted the argument of the prosecutor, who maintained that by failing to formally request an interpreter, Natividad had waived his right to language assistance and freed the state of any responsibility to provide it. "A defendant who passively observes in a state of complete incomprehension the complex wheels of justice grind on before him can hardly be said to have satisfied the classic definition of a waiver," the justices wrote. "This would be especially true with a Mexican national during his initial contact with our judicial system."[40] These words described Natividad's situation in the preliminary hearing as well as that of many other immigrants.

The justices concluded with an argument about the need for guaranteed interpretation services for Spanish speakers in Arizona courts. "The inability of a defendant to understand the proceedings," they wrote, "would be not only fundamentally unfair but particularly inappropriate in a state where a significant minority of the population is burdened with the handicap of being unable to effectively communicate in our national language." Certainly, the ideas that Spanish was a handicap and that English was a national language were easily contestable in a state that had once belonged to Mexico and that remained home to several Native American nations. Nevertheless, the court's ruling represented a significant challenge to the status quo. If a defendant could not understand court proceedings, the justices declared, "it would be as though [he] were to observe the proceedings from a soundproof booth or seated out of hearing at the rear of the courtroom, being able to observe but not comprehend the criminal processes whereby the state had put his freedom in jeopardy. Such a trial," they added, "comes close to being an invective against an insensible object, possibly infringing upon the accused's basic 'right to be present in the courtroom at every stage of his trial.'"[41]

The implications of the Negrón and Natividad cases were clear: the courts now needed to provide professional interpreters for speakers of limited English, which meant finding and training individuals who had the necessary skills. Most court authorities, however, had no idea where to begin, and only a few seriously tried. The earliest efforts took place in California, followed by New Mexico, New York, and Washington.[42] In California, the experiences of Holly Mikkelson, a career interpreter, professor, and advisor to judiciary committees, help illustrate the rocky path toward interpreter professionalization. Mikkelson, along with other young linguists, had her first work as a contracted interpreter at the 1976 hearings of the recently created Agricultural Labor Relations Board. By hiring interpreters for these hearings, state authorities sent a clear message that the voices of monolingual Spanish speakers were now welcome.[43]

In 1978 California authorities passed a law that established standards of competency for interpreters and required potential interpreters to take a test in order to certify their abilities.[44] This law was the first of its kind in the United States, yet, as Mikkelson recalled, the test "was kind of a joke." State authorities commissioned bilingual attorneys and Spanish professors to design the test, but none of them knew anything about interpreting. The test had multiple errors and did not even include the simultaneous mode of interpreting, which is integral to work in courtrooms.[45] When non-English speakers are on the witness stand, court interpreters use the consecutive mode to share their responses with the court, but for the questions that attorneys direct to linguistic minorities as well as all other dialogue on the record, interpreters generally use whispered simultaneous interpretation (also known as chuchotage) to keep non-English speakers abreast of the proceedings.[46]

The state government did not provide any training either. Interpreters who wanted to take the test, as Mikkelson noted, had to teach themselves. Given the situation, several interpreters in Los Angeles County who had recently formed the California Court Interpreters Association began developing practice materials for court interpreters. They also hosted the first conference on court interpreting and eventually became leaders in the national effort to professionalize court interpretation.[47]

Meanwhile, in 1978 a handful of interpreters in New York, including Dena Kohn and María Elena Cárdenas, formed the Court Interpreters and Translators Association (CITA), which began organizing symposia and publishing materials on court interpreting ethics, terminology, and practice. The first meeting took place in Kohn's living room. Shortly thereafter, interpreters in Brownsville, Texas, organized a Southwest chapter of the organization. Of those years, founding CITA member Nancy Festinger recalled, "there was a lot of *esprit de corps* ... and it was catching. Everyone around me was so determined to put court interpreting on the map, and the only way to achieve that was by working together." Sara García-Rengel added that "at the time there was this idea that [court] interpreters were sort of spies and would tell one side what they had learned from the other side." By establishing ethical standards in collaboration with regional court authorities,

CITA chipped away at those ideas. In 1989 CITA became the National Association of Judiciary Interpreters and Translators (NAJIT), which remains the profession's flagship organization.[48]

Notably, most court interpreters were women. The many reasons why women seem to have more talent for or interest in second languages is beyond the scope of this essay, but the way in which women built the interpretation profession deserves mention. Mikkelson describes interpreting as a "recessive activity" because good interpreters remain as inconspicuous as possible. Women, she continues, are often better at stepping out of the limelight than men.[49] Another scholar has described good translations or interpretations as "a pane of glass." Readers or listeners should only notice the interpreter when they find "scratches, bubbles," and "little imperfections" in the translated message.[50] In the courtroom, interpreters provide a crucial service, yet they are not the protagonists. Their role is closer to that of stenographers and clerks than it is to that of attorneys or judges. Perhaps for this reason, far more women filled the need for qualified interpreters. In time, Hispanic women became the majority in this profession.[51]

Unfortunately, the large presence of women may also help explain the struggle for respect that professional court interpreters faced. Initially, as Mikkelson recalled, nobody trusted them. Spanish-speaking defendants, witnesses, or victims were not used to working with government-hired interpreters and were not convinced that these individuals, especially Anglo American interpreters like Mikkelson, were going to help them. When interpreters did a good job, however, most of these doubts vanished.

Legal professionals, on the other hand, were a harder nut to crack. Judges, most of whom were men in the 1970s and 1980s, did not understand the role of interpreters. Mikkelson recalled one occasion when a judge required her to sit in the jury box instead of standing beside a Spanish speaker on the witness stand because he thought Mikkelson would whisper advice inappropriately to the witness. The judge apparently did not understand that it is impossible to provide a whispered simultaneous interpretation of court proceedings when one is positioned several yards away from the non-English speaker. In time, however, as the Judicial Council of California passed down instructions for judges regarding interpreters, judges became more comfortable with these individuals and their role. These instructions included swearing in interpreters before each case, a practice which has now become routine: *Do you solemnly swear to interpret the proceedings fully, completely, and accurately with no additions or omissions according to your best skill and judgment?*[52]

By far, the most persistent lack of trust involved attorneys, a challenge that exists to this day. Except for some hard-working public defenders, who grow accustomed to working with Spanish-speaking defendants and interpreters, lawyers do not like to feel dependent on interpreters, nor do they like any interference in their sacrosanct attorney-client relationships. Consequently, they often try to do the interpreter's job themselves or they question interpreters' word choices. Attorneys, however, have their own interests in mind, and they often overestimate their own abilities. Of all second languages, Spanish is particularly vulnerable to attorney interference. Not only is it the most common second language in the courtroom, but it is also the closest to English, and many English-speaking Americans have had at least some contact with it. To summarize the lament of one seasoned interpreter, attorneys who would not dare take a stab at Mandarin, Vietnamese, or Hmong often have no qualms about butchering Spanish.[53]

In some contexts, a well-intentioned effort to speak another language is admirable, but in the courtroom, attorneys' overestimation of their language skills leads to confusion and unfairness for non-English speakers. In my experience, attorneys usually fall for false cognates, such as *corte, sentencia, felonía, probación*, and *deposición*, and they rarely have any idea how to say basic terms such as *arraignment*, DA, *hearing, stipulation, enter a plea, waive your rights*, or *call the docket*.[54] I once heard a defense attorney who affirmed that he was bilingual change the crime of burglary (*allanamiento de morada*) to robbery (*robo*) because he did not know how to say the former. I can only imagine how confused the Spanish-speaking defendant must have felt. He may have broken into a building, but nobody in the courtroom—except his own defense attorney—had said anything about him stealing something. I also commonly hear attorneys of Hispanic origin converse in Spanish (sometimes rather sloppy Spanish) with their clients but switch into English for most legal terms. Since they attend law school in the United States, these attorneys know English legalese. How helpful would it be for English-speaking defendants if their attorneys uttered all legal terminology in Spanish?

Beyond terminology, attorneys or other courtroom staff rarely have any experience with the techniques of interpretation—simultaneous and consecutive, along with sight translation. The consecutive mode includes notetaking skills for responses on the witness stand that often run from three to five minutes. Sight translation refers to reading documents aloud in a different language (usually English into Spanish) so that defendants understand the forms they sign. These skills do not magically appear when someone learns a little Spanish or has a Hispanic name. As a federally certified interpreter in San Antonio recently wrote in an online post for her colleagues, "It is incumbent upon us to educate our clients . . . because too often the conduct and attitudes of legal professionals suggests a misperception of interpreting," namely the idea that interpreting requires nothing more than being reasonably bilingual, which overlooks "the enormous cognitive load imposed on the human brain by language transference processes."[55]

The experience of Cruz Reynoso in California, who left the CRLA and became a district judge, underscores the irreplaceable role of court interpreters. In his earlier career as an attorney, he himself had interpreted for clients. Of all lawyer-interpreters, Reynoso was probably one of the best, but, as he pointed out, it is impossible to make an argument before the court and interpret for someone at the same time. Even at moments when he was seated beside defendants, he said, "it was very difficult for me as a lawyer to both listen to the witnesses and respond to my client."[56] In 1982, as the first Chicano justice of the California Supreme Court, Reynoso reiterated the state's requirement that defendants of limited English proficiency have the option of receiving help from qualified interpreters. Laws of the Golden State, he wrote, "require that all persons tried in a California court understand what is happening about them."[57]

While the right to qualified interpreters became established in criminal court throughout several states, civil court was a different story. The 1978 civil case *Jara v. Municipal Court* in California turned many judges' reservations about the need for interpreters in civil cases into a significant precedent. In this case, plaintiffs sued Aurelio Jara in municipal court for damages from a car accident. To defend himself, Jara argued that he deserved an interpreter because he did not understand English, and he did not have the money to hire one. The municipal court rejected his request, and the state Supreme Court later upheld this ruling.

The reasoning of the high court in this case was surprisingly weak. In explaining their decision, the justices invoked several ideas about interpreting that the Negrón and Natividad cases had already rebutted or that were simply erroneous. "An interpreter for a witness [in criminal court] performs a different and much less burdensome function than an interpreter for a party [in a civil case]," they wrote. "The witness's interpreter is essential to permit the witness to understand questions asked and to inform counsel, judge and jury of the witness's responses. By contrast," they argued, "an interpreter for the litigant [in civil court] would interpret communications between the litigant and his counsel and all oral proceedings at trial."[58] In their reasoning, the judges assumed that Spanish speakers in criminal court only needed interpreters when they were on the witness stand, an idea that the Negrón and Natividad cases had already sundered. Moreover, they assumed that interpretation in civil court would bog down the proceedings, presumably because consecutive interpretation doubles the duration of all dialogue. The judges, however, did not understand that for all oral proceedings besides witness testimony, interpreters work simultaneously, which requires no extra time whatsoever. Only witness testimony and perhaps off-the-record attorney-client conversations, which are interpreted consecutively, take more time, but interpretation in these situations would be no less "burdensome" in civil court than in criminal court.

Adding insult to injury (and continuing with the metaphor of a burden), the judges argued that the lack of interpretation during all court proceedings besides witness testimony "has not been shown to constitute a substantial burden" to non-English speakers. Perhaps they had not read the rulings from New York or Arizona about the injustice of hearing only a "babble of . . . voices" in court or experiencing the U.S. legal system as if "from a soundproof booth." They culminated the inanity by stating that if interpretation were truly necessary, "members of [the defendant's] family, friends or neighbors—born or schooled here—may provide aid."[59]

The Jara case marked a significant step backward in the process of civil rights for linguistic minorities. Fortunately, not all judges were so set in the old ways. Justice Mathew Tobriner, who wrote the dissenting opinion, offered several convincing counterarguments. Regarding the role of court interpreters in civil as opposed to criminal cases, Tobriner argued that the majority's description of the interpreter's many functions "only illuminates the crucial purpose served by an interpreter for a non-English-speaking party." Thus, the idea that interpreters were not necessary in civil cases "would preclude the indigent defendant from any access to or participation in . . . communication [about him], and thus insure that for him the proceeding will be an empty and meaningless ritual."[60]

Tobriner also took the majority to task for their perspective on burdens. "I cannot agree," he wrote, "with the majority's assessment of the confusion, the despair, and the cynicism suffered by those who in intellectual isolation must stand by as their possessions and dignity are stripped from them by a Kafka-esque ritual deemed by the majority to constitute, nonetheless, a fair trial." Finally, regarding the idea that family or neighbors should serve as interpreters, Justice Tobriner declared, "Contrary to the majority's rather cavalier assumption, significant numbers of minority groups whose principal language is not English were neither born nor schooled here, and the defendant may not be able, therefore, to obtain assistance from his community." He continued, "In California, as in our nation as a whole, those people whose principal or sole language is not English are, unfortunately, most often part of the educationally and economically deprived subgroups, and may be the persons least likely to be able to provide for the defendant a competent and coherent translation of sophisticated court proceedings."[61]

Despite Justice Tobriner's persuasive dissent, many authorities remained reluctant to provide court-appointed interpreters for civil cases. One reason for this reluctance was money. As the interpretation profession developed, interpreters demanded competitive wages, which made some court officials less inclined to employ them. For previous generations of interpreters, as Alida Metcalf and other scholars have demonstrated, state funding was problematic because interpreter loyalties followed the money. Imperial states could use their resources to keep interpreters on their side. Yet as ethical standards of interpreter neutrality have developed from the Nuremberg trials onward, and as U.S. civil rights advocates argued for linguistic minorities' fundamental right to court interpreters, the larger challenge in U.S. courtrooms has not been interpreter bias; rather, it is the absence or underuse of professional interpreters altogether.

Though their claim may be met with derision, many professional interpreters today will say that their only loyalty is to the translation itself, an idea that has developed over the past few decades. Faithfulness to what has been said—rendering it precisely and accurately in the target language—is their goal, regardless of which party is speaking. A high level of accuracy, they would add, is the best way to achieve equity for linguistic minorities in the courtroom. Focus on their own professional craft is also what helps interpreters attenuate, at least to an extent, the vicarious trauma that comes with frequently listening to, visualizing, and repeating testimony of heinous crimes such as rape, murder, and child abuse.

In 1978 the federal government engaged in the process of interpreter professionalization with the passage of the Court Interpreter Act, which applied to interpreters in federal courts. "The Director of the Administrative Office of the United States Courts," the act stated, "shall establish a program to facilitate the use of certified and otherwise qualified interpreters in judicial proceedings instituted by the United States."[62] Unlike state governments that passed court interpreter legislation, the federal government was more prepared to follow through. In 1971 the Supreme Court had created the National Center for State Courts in an effort to make court proceedings throughout the nation more efficient and more just.[63] The National Center would eventually help oversee the certification of court interpreters throughout the nation. Holly Mikkelson recalled that the first federal interpreter exam was more accurate and rigorous than any of the states' early exams. Federal standards, along with the presence of federally certified interpreters in some states, served as an example for state courts.[64]

Besides California, states such as New Mexico, Washington, New Jersey, and New York had some of the most dedicated court administrators who took steps to find, certify, and fund courtroom interpreters.[65] In New Mexico, authorities even pioneered the idea of providing interpreters for jurors. The idea did not catch on. Court authorities in other states maintained that serving on juries required English proficiency.[66] The New Mexico experiment, however, indicates the extent to which a few administrators embraced inclusion in the courtroom.

Unfortunately, these examples were exceptional. Across the nation, most state governments were still not prioritizing interpreter programs, either because their states had relatively few linguistic minorities or because governments failed to notice the impact of language barriers. Yet as immigration from Mexico, Central America, and other regions continued, the need for court interpreters increased. The 1980 census revealed that 37 percent of residents in New Mexico were Hispanic, 21 percent in California, 19 percent in Texas, 16 percent in Arizona, and 12 percent in Colorado.[67] Overall, 14.6 percent of the national population was Hispanic. Of course, not all Hispanic residents were monolingual Spanish speakers, but many were. By 1990, 22.4 percent of the national population was Hispanic, with even larger concentrations in the Southwest—nearly 40 percent in New Mexico, 26 percent in California and Texas, and 20 percent in Arizona. Hispanic populations also increased significantly in New York, Florida, Illinois, and New Jersey.[68] With such growth, the needs of Spanish speakers were harder and harder to overlook.

By the late 1980s, academic scholars had also begun examining the role of court interpreters and, in some cases, the deficiencies of these individuals. In 1990 linguistics professor Susan Berk-Seligson published a study of pragmatics in the process of interpreting. Pragmatics deals with implications in dialogue, such as politeness, formality, or hedging. In her work, Berk-Seligson raked interpreters over the coals, arguing that the individuals that she observed consistently neglected pragmatics. Focusing solely on terminology, these interpreters changed witnesses' tones to sound more or less aggressive and to cast more or less blame than the witnesses intended. Such "inattention to pragmatic aspects of language," she wrote, "results in a skewing of a speaker's intended meaning." Furthermore, by committing this error, interpreters "introduce an element of coercion into the examination process." These problems, she concluded, call into question the "veritable explosion in the use of foreign language interpreting in American courtrooms."[69]

On one hand, Berk-Seligson's study indicated that court interpreters had room for improvement. They do sometimes fixate over terminology and neglect other skills. On the other hand, her indictment of interpreters' inattention to pragmatics tarred the whole profession and failed to acknowledge its place in the civil rights movement. Contributing to a long academic tradition of criticizing interpreters, Berk-Seligson emphasized the ways that interpreters could hurt, not help, linguistic minorities in court. However, she largely overlooked the experiences and voices of people such as Natividad, Negrón, and others who argued that if they were to have any hope of fair access to the U.S. legal system, they needed court interpreters.

As a useful counterpoint to Berk-Seligson's critiques, interpretation professor Elena M. De Jongh published an article in 1991 about the rigors of court interpretation. In this piece, De Jongh summarized several theoretical models about the work of interpreting, including listening, comprehending, restructuring, and delivering a message in the target language with the same register and level of nuance as the source language.[70] As the article made clear, professional interpreters, through training and practice, must develop the ability to carry out this work accurately and consistently, and despite shortcomings, this work was crucial to inclusion in the courts.

De Jongh also cited several pertinent statistics. In 1988 courts in the state of New York required interpreter services some 250 times per day. This same year, in Dade County, Florida interpreters helped in 154,645 proceedings. Across the nation, Spanish, by far, was the most common language for which interpreters were required. In 1988 Spanish interpreters helped in the U.S. district courts 46,064 times. Second and third on the list were interpreters of Haitian Creole (538 times) and Cantonese (520 times). Since 1980, in the federal district courts, 388 people had become certified for Spanish, and the passing rate for the federal oral exams in 1989 was 24 percent.[71] These statistics revealed a tremendous demand for interpretation services in the courts, especially for Spanish speakers, and a supply that was not keeping up. In nearly all states, court authorities could justifiably ask, "Where are all these professional interpreters that we are now supposed to be hiring?" Since criminal dockets could not sit while interpreters completed their training and passed their exams, informal interpretation still occurred far too often.

Government authorities slowly responded to these needs. In 1995 the National Center for State Courts oversaw the formation of the Consortium for Language Access in the Courts (CLAC), which helped states work together to create interpreter exams and certification programs. Washington, Oregon, Minnesota, and

New Jersey were the founding members, but other states, such as California and New York, soon joined.[72] For interpreters, the consortium, which eventually changed its name to the Council of Language Access Coordinators (still CLAC), ensured that training programs and certification exams in one state would be comparable to those in another. It also helped standardize wages, established annual continuing education requirements for interpreters, and provided reciprocity of credentials from state to state.

After its formation, the consortium, under the aegis of the National Center for State Courts, brought interpretation experts (including Holly Mikkelson) together to develop additional materials for state certification programs. In 1995 they published a 236-page report that provided instructions for strengthening state programs even if funds for training and testing were limited. To make progress, they wrote, state judicial councils needed "a pragmatic attitude about striking a balance between optimum and wholly unsatisfactory services." The report specifically recommended things such as "collaboration between states to share costs of test design," training for judges so that they could discern and dismiss clearly unqualified interpreters, and increased access to certified interpreters through telephone interpreting.[73] This last idea brought challenges of its own. Since communication is nonverbal as well as verbal, interpreters who cannot see the people for whom they interpret may struggle to understand them; plus, technology always has glitches. Overall, however, these ideas represented a sincere effort to help state authorities in the process of professionalization. In 1997 the National Center for State Courts followed up with an education program designed to help judges, lawyers, and court staff understand and work with interpreters.[74]

Over the past two and a half decades, the work of the consortium and the National Center for State Courts has helped more states improve the quality of court interpretation. In 2011 the South Dakota Supreme Court concluded a study of interpreters in its court system. The study indicated that at the time the state had no standards or training for court interpreters. As a result, "all too often not only does the limited English proficient (LEP)...individual face challenges in our judicial system, but the value and role of interpreters or translators is not clearly understood by judges and court personnel."[75] The resources of the Consortium and the examples of other states gave court authorities a clear idea of how to remedy this situation.

In Oklahoma interpreter professionalization is even more recent. In 2018, when I participated in a mandatory two-day training that preceded the first level of interpreter exams, I met several other participants who groused about the new requirements of local courts for interpreters to pass the state exams.[76] Up to that point, the staff in many courtrooms had allowed virtually anyone with a Hispanic name to provide interpretation. Many of my fellow participants had been working in that way for years, and, in their eyes, the changing requirements for state credentials amounted to little more than a bureaucratic hoop. Yet tellingly, many of them did not pass the first exams. By convincing courtroom staff to require credentialed interpreters, judicial authorities in Oklahoma, as in other states, are slowly training or, occasionally, removing the older generation of informal interpreters and replacing them with certified individuals. Certification does not mean perfection, but it does require high levels of fluency, accuracy, and ethical standards, which, in turn, gives linguistic minorities a greater chance of fully understanding and participating in court proceedings.

One of these ethical standards involves asking for repetitions or making corrections when necessary, instead of glossing over or changing unknown terms, such as *burglary* in the case of the marginally bilingual defense attorney and *mare* in the case of Boone Choate. Given the vastness of languages and legal systems, there is no shame in occasionally not knowing a word. The real shame lies in faking total proficiency before monolingual court authorities to the detriment of linguistic minorities. In cases of misunderstanding, professional interpreters simply pause the dialogue with a line such as, "Your honor, the interpreter needs to ask for clarification." (Interpreters in court speak of themselves in third person; if they were to speak in first person, listeners would assume they were speaking for the linguistic minority.)

I recall one case involving an incarcerated defendant from El Salvador whose arm was in a sling. In a conversation with the public defender, he complained that every time the prison personnel inspected his cell, *me tronchan la mano*. I had to pause and ask him what the verb *tronchar* meant. He then demonstrated how the officers would bend his injured arm behind his back, which obviously hurt.[77] As another example, that same defendant referred to *el hombre que me disparó*, which I interpreted as "the man who shot me." Seeing the sling, I assumed he had been shot in the arm or shoulder. As it turned out, however, he referred not to being shot but to being shot *at*. The original Spanish line could have referred to either meaning, but as he spoke with the attorney it became clear that he had injured his arm as he jumped out of the line of fire. Again, I had to pause the dialogue, this time to correct my earlier translation.

Ambiguity of this kind can also plague the witness stand. On another occasion, I interpreted the testimony of an immigrant woman from Mexico who had faced off a white male burglar in her living room in Oklahoma City. Although the prosecutor's initial questions required short answers—How did the burglar enter the house? How was he holding the knife? What did you do? I screamed, etc.—the interpretation soon became more difficult. After entering the living room, the burglar had advanced toward the victim brandishing the knife. Backing away, she had navigated around several pieces of furniture. The prosecutor wanted to know exactly where she had moved and how the defendant had pursued her. As the victim responded, it was clear that she was visualizing the interior of her own house. She even gestured with her hand to indicate where things were: "Well, you see, the sofa is here, so I backed over there [hand gestures], and then he came around the coffee table this way [more gestures], so I moved toward the kitchen doorway right here [again gesturing]." She went on for several minutes, sometimes pausing to wipe tears from her eyes as she relived the traumatic experience.

When she finished, the judge, the prosecutor, and everyone looked at me. On one page of my notepad, I had sketched an outline of her living room in an effort to follow her story, but it was no use. "Your Honor," I said, "the interpreter needs to ask for a repetition." Piece by piece, I then interpreted her story for the for the court. Although she continued gesturing, court interpreters do not mimic such gestures since the judge and others can see them for themselves. Regarding tone and emotion, interpreters do try to respect these elements of the dialogue, yet they also attenuate them in their own voice. A complete imitation can sound mocking.

In this particular case, the testimony ended on a relatively positive note because, unbeknown to the burglar, the victim's husband was in the bathroom taking a shower. When she screamed, the husband threw on a towel and came running out, and the burglar immediately fled out the front door. Later, when the husband was on the witness stand, the defense attorney pressed him for details regarding the appearance of the burglar. I suppose he wanted to emphasize that the husband could not reliably identify his client, the defendant, as the man who had entered the house. "When the man fled," the attorney asked, "did you follow him outside to get a glimpse of his face." "No," the elderly gentleman from Mexico responded, "I was wearing a towel and all covered in soap." Although his response stopped there, his tone seemed to say, "Would you, Mr. Defense Attorney, go running out to the road like that?"

As standards of professional practice have developed in recent decades, more and more college and university language departments have begun offering court and medical interpretation courses. Again, the West as region has helped lead the process. Among the first universities to offer such courses were the University of

New Mexico and National Hispanic University in San José, California. Several other universities in California also developed academic programs in interpretation. Since 1979 the University of Arizona has housed the National Center for Interpretation, which provides some of the best online training and continuing education classes for interpreters throughout the nation.[78] Many leading interpretation scholars also reside in the West. Roseann Dueñas González, directed the National Center for Interpretation and taught courses at the University of Arizona. Victoria Vásquez worked for the Pima County Superior Court in Tucson, Arizona. Holly Mikkelson taught for decades at the Middlebury Institute of International Studies in Monterey, California.

Currently, community colleges in many states across the country are beginning to offer certificate programs for court and medical interpreting. Admittedly, these shorter programs are easy targets for criticism, for they often underestimate the level of proficiency required before students can become professional interpreters, giving students the impression that all it takes to become an interpreter is memorizing a list or two of legal or medical terms. In the process of improvement, some of the more seasoned interpreter education programs in the West can serve as examples.

From the experiences of Gregorio Cortez, to those of Negrón and Natividad, to those of linguistic minorities in the twenty-first century, a case can be made for an arc of progress in the history of courtroom interpretation. Yet, like the civil rights movement itself, the process of professionalization remains incomplete. Additionally, it is important to remember that even if interpreters do a stellar job, which is not always the case, linguistic minorities will never be on exactly the same footing as English speakers. Sitting in a courtroom, English speakers pick up on bits and pieces of extraneous conversations that can familiarize them with judges and attorneys or with the world of the courtroom in general. Non-English speakers do not have that advantage. Rather than causing discouragement, these realities should prompt interpreters to hone their skills, and they should prompt court authorities to continually prioritize fair treatment of linguistic minorities.

Two final anecdotes, both civil cases, reiterate the potential of intermediaries in and out of the courtroom. In one, I interpreted a deposition for an elderly Mexican immigrant who had sold his truck to a car dealership. From what I gathered, the dealership used a bilingual Hispanic American employee, its intermediary, to selectively summarize parts of the all-English sales agreement in Spanish yet leave out certain clauses that would later allow the dealer to keep the truck but pay only a fraction of the promised amount. In the second case, I interpreted the testimonies of two construction workers who had painted a Montessori school in Oklahoma City. On the job site, they, like other subcontractors, had communicated with the owner of the school through the owner's Hispanic American foreman. Despite the trust the owner had placed in him, the foreman, as it turned out, had been skimming money off the owner's payments for construction materials. In a final heist, he took the fourteen-thousand dollar check that was intended to cover the labor and materials of the paint crew and skipped town.

In both cases, linguistic intermediaries in the business world used their position to bilk the parties that depended on them, especially monolingual Spanish speakers. Their examples underscore scholars' frequent and sometimes justifiable characterization of intermediaries as self-interested scoundrels and pawns of the powerful. Yet in both these cases, the victims and their attorneys paid and trusted a state-certified interpreter to help them present their evidence and seek redress in civil court. The development of this system of certification represents an additional chapter—and, in some ways, a *reinterpretation*—of the history of intermediaries in the West that grew mainly out of the U.S. civil rights movement and continues evolving to this day.

Notes

1. Taylor Cozzens, Oklahoma Certified Courtroom Interpreter; M.A. 2018 Spanish translation and interpretation, Middlebury Institute of International Studies; M.A. 2020 and PhD student, history, University of Oklahoma.
2. Spivak, "Can the Subaltern Speak?" 36–37; see also Macaulay, *Speeches by Lord Macaulay*, 359.
3. Tageldin, *Disarming Words*, 13–14; see also 18–28.
4. See Walters, *Silent Missions*; Márcio de Oliveira, *Attaché Extraordinare*; Rabe, *The Killing Zone*, 108–9, 125–27, 138, 147, 166–67; Rabe, *Kissinger and Latin America*, 61–62, 90–98, 125, 147, 230.
5. See, for example, Karttunen, *Between Worlds*; Townsend, *Malintzin's Choices*; Lamana, *Domination without Dominance*, 57–59; Valdeón, *Translation and the Spanish Empire in the Americas*; Nesvig, *Promiscuous Power*, 23–24, 33; Crandall, *These People Have Always Been a Republic*, 62–63.
6. Farriss, *Tongues of Fire*.
7. Yannakakis, *The Art of Being In-between*, 11, 30.
8. See Donnelly et al. *Operation Just Cause*, 16–17; Donoghue, *Borderland on the Isthmus*, 188; Larry Rohter, "Tuning in to the News beyond Noriega's Grip," *New York Times*, March 24, 1988; Arthur S. Brisbane, "U.S. Officials Defend Panama Strategy: Scowcroft Says Bush Personally Authorized Taking Custody of Noriega,"

Washington Post, October 9, 1989; Douglas Jehl, "Outspoken General Hopes to Change Panama's Ways," *Los Angeles Times*, January 20, 1990; Myra MacPherson, "Panama's Philosopher Pol: Ricardo Arias Calderon's Leap from Exiled Academic to Vice President," *Washington Post*, January 30, 1990.

9. Taylor, *Magistrates of the Sacred*, 5–6; see also Taylor, "Between Global Process and Local Knowledge," 148–49, 152–53.
10. Metcalf, *Go Betweens and the Colonization of Brazil*, 2.
11. See, of course, Limerick, *Legacy of Conquest*; for a more recent masterpiece, see Madley, *American Genocide*.
12. See also Szasz, *Between Indians and White Worlds*; Hosmer, "Reflections on Indian Cultural 'Brokers'"; Tong, *Susan La Flesche Picotte*; Merrell, *Into the American Woods*.
13. See Gramsci, *Selections from the Prison Notebooks*, 161 (161–68); see also, Martin, *Gramsci's Political Analysis*, 65–88.
14. Wrobel, *America's West*.
15. Dueñas González, Vasquez, and Mikkelson, *Fundamentals of Court Interpretation*, 35–70.
16. Paredes, *With a Pistol*, 62 (58–64).
17. Paredes, *With a Pistol*, 59.
18. Dueñas González, Vásquez, Mikkelson, *Fundamentals of Court Interpretation*, 48.
19. "Perovich V. United States, 205 U.S. 86 (1907)," U.S. Supreme Court, https://www.loc.gov/item/usrep205086/; "Vuko Perovich, Plff. In Err., v. United States," Cornell Law School Legal Information Institute, accessed July 11, 2022, https://www.law.cornell.edu/supremecourt/text/205/86; Naske, "The Case of Vuco Perovich," 2–9.
20. Dueñas González, Vásquez, Mikkelson, *Fundamentals of Court Interpretation*, 48–49.
21. Sommer, *Proceed with Caution*, 93.
22. Sommer, *Proceed with Caution*, 94.
23. Gaiba, *Origins of Simultaneous Interpretation*, 6.
24. For the development of professional interpretation prior to Nuremberg, see Baigorri-Jalón, *From Paris to Nuremberg*.
25. Gaiba, *Origins of Simultaneous Interpretation*, 106–8; emphasis in original.
26. Gaiba, *Origins of Simultaneous Interpretation*, 161–66.
27. Pinker, *Better Angels of Our Nature*, 249–94, esp. 289–90.
28. See the materials on court interpreting from the 1990s cited in notes 73–75.
29. "Confrontation—Right to a Translator"; see also "United States ex Rel. Negron v. State of N.Y.," October 15, 1970, Casetext, https://casetext.com/case/united-states-ex-rel-negron-v-state-of-ny.
30. "The Bill of Rights: A Transcription," accessed June 30, 2023, https://www.archives.gov/founding-docs/bill-of-rights-transcript.
31. Mary Ellen Leary, "Children Who Are Tested in an Alien Language: Mentally Retarded?" *New Republic*, May 30, 1970; CRLA Records, box 65, folder 6.
32. See Glick and Jourdane, *Soledad Children*.

33. Leary, "Children Who Are Tested."
34. As examples of CRLA litigation, in 1967 the agency sued the Federal Department of Labor for acquiescing to the demands of California growers and bringing temporary Bracero laborers across the border, despite the availability of local farmworkers. In 1969 it again filed suit against the federal government for allowing growers to still use the pesticide DDT. See "Braceros in California: Summary of the CRLA Brief to the Department of Labor," September 19, 1967, CRLA Records, carton 174, folder 4. See also Cole and Foster, *From the Ground Up*, 221n32; Sze, "Denormalizing Embodied Toxicity," 111.
35. Leary, "Children Who Are Tested."
36. "A Brief Analysis of the 1969–1970 Caseload," 8–10, CRLA Records, box 7, folder 9; see also Leary, "Children Who Are Tested."
37. See "California Code, Government Code 68560," FindLaw, accessed June 23, 2022, https://codes.findlaw.com/ca/government-code/gov-sect-68560.html.
38. Judicial Council of California, "Fact Sheet: Court Interpreters Program."
39. "Opinion: State v. Natividad, Supreme Court of Arizona," Casetext: Smarter Legal Research, accessed June 23, 2022, https://casetext.com/case/state-v-natividad/.
40. "Opinion: State v. Natividad, Supreme Court of Arizona."
41. "Opinion: State v. Natividad, Supreme Court of Arizona."
42. Dueñas González, Vasquez, and Mikkelson, *Fundamentals of Court Interpretation*, 71–79.
43. Holly Mikkelson, in conversation with author, June 30, 2022.
44. Judicial Council of California, "Fact Sheet."
45. Holly Mikkelson, in conversation with author, June 30, 2022.
46. Some Asian languages are exceptions to this rule because their sentence structures differ drastically from that of English, making simultaneous interpretation impractical; in these cases consecutive is the best option.
47. Holly Mikkelson, in conversation with author, June 30, 2022; see also "About Us," CCIA, accessed July 6, 2022, http://www.ccia.org/about-us.html.
48. Janis Palma, "NAJIT: The First Forty Years," National Association of Judiciary Interpreters and Translators, accessed February 4, 2025, https://najit.org/wp-content/uploads/2020/12/NAJIT-The-First-Forty-Years.pdf.
49. Holly Mikkelson, in conversation with author, June 30, 2022.
50. See the quotations from Norman Shapiro (and Willard Trask) in Venuti, *Translator's Invisibility*, 1, 7.
51. In 2022 the California list of official Spanish-English interpreters included 1,319 individuals. Judging by their names, between 70 and 75 percent of these individuals are women, and just over 50 percent of all interpreters are Hispanic women. The statistics in many other states are similar. In Washington, nearly 70 percent of all interpreters are women, and some 45 percent are Hispanic women. In Oklahoma, around 70 percent of all interpreters are women, and some 55 percent are Hispanic women. These percentages are approximate, of course, because a name alone does not fully reveal ethnicity and gender identity, but a long list of names can provide a

panorama. See "Search for an Interpreter," California Courts: The Judicial Branch of California, accessed July 15, 2022, https://www.courts.ca.gov/35273.htm; "Court Interpreters," Washington Courts, accessed July 15, 2022, https://www.courts.wa.gov/programs_orgs/pos_interpret/; "Certified Courtroom Interpreters," Oklahoma State Courts Network, accessed July 15, 2022, https://www.oscn.net/static/forms/aoc_forms/interpreter.asp.

52. Holly Mikkelson, in conversation with author, June 30, 2022; the wording of the interpreter's oath varies slightly from state to state.
53. Kathleen Shelly, "I Can't Get No Respect: Lamentations of a Language Professional," NAJIT blog, October 26, 2012, https://najit.org/i-cant-get-no-respect-lamentations-of-a-language-professional/.
54. Regarding the false cognates, the term *corte* does mean *court*, but legally it only refers to the high court, supreme court, or *corte de última instancia*; for trial and appeals courts, the terms *juzgado* and *tribunal* are correct. The term *sentencia* also exists, but in Spanish it only refers to the judgment or verdict, whereas *sentence* in English refers to the punishment (*pena*); to pass sentence is to *dictar la pena*. A *felonía* in Spanish is a minor crime, while felony in English, of course, is a serious crime (*delito grave*). Interpreters debate the best translation of *probation*—*libertad vigilada, libertad condicional*, etc.—but it is certainly not *probación*. A deposition is a *declaración jurada*.
55. Janis Palma, "Interpreters Are Not Tools," NAJIT, July 11, 2022, https://najit.org/interpreters-are-not-tools/.
56. Kristina Horton Flaherty, "Cruz Reynoso Honored as a 'Legal Giant,'" *California Bar Journal*, October 2009, https://archive.calbar.ca.gov/archive/Archive.aspx?articleId=96466&categoryId=96412&month=10&year=2009.
57. Maria L. La Ganga, "Cruz Reynoso, California's First Latino State Supreme Court Justice, Dies at 90," *Los Angeles Times*, May 7, 2021, https://www.latimes.com/obituaries/story/2021-05-07/cruz-reynoso-california-supreme-court-justice-died.
58. "Jara v. Municipal Court," Stanford Law School: Supreme Court of California Resources, accessed July 12, 2022, https://scocal.stanford.edu/opinion/jara-v-municipal-court-28075.
59. "Jara v. Municipal Court."
60. "Jara v. Municipal Court."
61. "Jara v. Municipal Court."
62. See 28 U.S. Code 1827 Interpreters in Courts of the United States, Legal Information Institute, Cornell Law School, accessed June 23, 2022, https://www.law.cornell.edu/uscode/text/28/1827.
63. See "Mission and History: National Center for State Courts," accessed July 8, 2022, https://www.ncsc.org/about-us/mission-and-history.
64. Holly Mikkelson, in conversation with author, June 30, 2022.
65. Dueñas González, Vasquez, and Mikkelson, *Fundamentals of Court Interpretation*, 71–79.
66. Holly Mikkelson, in conversation with author, June 30, 2022.

67. U.S. Dep. Of Commerce, Bureau of the Census, "1980 Census of Population, Persons of Spanish Origin by State, 1980: Supplementary Report." For comparison, see U.S. Census Bureau, "1970 Census of Population, Subject Reports: Persons of Spanish Origin."
68. U.S. Dep. Of Commerce, Economics and Statistics Administration, and Bureau of the Census, "We the American Hispanics," September 1993.
69. Berk-Seligson, *Bilingual Courtroom*, 1–3, 194–97.
70. De Jongh, "Foreign Language Interpreters in the Courtroom," 285, 288–90.
71. De Jongh, "Foreign Language Interpreters," 286–87, 294.
72. "About Us: National Center for State Courts," accessed July 8, 2022, https://www.ncsc.org/consulting-and-research/areas-of-expertise/interpreter-info/about-us.
73. National Center for State Courts, "Court Interpretation," 1–5.
74. National Center for State Courts, "Managing Language Problems."
75. South Dakota Supreme Court, "Supreme Court's Committee."
76. Most states now have two levels of interpreter credentials: registered (level 1) and certified (level 2). Federal certification is even higher. In Oklahoma, as in other states, court staff are supposed to provide certified interpreters for felony cases, but because of a shortage of certified individuals, the courts do not always comply with this rule.
77. According the dictionary of the Real Academica Española, *tronchar* refers to the hand motion of breaking the stem (*el troncho*) of a vegetable or breaking anything else in a similar way. The adjective *tronchada* is also used to describe, for example, the twisted nature of a pig's tail. See Real Academica Española, s.v. "tronchado," accessed May 21, 2024, https://dle.rae.es/tronchado?m=form.
78. "The University of Arizona College of Humanities: National Center for Interpretation," accessed July 15, 2022, https://nci.arizona.edu/training/citi.

Bibliography

ARCHIVAL SOURCES

CRLA Records (M0750). Department of Special Collections and University Archives. Stanford University Libraries.

PUBLISHED WORKS

Baigorri-Jalón, Jesús. *From Paris to Nuremberg: The Birth of Conference Interpreting.* Translated by Holly Mikkelson and Barry Slaughter Olsen. Philadelphia: John Benjamin's, 2014.

Berk-Seligson, Susan. *The Bilingual Courtroom: Court Interpreters in the Judicial Process.* Chicago: University of Chicago Press, 1990.

Cole, Luke W., and Sheila R. Foster. *From the Ground Up: Environmental Racism and the Rise of the Environmental Justice Movement.* New York: New York University Press, 2001.

"Confrontation—Right to a Translator (United States ex rel. Negrón v. State of New York)." *St. John's Law Review* 46, no. 3 (1972): 468–70.

Crandall, Maurice. *These People Have Always Been a Republic: Indigenous Electorates in the U.S.-Mexico Borderlands, 1598–1912*. Chapel Hill: University of North Carolina, 2019.

De Jongh, Elena M. "Foreign Language Interpreters in the Courtroom: The Case for Linguistic and Cultural Proficiency." *Modern Language Journal* 75, no. 4 (1991): 285–95.

Donnelly, Thomas, et al. *Operation Just Cause: The Storming of Panama*. New York: Lexington Books, 1991.

Dueñas González, Roseann, Victoria F. Vasquez, and Holly Mikkelson. *Fundamentals of Court Interpretation: Theory, Policy, Practice*. Durham NC: Carolina Academic Press, 1991.

Donoghue, Michael E. *Borderland on the Isthmus: Race, Culture, and the Struggle for the Canal Zone*. Durham: Duke University Press, 2014.

Farriss, Nancy. *Tongues of Fire: Language and Evangelization in Colonial Mexico*. New York: Oxford University Press, 2018.

Gaiba, Francesca. *The Origins of Simultaneous Interpretation: The Nuremberg Trial*. Ottawa: University of Ottawa Press, 1998.

Glick, Marty, and Maurice Jourdane. *The Soledad Children: The Fight to End Discriminatory IQ Tests*. Houston: Arte Público Press, 2019.

Gramsci, Antonio. *Selections from the Prison Notebooks*. Edited and translated by Quintin Hoare and Geoffrey Nowell Smith. New York: International Publishers, 1971.

Hosmer, Brian. "Reflections on Indian Cultural 'Brokers': Reginald Oshkosh, Mitchell Oshkenaniew, and the Politics of Menominee Lumbering." *Ethnohistory* 44, no. 3 (1997): 493–509.

Judicial Council of California. "Fact Sheet: Court Interpreters Program." September 2023. https://languageaccess.courts.ca.gov/sites/default/files/partners/default/2024-01/cip%20fact%20sheet.pdf.

Karttunen, Frances. *Between Worlds: Interpreters, Guides, and Survivors*. New Brunswick: Rutgers University Press, 1994.

Lamana, Gonzalo. *Domination without Dominance: Inca-Spanish Encounters in Early Colonial Peru*. Durham NC: Duke University Press, 2008.

Limerick, Patricia Nelson. *Legacy of Conquest: The Unbroken Past of the American West*. New York: W. W. Norton, 1987.

Macaulay, Thomas Babington. *Speeches by Lord Macaulay: With His Minute on Indian Education*, edited by G. M. Young. London: Oxford University Press, 1952 [1835].

Madley, Benjamin. *An American Genocide: The United States and the California Indian Catastrophe, 1846–1873*. New Haven: Yale University Press, 2017.

Márcio de Oliveira, Frank. *Attaché Extraordinare: Vernon A. Walters in Brazil*. Washington DC: National Defense Intelligence College, 2009.

Martin, James. *Gramsci's Political Analysis: A Critical Introduction*. New York: St. Martin's, 1998.

Merrell, James. *Into the American Woods: Negotiators on the Pennsylvania Frontier*. New York: W. W. Norton, 1999.

Metcalf, Alida C. *Go Betweens and the Colonization of Brazil: 1500–1600*. Austin: University of Texas Press, 2005.

Naske, Claus-M. "The Case of Vuco Perovich." *Pacific Northwest Quarterly* 78, no. 1/2 (1987): 2–9.

National Center for State Courts. "Court Interpretation: Model Guides for Policy and Practice in the State Courts." Williamsburg VA: State Justice Institute, 1995. https://www.ncsc.org/__data/assets/pdf_file/0029/19694/court_interpretation_model_guides_for_policy_and_practice_in_the_state_courts.pdf.

———. "Managing Language Problems: A Court Interpreting Education Program for Judges, Lawyers, and Court Managers," 1997. https://www.ojp.gov/pdffiles1/Digitization/173730ncjrs.pdf.

Nesvig, Martin Austin. *Promiscuous Power: An Unorthodox History of New Spain*. Austin: University of Texas Press, 2018.

Paredes, Américo. *With a Pistol in His Hand: A Border Ballad and Its Hero*. Austin: University of Texas Press, 1998 [1958].

Pinker, Steven. *The Better Angels of Our Nature: Why Violence Has Declined*. New York: Penguin Books, 2012.

Rabe, Steven G. *The Killing Zone: The United States Wages Cold War in Latin America*. New York: Oxford University Press, 2012.

———. *Kissinger and Latin America: Intervention, Human Rights, and Diplomacy*. Ithaca: Cornell University Press, 2020.

Sommer, Doris. *Proceed with Caution, When Engaged by Minority Writing in the Americas*. Cambridge: Harvard University Press, 1999.

South Dakota Supreme Court. "Supreme Court's Committee to Study the Use of Interpreters and Translators in the South Dakota Court System: 2011 Report to the South Dakota Supreme Court," November 18, 2011. https://ujs.sd.gov/uploads/committees/2011_interpreter_committee_report_final.pdf.

Spivak, Gayatri Chakravorty. "Can the Subaltern Speak?" In *Can the Subaltern Speak? Reflections on the History of an Idea*, edited by Rosalind C. Morris, 21–80. New York: Columbia University Press, 2010 [1985].

Szasz, Margaret Connell. *Between Indians and White Worlds: The Cultural Broker*. Norman: University of Oklahoma Press, 1994.

Sze, Julie. "Denormalizing Embodied Toxicity: The Case of Kettleman City." In *Racial Ecologies*, edited by Leilani Nshime and Kim D. Hester Williams, 107–22. Seattle: University of Washington Press, 2018.

Tageldin, Shaden M. *Disarming Words: Empire and Seductions of Translation in Egypt*. Berkeley: University of California Press, 2011.

Taylor, William. "Between Global Process and Local Knowledge: An Inquiry into Early Latin American Social History, 1500–1900." In *Reliving the Past: The Worlds of Social History*, edited by Olivier Zunz, 115–90. Chapel Hill: University of North Carolina Press, 1985.

———. *Magistrates of the Sacred: Priests and Parishioners in Eighteenth-Century Mexico*. Stanford: Stanford University Press, 1996.

Tong, Benson. *Susan La Flesche Picotte, M.D.* Norman: University of Oklahoma Press, 1999.

Townsend, Camilla. *Malintzin's Choices: An Indian Woman in the Conquest of Mexico.* Albuquerque: University of New Mexico Press, 2006.

U.S. Census Bureau. "1970 Census of Population Subject Reports: Persons of Spanish Origin," June 1973. https://www.census.gov/library/publications/1973/dec/pc-2-1c.html.

U.S. Department of Commerce. Bureau of the Census. "1980 Census of Population, Persons of Spanish Origin by State, 1980: Supplementary Report." https://assets.nhgis.org/original data/modern-census/1980PL_80-S1–7.pdf.

U.S. Department of Commerce. Economics and Statistics Administration and Bureau of the Census. "We the American Hispanics," September 1993. https://www.census.gov/library/publications/1993/dec/we-02.html.

Valdeón, Roberto A. *Translation and the Spanish Empire in the Americas.* Philadelphia: John Benjamins, 2014.

Venuti, Lawrence. *The Translator's Invisibility: A History of Translation.* London: Routledge, 1995.

Walters, Vernon A. *Silent Missions.* New York: Doubleday, 1978.

Wrobel, David. *America's West: A History, 1890–1950.* Cambridge: Cambridge University Press, 2017.

Yannakakis, Yanna. *The Art of Being In-between: Native Intermediaries, Indian Identity, and Local Rule in Colonial Oaxaca.* Durham: Duke University Press, 2008.

Dueling Interpretations

From the editors: In the following exchange, members of the New York State Senate are investigating the history of government-Indigenous treaties and annuities. In this particular case, historical agreements have been complicated by federal (United States and Canada) and Native divisions (Cayuga, Seneca, and Six Nations peoples). Excerpts from two committee meetings follow, the first held in Bradford, Ontario, on November 21, 1889. The teams are as follows:

CANADIAN-BASED INTERESTS
Attorney C. H. Ritchie (Canadian government)
General J. C. Strong (Cayuga Nation)
James Styres (interpreter)

U.S.-BASED INTERESTS
New York Senate committee members

Attorney J. G. Johnson (Seneca Indians)
Reid Winne (interpreter)

The first meeting reveals that, as the Canadian side proposes to call its next witness, the New York State delegation and its interpreter Reid Winne have come to distrust the translations offered by the Canadian interpreter, James Styres.

Testimony Taken before the Senate Committee

RITCHIE: There is another aged witness here whom I propose calling in anticipation so that we may get his evidence.

JOHNSON: If the court please, in view of the fact that the interpreter and the witness have a common interest, and it is utterly impossible for the commission to know what is being said, or the form or manner of expressing it, I would ask that Mr. Winne from this time on be authorized to interpret, for the reason that Mr. Winne, whose interest is certainly not in common with that of the witness or the party that is prosecuting, and that they have to guard against it, the presence of two interpreters from whom they may have the fullest knowledge, and can know in an instant if he deviated in any way that there be a substitution of interpreters.

RITCHIE: I do not know. It stands in the same position, I understand. I understand that the interests are practically identical, if they are interested at all.

STRONG: Precisely identical.

JOHNSON: Oh, no; Mr. Winne represents the Western band, from whom you propose to divert the money.

RITCHIE: Then he has an interest.

JOHNSON: I thought it was so easy for the interpreter, by inflection or form of the interrogatory, to indicate how he desired, or imagined the counsel desired, the question to be answered, and particularly with what has to come from the suggestions that are made from the counsel, *pro* and *con*, so that the direction is pointed out, and it seems to me to be no more than fair that that course should be taken from which no possible injury could come to any person.

RITCHIE: It seems to me the same injury would come, if as a matter of fact he could by inflection, or by any method outside of the direct language; your man may do it as well as this interpreter.

JOHNSON: But, I say, the interpreter himself is a party in interest.

STRONG: To do away with anything of that kind, here (Styres) is the official interpreter of the government.

JOHNSON: The official interpreter, as we understand, is not satisfactory at all.

STRONG: I do not see why Mr. Winne is not just as much interested as Mr. Styres, and as a little of the start we had here would indicate, Mr. Styres seems to understand our language as well as Winne, if not better, and it seems to me their interests are identical, one antagonistic and one favorable.

JOHNSON: With a willing witness and willing interpreter you have a twofold cord with which to bind us. My interpreter sits there and tells me that your interpreter does by the manner and form of asking the question indicate clearly the form of the answer in many cases that is desired.

STRONG: Let him mention that instantaneously at the time, and let the interpreter correct it.

JOHNSON: He has, but it seems to me we had better have a correction of the whole thing.

STRONG: I do not see how you get a correction by changing one interpreter for the other.

JOHNSON: The witness is a willing witness, one anxious to do your bidding, one schooled partially through the examination of the counsel, and who understands partially the facts desired to be proved by him.

LAUGHLIN: Well, gentlemen, of course the interpreter ought to give only the language put in his mouth by counsel to the witness from whom he asks a question. The interpreter ought also to give just the exact language as near as he can translate it of the witness who answers the questions. Mr. Winne, I understand, is here as an interpreter, and the committee at Buffalo authorized the counsel to request his attendance. I think perhaps we ought to use him as our interpreter, if our Government expects to pay his expenses here.

STRONG: I supposed he was being used in that capacity now.

LAUGHLIN: I understand there are only a few more witnesses to be sworn this afternoon, and in as much as the request has been made, certainly I can not see any objection to letting Mr. Winne interpret this afternoon.

STRONG: Well, we will submit to the decision of course.

LAUGHLIN: I do not see what objection there can be and the two interpreters are here; they can watch your interests as closely as Winne has, and Mr. Winne can act as interpreter this afternoon, and Mr. Styres can sit over by General Strong.

RITCHIE: Has he got good lungs?

WINNE: I think I have got good lungs; I think I can be heard whenever I want to be, I do not think I have got consumption yet.

LAUGHLIN: Now, Mr. Winne, you understand when the counsel asks the witness a question you ask it in just the same language, the same words as near as you can interpret them, and give us everything that the witness says in reply, tell use everything. If you do not, why Mr. Styres or these other gentlemen here will correct you. That is your sworn duty you understand, you were sworn yesterday as an interpreter.

WINNE: Yes, sir.

•

From the editors: Another meeting, held six days later in Buffalo, New York, features the same individuals. The committee is soliciting the testimony of David Hill (b. 1810), a leader of the Canadian Seneca for more than fifty years. Attorney Ritchie, for the Canadian government, is asking about Hill's understanding of two histori-

cal meetings held sixty years earlier, one in Canada, the other in the United States. Ritchie is attempting to understand—through Mr. Styres's interpretations—if these meetings transpired around the same time.

> RITCHIE (TO STYRES): Ask him again how near together were these meetings held, the meeting in Canada and the meeting in the States, in connection with this question of the mode of electing chiefs.
>
> HILL (VIA STYRES): Just about.
>
> RITCHIE: About what?
>
> HILL (VIA STYRES): About the council over there.
>
> RITCHIE: About that same time?
>
> HILL (VIA STYRES): Yes, sir; that was the cause of it; they wanted to hold the council; some wanted to have chiefs and the others wanted to have head officers.
>
> RITCHIE: Then the two meetings were held about the same time; the meeting in the United States and the meeting in Canada at Middleport were held pretty near the same time?
>
> HILL (VIA STYRES): Yes; somewhere.
>
> RITCHIE (TO STYRES): Then, did you correctly interpret him when you said some time ago that there was eighteen years elapsed between the two?
>
> STYRES: That is what he says now.
>
> RITCHIE: What?
>
> STYRES: He thinks it was somewhere about eighteen years apart.
>
> RITCHIE (RESUMING TO HILL): You said a moment ago that he said they were both held about the same time; how do you account for that?
>
> STYRES (INTERPRETING HILL): He says he is himself Indian, and that is the way he expresses it; he says eighteen years is not so very long; he says you white folks, they think every word you put down on a paper, but he don't put it down on a paper.
>
> RITCHIE (TO STYRES): But what I want to get at is what he means; whether he thinks they were held about eighteen years apart?
>
> JOHNSON: What language is he speaking?
>
> STYRES: Onondaga.
>
> RITCHIE: Well, the two interpreters between them could ascertain what he means. Does Mr. Winne hear him?
>
> WINNE: I hear him, but do not exactly understand always.
>
> RITCHIE: You do not understand that eighteen years is only a little while?

Dueling Interpretations

WINNE: Oh, yes; I understand that eighteen years is a long while, but to his (Hill's) understanding eighteen years is a very little while.
JOHNSON: That is, that the Indian says he only means a little while?
WINNE: He says he understands one way and the white people another.
RITCHIE: What would you understand now? I am asking him whether these two councils were held about the same time, one in the States, and within a month or two afterwards, calling another on the other side, or perhaps a year or two? Is that the way you understand, or do you understand that there was that great lapse of time between the two meetings? Perhaps Mr. Styres can ask him again what he means about it.
WINNE: He says if you do not understand him, he do [*sic*] not think he can make you understand.[1]

Notes

1. New York Committee on Indian Affairs, *Testimony Taken before the Senate Committee on Indian Affairs Relative to the Cayuga Indians Under Resolution of May 15, 1889* (Albany: James B. Lyon, State Printer, 1890), 109–11, 268–70.

9

Puente, ຂົວ, Bridge

Interpreting for Social Transformation in Storm Lake, Iowa

ANDREW OFFENBURGER

Puente, ຂົວ, bridge: each of these terms describes a physical structure linking two points, across water or land. The words—themselves a series of lines and curves recognized by speakers of Spanish, Lao, and English—correspond to a particular sound, intelligible to certain people. We readers recognize one of these terms more than others. We cling to it for meaning. If you are reading this chapter, published in English, "bridge" likely resonates most forcefully. But for multilingual midwestern towns like Storm Lake, Iowa, each of these terms feels natural to a significant percentage of its population. All others feel foreign. This language variation—including dozens of others in the town—decenters English as a dominant language and shapes plural perceptions of everyday life in rural Iowa. Interpreting these languages therefore becomes a necessary act of self-identification, of group formation, of community policing.

Set in the expansive, flat prairie of northwest Iowa, amid a checkerboard of county roads and waving tassels, Storm Lake's meatpacking plants process pork as much as they do dreams for immigrant laborers from dozens of nations.[1] What is the town's population? Ask any resident, and the most consistent response will include "about": "about twelve thousand," or "about fourteen thousand," perhaps. No one is quite sure. Beyond the grasp of census workers, an untold number of undocumented immigrants squeeze into apartments, working toward a better future. Ever since the early 1990s, the pull effect of working at Iowa Beef Processors (IBP)—and now Tyson Fresh Meats—has redefined Storm Lake.[2] In a state with 90 percent self-identified Caucasians, the local school district enrolls nearly three thousand students, "more than 85% non-Caucasian." A total of thirty-one languages other than English are spoken in the school district, with about two-thirds learning English.[3] A majority speaks Spanish as a native tongue, while residents of Asian descent account for 20 percent of the town's population.[4]

In the early 1990s, much to their credit, local officials recognized the forces transforming the town and took steps to add a "community service officer" (CSO) to its police force. This need became all the more evident in 1992, when a fire erupted at a house and its Spanish-speaking residents nearly died for lack of interpretive services. The following week, the city made hiring a CSO proficient in Lao or Spanish a "top priority" for the next year.[5] Within two years, it had hired two women who had been living in town for some time: Graciela Vrieze, from northern Mexico, and Pom Kavan, from Laos.

In early news reports, local officials repeatedly described the CSO and other interpretive positions as "bridges." These jobs were created to "bridge language and cultural barriers," to "bridge the gap between the people," to serve as a "bridge to bring cultures together," to be "a bridge between Laotian people and officers," and to "bridge the cultural gap."[6] While a "bridge" can be a useful metaphor easily understood, the image it conveys—of an unchanging physical structure between distinct entities—misses the required flexibility and fluidity of the position, as well as the multiple, overlapping obligations that interpreters have within their communities.

In the case of Storm Lake, community ties strained beneath the weight of national immigration debates in 1996, a moment of crisis when the federal government raided local meatpacking plants to deport undocumented workers. During the raid and soon after, Storm Lake relied on the cultural flexibility of CSOs. These critical interpreting positions offered some sense of continuity for a town trying to span a number of gaps: between legal and illegal, and between the demands of industrial agriculture and immigrant workers. The historical moment exposed the immense challenges and conflicting loyalties of serving as a CSO. Here, "bridge" itself failed as a metaphor, obscuring the complicated reality of lived experiences.

This chapter follows the lives and careers of Graciela Vrieze and Pom Kavan, who each worked as CSOs in Storm Lake for three decades. Their examples reveal continuities in interpreting, from western frontiers and borders to the present day. At the same time, the examples of Vrieze and Kavan—the former crossing the border through marriage, and the latter fleeing by boat as a refugee—illustrate how individuals of humble origins used their linguistic skills to shape community formation through the power of the police. Their experiences interpreting cultures for thirty years in Storm Lake, Iowa, convey the power and also the limits of puente, ಜೂ, and bridge.

Graciela Vrieze

Born in southern Mexico and raised in the border town of San Luis Río Colorado, twenty miles east of Mexicali and across the border from Yuma, Arizona, Graciela Vrieze arrived in Storm Lake through marriage. She first met her husband, Terry, from southern Minnesota, when he was stationed as a marine in Yuma. Though the crossing of these two individuals was by chance—she unexpectedly met him through a friend of a friend—historical forces shaped the borderlands, leading Graciela and Terry to live on neighboring sides of the border.

After a quick courtship of a few months, the pair wed and moved to Storm Lake, near her in-laws and where IBP was actively hiring. Work at IBP, and life in Storm Lake, took some adjustment for the new arrival from Mexico. So much was new: living in the Midwest, its unusual daily rhythms, its more verdant landscape, its . . . smells. "First of all, I had never smelled pigs," Vrieze remembered with a smirk. "It was awful. . . . I started gagging so bad! My husband was laughing. . . . As the weeks went by, I started getting used to it. . . . I felt like a drama queen." Life in rural Iowa required adjustment, sure, but the structure of finding employment set her on a path to finding her place in a new community.

Vrieze landed a position with the processing plant, working partly "on the line" and also as an interpreter in its orientation classroom. "They pulled me out every time they need[ed] somebody," she recalled. "At that time, when I first started, there wasn't very many Hispanics. But as the years went by, they started coming. And [interpreting] was needed. I was basically more in the classroom."[7] The demand for translation, to explain rules and regulations, intensified the need for bilingual interpreters in a rapidly globalizing rural town. The need originated from the economic pull of the processing plant, which recruited labor from Latin America and Southeast Asia, but the national origins of IBP's workers fluctuated with global developments. Storm Lake's immigrants tended to come in waves. Reading a list of some of them—Vietnam, Laos, Mexico and Central America, Sudan, Micronesia—is to follow a chronology of global migration from the 1970s to today. To call this a ready labor supply might resonate with economic historians, but such a phrase obscures the social disruptions leading to willing and often desperate migrants seeking safety, security, and a new home. This pattern did not

FIG 7. Graciela Vrieze. Digital watercolor by Ricky Hadi, based on a photograph of Graciela Vrieze by the author.

apply directly to Vrieze, who arrived as a spouse, but it did affect her employability and relationships with other new arrivals.

Within a year or two, with increasing numbers of Spanish-language residents in town, Vrieze found additional opportunities as a translator. She helped workers in their daily lives outside the plant, accompanying them to the doctor, for instance. She negotiated terms between renters and their landlords. "Pretty soon the hospital found out that I spoke Spanish, and they started calling me," she said. Vrieze volunteered as an interpreter in the obstetrics department over a period of three years, winning recognition as volunteer of the year and becoming enmeshed in a new community that needed and valued her unique skills. In 1993, five years after Vrieze moved to Storm Lake, the City Council advertised a new position of cultural liaison for the police department. Rather than fighting crime "directly," the local *Pilot Tribune* reported, Vrieze would "perform outreach and educational programs" in uniform, though unarmed.[8]

Vrieze's move from private enterprise (IBP) and volunteering for the hospital to the center of community power (SLPD) brought with it some social strains. Line workers with and without documentation, friends, and acquaintances she had assisted with translation celebrated her advancement, for sure, but this new position left her potentially vulnerable to uninformed suspicions that she would "sell out" her people. "It was like hearsay, you know?" Vrieze said. "I know that the rumors were out there. They didn't tell me directly. . . . It hurt my feelings, because they obviously didn't know me." Vrieze felt these frustrations acutely because, by the middle 1990s, she knew a large swath of Storm Lake residents by either working with them on the line, assisting them in delivering children, or working to alleviate problems as a CSO before they could lead to larger issues. The nickname "Gracie" became a single-word institution in Storm Lake. "I would say probably 95% of the population in Storm Lake knows my phone number," she said without a smile, a simple statement of fact. "I've had my house phone number for thirty years. . . . The same phone number. Thirty years."[9] The consistency she brought to her profession and to her community stood in stark contrast to the rapid social change in the small Iowa town.

As much as city officials and the general public hoped she could bridge increasing differences in the community, and despite her broad name recognition, Vrieze's new position came with an unanticipated personal cost. "We [CSOs] have to keep things separately," she said. "Work is one thing. Friendship is another thing. You can't really mix it. . . . It's a change of way you conduct yourself in public and you work for the police station. . . . I kind of pulled myself out a little bit from the rest of my friends." The work of interpretation, of bringing separate communities together through cultural flexibility, for Vrieze and other CSOs, occasionally strained personal relationships in extended social networks. The same can be said of how line workers viewed her marriage to an American of western European descent. Intercultural connections can test the sense of being a fully vested member of a single community.

This paradox of cultural flexibility and strained relations emerged most forcefully on Friday, May 10, 1996, when U.S. Border Patrol agents stormed IBP—working with the company and with the SLPD—in a raid to gather and deport seventy-eight undocumented immigrants. It was the culmination of a two-year investigation by the SLPD and received coverage in national media outlets.[10] The experiences, like the images, of the raid tore at the community. Communication broke down, and information about who had been detained and why traveled through informal networks among immigrants. Families relied on word of mouth to learn if a member had been detained, fairly or otherwise. It seemed especially insensitive, to local residents, to have happened leading into Mother's Day weekend. Vrieze, who could have been especially useful to agents and local officials, was not in Storm Lake. Months prior, she had scheduled a two-week family vacation. She was in California, at Disneyland.

According to Vrieze, she first learned of the raid in an accusatory phone call. A friend asked, "Hey, why didn't you tell us? Immigration is over here. Why didn't you tell us that they'd come in?" Given her position, it was a fair question. Compounding the problem, Vrieze recalled that one of the agents looked like her, and that many residents thought she personally assisted federal authorities. "I got blamed for not telling them... And at the time, I had no clue."[11] When she returned to Storm Lake, Vrieze said, she realized that several of her friends had been swept up in the raid, as well. And yet the heat of the moment had dissipated. "Everything was back to normal," she claimed.

To the contrary, the sweep by federal authorities working in conjunction with IBP and the SLPD proved to be a pivotal event in Storm Lake history. The town would have to establish a new normal. Saying "the raid" to any longtime resident elicits painful memories, if distant, that continue to mark the community like a scar. Townsfolk recall those who left, like eight-year-old Julio Barroso, who had been featured, a month before the raid, in a heartwarming newspaper profile, "sharing the gift of a new language." Four weeks later, he and his family were gone.[12] The roundup of undocumented workers affected the lives of most Storm Lakers. If Vrieze's position as a bridge was vital to the community before the raid, it would be essential to the town thereafter.

Pom Kavan

As with the case of Vrieze, Pom Kavan embodied Storm Lake's immigrant community as a CSO for nearly thirty years. Just over five feet tall and with a cheery if guarded disposition, Kavan does not brandish an aura of state authority. Yet her position as an appointed Lao and Tai-Dam interpreter for the Southeast Asian community in town, under the umbrella of the police department, carried immense potential power.

Although she was born in Laos, Kavan's family emigrated from Southeast Asia in 1981, when the Tai Dam people feared reprisals from North Vietnam for their resistance to communism. Her family of twelve crossed the Mekong River to a refugee camp in Thailand, where they spent more than a year waiting for an organization to resettle them in the United States. Though she does not recall being scared, Kavan tells the story with alarming candor. "I was younger so I didn't have any feeling," she said in a 2021 interview.

> I just go where my parents go, where my grandparents go. We just follow them because you just follow the adults. Your mom says "go," we go. . . . But my aunt, the adults, were scared because we have to cross the Mekong River to get to Thailand [refugee] camp. If you have money to pay that person, somebody will bring you over on a boat. . . . And if you can't afford to pay that person, you come with them but you hang onto the boat; or some adults with no family would have to swim across the river, because the younger ones get to be in the boat. And my aunt had to swim, hang on to the boat because my grandfather didn't have enough money for everybody to get on the boat. So she's hanging on to the boat.
> And then, I remember hearing stories, if they can't make it across—at that time there were communist soldiers, because they stand-guard the river, because they don't want people to leave the country—so when people crossed the rivers they had to sneak out. You either make it or you don't. And I hear stories that people didn't make it 'cause the soldiers will see you and they will shoot you, and they did. People would try to cross in the middle of the night because that's when they can't see you and I hear some stories like some of them would have to pretend like they gonna go fishing because they don't wanna alert people, or the communists that they are leaving. I know my grandfather's nephew, his family, a couple of his siblings, were shot on the river. Another girl that I know of, her sister and her brother-in-law were shot, and her nephew was shot. They didn't make it across. Yes, that's from the stories that I hear.[13]

Kavan's family spent a year in Thailand and later the Philippines. Though the transition certainly challenged her family, she, then thirteen years old, managed to find inspiration through language. "When I was in [the camps], when I was attending class, there's an Asian person that teaches class," she said. "And I remember sitting in a classroom, it was like wood bench and a table—that's our classroom tables—and we were provided pencil and notebook. And I remember sitting there and listening to him teaching English class. In the back of my mind I'm like, 'I

FIG 8. Pom Kavan. Digital watercolor by Ricky Hadi, based on a photograph of Pom Kavan by Morgan Krull, Storm Lake, Iowa.

really want to do that. I want to teach English, I want to be an interpreter, I want to translate.'... You know, when you don't know English, it sounds like [a] foreign language, like [makes buzzing noises]. You don't understand it. I'm like, 'That is so cool!'"

Kavan's ability as a child to find the "cool" amid such dire circumstances can be explained by childhood innocence, sure, but also by her captivated intellect. The "buzzing noises" she used to describe what English sounded like to a young speaker of Lao underscores just how "foreign" her future would be. While she and her family had been waiting in refugee camps, Iowa governor Robert Ray saw a *60 Minutes* report on the "Boat People" of Southeast Asia. Correspondent Ed

Bradley's team captured images of emigrants like Kavan's family desperate to leave the region, adrift in makeshift boats, floating from persecution with little hope of salvation. Ray petitioned President Gerald Ford for permission to relocate thousands of Tai Dam refugees. In this fashion, from the military entanglements of the Vietnam War to the Cold War struggle against communism, a thirteen-year-old girl who found English so exotic settled on the strange wind-swept lands of Spencer, Iowa, in February 1981.

For the next several years, Kavan adjusted to American life. She graduated from high school and married another Tai Dam refugee, Choung Kavan. Choung had been working at IBP, acting as an interpreter for its Southeast Asian workers. Pom saw the possibilities of using her own training in the language, and in 1992 joined the school district as a paraprofessional teacher of English as a second language. She translated at parent-teacher conferences. By 1994 she and her husband had two children, Jesse and Samantha (named after characters from the television show *Full House*). Kavan then began working as the SLPD's second CSO.[14]

The origins of Kavan and Vrieze, the first two CSOs hired in the earliest stages of Storm Lake's social transformation, illustrate the strength of the pull factors of American industry and of the military. At first glance, what are the chances that two young women, one in her twenties in Mexico and the other in her teens in Southeast Asia, would relocate to the northwest corner of Iowa, train to attain fluency in English, and become vital to maintaining peace within the police force, in a land so removed from home? Teasing apart the deeper entanglements of U.S. foreign policy, border control, and the breaking of unions, from 1965 to the present, makes this scenario plausible. Adding the draw of economic opportunity and a safe community makes it, at least in Storm Lake, commonplace.

Thousands of stories similar to Vrieze's and Kavan's, of people seeking to improve their lives, or of following loved ones, have caused Storm Lake to scramble to address its growing immigration, legal or otherwise. The town's transformation originated in 1981, when IBP took over production from Hygrade and broke the unions.[15] Blue-collar meatpackers who had once thrived on union-brokered salaries were now a distant memory. IBP recruited new employees from California, Mexico, and Central America at a fraction of the cost.

The rapid influx of new residents threatened to upset the social order, as some of the earliest families from Southeast Asia began to be joined by others from Latin America. Tensions within the community began to rise such that, by 1994, local leaders and officials formed an ad hoc committee to "defuse cultural tension and promote harmony.... Complaints have been heard that Latinos, Southeast

Asians and Africans are treated rudely in stores and clinics around town."[16] Concern spiked in 1996 to the point that one local newspaper started a special report that February on "Diversity: The Progress Files."[17]

The tensions emerging in early 1996 foretold of the town's turning point that year, when Immigration and Naturalization Services (INS) raided the IBP plant. Helicopters hovered above the scene; regional and national media appeared instantly on the ground. The event sowed deep discord in the community and appeared to be little more than a photo-op of federal power. In a plant employing more than twenty-five hundred people, only seventy-eight were deported, many of them returning with time.

Police Chief Mark Prosser initially supported the raid, based in part on a mistaken belief that rising crime rates were attributable to undocumented immigrants. From this position, he had been cooperating for two years with corporate and federal authorities, and he even worked to open an INS office in town. After witnessing the raid on the facility, though, seeing its social effects on his community, and recognizing the public relations spectacle, he felt duped, convinced it was all mere spectacle. Prosser vowed to change course and work with residents for a more humane approach to policing. "In retrospect, I don't think the taxpayers' money was well spent, given the number of illegals who were here," Prosser said months later. "I've come to a conclusion. The emphasis has to be on legalization, not arrests. There's just got to be a better way." Editorialist Art Cullen put it simply: "We need to make life work for people of all cultures in Storm Lake, because they will keep coming no matter what."[18]

CSOs like Vrieze and Kavan became absolutely essential figures in a new approach to police-community relations.[19] While Kavan and the Southeast Asian community did not feel directly threatened, the residual effect of feeling watched, of needing to carry papers when doing one's daily routine, took hold. Vrieze, who was in charge of police-Hispanic relations, certainly felt the sting of unspoken suspicions in the community. Post-raid, these two individuals would play a central role in negotiating police power with a suspicious immigrant community. The interpretive skills that had begun on the margins of their lives, as something "cool" for Kavan and as a love story for Vrieze, had now turned into a profession upon which the peace and security of an entire town depended.

Within a year, the SLPD had shifted resources to prioritize communication in the hopes of regaining trust. The department had ample evidence that it could work. In one section of town, a spike of petty crimes was cut in half through door-to-door surveys conducted in three languages, which led to small, concrete solutions like "cutting back trees for better lighting, starting foot patrols and generally increasing police visibility in the neighborhood."[20] In her years as CSO, while Kavan interpreted for high-profile cases, such as a double homicide in 1996, her value to the community lay in acting as a cultural go-between, helping "bridge cultural and language gaps throughout the community." This included assignments like these door-to-door surveys, translating a "statewide multilingual domestic violence handbook for patrol officers," and interpreting for visiting health clinics.[21]

Indeed, much of Kavan's work was pedestrian: explaining to the Southeast Asian community why trash must be picked up, how to contact the police, and *why* they should trust the SLPD. Over time, the earned trust enabled victims to seek her help. One of her proudest moments came when a Hmong resident approached her. "I don't speak Hmong," Kavan said, "but she speaks some Laotian and she came to me, and I think, because you know who I am and I look familiar to her, she came in and talked to me about [a sexual assault]." The pair worked through broken Lao to press charges in the courts.[22]

The example of Pom Kavan affirms that, though language may be the operating medium, the primary role of an interpreter is cultural intermediation. Scholars to date have examined most frequently the interpreter's role between Indigenous populations, a state power, and settler colonists.[23] Whether responsible for translating from one language to another between peoples, or negotiating as a broker of trade, customs, or captives in a fluid borderland, interpreters have a paradoxical role. They inhabit a position of great potential power but are typically assumed to act as a disinterested third party. Through words, interpreters deliver units of meaning from origin to destination and back, all the while capable of rounding corners of meaning, substituting synonyms to color reception, or manipulating context to serve self-interest. Syntax carries power.

In the history of the American West, this power was deployed most frequently—at the earliest stages of intercultural contact—through traders or the military. The classic example of Bent's Fort as a meeting place of numerous Indigenous and Euro-American cultures saturates Western histories for good reason. In addition to early interpreters negotiating goods and peace, a generation of intercultural families, notably personified by William Bent and Owl Woman, served the interests of all sides, at least until the window of opportunity closed, and mixed heritage unions became a liability in the peak stages of settler colonialism.[24] The military's reliance on interpreters never stopped in 1804, 1846, nor 1890, as the imperial march of American forces turned outward from the American West to other global venues. Dual or trilingual specialists served in Cuba and the Philippines during the Spanish-American War, in World Wars I and II, the Korean War, the Vietnam War, and up through U.S. entanglements in the Middle East and Afghanistan since 1990. Wherever goes empire, so go interpreters.[25]

Another feature of American empire has reshaped the domestic United States, as well: immigrants from zones of imperial encounter arriving on the mainland. Historians like Matthew Jacobson and Paul Kramer have examined this bidirectional flow of ideas and people in the late nineteenth and early twentieth centuries. The relationship continues today, whether from a militarized border, where Vrieze first met her veteran husband, or from the migrations of people like Kavan, from a land shaped in part by American foreign wars. Vrieze and Kavan could never have anticipated their paths would cross in a little-known corner of rural America, but U.S. entanglements in foreign wars and capitalist expansion account for many circumstances that brought Vrieze and Kavan together as CSOs in Storm Lake, Iowa.[26]

Though shaped by larger forces, it's notable that the cases of Kavan, Vrieze, and now other CSOs do not entrench either police power or the aims of a state. One might be able to make such an argument before 1996, when Prosser's SLPD aligned itself with an aggressive INS posture. Inroads with the communities of newcomers, documented or not, could have fed into a system of governmental observation and control. After that pivotal year, as the police chief saw the damage perpetrated on his community, his officers began to prioritize linguistic and cultural interpreters to build trust. The SLPD would only report residents to federal authorities if they had committed a crime. This adjustment means that, for Kavan and her fellow interpreters, their work continues *not* as a channel of state power but as one that operates in the reverse. By connecting with local residents, the CSOs have demonstrably decreased crime and reduced the chance that an undocumented resident would be deported. Interpretation therefore serves the community. The role of interpreter, unlike so many examples in early American history, has been modified to minimize criminal encounters and avoid, whenever possible, ruptures to families and the community.

When not working for the department, Kavan can be found among many social circles, participating in all types of public service organizations, and practicing her faith at both the Storm Lake Buddhist temple and at St. John's Lutheran Church. "I can believe in Buddha," she said. "I believe in God, because we all believe the same thing. The purpose is the same thing: peace.... When I pray at night I pray in English, I don't know why but it comes out [in English] ... It comes naturally when I pray at night or in the morning when I pray to God. I still do attend Buddhist temple, go to Buddhist temple for functions and other occasions. You know, when I go there, I pray in the language, our language, to Buddha. You know, it all comes down to the same purpose. You want good. You want to do good."[27]

Notes

1. Though ominous for reasons to be discussed, "processing dreams" does not necessarily carry a negative connotation. Numerous informants have emphasized that working in plants like Tyson's pork processing center in Storm Lake has, indeed, made a more comfortable life possible for any who seek it. Recent anthropological and historical work have exposed the lived experience of working in meatpacking plants. See esp. Pachirat, *Every Twelve Seconds* and Striffler, *Chicken*.
2. In Iowa, the town of Perry underwent similar transformations at the same time, though the outcomes of there and in Storm Lake diverged to a great degree after 2000. See Fink, *Cutting into the Meatpacking Line* and Cullen, *Storm Lake*. Denison experienced a significant influx of Latinx workers after 1980. Juffer, *Intimacy across Borders*. Marshalltown offers an interesting case study on the reception of Latinx immigrants, discussed in Grey and Woodrick, "'Latinos Have Revitalized Our Community.'"
3. "Storm Lake School District's Demographics Shows [*sic*] City's Diversity," Storm Lake Community School District press release, December 16, 2019. Available at https://stormlakeradio.com/local-news/2019/12/16/storm-lake-school-districts-demographics-shows-citys-diversity.
4. Though other communities in California or the Southwest may mirror the dynamics of this one small town, its location in rural Iowa makes it somehow exceptional, drawing the eye of national news crews. The inversion of racial demographics surprises most other Americans as somehow un-midwestern. Contemporary Storm Lake reframes midwestern history as an inversion of this tale, as a region defined by its international connections. On the Midwest's global connections, see Longworth, *Caught in the Middle* and Hoganson, *The Heartland*. Older, seminal works that framed the field of midwestern history include Shortridge, *Middle West*; Cayton and Gray, *Identity of the American Midwest*; Lauck, Whitney, and Hogan, *Finding a New Midwestern History*; Barnhart, "'Common Feeling'"; and Hart, "Middle West."
5. Dana Larsen, "Ethnic Officer Is City's Top '93 Goal," *Storm Lake Pilot Tribune*, December 16, 1992.
6. "First Police Ethnic Expert Faces 'Unknown,'" *Storm Lake Pilot Tribune*, June 9, 1993; Kerry McCullough, "New IBP Pot Is Building Bridges for the Community," *Storm Lake Pilot Tribune*, February 28, 1996; "500 Come to Family's Aid," *Storm Lake Pilot Tribune*, January 18, 1995; Mary Cullen, "Pom Serves as a 'Bridge,'" *Storm Lake Times*, January 4, 1995; "Lao Community Officer Excited at Rare Opportunity," *Storm Lake Pilot Tribune*, June 11, 1994, .

7. Interview with Graciela Vrieze, June 7, 2022, Storm Lake, Iowa. Vrieze found the line work especially difficult in those early days; she had worked previously as an administrative assistant to a lawyer in her hometown, "typing and doing all the paperwork and stuff for the courthouse."
8. "First Police Ethnic Expert Faces 'Unknown.'"
9. Interview with Graciela Vrieze.
10. "Sweep Brings in 78 Illegal Aliens," *Storm Lake Times*, May 15, 1996. A later article noted that the national coverage was possible, in part, because reporters had been "tipped to the sweep by sources in Washington." "What Really Prompted the Sweep?" *Storm Lake Times*, May 18, 1996.
11. Interview via Zoom with Graciela Vrieze, conducted by Madeline Phaby, April 26, 2022.
12. The story of Barroso has been covered over the years by the *Storm Lake Times*, which originally ran the profile, as well as a follow-up notice the following month. Over the years since, the *Times* has updated readers on Borroso's life in Mexico. See Tim Gallagher, "Sharing the Gift of a New Language," *Storm Lake Times*, April 24, 1996; "Julio Is Gone," *Storm Lake Times*, May 15, 1996; Tom Cullen, "Where Did Julio Go?" *Storm Lake Times*, August 1, 2018; Art Cullen, "Julio Is gone," *Storm Lake Times*, August 1, 2018; and Tom Cullen and Karina Guerrero, "Julio Barroso Hopes to Come Home to Storm Lake," *Storm Lake Times*, December 18, 2020.
13. Interview with Pom Kavan, conducted by Morgan Krull and Olivia LeRoux, March 23, 2021.
14. Cullen, "Pom Serves as a 'Bridge.'" This article, as with many written by Mary Cullen, features a favorite recipe of Kavan's for stir fry shrimp or beef, though she is quick to clarify the separate duties between herself and her husband: "He cooks and I clean," she said.
15. On the effects of industrial agriculture, see esp. Stull, Broadway, and Griffith, *Any Way You Cut It*; Fitzgerald, "A Social History of the Slaughterhouse"; and Jacques, "The Slaughterhouse, Social Disorganization, and Violent Crime in Rural Communities." Mark Grey worked to collect oral histories in Storm Lake shortly after the union broke. See esp. Grey, "Turning the Pork Industry Upside Down."
16. "Leaders Meet to Promote Harmony," *Storm Lake Times*, October 15, 1994. The meeting built on previous work by the "Task Force on Unmet Needs." Kavan attended the meeting and offered a first step toward peace. "A simple smile would do it," she said. "Laotians take a lot from facial expressions."
17. *Storm Lake Pilot-Tribune*, February 28, 1996.
18. Art Cullen, "Legalizing the Illegal," *Storm Lake Times*, January 22, 1997.
19. Interview with Mark Prosser, February 17, 2021. See also Katie Johnston, "Immigration Doesn't Ruin a Community—It Enhances It," *Storm Lake Times*, December 10, 2021.
20. Art Cullen, "Community Policing on Track in SL," *Storm Lake Times*, June 7, 1997.
21. "Officer Awards: Selected by Peers," *Storm Lake Pilot-Tribune*, March 6, 2001.
22. Interview with Pom Kavan, conducted by Andrew Offenburger with the students of "Researching Midwestern History," February 23, 2022.

23. Kawashima, "Forest Diplomats"; West, *Contested Plains*; Gump, *Dust Rose Like Smoke*; Scully, "Malintzin, Pocahontas, and Krotoa."
24. West, *Contested Plains*.
25. The example of Navajo code talkers in World War II should remind us of the explicit desire to occlude meaning from words that accompanies international espionage. If interpretation serves as a channel of power, so, too, does its negation.
26. Jacobson, *Barbarian Virtues*; Kramer, *Blood of Government*; Immerwahr, *How to Hide an Empire*.
27. Kavan interview, March 2021.

Bibliography

Barnhart, Terry A. "'A Common Feeling': Regional Identity and Historical Consciousness in the Old Northwest, 1820–1860." *Michigan Historical Review* 29, no. 1 (2003): 39–70.

Cayton, Andrew R. L., and Susan E. Gray, eds. *The Identity of the American Midwest: Essays on Regional History*. Bloomington: Indiana University Press, 2001.

Cullen, Art. *Storm Lake: A Chronicle of Change, Resilience, and Hope from a Heartland Newspaper*. New York: Viking Press, 2018.

Fink, Deborah. *Cutting into the Meatpacking Line: Workers and Change in the Rural Midwest*. Chapel Hill: University of North Carolina Press, 1998.

Fitzgerald, Amy. "A Social History of the Slaughterhouse: From Inception to Contemporary Implications." *Human Ecology Review* 17, no. 1 (2010): 58–69.

Grey, Mark A. "Turning the Pork Industry Upside Down: Storm Lake's Hygrade Work Force and the Impact of the 1981 Plant Closure." *Annals of Iowa* 54 (1995): 244–59.

Grey, Mark A., and Anne C. Woodrick. "'Latinos Have Revitalized Our Community': Mexican Migration and Anglo Responses in Marshalltown, Iowa." In *New Destinations: Mexican Immigration in the United States*, edited by Victor Zúñiga and Rubén Hernández-León, 133–54, New York: Russell Sage Foundation, 2005.

Gump, James O. *The Dust Rose Like Smoke: The Subjugation of the Zulu and the Sioux*. Lincoln: University of Nebraska Press, 1994.

Hart, John Fraser. "The Middle West." In *Regions of the United States*, edited by John Fraser Hart, 258–92. New York: Harper and Row, 1972.

Hoganson, Kristin L. *The Heartland: An American History*. New York: Penguin Books, 2019.

Immerwahr, Daniel. *How to Hide an Empire: A History of the Greater United States*. New York: Picador, 2019.

Jacobson, Matthew Frye. *Barbarian Virtues: United States Encounters Foreign Peoples at Home and Abroad, 1876–1917*. New York: Macmillan, 2000.

Jacques, Jessica Racine. "The Slaughterhouse, Social Disorganization, and Violent Crime in Rural Communities." *Society and Animals* 23 (2015): 594–612.

Juffer, Jane. *Intimacy across Borders: Race, Religion, and Migration in the U.S. Midwest*. Philadelphia: Temple University Press, 2013.

Kawashima, Yasuhide. "Forest Diplomats: The Role of Interpreters in Indian-White Relations on the Early American Frontier." *American Indian Quarterly* 13, no. 1 (1989): 1–14.

Kramer, Paul A. *The Blood of Government: Race, Empire, the United States, and the Philippines.* Chapel Hill: University of North Carolina Press, 2006.

Lauck, Jon K., Gleaves Whitney, and Joseph Hogan, eds. *Finding a New Midwestern History.* Lincoln: University of Nebraska Press, 2018.

Longworth, Richard C. *Caught in the Middle: America's Heartland in the Age of Globalism.* New York: Bloomsbury, 2008.

Pachirat, Timothy. *Every Twelve Seconds: Industrialized Slaughter and the Politics of Sight.* New Haven: Yale University Press, 2011.

Scully, Pamela. "Malintzin, Pocahontas, and Krotoa: Indigenous Women and Myth Models of the Atlantic World." *Journal of Colonialism and Colonial History* 6, no. 3 (2005).

Shortridge, James R. *The Middle West: Its Meaning in American Culture.* Lawrence: University Press of Kansas, 1989.

Striffler, Steve. *Chicken: The Dangerous Transformation of America's Favorite Food.* New Haven: Yale University Press, 2005.

Stull, Donald D., Michael J. Broadway, and David Griffith. *Any Way You Cut It: Meat Processing and Small-Town America.* Lawrence: University Press of Kansas, 1995.

West, Elliott. *The Contested Plains: Indians, Goldseekers, and the Rush to Colorado.* Lawrence: University Press of Kansas, 1998.

Interpreting for and in Vietnam

From the editors: The example of Pom Kavan (chapter 9) and the experiences of Zachary Guiliano (chapter 10) address the importance of interpreters "on the ground" in the American West and beyond it, as the United States became entangled in the Cold War and the global war on terror. In two separate anecdotes below, we get a glimpse of interpreting at two levels of international engagement during the Vietnam War.

The first is from Ambassador Nguyen Dinh Phuon, who served as Vietnam's interpreter at the Paris Peace Talks between Vietnam and the United States, from 1968–73. He interpreted conversations between Le Duc Tho and Henry Kissinger. Note the dueling interpreters with divergent interests, a scene that echoes the preceding vignette of Seneca, Cayuga, U.S., and Canadian discussions. The ambassador is responding to questions posed by Ian Andersen at the Hotel Metropole, Hanoi, on June 15, 2003.

Interview with Vietnam Peace Talks Interpreter

ANDERSEN: Did you feel as you were working that you could distance yourself from the process and just be the interpreter, or were you in fact very much involved personally and engaged in the process?

NGUYEN: As an interpreter, we must act as not being involved in the negotiations, but as Vietnamese, then you must pay attention to the content of the idea, and how to express the idea clearly and not as an interpretation, but we must express it in an English way, not to be very peculiar or queer. Because on the American side, there was also an interpreter who spoke Vietnamese.

ANDERSEN: And did he interpret as well for the American delegation, or did you do all the work?

NGUYEN: For some time at the beginning, I was interpreter for both sides. But after some time, because the meeting lasted very long, therefore, we proposed to the American side that the interpretation should be done by each side. Then I had to translate for the Vietnamese side, and not for the American side.

ANDERSEN: Did you feel that was an improvement for your working conditions?

NGUYEN: Yes.

ANDERSEN: Did you feel it was an improvement also in the understanding, or did it work better when you were doing both ways?

NGUYEN: Yes, because the American interpreter, interpreted from English to Vietnamese.... and me from Vietnamese into English....

ANDERSEN: How did you perceive the situation as an interpreter? Was it particularly difficult from an interpretation point of view?

NGUYEN: Certainly, it was difficult. Interpretation is a difficult job. But interpretation for negotiation conference is all the more difficult. Because it is a political matter, and the position of each side, you must practice to interpret correctly. Because our interpretation may be wrong in terms of the meaning, the nuances of the words used.

But other times when I was doing the job, I did not think about the difficulty, but I think more of the *content* of the interpretation. I was not being trained to be an interpreter, but how to express Le Duc Tho's views, it was my main occupation then.... At every session, it is not only the question of language, but it is a question of the content of the idea. How to express the idea clearly and understandably for the other side. Therefore the words were chosen carefully, and not to misinterpret [the idea].[1]

▪

From the editors: Douglas Bekke served as first lieutenant in the U.S. Army during the Vietnam War. In November 1970, he was assigned to a Special Forces Camp at Dong Da Thin. He and others in his unit were in charge of training Cambodian allies. The following excerpt comes from his written piece, "Lost in Translation," published by the Minnesota Remembers Vietnam project, a Minnesota PBS Initiative. He was also interviewed in 2004 with the Veterans History Project, the recording of which is available at the Library of Congress.

Consider the parallels between Bekke's experiences here, and those recounted by Zachary Guiliano (chapter 10).[2]

The fundamental problem existed of finding interpreters/translators to assist with the training. In our unit we had a number of Cubans who were native Spanish speakers, 2 who spoke Navajo, and a few with the various languages of South Vietnam. Others spoke European languages, but only the 2 French speakers were occasionally useful in training the Cambodians.

So what do we do? . . .

Soon translators/interpreters were showing up at the camp. I'm not sure what the hiring process was, who sought them out, or who actually hired them. I'm pretty sure that on some level the VNSF were involved.

Some of the interpreters were pretty good and some left a lot to be desired. Some of the Americans were able to work effectively through the interpreters and some just couldn't alter their textbook-Ft. Benning-school-presentation format to be effective.

As best I could understand it, most of our interpreters were at least part Cambodian, and I'm sure spoke both Cambodian and Vietnamese well, if not both as native speakers, but they had varying degrees of English language proficiency. So you just never knew if what you were saying was getting properly translated. . . .

One day I was teaching a class on retrograde operations. I was pretty pleased with how things were going and I thought I was being pretty effective. I didn't have much confidence in the translator for that class. To help him, I tried to use the blackboard effectively and I simplified my language as best I could, avoiding unnecessary technical terms and American army jargon. After an hour we took a break and one of the Cambodian officers who spoke a little English came up to me and said that for an hour all the translator had been saying over and over was "pay attention or you are going to die!" I tried to get another translator but couldn't. What could I do? I felt like that morning I had completely failed the Cambodians and was wasting my time and theirs.

Word choice could be problematic. The first time we taught a class on the M-16 rifle whenever we mentioned the rifle bolt we noticed that the Cambodians were snickering. We shortly found out that "bolt" in Cambodian is a slang term for a penis. OK, so what was another word we could use in the future to describe that part of the rifle? . . .

I often think about our translators and what their fate might have been. After we left, did they go to Cambodia and meet a horrible death? Were they captured by the Communists and sent to years of hard labor in "re-education camps" because they had worked for the Americans? Did they escape to the United States with other refugees? Did some of them show their secret loyalty as Viet Cong and join the "Liberation"? We could never get beyond the fundamental problem of doubt about who we were employing, who we could really trust, and what our translators were really saying and thinking.

Notes

1. Nguyen Dinh Phuon, "Interview with Vietnam Peace Talks Interpreter," interview by Ian Andersen, posted December 11, 2012, by EU Interpreters, YouTube video, https://www.youtube.com/watch?v=qrPnoLPWny0.
2. The following section was reproduced courtesy of Doug Bekke.

10

Keeping Faith

Interpreters in the Global War on Terror

ZACH GUILIANO

Little about the failed U.S.-led war in Afghanistan makes sense without illuminating the role of interpreters. In the early weeks of the war, interpreters were vital in facilitating meetings (which, in the Afghan way, certainly included much-needed food) between U.S. forces and their new Afghan allies. As American leaders clumsily fumbled about the quicksand of nation building, interpreters were present with the Marines on the ground as well as within the walls of the presidential palace. Despite their priceless service to their U.S. partners, tens of thousands of Afghan allies, interpreters, and their families were left behind in a hasty retreat. As of July, 2025, they are still left to their own devices amid economic collapse, famine, and persecution by a hostile Taliban government.[1]

Like many other important "background" roles, it can be easy to take interpreters for granted. For both interpreter and "interpretee," competency begets trust. If interpreters are good at their jobs and all involved parties are cordial, what follows is a mostly seamless process of patient conversation where everyone waits their turn to speak. Inversely, poor interpreters (and poor interpretees) produce noticeably shoddy work. The consequences of poor communication can be less predictable, and in situations with interpreters, it is virtually impossible for both parties to know what the other is truly saying. In retrospect, I placed more faith in some of the interpreters I worked alongside in Afghanistan than I had ever vested in anybody else I served alongside. Regretfully, I did not appreciate that at the time.

Comparisons between the Vietnam War and the Global War on Terror (GWOT) are widespread, such as the very directly titled PBS Frontline documentary, *Obama's Vietnam*. However, while this is an accurate comparison, it could be more historically accurate to draw a direct connection from the Indian Wars to Vietnam to the GWOT. In fact, once this comparison is posited, it is entirely reasonable to propose that the Indian Wars never truly ended and that the United States merely exported them abroad.

Cuba, Puerto Rico, the Philippines, Korea, Vietnam, Panama, Somalia, Afghanistan, Iraq, and Syria (among countless others) are directly linked to the Indian Wars by three broad factors: U.S. troops waging war against Indigenous populations, economic imperatives leading to these interventions, and even tactics that bear direct resemblance to each other.[2] Writing on the very first page of *Custer Died For Your Sins*, Vine Deloria Jr. said in the 1988 edition that "Indians raised the question of the American past, and since this bloody past was then being revived in the search-and-destroy missions in Vietnam ... it was apparent that few people in the government heeded the lessons of history."[3] It follows that since Vietnam can be compared to the Indian Wars, so can the GWOT.

American troops who struggled to adapt their equipment and combat tactics to the enemy and the terrain of, say, Apachería, struggled in ways that foreshadowed the work of troops in Afghanistan. In the nineteenth century, Army leaders and quartermasters made troops rely on horses that were ill-suited to the climate and terrain; in the twenty-first, military leaders ordained that aviation troops should fly and maintain helicopters equally inadequate to the environment.[4] In one era, troops were ill-prepared for prolonged foot movements against a highly mobile, nigh invisible enemy; in the later era, troops were ordered to walk for a day or more at a time with their body weight on their back in some of the highest elevations a human can reasonably endure.

In *Making the Forever War*, Marilyn Young writes outright that the motives and strategy of the GWOT were directly informed by the Indian Wars. According to Young, the economic crises and racial tensions of Reconstruction found a unitary outlet through the wars again Indigenous peoples of the Great Plains and the first of "exported" Indian Wars, the Spanish-American War.[5] Even a brief examination of the cultural and political narratives of the Indian Wars will reveal a similarity with the narratives of the GWOT. A "savage" enemy, uncivilized and ruling over a people in desperate need for Western democracy would easily be beaten if enough troops, resources, and money could be leveraged to fight them for a single campaign season.

This continuity appeared time and again throughout the GWOT, from Bush Jr.'s ironic "Mission Accomplished" spectacle to the promised silver bullet of "Hearts and Minds." The year 2017 saw the first-ever combat use of the Mother of All Bombs (MOAB) during an operation meant to destroy a nascent ISIS affiliate, the Islamic State in Khorasan; the deployment of a MOAB, by its mere name, could be interpreted as signaling some sort of finality. The operation resulted in hundreds of dead insurgents, but the targeted group remained intact and claimed credit for the Abbey Gate bombing at Hamid Karzai International Airport during the American withdrawal in August 2021.

A popular axiom about the GWOT, and Afghanistan in particular, says "[Coalition Forces] have the watches, but [the Taliban] have the time." When fighting an insurgent, Indigenous population—whether it is in Apache or Afghan territory—victory is more up to Fortuna than to the morale and commitment of a nation's troops and polity. In the case of the Indian Wars and the GWOT, the role of interpreters in Fortuna's blessings was either undersold or outright ignored by the United States, as analyzed and predicted by Deloria.

It will not surprise the average reader that the U.S. military has a dizzying number of contingency plans. For example, as the Russian invasion of Ukraine unfolded, observant Americans might have seen footage on social media of massive freight trains crossing Atlanta, laden with M1A2 Abrams tanks and fuel trucks bound for equipment depots in Western Europe. What might be surprising to many, though, is that the United States had no preexisting plan for military action in Afghanistan, according to Bob Woodward's 2002 book, *Bush at War*. What this meant was that every facet of invading a country had to be planned from scratch: infiltration, logistics and sustainment, air support (and all the necessary naval and ground movement), to say nothing of overall strategy. The need to plan from square one was compounded by outdated intelligence and maps. Al-Qaeda, the Taliban, and their allied warlords were not the only threats in Afghanistan; the Soviet Union left behind untold amounts of unexploded ordinance, and it was not uncommon for Afghans to be killed or maimed by these years after the Soviets were gone.[6] And it was in this environment that the Bush administration, backed by an emotionally charged American public, demanded as immediate an action as possible after September 11, 2001.

The finer details were still being worked out when ten personnel from the CIA's Special Activities Division, callsign Jawbreaker, arrived in the formidable Panjshir Valley, Afghanistan, to link up with the anti-Taliban Northern Alliance. U.S. planners understood that money talks, and in addition to the massive suite of communications and intelligence equipment, Jawbreaker brought along $3 million in cash for operational expenses (with millions more to follow). Jawbreaker's commanding officer, a career CIA agent, spoke Pashto and Dari, the two most widespread spoken languages in Afghanistan. One of the other team members spoke Farsi and Dari (related languages that can incorrectly be grouped as "Persian"). Eventually, Jawbreaker would be supplemented by more CIA and SOF personnel, including operational detachments from 5th Special Forces Group who were trained to speak local languages. Concurrently, the British government approved the deployment of veteran MI6 agents to Afghanistan's south, most of whom had previously worked with the Afghans during the Soviet war.[7]

As Jawbreaker's operational scope expanded beyond making contact with the Northern Alliance and the United States became engaged in combat, the need for interpreters must have been apparent. Because the Bush administration's plan relied on the presence of small numbers of highly elite combatants, it was inevitable that the Americans who could not speak the languages would have to operate independently from the ones who did. The interpreters brought on in the early months proved capable and facilitated meetings between invading U.S. troops and anti-Taliban warlords, such as future president Hamid Karzai near Kandahar. Despite their importance, little has been said of these men who did such vital work, even in the current era of more heightened awareness of interpreters' existence. Doug Stanton's 2009 book *Horse Soldiers* is one of the most in-depth perspectives on the U.S. invasion (detailing the events surrounding a Special Forces team that participated in history's most recent cavalry charge) and features accounts from an Afghan named Najeeb Quraishy who eventually becomes an interpreter for foreign journalists. His time with the Special Forces team is short, as the commander suspects Najeeb's friendly questions mean he is a Taliban spy. This early display of distrust would play out time and again throughout the war between countless Americans and Afghans.

The invasion of Iraq, conversely, was planned based off preexisting "blueprints" (which were likely refined during the ten years of "peacekeeping operations" in Northern Iraq prior to 2003) that recognized the density and importance of Iraq's many ethnic and religious groups and the role they could play in a post-Saddam, pro-U.S. Iraq. For this reason, when the U.S.-led coalition invaded Iraq in March 2003, many units had interpreters embedded with them when they stepped off. This process, though better than the ad hoc plan for invading Afghanistan, was plagued with what the corporate world would call "staffing issues." Evan Wright, in his 2004 book *Generation Kill*, indicated that even the elite U.S. Marine Corps 1st

Reconnaissance Battalion only had one interpreter for the whole battalion. This meant a ratio of one interpreter for approximately four hundred combat troops spread across hundreds of miles of combat space. This interpreter, called Meesh, was seen by the Marines as lazy and incompetent. Ironically, Wright's book would be made into an HBO miniseries a few years later, and the one-sided portrayal of Meesh would be many Americans' only look at what interpreters are like.

Not all interpreter experiences are equal, and this can vary across cultures. Although the GWOT was waged across the Islamic *Ummah* (and still is, albeit mostly through our regional allies), it is important to remember two things: first, commonality in language is only one element of a shared culture, and just as the legions of English speakers within the United States have multitudes of cultural views there are significant differences between many groups of Afghans and Iraqis. Second, it is important to consider that an interpreter's performance in war is directly affected by how they, or their people, feel about that war.

The interpreters I worked with, or "terp(s)" for short, were all Afghan-born men who had immigrated to the United States and obtained citizenship. I believe all of them were young during the Soviet-Afghan War, and one of them—the oldest, reverently called Mr. Wardak—fought in the war as a member of the *mujahedin*. I knew many of them by only one name, such as Haroon or Ghani. As with any type of work, we considered some interpreters better at their jobs than others. Thus, we had preferred interpreters and those who we worked with simply because nobody else was around. A few interpreters were basically "one of the boys," whereas others were little trusted.

I cannot speak for my comrades, but these sorts of cognitive processes worked automatically and with little to no consideration on my part. When I criticized poor interpretive performance, I did it without recognizing that I could not speak Pashto, Dari, and/or even more obscure languages. This criticism came without thinking about the less spoken of, and far more intangible translation of worldviews. Culture impacts every facet of one's expectations, from mission outcomes, acceptable rules of engagement, policy goals, and even work ethic. As my friends and I puzzled over the Afghans' habit of arriving at their own pace (what we mocked as "*Inshallah* time"), I wouldn't realize until years later how equally puzzling our breakneck speed of work was to the Afghans.[8]

Many of the micro-scale interactions were also occurring on a grand scale between the Afghan National Security Forces (ANSF) and International Security Assistance Force (ISAF). ISAF was established in December 2001 to help build, train, and advise the ANSF; although an international coalition had formed, the

United States still held overall command. To this end, Afghanistan was crudely divided into a quadrant of four Regional Commands, with Germany commanding RC-North, Italy commanding RC-West, and the United States directly controlling operations in RC-East and RC-South (this command would be split in 2010 to include RC-Southwest, which was committed to the hotly contested province of Helmand). The area around Kabul became its own Regional Command, with rotational command from states such as France, Turkey, and New Zealand.

If you feel that this explanation of basic operational ordering needed its own interpretation, I congratulate you on a lesson learned and invite you to empathize with how this confusing command structure must have felt to Afghans. General Stanley McChrystal (U.S. Army) assumed control of the war in conjunction with a surge in U.S. troop numbers and a shift in focus from combat operations to "indirect counterinsurgency" in 2008. Indirect counterinsurgency, or COIN for short, is the infamous "hearts and minds" approach first made known to the U.S. public during the Vietnam War. Similarly to the Vietnam War, President Obama would shift operations from U.S.-led efforts to that of "Afghanization," or enabling Afghan forces to take the lead. This concept was inspired directly by the process of Vietnamization under Nixon. Perhaps the president and senior defense officials needed a sort of historical interpreter to explain to them that using concepts from a failed, unpopular counterinsurgency was not a formula for victory.

With a doubling down on nation-building came a focus on ensuring—nominally—that ISAF operated with a mind toward Afghan cultural norms. The intelligence community began to buzz over "human terrain," or the many depths and positions held by various local peoples. Conventional and SOF units began introducing teams of females who would be in a better position to respectfully search and interview Afghan women. These proved to be superficial dressing on a fatal wound. If confusing jargon and arbitrary command structures were the only problems in ISAF's enterprise, perhaps the war would have been prosecuted less sloppily.

Emblematic of the shoddy strategic framework set forth from the highest levels is what I will call the Helicopter Puzzle. The U.S. Department of Defense insisted the Afghan Air Force be equipped with modern U.S. aircraft. Small amounts of Soviet-era, legacy helicopters were present within the ANSF for much of the war but were eventually phased out of service. Because of a mixture of logistics, the fact that certain portions of the systems are classified, and the sheer complexity of the avionics (that is, the systems which control the aircraft), American helicopters could only be serviced by U.S. mechanics. This was mostly done in-house by U.S. military personnel supplemented by contractors, but as troop numbers were lowered the U.S. military increasingly relied on private contractors to bolster capabilities.

On March 10, 2021, Special Inspector General for Afghanistan Reconstruction (SIGAR) John F. Sopko said "contractors currently provide 100 percent of the maintenance for Afghan Air Force UH-60 helicopters and C-130 cargo aircraft, and a significant portion for Afghan light combat support aircraft."[9] Further, Sopko correctly emphasized that these vital airframes would only be operable without maintenance for "a few months," and as the U.S.-backed Afghan government began to collapse in June 2021 there was a sharp increase in reports of military helicopters making emergency or crash landings.[10] By the end of the month the lion's share of Afghan air mobility would be grounded, and the total collapse of Afghan government forces began as logistics could no longer cope with Afghanistan's terrain. In late 2021 the SIGAR's office reported what many U.S. servicemembers already knew: there was never anything resembling an overarching strategy for the war in Afghanistan.

The widely reported issues within the Afghan National Army (ANA), such as irreconcilable cultural differences, open corruption within senior ranks, low morale, rampant narcotics abuse, and high desertion rates translated to an overt lack of respect from the ISAF advisors sent to train them.[11] An Afghan infantryman being stoned on *khat* could be either viewed as merely lack of professionalism or a symbol of their nondedication, even if we quietly acknowledged that our morale would be low under the same conditions. Perhaps ISAF and U.S. government officials needed an interpreter to tell them that serving in a civil war under a corrupt government would damage one's mental health to the point of narcotics abuse. Narcotics have killed more U.S. troops and veterans in the post-9/11 era than the Taliban or al Qaeda. But even as the U.S. military and veteran community reeled from and decried the U.S. veterans' suicide epidemic, the cultural norm was to derisively chalk the shortcomings of the ANA as just "Afghans being Afghans."

It does not take an interpreter to see when one is held with disdain by someone who is supposed to be a mentor, peer, or ally, even if the observer does not speak the language, is "uneducated," or illiterate. Apparently, it takes an interpreter to point out that actions speak louder than words. In retrospect it is easy to understand why tens of thousands of ANA soldiers turned over their weapons to the Taliban and went home.

Caught in the middle of the clueless foreign army and the generally unenthusiastic Afghans were the interpreters. Military personnel and their interpreters were bonded by the war itself, as it is unlikely any of us would ever have a chance to work or socialize with one another in other circumstances. For the Americans, interpreters, and Afghans in the Tactical Operations Center (TOC) I worked in, we mutually enjoyed watching sports (particularly American football) and food. Despite our proximity and shared mission, without the interpreters present the language barrier would be an insurmountable obstacle. One of the Afghans, a man about my age, spoke English quite well, and several could speak to us in broken conversation; our own knowledge of Pashto was the greeting *Salaam Alaykum*, and perhaps some other words for "hello." The interpreters acted as a bridge, helping us ask after one another's families and discussing the whereabouts of Taliban in the same conversation.

The bridge was maintained under strict scrutiny, though. When lives are on the line (whether immediately or in the general sense), it is important that an interpreter relay translation accurately, without losing nuance or adding uncertainty. And, an interpreter must translate quickly, to preserve the flow of conversation. But these necessary guidelines can squeeze interpreters, as they struggle to speak two languages at once while perhaps not *literally* translating every single word. A unique confluence of the Afghan-American relationship was the short and to the point Americans and the meandering, sometimes poetic speech of Afghans.

When I first met the commander of our Afghan partner force, an ANA colonel named Amanullah, one of my American counterparts had me take notes while they chatted. This was standard, as two sets of ears and an extra notepad is better than one. Amanullah (as I learned) was boastful, and this would be my first taste of many dramatic tirades. While discussing potential Taliban activity within a part of the province, the conversation took a decidedly one-sided turn. Amanullah began talking at length, speaking for perhaps two minutes or more with little pause. Mr. Wardak haltingly tried to interpret what was said, but Amanullah's concluding remarks were burned into my ears. "If I am wrong," about certain men being members of the Taliban, "you can cut off my head and place it on the wall of my house."

I recall a conversation—or debate—later in the deployment following a question about how we obtained satellite imagery. The Afghan partners present fell into two camps. In the first were those who accepted our crude, non-expert explanation of how satellites work, and in the second were those who simply could not understand. Our limited knowledge of orbital physics quickly clashed with our interpreter's blameless inability to translate it, and the whole exercise buckled under our requirement of dancing around the big, classified elephant in the room:

our Afghan partners were not American, and thus were held at arms' length about our collection capabilities.

In clear sight and speaking distance of the truth, I'm unsure how often the Afghans knew we kept so many "small" or "inconsequential" secrets from them, if at all. Finally, one of the Americans told the second group that the United States had installed a large camera on the moon. Seeing the lie for what it was, the final holdouts said through our interpreter that this could not be, because "the moon is only the size of an elephant."

The vital principles of speed and accuracy are held in delicate balance by patience, as is important in building rapport and trust. Mr. Wardak was held in high esteem—we did not call any of the other terps "mister"—but his propensity for slower, literal translation would land him in relatively hot water when seconds or minutes mattered. On the other end of the spectrum was Ali, whose poor performance could not have been more textbook. Although characterized by poor performance, Ali faced the same stressors as Wardak, who did not or could not always hide the stress of the job from showing on his face.

Patience goes both ways. Once, I returned from a workout to two of the Americans giving a class to the Afghans, assisted by a clearly stressed Mr. Wardak. The Afghans quietly and respectfully sat listening to a class on the geography of Afghanistan, of all things. As the two Americans patronizingly indicated a province on the map, they would tell the Afghans its name. Somewhat panicked, I quietly asked one of my superiors what they were doing, and he had no good answer. We could only watch as the two Americans embarrassed themselves and by extension, us. While this incident did not lead to any ill will, I've thought of it often. I could not see any U.S. military officer sitting down in good faith for a geography lesson taught by foreigners on the fifty states. The Afghans, as well as the workhorse Mr. Wardak, allowed the angels of their better nature to prevail and not let it become an incident.

Although interpreters fill a necessary gap in language between two parties, it is immediately apparent when they are not doing their job well. Ali would simply disappear for lengths of time and had a habit of heavily abridging what was said when speaking English but speaking for double or triple the amount of time to translate from English. There is a degree of leeway allowed for interpreters, as they may have to *explain* a specific concept or phrase due to a lack of direct translation. However, we suspected that Ali was breaking the cardinal rule of interpretation by putting words in our mouths. This was especially problematic for the operating environment, where Ali very likely overstepped his role from interpreter into a direct military position.

Equally problematic was the lack of trust, which neuters any collaborative effort. We would only work with Ali if we had no other option available. This meant that the times Ali worked alone, we would speak as little as possible with our Afghans if at all. Resentment built within the American "camp," as we could not trust him; the other interpreters began being called in during their time off to compensate. Although I never spoke to the Afghans about it, Ali clearly carried himself as "one of the Americans," and this attitude precipitated a physical fight with one of Amanullah's bodyguards (to say nothing of his many off-color, concerning remarks) and eventually resulted in Ali's removal.

The necessity of interpreters in a war like Afghanistan is obvious, but the ways they were employed as assets by the U.S.-led mission bears further study. In writing this, I have done a great degree of reflecting on my own experiences. I was naturally curious to see what other veterans' experiences may have been elsewhere.

One friend, a former infantryman who did two deployments to Iraq and one to Afghanistan with the 82nd and 101st Airborne Divisions, said he felt that the U.S. military did not do enough to educate its combatants on local languages, customs, and culture. This in turn led to an overreliance on interpreters, which he believed hamstrung U.S. efforts to win over the "hearts and minds" of local populaces. His deployments occurred between 2006 to 2012, and over coffee one morning not long after New Year's Day, 2022, he told me he felt vindicated in these views because, in his eyes, it is no wonder local populations in Iraq or Afghanistan would accept extremists in charge of them. The only words his units (and he assumes many other combat units) were taught in Arabic were "hello," "move away," and "stop or I will shoot." As he put it, if an armed, foreign occupier arrived in Denver with the same behavior there would be no shortage of American insurgents.

One GWOT veteran I spoke to (who asked that I use as little identifying information as possible) related to me a time they were forced by circumstance to be an interpreter during a special operations deployment in 2016. Allied casualties had been Medevac'd to their relatively remote base, and they were the only person on hand who could speak both English and Arabic. Although this veteran speaks Arabic, they are not a native speaker. Nor are they medically trained. Shouting over the din of helicopter rotors and standing above the grisly reality of combat, this veteran—suffering from a bout of food poisoning—had to relay the various injuries and circumstances behind them to the medic, also an American. This event stands out in that veterans' mind as strange, because a bureaucracy as large and well-funded as the Department of Defense still could not figure out how to embed adequate numbers of qualified interpreters.

The veteran who previously ran a now-defunct popular social media page called Syrian Summers, dedicated to veterans' experiences in that theater, said he and many other Syria veterans had noticeably different experiences than their Iraq and Afghanistan campaign peers. I not only learned of the deep friendship he had formed with his unit's interpreter, Adam, but was also treated to a flurry of photographs of the two of them. The general opinion among this small cohort of American military life is that the Kurds are more eager to fight and are far more appreciative of their American comrades. It could be so because the Kurds are not fighting a civil war framed as nation-building but a generations long struggle for independence and international recognition.

To that end, where many Iraq and Afghanistan veterans met a lack of enthusiasm from their partners and interpreters, there is a sense of genuine trust between Kurds and Americans who have served alongside one another. These circumstances led to noticeably different treatment between U.S. forces, partner forces, and local nationals. In addition to the veteran mentioned above, an old friend of mine who has seen time in Afghanistan, Iraq, and Syria indicated Kurdish partners were free to enter, exit, and roam American bases at will the way U.S. personnel do on their own bases stateside. In contrast, during my time in Afghanistan, our Afghan partners had to submit to rigorous security protocols as a matter of standard operating procedure.

There was a palpable strain between us and the Afghans, although I think few of us could put words to it at the time. I was in Jalalabad in 2013, and the year before was the height of "green on blue" attacks, when Afghan partners (green) turned their weapons or detonated explosives against their U.S. allies (blue).[12] One high profile green on blue attack killed several CIA personnel, and in another a U.S. general was killed. Early in my deployment, perhaps three weeks in, the senior noncommissioned officer in our TOC was leading a period of instruction for our Afghan partners on the M9 pistol. Mr. Wardak dutifully translated the short class before we headed outside to supervise their qualification.

As everyone began heading outside, the senior NCO quietly told another enlisted American and I that we were on "guardian angel" duty. Guardian angel was the code phrase used for U.S. troops who would stand watch to stop a green on blue attack before it could progress. In other words, those two words meant that I not only was expected to distrust my Afghan partners while they handled

Keeping Faith

weapons but that I was also expected to kill them without hesitation. What good would a guardian angel be otherwise? Whether or not the code phrase worked, the fact that two of the American soldiers present were the only people wearing body armor and carrying assault rifles belied our purpose. Looking back on this event and the title bestowed on me, I am reminded of Jefferson-Tatum's "violence of translation," as referenced by Farina King earlier in this volume.

Despite this unease, we still regarded one another as human and learned from one another. Following a rocket attack, some of the Afghan partners, our interpreter Ali, and myself were sheltering in a small bunker. I pulled security at the entrance while they talked among themselves. Ali said the Afghans were teasing me for being "ready for battle," and I responded that someone had to protect the officers because they were not allowed to do it themselves.[13] The Afghan second-in-command became quite the fan of Tony Romo and the Dallas Cowboys. Amid daily greetings of handshakes and hugs, I learned a hand on the heart meant sincerity. It is a gesture I reflexively use to this day.

I would be remiss if I did not acknowledge the good. As humans always do, we all bonded over our mutual need to eat, and our love for good food. This shared enthusiasm for gastronomy evolved into a full-blown weekly event. Having purchased a toaster oven for our TOC, we next set our Afghan partners to task on getting locally made naan and cheese. On the American end, we began requesting—pleading, really—for our families and friends to send us cans of tomato sauce, packaged pepperoni, and any other pizza topping we could think of. The weekly pizza nights became a huge success, eventually pulling thirty or more people a week into our building—many of whom had not significantly interacted with our Afghan partners until that point.

To this day I believe in the importance of these gatherings between our Afghan partners, interpreters, and the U.S. personnel who did not regularly work with Afghans. All of us got to go back to the United Sates when our time was up, while the Afghans had no such luxury. Regardless of motivation, by merely choosing a side they had sentenced themselves and perhaps even their families to death. Although our interpreters were U.S. citizens, many of their families were not. And, it bears repeating, many interpreters used by the U.S. were local Afghans who were promised U.S. citizenship for their aid. It bears further emphasis that many of these people have been left to die at the hands of a hostile government.

What kind of quandaries does "choosing a side" in a civil war present for an interpreter? How long can an interpreter be resilient in the face of combat stress, death threats, or violence against their families? These questions are even more important for a culture like that of Afghanistan, where loyalty to a nation is far subservient to the duty one has to their family, tribe, or ethnicity. The use of interpreters in Afghanistan takes on an eerie familiarity if we consider their context and the historical context of interpreters in the Indian Wars. In both instances, interpreters were simultaneously considered unimportant background actors while being deeply distrusted by their interpretees (to say nothing of the lack of trust between the warring parties).

As we delve deeper into an age of information, where narratives are often as important as the events themselves, it would be wise to consider how much has changed between the Indian Wars and their early twenty-first-century cousins in west and central Asia. How much wasted money, bloodshed, and heartache could have been avoided if each party sat down in good faith and negotiated peace sooner? Or were the generation long American experiments in Afghanistan, Iraq, and beyond unavoidable foreign policy crunches? And, how much of these things could have been avoided if the U.S. government and military had placed the same amount of faith in interpreters as we the interpretees did? Imagine what the world could be if interpreters weren't considered a background role but were empowered to help interpretees cut through the unknowns of cross-cultural dialogue.

I extend my deepest thanks to people courageous enough to involve themselves in a conflict as a noncombatant. The services provided by even the least capable of interpreters has the potential to deescalate violent situations and save lives. As the saying goes, "the pen is mightier than the sword." Maybe we can amend this saying to "the interpreter is mightier than the drone operator."

I implore my fellow Americans to think like an interpretee and gladly approach situations on which they do not have a grasp with trust that their interpreters will guide them. Conversely, I plead with our many societal interpreters to use their authority for truth. I implore my fellow veterans—as well as my comrades still in uniform, and those at government agencies—to consider the ways we as interpretees could have helped make our interpreters' lives easier. I also invite this group of Americans to share their stories, even if they are not Hollywood caliber screenplays. Posterity will look back on this generation of war with confusion, and now is our chance to help future generations interpret one of the most embarrassing, shameful chapters of American imperialism.

To my Afghan allies whose lives are at risk for simply being stranded in their homelands, whether you are interpreters or partners in military or government operations: Keep the faith. You are not, and cannot be, forgotten.

Notes

1. I originally wrote the first draft of this chapter in June 2022, including this line. In the last two years, it has come to light that the Department of State is processing Special Immigrant Visas at a glacial pace, with more than one hundred thousand applications and no diplomatic facilities in Afghanistan for applicants to work through. I have experienced this frustration firsthand, as pleas to the State Department on behalf of my friend, pseudonymed Mohammad to protect his identity, have been met with copy/pasted responses from an unmonitored email address telling me that my message was received.
2. Including actors whose intentions are less-than-honorable or outright rogue, such as Confederate colonel Joel M. Bryant, discussed by Alice Baumgartner earlier in this volume.
3. Deloria Jr., *Custer Died for Your Sins*, vii.
4. Lahti, *Wars for Empire*, 56–60.
5. Young, *Making the Forever War*, 128–30.
6. Rasmussen, "Afghans Live in Peril among Unexploded Nato Bombs that Litter Countryside," *Guardian*, January 29, 2015.
7. Woodward, *Bush at War*, chap. 10.
8. Taken from the Afghan habit of saying *Inshallah*, or "God willing" in response to future events. This world view is not unique to Afghans, as many Muslims believe that only God can guarantee life. So, when invited to a briefing "tomorrow at 0900," they would say "God willing I will be there." The implication is not just their attendance, but that God willing they would also be on time (which they often weren't).
9. Sopko, "Remarks on 2021 SIGAR High-Risk List."
10. Sopko, "Remarks on 2021 SIGAR High-Risk List."
11. For a better, deeper look into this aspect of U.S.-Afghan relations please see the 2013 VICE documentary *This Is What Winning Looks Like*.
12. Roggio and Lundquist, "Green-on-Blue Attacks in Afghanistan."
13. Jokes are often less funny when explained, but context is important: The compound we worked on was heavily fortified, and there were two guard towers nearby. Also nearby was an idling armored vehicle with an infantry squad (that is to say, trained professionals) and several heavy machine guns, as well as several other squads nearby. The danger had passed with the rocket impacts, but SOP dictated that I be ready at that bunker with my rifle.

Bibliography

Deloria, Vine, Jr. *Custer Died for Your Sins*. Second edition. Norman: University of Oklahoma Press, 1988.

Lahti, Janne. *Wars for Empire*. Norman: University of Oklahoma Press, 2017.

Roggio, Bill, and Alexandra Lundquist. "Green-on-Blue Attacks in Afghanistan." Foundation for Defense of Democracies, 2017.

Sopko, John F. "Remarks on 2021 SIGAR High-Risk List." Special Inspector General for Afghanistan Reconstruction. Center for Strategic International Studies, 2021.

Woodward, Bob. *Bush at War*. New York: Simon and Schuster, 2002.

Young, Marilyn. *Making the Forever War*. Amherst: University of Massachusetts Press, 2021.

Call Me Phillip Morris

From the editors: In the beginning of the documentary "The Interpreters" (2019), Sargent Paul Braun explains how American forces entirely relied upon linguistic intermediaries in both Iraq and Afghanistan after September 11, 2001. Within his opening narration, the interpreters are placed in an unenviable position: between their own people, who think of them as traitors, and American soldiers, who question their motivations. Braun describes how he came to know his unit's interpreter, "Phillip Morris," near Basra, Iraq, in 2009. The documentary then details Morris's seven-year journey to the United States to rejoin his "brother from a different mother," and how his successful case was one of but thousands waiting for clearance from the U.S. State Department.

"The Interpreters"

> BRAUN: As American soldiers, we had difficulty communicating with the Iraqis. It was common for us to employ local nationals or other Iraqis that would serve as an interpreter or a translator for the soldiers.
>
> The interpreters were considered to be traitors to their country, traitors to their religion. They'd have to wear a mask over their face and always use a fake name, but after a while, people found out who they were.
>
> We kept hearing reports of an interpreter turning on the soldiers, helping coordinate an attack or a suicide bomb, and blowing himself up and killing soldiers.
>
> Several interpreters were offered to us. We can't call an interpreter by their real name. And that's when he lit up a cigarette, and said, "You will call me Phillip Morris." And that's how we ended up with his name.
>
> MORRIS: You know, [Sargent Braun] came with his mohawk, with his gray hair, with his full gear, with his rifle, and he gave me this serious look.

FIG 9. Phillip Morris. Based on a photograph in "'From Being Alone To A Whole Family,' An Iraqi Interpreter's Dream Fulfilled," *Morning Edition*, National Public Radio, February 3, 2017.

>"If you try to mess with me or with my soldiers, I will kill you." (Morris laughs.)
>
>BRAUN: And he starts to laugh. And I'm like, "What do you think is so funny about this?" And he said, "Someday, you and I will sit in America, and laugh about this conversation over tea."[1]

Notes

1. Andrés Caballero and Sofian Khan, dirs., *The Interpreters*, New York: Capital K Pictures, 2019.

CONTRIBUTORS

ALICE BAUMGARTNER is an assistant professor of history at the University of Southern California. She received a PhD in history from Yale University and an MPhil in Latin American studies from the University of Oxford. Her first book, *South to Freedom: Runaway Slaves to Mexico and the Road to Civil War*, published in 2020, was named a *New York Times* Editors' Choice, and a finalist for the *Los Angeles Times* Book Award. Her articles have appeared in the *Journal of American History*, the *Journal of Southern History*, and the *Western Historical Quarterly*, among others.

PAUL CONRAD teaches Native American history and literature at the University of Texas at Arlington. He is the author of *The Apache Diaspora: Four Centuries of Displacement and Survival* (University of Pennsylvania Press, 2021). He is currently working on a new project examining the role of boarding school alumni in Apache communities in the twentieth century.

TAYLOR COZZENS is a PhD candidate in the University of Oklahoma History Department. While his dissertation deals with agriculture in the modern Andes, he has a long-running interest in the history of intermediaries. Prior to graduate studies in history, Taylor studied Spanish translation and interpretation, and he works regularly as a certified courtroom interpreter in central Oklahoma.

NICOLE EUSTACE is a professor of history at New York University, where she has leadership roles in both the history of women and gender program and the Atlantic history workshop. A historian of the early modern Atlantic and the early United States, she specializes in the history of emotion. She is author of Pulitzer-Prize winning *Covered with Night: A Story of Murder and Indigenous Justice in Early America* (2021), *Passion Is the Gale: Emotion, Power, and the Coming of the American Revolution* (2008), and of *1812: War and the Passions of Patriotism* (2012). She is also coeditor of *Warring for America: Cultural Contests in the Era of 1812* (2017).

ZACH GUILIANO is a veteran of the United States Army and served five years as an intelligence analyst. During his 2013 counterterrorism deployment to Jalalabad, Afghanistan, Zach had to navigate a complex operational and strategic environment while interacting with Afghan allies through interpreters. His experiences led to over a decade of professional and academic research into insurgencies and revolutions, and how they are impacted or driven by relevant players' perceptions of one another.

FARINA KING, PhD, a citizen of the Navajo Nation, is the Horizon Chair of Native American Ecology and Culture and Associate Professor of Native American Studies at the University of Oklahoma. King specializes in twentieth-century Native American Studies, especially Indigenous experiences in boarding schools. She is the author of *The Earth Memory Compass: Diné Landscapes and Education in the Twentieth Century*, and coauthor with Michael P. Taylor and James R. Swensen of *Returning Home: Diné Creative Works from the Intermountain Indian School*.

MARK W. LENTZ, associate professor of Latin American history and the History Program coordinator at Utah Valley University, is a historian of colonial Mexico, Central America, and the Atlantic World. His current interests include interpreters in the conquest and colonization of Yucatan and interethnic relations in colonial and early national Mexico and Guatemala. He recently published articles on Indigenous-African relations in eighteenth-century Guatemala and Belize and the role of Jesuits in translation, conversion, and pedagogy in colonial Yucatan, and an article on creole and African-descent fluency and literacy In indigenous languages in the *Hispanic American Historical Review* that won the 2018 Best Article Prize at RMCLAS. His first monograph, *Murder in Mérida, 1792: Violence, Factions, and the Law*, was published in June 2018 with the University of New Mexico Press's *Diálogos Series*. He was the 2015–16 R. David Parsons fellow at the John Carter Brown Library in Providence, Rhode Island. He received his PhD from Tulane University in 2009.

BRANDON MORGAN is associate dean in the School of Liberal Arts and a professor of history at Central New Mexico Community College (CNM) in Albuquerque, New Mexico, where he teaches Latin American, New Mexican, and American history courses. He earned his PhD from the University of New Mexico in 2013. His first book, *Raid and Reconciliation: Pancho Villa, Modernization, and Violence in the U.S.-Mexico Borderlands*, was published with the University of Nebraska Press in August 2024.

CAM SHRIVER is a Myaamia research associate at the Myaamia Center and a visiting assistant professor of History at Miami University. He is currently building a GIS database of Myaamia reserves and land transactions in nineteenth-century Indiana, as requested by tribal government. Dr. Shriver completed his PhD in history at Ohio State University in 2016. In addition to his work for the tribe, he is also revising a book manuscript entitled "The Contest for Information in the Colonial Great Lakes," which details changing surveillance efforts between Miami-Illinois speakers and colonizing empires in the eighteenth century. He has taught American history and, most recently, "Introduction to the Miami Tribe," at Miami University.

INDEX

Page numbers in italics indicate illustrations.

Aakaawita "Porcupine," 62, 63, 64
Abbey Gate bombing, 249
activism, 112, 121, 126; environmental, 2
Adam (interpreter), 257
Adams, John Quincy, 136
Administrative Office of the United States Court, 207
Afghan Air Force, 252
Afghanistan war, 248, 249; interpreters and, 247
Afghan National Army (ANA), 253, 254
Afghan National Security Forces (ANSF), 251
Afghan partners, 251, 257, 258, 259; collection capabilities of, 255; relationship with, 254
Agricultural Labor Relations Board, 202
Aguilar, Juan de, 26
Aikau, Hokulani, 159
Ainsa, Jesus M., 99
Algonquian groups, 43, 44, 48
Algonquian language, 47, 50
Ali (interpreter), 245, 256, 258
Allard, John, 127n11
al-Qaeda, 249, 253
Amanullah, Colonel, 254
American Indian Program, 158
American West, 1, 108, 111, 243; focus on, 7; history of, 2–3, 193
America's West (Wrobel), 195
ANA (Afghan National Army), 253, 254
Andersen, Ian: questions by, 243–46

Anglo-Powhatan War (1609), 42
Apache (town), 119
Apache language, 112, 116
An Apache Lifeway (Opler), 112, 118, 124, 127n11, 130n52
Apaches, 110, 112, 113, 117, 120, 121, 135
Apache Voices (Robinson), 119
Aragón, Alfredo, 143
Archivo General de Indias, 24
Archivo Histórico de la Secretaría de Relaciones Exteriores, 89, 90, 99
Archivo Histórico Génaro Estrada, 140, 149
Arévalo, Alonso Ruiz de, 21–22, 23, 27, 28, 29, 32n1, 35n44; ancestry of, 25; death of, 32; illegitimate status of, 25; as interpreter general, 18, 19, 31; pension for, 25; probanza hearing of, 26; royal confirmation and, 17
Arizona Supreme Court, 201
An Artist in Treason: The Extraordinary Double Life of General James Wilkinson (Linklater), 39
Arviso, Jesus, 161, 162
Arviso, Steven, 154
Arze, Martín Ruiz de, 29
Ashton, J. Hubley, 96
Assistance of Counsel, 199
ayánni bitó, 154, 155

Baca, Angelo, 159
Baldwin, Daryl, 75, 77n10
Baldwin, Jarrid, 77n10

Ball, Eve, 110, 111, 112, 114, 117, 120, 125, 127n12, 129n41; Apache culture and, 126; Daklugie and, 115, 118, 119, 122; informants and, 129n33; Kaywaykla and, 121; oral histories by, 118, 127n12, 129n32
Barrett, Stephen M., 115, 116
Barrio de San Cristóbal, 26
Barron, Joseph, 71
Barroso, Julio, 232, 240n12
Battle of Fort Dearborn (1812), 72
Battle of the Wabash (1791), 62, 64
Baumgartner, Alice, 7, 8, 140, 260n2
Báxoje, 72
Begay, Nanabah Bia, 164–74; Diné/LDS lifeways and, 162; oral history of, 167, 168, 169, 172, 174, 178n67; recollections of, 166; recording of, 168; testimony of, 172–74; Yellowhair and, 172, 173
Bekke, Douglas, 244
Bell, General, 151n10
Benally, Moroni, 163, 177n29
Benally, Ruby Whitesinger, 164
Bent, William, 237
Bent's Fort, 85, 237
Berk-Seligson, Susan, 208, 209
Beyal, Clyde, 161
bilingualism, 19, 20, 21
Bisbee, 144, 145, 150
Bishop, Clarence, 176n22
Biye, Hastiin Biyo Łání Yęę, 157
Blackfoot, 85
Blackhawk, Ned, 42, 73
Black Perspectives (website), 90
Blair, J. R., 141, 145, 147
Blaisdell, Francis, 94
Blessingway, 171
Blue Jacket, 67
Boat People, 234
Bonillas, Ygnacio, 148
Book of Mormon, 159, 163; Diné teachings and, 161; translating of, 156
Borah, Woodrow, 22

borderlands, 7, 8, 149; history of, 2–3; interpreters in, 10
Boxer, Elise, 159
Bradley, Ed, 234–35
Braun, Albert, 115
Braun, Paul, 262–63
Breckinridge, William, 136
Briceño, Diego, 26
bridge, 227; limits of, 229
Briggs, Scotty, 183, 184, 185
Brigham Young University, 120, 122, 158, 166
Brown, Eugene, 74
Brown, Wallace, 163–64
Bryant, Doña Mariana, 89; testimony of, 94–95, 101
Bryant, Joel M., 92, 93, 99, 260n2
Buchanan, Golden, 176n22
Buddhists, 239
Buffalo Bill Historical Center, 4
Burak, Sarah E., 160
burglary, 9, 211; robbery and, 204
Burkybile, Sharon, 74
Bush, George W., 249
Bush at War (Woodward), 249
BYU Indian Education Program, 158

California Board of Education, 200
California Constitution, 200
California Court Interpreters Association, 202
California Rural Legal Assistance (CRLA), 199, 200, 205, 216n34
California Supreme Court, 205
Callen, Mr., 151n10
Calloway, Collin, 42
Calotmul, 31
Camp Furlong, 144
Cañedo, Juan de Dios, 93
Cantonese, interpreting, 209
Cárdenas, Juan de, 26
Cárdenas, María Elena, 202
Carlisle, John G., 136

Carlisle Indian Industrial School, 74, 114, 115, 120
Carranza, Venustiano, 142, 147, 149, 150; death of, 148; diplomacy of, 145
Carreón, Juan, 141
Casas Grandes, 148
Catlin, George, 59, 108
Cato, 45
Cayuga nation, 44, 222, 243
Center for Southwestern Research, 166
certification exams, 210, 211, 214, 218n76
Charles II, 46
Charles Redd Center for Western Studies, 166
Chesapeake-Leopard affair, 70
Chevrolet Nova, *no va* and, 11n6
Chi, Gaspar Antonio Herrera de, 26, 27, 28, 29, 31; biographical sketches of, 20, 24, 25; death of, 18, 32; as interpreter general, 19, 23; testimony for, 22; translating by, 17–18
Chihuahua, 113, 139, 142, 143, 148
Chihuahua City, 92, 93, 94, 95, 99
Chinle, 165, 173, 174
Chino, Wendel, 125
Chiricahua Apaches, 111, 112, 113, 115, 116, 117, 119, 121, 122, 123, 125, 126, 127; factionalism of, 128n18; Geronimo and, 124; relations with, 114
Chivington, John, 85
Choate, Boone, 195, 196, 198, 211
Chontal Maya, 17, 27, 29, 30, 32n1
Christianity, 46, 52; Diné and, 155, 158
Christian names. *See* English names
Christy, Howard Chandler, 73
Church History Department, 164, 166
Church History Library, 164, 165, 167, 168
Church of Jesus Christ of Latter-day Saints, 155, 156, 158, 176n14
CIA, 193, 249, 250, 257
Cisneros, Marc, 193
CITA (Court Interpreters and Translators Association), 202, 203

citizenship, 95, 133, 251, 258
civil cases, 206, 207, 213
civility, 46, 54n11; English connotation of, 48
Civility, Captain, 45–46, 47, 48, 52
civilization, 66, 135; American, 65; plan, 68; primitivism and, 74; savagery and, 73
civil rights, 195, 206, 207; movement, 194, 198, 214
civil war, 257, 258
Civil War (U.S.), 90, 93, 95, 96
Club Patriótica, 138–39, 141, 146, 147, 150
Cocomes, 24
Cohen, Matt, 54n3
Cold War, 192, 235, 243
Colima, 30
Collier, John, 9, 153
colonialism, 159, 163; interpreters and, 41, 192, 127n6; Spanish, 193. *See also* settler colonialism
Colonia Mexicana, 139, 140, 142, 146, 147, 148
Columbus, 138, 139, 141, 148, 149, 150, 151n10; context of, 142–47; raid in, 140
Columbus Courier, 140, 142, 143, 144, 147, 148; on Landín, 146
Colvin, Gina, 162–63
Commerce Clause, 151n22
Commissioner of Indian Affairs, 133
communications, 3, 10, 45, 66, 231–32; civil cases and, 206; cross-cultural, 44, 127n7; facilitating, 2; poor, 247; prioritizing, 236; systems, 54n3; verbal, 91
community service officer (CSO), 231, 232, 235, 236, 237, 238; cultural flexibility and, 228
Complaints of Trade, 50
Conestoga, 43, 44, 46, 47, 49, 53, 56n31; community at, 50; conclave at, 50
Conolly, Jonathon, 98
Conrad, Paul, 9, 193–94
Consortium for Language Access in the Courts (CLAC), 210

Index 271

Consulate General (El Paso), 138
Cooke, Sherburne F., 22
Coo-rux ruh-rah-ruk-koo (Afraid-of-a-bear), 136
Corn Pollen, 172, 178n62
Cortez, Gregorio, 195–96, 213
Cortez, Romaldo, 195, 196
cosmology, Diné, 163
Costa, David, 77n10, 77n12
Council of Indies, 31
Council of Language Access Coordinators (CLAC), 209
Court Interpreter Act (1978), 207
Court Interpreters and Translators Association (CITA), 202, 203
Cozumel, 25, 27
Cozzens, Taylor, 5, 7, 8, 9
Crabb, Henry A., 99
Creel, Reuben, 93, 99
creoles, 19, 28, 32; literacy/fluency and, 30, 31; Mayas and, 31
CRLA. *See* California Rural Legal Assistance (CRLA)
CSO. *See* community service officer (CSO)
Cullen, Art, 236
Cullen, Mary, 240n14
cultural gaps, 228, 237
culture: Afghan, 259; American, 163; Apache, 116, 118, 119, 122, 124, 125, 126; Chiricahua, 121, 122; Diné, 158, 162, 163; Euro-American, 237; hybrid, 193; Indigenous, 124, 237; Mormon, 162–63
Cunill, Caroline, 19, 20, 28, 33n12
Cushing, Caleb, 96, 97
Custer Died For Your Sins (Deloria, Jr.), 248

Daklugie, Asa, 111, 112, 113, 114, 116, 117, 120, 123, 127n12, 128n30; Apaches and, 121; Ball and, 115, 118, 119, 122; Kenoi and, 126; watercolor of, *118*; work of, 129n42
Daklugie, Maude, 18
Daklugie, Ramona, 118, 120

Dandy, Jim, 160, 161
Daniel, Burrill, 8, 91; case of, 89–90, 92–96, 98–99, 101; slavery and, 99–100
Daniel, Luis, 93
Dari language, 250, 251
Davis, Jefferson C., 91
"The Days When We Went Gipsying" (song), 86
Debo, Angie, 110, 117, 120, 127n12
Defensor de los Naturales, 27
de Jongh, Elena M., 209
de Landa, Diego, 24
de la Puente Luna, José Carlos, 33n10
de las Casas, don Guillén, 28
Delaware language, 50, 65
Delawares, 43, 62, 69, 70
Deloria, Vine, Jr., 74, 249
de Luna y Arellano, don Carlos, 17
Deming, 146, 147, 150n2
Deming Graphic, 140, 143
Deming Headlight, 140
de Mora, Diego, 17, 18
Derecho indiano, 22
Deroine, Jeffrey ("Doraway"), 108; watercolor of, *109*
Des-to-dah, 135–36
Destodah, Max, 135–36
de Yanguas, Geronimo, 17
Diana v. Board of Education, 199, 200
Diné, 7, 154, 157, 160, 162, 163–64, 175, 175n6; Americanization of, 176n15; Christianity and, 155; generalizations about, 176n16
Diné Bikéyah, 154, 155, 157, 161, 174
Diné bizaad, 6, 154, 155, 156, 160, 161, 163, 165, 166, 167, 168, 172, 173, 174, 175; spiritual power of, 164
Diné dóó Gáamalii, 156, 158–59, 160, 164–74; thought sharing by, 171
Diné dóó Gáamalii (King), 155, 164, 165
District of Alaska, 91
diversity: diminishing, 22–28; linguistic, 22–28, 30

"Diversity: The Progress Files," 236
Diyin Dine'é, 171
Dong Da Thin, 244
"Don Pedro de Dueñas" (Jurado), 33n10
Dorados, 148, 151n24
Doris Duke Collection of American Oral History, 166
Dueñas González, Roseann, 195, 196, 197, 213
Duke, Doris, 166
Dunn, Mary, 43, 55n13
Dunn, Richard S., 43, 55n13
Dutch Reformed Church, 115

The Earth Memory Compass (King), 166
Edwards, Abraham, 78n23
Edwards, Alexander H., 78n23
Eepihkanita, 62, 63
El Paso, 93, 139, 140, 142, 148
El Paso Herald, 148
El Salvador, 147, 149, 194, 211
emancipation, 90, 98, 99, 100, 101, 102
Emancipation Proclamation, 99
Embry, Jessie, 164
enfermedad/enfermo, 18
English language, 86, 111, 227; limited, 195; proficiency in, 245; teaching, 234; translating, 116
English names: substituting Indian names with, 134
españoles, 21; tacit, 22, 23
Estrada, Juan de (Juan Duro), 26
Eustace, Nicole, 7, 8, 9
Evanoff (half-breed), 91
Exploratory Travels (Pike), excerpt from, 13–14

Fall, Albert B., 151n6
false cognates, 204, 217n54
fani mingo, 47, 48
Fanni Mingo, 48
Fanshaw, Buck, 183, 184, 186, 187
Farriss, Nancy, 193

Farsi language, 250
Fatty, David, 113
Favela, Juan, 141
Festinger, Nancy, 202
Five Nations, 44, 50, 51, 55
Ford, Gerald, 235
Fornoff, Fred, 144, 151n10
Fort Apache, 124
Fort Benning, 245
Fort Bliss, 151n10
Fort Dearborn, 72
Fort Marion, 114
Fort Sill, 115, 116
Fort Sumner, 162
Fort Wayne, 65, 66, 67, 72, 78n23
Fort Wayne Indian Agency, 66
Forzan, Génaro, 141, 143, 146
Four Sacred Mountains, 162
Fourteenth Amendment, 200
Franciscans, 17, 24, 25, 29, 32
Frazer, Mr., 13
Freedmen's Bureau, 91, 100
freedpeople, 98, 100
French, John, 46

Gáamalii, 156, 157
Gaiba, Francesca, 197, 198
Ganawese migrants, 43
García, Andrés G., 142
García, Antonio, 31
García Bernal, Manuela Cristina, 34n24
García de Palacio, Diego, 27, 29
García-Rengel, Sara, 202
Gatewood, Charles, 111
Generation Kill (Wright), 250
Geronimo, 113, 114, 115, 116, 117, 121, 123; Chiricahuas and, 124; interpreting, 128n30; surrender of, 127n13
global war on terrorism (GWOT), 7, 249, 251; and Indian Wars compared, 248; and Vietnam War compared, 247
Gómez, Reysedel, 139, 141, 146, 147
Gónzalez, Blas, 24, 26

Gookin, Charles, 46
Göring, Hermann, 197
Grant, Ulysses S., 113
Graubart, Karen, 33n14
Graves, J. K., 91
Great Lakes, 7, 44, 64, 66
Grey, Mark, 240n15
Guiliano, Zachary, 7, 9, 243, 244
GWOT. *See* global war on terrorism (GWOT)

Hadi, Ricky: watercolors by, *60, 63, 109, 118, 122, 167, 230, 234*
Haitian Creole, interpreting, 209
Haltman, Kenneth, 4–5
Hamburg, Don Jacobo, 92, 94, 95
Hamid Karzai International Airport, 249
Hampton Institute, 114
Harrison, William Henry, 66, 67, 72, 78n26; criticism by, 69–70; Wells and, 69–71
Haskell Institute, 74
Haudenosaunee, 44, 51, 54n9
The Heartbeat of Wounded Knee, 127n13
Heckewelder, John, 65
Heiss, Matthew, 9, 164–65, 166, 167, 169, 170, 172, 173; Yellowhair and, 174
Helicopter Puzzle, 252
helicopters, 236, 248, 252, 253, 256
Henry, George: watercolor of, *60*
Herbert, Hillary, 136
Hercules, 45, 46
Herrera, Francisca China Couoh de, 23
hijo natural, 17, 25
Hill, David B., 136, 224, 225
Hill, Jane H., 53n2
history: Apache, 116, 118, 119, 120, 122; Chiricahua, 121, 123; Diné dóó Gáamalii, 172
Hmong language, 204, 237
HMS *Leopard*, 70
Ho-Chunks, 72, 78n23
Hocobén, 31
Holy People, 171

Holy Spirit, 172
Honorable Counsel, 97
Hopi-Hopi (elder), 166, 167, 168
Hopis, cooperation among, 79n58
Horse Soldiers (Stanton), 250
Hotel Metropole, 243
housing, racist, 140, 150
hózhǫ́, 158
humor: miscommunications and, 1, 6; misinterpretation and, 9
Hwééłdi, 162

IBP. *See* Iowa Beef Processing (IBP)
identity, 8, 14; Diné, 156, 158–59; Diné dóó Gáamalii, 175; dual, 160; gender, 216n51; Latter-day Saint, 176n14; mestizo, 21; racial, 22
Ilts'á idits'agí, term, 116
Immigration and Naturalization Services (INS), 236, 238
imperialism, 69, 73, 193, 195, 259
Indeh: An Apache Odyssey (Ball), 112, 119, 120, 121, 127n12
Indian Affairs, 123
Indiana Territory, 69
Indian Claims Commission, 123
Indian Committee, 176n22
Indian Department, 133, 135
Indian names: substituting English names for, 134; unpronounceable, 135
Indian Office, Indian names and, 135
Indian Student Placement Program, 158, 160, 161, 177n36
Indian Wars, 7, 85, 249, 259; and GWOT compared, 248
Indigenous Pacific Islanders, 159
Indigenous peoples, 8, 9, 42, 47, 49, 50, 51, 159, 161, 248; armed conflict by, 52–53
indio conquistador, 26
Industrial Workers of the World (IWW), 144
Informe contra idolarum cultures del obispado de Yucatan (Chi), 24

INS (Immigration and Naturalization Services), 236, 238
International Court of Justice, 198
International Security Assistance Force (ISAF), 251, 252, 253
interpretation, 3, 7, 168, 197, 199, 201, 202, 208; academic programs in, 212–13; in civil court, 206; community and, 238; constitutional, 91; courtroom, 7, 213; cultural, 133; Diné Latter-day Saint, 163–64; emergence of, 126; and interpreter generation, 111, 122; point of view of, 244; power/negation and, 241n25; radical, 91; techniques of, 204; translation and, 6; roots of, 113–14
interpreters, 8, 31, 32, 126, 154, 245, 257; Afghan, 259; ancestry of, 20; certification of, 211, 213, 214; Chiricahua, 113, 115–25; as choke points, 61; colonialism and, 41, 192, 127n6; court, 192, 195, 197, 208; credentialed, 32, 204–5, 211; as cultural brokers/intermediaries, 2; definition of, 41, 116; Diné, 155–56, 161–63, 175; Diné dóó Gáamalii, 164–74; educating, 212–13; empowerment of, 9; ethical standards of, 207; funding, 208; Hispanic, 211; history of, 6; Indigenous, 30, 41, 53, 192; informal, 211; lawyers and, 204; mestizo, 18, 19, 20, 22, 30; nation building and, 247; professional, 207, 209, 210–11, 212–13; qualified, 29, 257; role of, 128n25, 208, 247, 256; significance of, 5; Spanish-English, 192, 209, 216n51; studies of, 4, 20; substituting, 223; testimony and, 192; working with, 251
"The Interpreters" (documentary), 262–63
interpreters general, 17, 19, 23
Intérpretes y trasuntos (Machua Chávez), 20
Intertribal Ceremonial buffalo riding competition, 154
In the Days of Victorio (Ball), 112, 119, 120, 121, 127n12

Iowa Beef Processing (IBP), 227, 229, 231, 232, 235, 236
Ioway, 108
Iraq war, 248, 250, 251
Ironstrack, George, 73
Iroquoian language, 44, 47, 50
Iroquois, 43, 44, 48
ISAF (International Security Assistance Force), 251, 252, 253
Ishkey, 113
Islamic State of Khorasan, 249
Iyanbito, 154, 155, 156

Jacobson, Matthew, 238
Jara, Aurelio, 205, 206
Jara v. Municipal Court (1978), 205
Jawbreaker, 249–50
Jefferson, Thomas, 68, 69
Jefferson-Tatum, Elana, 158, 258
Jim (Haida boy), 100
Johnson, Andrew, 91
Johnson, J. G., 222, 223, 224, 225, 226
Johnson, Lyndon B., 199
Johnston, John, 67, 68, 69
Judicial Council of California, 203
Judiciary Commission, 91
Juh, 113
Junta Colonizadora Palomas, 139
Jurado, Carolina, 33n10

kaapia, role of, 68, 76
Karzai, Hamid, 250
Kavan, Choung, 235
Kavan, Jesse, 235
Kavan, Pom, 194, 228, 240n14, 243; cultural/language gaps and, 237; police-community relations and, 236; watercolor of, *234*; work of, 232–39
Kavan, Samantha, 235
Kaywaykla, James, 119, 120, 121
Kenoi, Samuel E. ("Sammy"), 112, 113, 114, 115, 116, 119, 121, 123, 127n11, 129n43, 130n47; Daklugie and, 126; interpreting

Index   275

Kenoi, Samuel E. (*continued*)
by, 110–11; Opler and, 122, 124, 125, 130n46; watercolor of, *122*
Kickapoos, 63, 78n23
Kiihkayonki, 64, 66
Kiilhsoohka, 74
Kimball, Spencer W., 161, 170, 175, 176n22; legacy of, 158–59; Polacca and, 162
Kineepikwameekwa Siipiiwi "Eel River," 62
King, Farina, 6, 7, 9, 194
kinship networks, 73, 123
Kissinger, Henry, 243
Kohn, Dena, 202
Korean War, 238
Kramer, Paul, 238
Ku, don Pedro, 26, 29
Kurds, civil war and, 257

La Ascención, 139, 148, 151n24
Lacy, Charlotta, 156
Lamanites, 158, 159, 161, 165
Landín, Antonio, 138, 145, 194; Blair and, 147; consular services and, 149; as cultural bridge, 150; as interpreter/interpretee, 139–42; López and, 142; Mann Act and, 148; propaganda of, 146
Landín, Timotea Fontes de, 147, 148
language: barriers, 194; bridge, 228; derogatory, 198; Diné, 158; gaps, 237; Hispanic, 162; Indigenous, 19, 30, 68, 193; pragmatic aspects of, 208
language skills, 193; community formation and, 228–29; overestimation of, 204
language specialists, 237–38
Lao language, 232, 234, 237; speaking, 227, 228
La Prensa, 140, 147
La República, 140, 148
Las lenguas indígenas (Cunhill and Testino), 20
Latinx, 159

Latter-day Saint converts: Diné, 155, 157, 159–61, 165, 166, 174, 175, 177n29; Native American, 164, 177n29
Laughlin, 224
League of Nations, 89
Leary, Mary Ellen, 199
Le Duc Tho, 243, 244
Lee, Fitzhugh, 136
Lee, George P., 165, 175n6
Lehi, 159
Lenapes, 43, 54n7
Lentz, Mark, 7, 8
Library of Congress, 244
Limerick, Patricia (Patty), 4–5, 140
Lindsay, Washington E., 144
Linklater, Andro, 39
Loaysa, Jofre de, 27, 32n1
Locke, John, 51, 52, 53, 56n27
Lockwood, Hunter Thompson, 77n10, 77n12
London, Jack, 151n10
Long, Clayton, 8, 156
López, Leopoldo G., 139, 141, 146, 147, 148; Landín and, 142
López de Cogolludo, friar, 24
Los Angeles County, interpreters in, 202
"Lost in Translation" (Dong Da Thin), 244

Máamalii, 157
Macaulay, Thomas Babington, 192
Machua, Paulina, 20
Macmanus, George L., 99
Making the Forever War (Young), 248
Maldonado, Pablo, 25
Malliefert, Salvador, 150n2
Mandarin language, 204
Maní, 17, 24
Maní Land Treaty, 24
Mann Act, 148
"Man Who Double-Crossed the Founders," excerpt from, 39
"Many Tongues of the King" (Luna), 33n10

Māori peoples, 159
Masters, Adrian, 21, 22, 31
Maungwudaus, 10, 59; watercolor of, *60*
Mayas, 21, 23, 33n13; competition with, 28–32; creoles and, 31; disappearance of, 19, 20; fluency/literacy in, 19; mestizos and, 23; population of, 22; social standing of, 21
McChrystal, Stanley, 252
McCombs, Edward W., 165, 166
McCombs, Ruth Ann, 165
McGuffey House and Museum, 6
McKee, Alexander, 67
McPherson, Robert, 159, 160
Meesh, 251
"The Mellow Horn" (song), 86
Menard Family Center for Democracy, 5
"Mentally Ill Manual," 200
Mérida, 17, 26, 27
Merrell, James H., 41, 54n10, 62
Merritt, Jane T., 42
Mertz, Elizabeth, 100
Mescalero Apaches, 115, 119, 123, 125
Mescalero Reservation, 115, 118, 128n22
mestizos, 18, 19, 22, 33n13; competition with, 28–32; exclusion of, 22; interpretation by, 20; legal and social status of, 22; Mayas and, 23; opposition to, 30; as racial category, 23; rights of, 31; social standing of, 21
Metcalf, Alida, 193, 207
Mexican Consular Agency, 145, 150n2
Mexican Independence Day, 138, 139, 146, 149
Mexican Revolution, 140, 147, 148, 149
Mexican Secret Service, 140, 141
Mexico City, 99, 140, 146, 149
México de Afuera, 139, 150n2
Miami language, 64
Miami Nation, 67, 69, 75, 76
Miamis, 61, 63, 65, 67, 69, 70, 71; foreign policy of, 76; Potawatomis and, 72

Michoacán, interpreters in, 30
Middlebury Institute of International Studies, 213
middle ground, 42, 54n4, 72, 73
Mihsihkinaahkwa "Little Turtle," 62, 64, 65, 66, 68, 70, 71–72, 73, 74; translating for, 69; Wells and, 72, 75
Mikkelson, Holly, 195, 196, 201, 202, 203, 207, 210, 213
Militia Act (1862), 95
Mingos, 47, 48
Minnesota Remembers Vietnam project, 244
"The Minstrel's Returned from the War" (song), 86
"Minutes of a Meeting Held at Miami," 153
miscommunications, 170; humor and, 1, 6; irritation from, 1–2; violence and, 2
Missasaugas, 59
Mississinwawy Chiefs, 72
Mitchell, Robert Byington, 92, 96, 97
Mohammad, 260n1
Montejo, Francisco de, 21, 26
Mora, Diego de, 27
Morgan, Brandon, 7
Morgan, Thomas J.: letter from, 133–35
Mormon, term, 176n14
Mormonism, 156, 159, 160
Mormon Temple, 9
Morris, Phillip, 262–63; watercolor of, *263*
Morris, W. T., 195, 196
Moseley, Perrow G., 143, 150n5
Moye, Charles, 92, 93, 95
Mt. Vernon Barracks, 114
muhjahedin, 251
Muller, Henry, 93, 94
Muñoz, Francisca, 26
Muñoz, Francisco, 26
Murphy, Thomas, 159
Myaamia, 62, 63, 65, 66, 68, 72, 73–74, 75, 76, 77n10, 77n21, 79n58; foreign policy of, 67; politics of, 71; resistance by, 61

Index   277

Myaamiaataweenki, 64, 66, 74–75, 76
Myaamia Center, 5, 6

Naaltsoos Mormon Wolyéhígíí, 156
Nahuatl, 23, 26, 27, 29, 30, 32, 32n1
Nairne, Thomas, 47
Nájera, Gaspar de, 23, 72–73
National Archives and Records Administration, 90
National Association of Judiciary Interpreters and Translators (NAJIT), 203
National Center for Interpretation, 213
National Center for State Courts, 207, 209, 210
National Hispanic University, 213
Native American and Indigenous Studies Association, 157
Native Americans, 41, 71, 159, 165, 201; transforming, 68
Native Hawaiians, 159
Natividad, José, 200, 201, 205, 209, 213
Na-to-mah, 85
Navajo code talkers, 241n25
Navajo language, 154, 245
Navajo Nation, 156, 163, 164, 165, 176n15, 176n16
Navajo religion, 163, 170, 171
Navajo Tradition, Mormon Life (McPherson, Dandy, and Burak), 160
Ndé groups, 113
Negrón, Rogelio Nieves, 198, 200, 201, 205, 209, 213; interpreters and, 199
New York State Senate, testimony before, 222–24
New York Times, 151n6
Nguyen Dinh Phuon, interview of, 243–44
Nicholas, Daniel, 123, 125, 127n11, 130n47
Nieto, Antonio, 21–22, 23, 29, 31, 32, 33n13; as interpreter, 28; mixed ancestry of, 22
Nixon, Richard, 252
Northern Alliance, 249, 250
Nuremberg trials, 197, 198, 207

Oaxaca, interpreters in, 30
Obama, Barack, 252
Obama's Vietnam (PBS documentary), 248
Obregón, Alvaro, 148, 149
Offenburger, Andrew, 5, 7, 140, 194
Office of Indian Affairs, 100, 108; letter from, 133–35
Ohio Country, 64
Ohio River, 43, 62
Ojibwas, 10, 59
Ojitos hacienda, 142
Olivares, don Manuel de, 31–32
Oneida nation, 44
Onondaga, 45, 225
Opler, Morris Edward, 111, 112, 117, 118, 123, 130n52; Apaches and, 125, 126, 127n10; Kenoi and, 122, 124, 125, 130n46
oral history, 118, 126, 127n12, 159–60, 167, 168, 169, 172, 173, 178n57, 240n15; Diné, 166; Diné dóó Gáamalii, 164; interviews for, 174; Latter-day Saint, 164; Navajo Nation, 164–65; stake, 174; translating, 166
Osages, 10, 153
Owl Woman, 237

Palacio, don Diego de, 25, 27
Palomar, Martín de, 23
Palomas, 139, 141, 147, 149
Palomas Land and Cattle Company, 143
Palomino, Francisco de, 27
Panama, 248; invasion of, 193
Paredes, Américo, 195, 196
Paris Peace Talks, 243
Parks, G. E., 144, 145
Pashto language, 250, 251, 254
Pavlik, Steve, 160
Paxton Boys, 56n31
PBS Frontline, 248
Pech, don Juan, 27
Penn, William, 42, 50, 52, 53, 54n11, 55n13, 136; diplomacy and, 43; Indigenous people and, 43–44

Pennsylvania Council, 47
Pequot War (1637), 42
Perovich, Vuco, 196, 197
Perovich v. United States (1907), 196
Pershing, George, 144
Pershing Punitive Expedition, 143, 144
Peterson, Orlando, 90
Phelps Dodge Company, 144, 145
Pierce, Franklin, 136
Pike, Zebulon, 13
Pilot Tribune, on Vrieze, 231
Pima County Superior Court, 213
Pinelo, Antonio de León, 31
Pinker, Steven, 198
Pinšiwa, 67
Polacca, Howela, 161, 162
Polacca, Ruth, 161, 163–64, 170; Kimball and, 162
policework, 7, 227, 236
Potawatomis, 69, 72, 74, 79n58
Pratt, Richard, 115
Presbyterians, 157, 158
Prewitt & Pender, 146
primitivism, civilization and, 74
probanzas, 18, 22, 25
Prophet, 67, 70, 71, 78n33
Prophetstown, 72
Prosser, Mark, 236, 238
puente, 227, 229
Putnam, General, 64

Quakers, 68
Quapaws, 10
Quraishy, Najeeb, 250

Race and Slavery Petitions Project, 99
racism, 22, 53, 111, 151n22
Ramah, 157, 176n16
Ration, Tom, 166, 167
Ray, Robert, 234
reales cédulas, 19, 31, 33n13
Reconstruction, 248
Red Cross, 140

re-education camps, 245
Reformed Church, 157
Regional Commands (RC), 252
Relacion de las casas de Yucatan (de Landa), 24
relación de méritos, 26
Relaciones geograficas, 24
república de españoles, 30
Reynoso, Cruz, 199, 205
Richardsville, Jean Baptiste, 67
Richter, Daniel K., 42, 43
Riggs, G. E., 145
Riggs, Lee, 141
Ritchie, C. H., 23, 222, 224, 226
robbery, 9, 191; burglary and, 204
Robinson, Sherry, 119, 129n33, 129n41
Rodríguez, Antonio, 31
Rodríguez, Marcos, 28, 29
Rojas, Alonso de, 23
Rojo, Bartolomé, 26, 35n44
Romo, Tony, 258
Rosseau, Pierre, 13
Roughing It (Twain), excerpt from, 183–88
Rousseau, Jean-Jacques, 65
Royal Navy, 70

Sacred Corn Pollen, 170, 171
Salaam Alaykum, 254
San Antonio, 140, 204–5
San Carlos and Fort Apache reservation, 113–14
Sánchez de Aguilar, Pedro, 24, 143
San Cristóbal, 26
Sand Creek Massacre (1864), 85
San José, 213
San Luis Río Colorado, 229
San Salvador, 149
Santa Cruz Wharf, 10n1; story about, 1–2
Santiago, 26
Sauteurs, 14
Say-say-gon, 59
Schurz, Carl, 74
Schwaller, Robert F., 21, 23

Schwartz, Ana, 54n6
Schweninger, Loren, 99
sea lions, dogs and, 1–2
Second-Jumper, Sigfried, 121
Secretaría de Relaciones Exteriores, 93, 140, 141, 145, 149
Seneca Indian School, 74
Seneca nation, 44, 46, 51, 222, 224, 243
September 11th, 249, 262
settler colonialism, 8, 41–42, 44, 46, 47, 49, 51, 53, 73, 113, 194; destructiveness of, 112; peak stages of, 237. *See also* colonialism
Seward, William, 96
Shakespeare, William, 136
Shapiro, Norman, 101
Shawnee Nation, 46
Shawnees, 43, 67
Shoshone Agency, 136
Shriver, Cameron, 7, 9, 193
Sickel, Colonel, 144
Silva, Maria País de: petition of, 100
Simon, Hemoperekei, 159
Sioux, 13, 14
Sitka Indians, 100
Six Nations, 44, 45, 222
60 Minutes, 234
"Slave, Trader, and World Traveler" (Olson), excerpt from, 108
slavery, 52, 91, 92, 97, 100, 101, 102n7, 103n58; abolishing, 98, 99; coolie, 104n59; definitions of, 7, 89, 98; translation of, 90; white, 104n59
Slocum, Herbert, 143, 151n6
SLPD. *See* Storm Lake Police Department (SLPD)
Smith, Charlie, 130n52
Smith, J. B., 144
Smith, John Simpson, 85–86
Smith, Joseph, Jr., 159
Smith, Phillip L., 9, 164, 178n59, 178n60; translation by, 169, 170, 171
sobriquets, adopting, 134, 135

Sommer, Doris, 197
Sopko, John F., 252
Sopuerta, Hernando de, 23
South Dakota Supreme Court, 210
Southwest Indian Mission, 158, 174
Soviet-Aghan War, 251
Soviet Union, Afghanistan and, 249, 251
Spaniards, 14, 32; arrival of, 22
Spanish-American War, 238, 248
Spanish language, 30, 96; attorney interference with, 204; fluency/literacy in, 19; interpretation of, 202, 209, 211; speaking, 227, 228
Special Activities Division (CIA), 249
Special Forces, 244, 250
Special Immigrant Visas, 260n1
Special Inspector General for Afghanistan Reconstruction (SIGAR), 253
spiritual ways, 172; Diné, 158, 160, 175n6; Latter-day Saint, 160
Spivak, Gayatri, 192
Stanford-Binet Intelligence Test, 199
Stanton, Doug, 250
Steer, Alfred, 198
Stepetin, Haliehana Alag̃um Ayagaa, 158, 176n18
Stickney, Benjamin, 78n23
St. John's Lutheran Church, 238
St. Louis, 13; Sioux chiefs to, 14
Stone, E. B., 143
Storm Lake, 194, 230, 231, 232, 238, 239n1; immigration debates and, 228–29; midwestern history and, 239n4; oral history in, 240n15; redefining, 227–28; transformation of, 235, 239n2
Storm Lake Buddhist temple, 238, 239
Storm Lake City Council, 230
Storm Lake Police Department (SLPD), 231, 232, 235, 236, 237, 238
Storm Lake Times, 240n12
Strong, J. C., 222, 223, 224
Styres, James, 222, 223, 224, 225, 226
Sumner, Charles, 91

Susquehanna River Valley, 43, 44, 45, 47, 48, 49, 50, 52
Susquehannock language, 49
Susquehannock Nation, 47
Susquehannocks, 43, 44, 54n9; Civility and, 45; Lenape and, 54n7
Syrian Summers (social media page), 257

Tactical Operations Center (TOC), 254, 257, 258
Tádídíín, 171, 178n62
Tageldin, Shaden M., 192
Tai-Dam language, 232
Tai Dam refugees, 235
Taliban, 247, 249, 250, 253, 254
Tallchief, Henry, 153
Taos Trail, 85–86
Taquatarensaly, 44–45, 46–47, 48, 50, 52, 53
Taylor, William, 193
Tecumseh, 67, 71, 72, 78n23
Tecun, Arcia, 159
Tenskwatawaw (the Prophet), 70
Terrazas, Don Luis, 92, 94, 95, 96, 97
Terry, Frank, 133
Testino, Luis Miguel Glave, 20
Thirteenth Amendment, 90, 91, 97, 99–100, 102n7
This Is What Winning Looks Like (documentary), 260n11
Thornton, Edward, 97, 98
Thurman, Allen G., 137
Tizimin, 29, 31
Tobriner, Mathew, 206, 207
TOC (Tactical Operations Center, 254, 247, 248
Tomás (freedman), 93
Townsite Company, 145
translation, 3, 20; ambiguity in, 211–12; framework of, 91; interpretation and, 6; professional/ethical standards for, 198; violence of, 158, 258
Translation Division, 198

translators, 245; court-appointed, 8; Diné, 155–56; Indigenous, 53; Maya, 20; mestizo, 20, 21
Treaty of 1868, 162
Treaty of Fort Wayne (1809), 72
Treaty of Friendship and Commerce, 141
Treaty of Greenville (1795), 64, 69, 75
Truett, Samuel, 145
Tsaltaykoo, 113
Tuba City, 165, 176n13
Turner, Elizabeth, 90, 102
Tuscarora Nation, 46
Twain, Mark, 183
Two Treatises of Government (Locke), 51
Tyson Fresh Meats, 227, 239n1

Uchtdorf, Dieter F., 162
Ukraine, Russian invasion of, 249
Ummah, 251
United Nations, 198
Upham Hall, 6
U.S. Army, 62, 100, 244, 252
U.S. Boarding School for Crow Indians, 133
U.S. Border Patrol, 231
U.S. Constitution, 199
U.S. Department of Defense, 252, 257
U.S. Department of Education, settlement by, 200
U.S. Department of Labor, 216n34
U.S. Department of State, 96, 100, 193; Special Immigrant Visas and, 260n1
U.S. Department of the Interior, letter from, 133–35
U.S. Legation, 96
U.S. Marine Corps, 247, 250
U.S.-Mexico Claims Commission, 8, 89, 90, 101; Daniel and, 92–96, 96–98, 98–99
U.S.-Mexico War, 93
U.S. Supreme Court, 207
U.S. War Department, 68, 70

Van Winkle, Rip, 136

Vargas, Diego de, 21, 23, 28, 32, 33n13
Vásquez, Victoria, 23, 195, 196
Vavel, Hidado, 143
Velasco, Diego Fernández de, 27
Venuti, Lawrence, 101
Vietnamese language, 204; interpreting from, 244
Vietnam War, 235, 238, 243, 244, 245, 252; and GWOT compared, 248
Villa, Francisco "Pancho," 138, 142, 143, 145, 148, 150n5; raid by, 140, 146, 147
violence: eruption of, 8; miscommunications and, 2; personal, 188; of translation of, 158, 258
Volney, Comte de, 65, 80n70
Vrieze, Graciela, 194, 238, 240n7; police-community relations and, 236; watercolor of, *230*; work of, 229–32
Vrieze, Terry, 229

Waapaahsiki Siipiiwi "Wabash River," 62
Wabash River, 62, 63, 71
Wadsworth, William Henry, 97
Wah-To-Yah, Taos Trail and, 85–86
Walker, Mildred, 74
Walters, Vernon, 192, 193
Wa-nan-go-peth, 64, 77n10
Wardak, Mr., 245, 251, 254, 257
War of 1812, 72, 75
Washington, George, 62, 136
Wayne, Anthony, 64, 66, 73
Welcome (ship), 55n13
Wells, Samuel, 63, 64
Wells, William, 63–64, 99, 193, 77n9, 77n15, 78n23, 78n33; council house/blacksmith shop and, 67; criticism of, 69–70; geopolitical context for, 71; Harrison and, 69–71; interpretation and, 61, 65, 66, 67; Mihsihkinaahkwa and, 72, 75; Myaamia community and, 75; painting of, 73; translation and, 68–69; watercolor of, *63*; youth of, 62
Wells Street, story behind, 72
Western History Association, 5
Wheeler, Sheriff, 145
Wheeler-Howard Indian Rights Bill (1934), 153
White, Richard, 42, 72, 73
Whitt, Sarah, 114
Wilde, Fearing B., 136
Wilkinson, James, 39
William, Morgan, 157
Willoughby, Rany Tam, 92
Window Rock, 163, 165
Winne, Reid, 222, 223, 224, 225, 226
Wolcott, James, 75
Woodward, Bob, 249
Worley, Henry, 46, 55n13
Wright, Evan, 250, 251
Wrobel, David, 5, 195

Xiu, Jorge, 24, 26
Xol, 229

Yannakakis, Yanna, 128n25, 193
Yazzie, Arnold, 163
Yazzie, Renata, 157, 158
Yellowhair, Helena, 9, 165, 166, 168, 169, 170, 178n60, 178n67; Begay and, 172, 173–74; interpretation of, 171–72; watercolor of, *167*
Yellowhair, Salena, 169, 170
Yobain, 17, 18, 27
Young, Robert W., 157, 176n15
Yucatan, 7, 24, 29; population of, 22, 34n24; translation in, 20
Yucatec Maya, 23, 26, 27, 29, 30, 31, 32n1

Zamacona, Manuel Maria de, 97

www.ingramcontent.com/pod-product-compliance
Lightning Source LLC
Chambersburg PA
CBHW030610230426
43661CB00053B/1927